"This is a splendid and very readable book on housing and urban planning for degrowth. The degrowth perspective implies a decrease in the social metabolism and an increase in communality and conviviality. There are many chapters on actual types of degrowth housing in many countries and fundamental discussions of top-down versus bottom-up urban planning leading to these objectives. This book should become a textbook for courses in architecture, and urban and rural planning."

Joan Martinez Alier, Emeritus Professor of Economics and Economic History and Senior Researcher at the Institute of Environmental Science and Technology, Autonomous University of Barcelona, and Co-director of the EJAtlas (www.ejatlas.org)

"Degrowth is not just a theory — it is practice and it has policy implications. This fantastic collection of new essays shows how a degrowth mindset opens new ways of thinking alternatives and solutions to what is becoming a truly global housing crisis."

Giorgos Kallis, ICREA Research Professor at Universitat Autònoma de Barcelona, and a co-editor of Degrowth: A Vocabulary for a New Paradigm (2014)

"This book brings together astonishingly rich views on sustainable urban development, wholly local but with a global coverage. It fits in with trends away from evermore centralised decision making for growth towards local independence. Decentralised autonomy can halt encroachment of global organisations in private life, with communal housing at its core."

Gjalt Huppes, Senior Researcher, Institute of Environmental Sciences (CML) at Leiden University, Netherlands

Housing for Degrowth

'Degrowth', a type of 'postgrowth', is becoming a strong political, practical and cultural movement for downscaling and transforming societies beyond capitalist growth and non-capitalist productivism to achieve global sustainability and satisfy everyone's basic needs.

This ground-breaking collection on housing for degrowth addresses key challenges of unaffordable, unsustainable and anti-social housing today, including going beyond struggles for a 'right to the city' to a 'right to metabolism', advocating refurbishment versus demolition, and revealing controversies within the degrowth movement on urbanisation, decentralisation and open localism. International case studies show how housing for degrowth is based on sufficiency and conviviality, living a 'one planet lifestyle' with a common ecological footprint.

This book explores environmental, cultural and economic housing and planning issues from interdisciplinary perspectives such as urbanism, ecological economics, environmental justice, housing studies and policy, planning studies and policy, sustainability studies, political ecology, social change and degrowth. It will appeal to students and scholars across a wide range of disciplines.

Anitra Nelson is an activist-scholar, Associate Professor in the Centre for Urban Research at RMIT University, Melbourne (Australia), and author and editor of several books including *Small Is Necessary: Shared Living on a Shared Planet* (2018) and *Life Without Money: Building Fair and Sustainable Economies* (ed.) (2011).

François Schneider has supported degrowth since 2001. Co-founder of Research & Degrowth (http://degrowth.org/) and initiator of degrowth conferences, he is Associate Researcher at the Institute of Environmental Science and Technology (ICTA), Autonomous University of Barcelona. In 2012, he started the experiential project Can Decreix, 'house of degrowth' in Catalan.

Routledge Environmental Humanities
Series editors: Iain McCalman and Libby Robin

Editorial Board

Christina Alt, St Andrews University, UK
Alison Bashford, University of Cambridge, UK
Peter Coates, University of Bristol, UK
Thom van Dooren, University of New South Wales, Australia
Georgina Endfield, University of Nottingham, UK
Jodi Frawley, University of Sydney, Australia
Andrea Gaynor, The University of Western Australia, Australia
Tom Lynch, University of Nebraska, Lincoln, USA
Jennifer Newell, American Museum of Natural History, New York, US
Simon Pooley, Imperial College London, UK
Sandra Swart, Stellenbosch University, South Africa
Ann Waltner, University of Minnesota, US
Paul Warde, University of East Anglia, UK
Jessica Weir, University of Western Sydney, Australia
International Advisory Board
William Beinart, University of Oxford, UK
Sarah Buie, Clark University, USA
Jane Carruthers, University of South Africa, Pretoria, South Africa
Dipesh Chakrabarty, University of Chicago, USA
Paul Holm, Trinity College, Dublin, Republic of Ireland
Shen Hou, Renmin University of China, Beijing, China
Rob Nixon, Princeton University, Princeton NJ, USA
Pauline Phemister, Institute of Advanced Studies in the Humanities, University of Edinburgh, UK
Deborah Bird Rose, University of New South Wales, Sydney, Australia
Sverker Sorlin, KTH Environmental Humanities Laboratory, Royal Institute of Technology, Stockholm, Sweden
Helmuth Trischler, Deutsches Museum, Munich and Co-Director, Rachel Carson Centre, Ludwig-Maximilians-Universität, Germany
Mary Evelyn Tucker, Yale University, USA
Kirsten Wehner, National Museum of Australia, Canberra, Australia

The *Routledge Environmental Humanities* series is an original and inspiring venture recognising that today's world agricultural and water crises, ocean pollution and resource depletion, global warming from greenhouse gases, urban sprawl, overpopulation, food insecurity and environmental justice are all *crises of culture*.

The reality of understanding and finding adaptive solutions to our present and future environmental challenges has shifted the epicentre of environmental studies away from an exclusively scientific and technological framework to one that depends on the human-focused disciplines and ideas of the humanities and allied social sciences.

We thus welcome book proposals from all humanities and social sciences disciplines for an inclusive and interdisciplinary series. We favour manuscripts aimed at an international readership and written in a lively and accessible style. The readership comprises scholars and students from the humanities and social sciences and thoughtful readers concerned about the human dimensions of environmental change.

Housing for Degrowth
Principles, Models, Challenges
and Opportunities

Edited by Anitra Nelson and
François Schneider

First published 2019
by Routledge
2 Park Square, Milton Park, Abingdon, Oxon OX14 4RN

and by Routledge
711 Third Avenue, New York, NY 10017

Routledge is an imprint of the Taylor & Francis Group, an informa business

© 2019 selection and editorial matter, Anitra Nelson and François Schneider; individual chapters, the contributors.

The right of Anitra Nelson and François Schneider to be identified as the authors of the editorial material, and of the authors for their individual chapters, has been asserted in accordance with sections 77 and 78 of the Copyright, Designs and Patents Act 1988.

All rights reserved. No part of this book may be reprinted or reproduced or utilised in any form or by any electronic, mechanical, or other means, now known or hereafter invented, including photocopying and recording, or in any information storage or retrieval system, without permission in writing from the publishers.

Trademark notice: Product or corporate names may be trademarks or registered trademarks, and are used only for identification and explanation without intent to infringe.

British Library Cataloguing-in-Publication Data
A catalogue record for this book is available from the British Library

Library of Congress Cataloging-in-Publication Data
A catalog record for this book has been requested

ISBN: 978-1-138-55805-2 (hbk)
ISBN: 978-1-315-15120-5 (ebk)

Typeset in Goudy
by Apex CoVantage, LLC

Printed and bound in Great Britain by
TJ International Ltd, Padstow, Cornwall

Contents

List of figures	x
List of tables	xi
Foreword	xii
JOAN MARTINEZ-ALIER	
Acknowledgements	xv
List of abbreviations	xvii
List of contributors	xix

PART I
Simple living for all — 1

1 Housing for growth narratives — 3
   ANITRA NELSON

2 Housing for degrowth narratives — 14
   FRANÇOIS SCHNEIDER

PART II
Housing justice — 31

3 From the 'right to the city' to the 'right to metabolism' — 33
   ELISABETH SKARðHAMAR OLSEN, MARCO OREFICE
   AND GIOVANNI PIETRANGELI

4 How can squatting contribute to degrowth? — 44
   CLAUDIO CATTANEO

PART III
Housing sufficiency   55

5 Rethinking home as a node for transition   57
PERNILLA HAGBERT

6 Framing degrowth: the radical potential of tiny house mobility   68
APRIL ANSON

7 Housing and climate change resilience: Vanuatu   80
WENDY CHRISTIE AND JOHN SALONG

PART IV
Reducing demand   97

8 Christiania: a poster child for degrowth?   99
NATASHA VERCO

9 Refurbishment vs demolition? social housing campaigning for degrowth   109
MARA FERRERI

10 The Simpler Way: housing, living and settlements   120
TED TRAINER

PART V
Ecological housing and planning   131

11 Degrowth: a perspective from Bengaluru, South India   133
CHITRA K. VISHWANATH

12 Low impact living: more than a house   145
JASMINE DALE, ROBIN MARWEGE AND ANJA HUMBURG

13 Neighbourhoods as the basic module of the global commons   156
HANS WIDMER ('P.M.') WITH FRANÇOIS SCHNEIDER

14 The quality of small dwellings in a neighbourhood context   171
HARPA STEFÁNSDÓTTIR AND JIN XUE

PART VI
Whither urbanisation? 183

15 Housing for degrowth: space, planning and distribution 185
JIN XUE

16 Urbanisation as the death of politics: sketches of degrowth municipalism 196
AARON VANSINTJAN

17 Scale, place and degrowth: getting from here to 'there' – on Xue and Vansintjan I 210
ANDREAS EXNER

18 Geography matters: ideas for a degrowth spatial planning paradigm – on Xue and Vansintjan II 217
KARL KRÄHMER

19 'Open localism' – on Xue and Vansintjan III 223
FRANÇOIS SCHNEIDER AND ANITRA NELSON

PART VII
Anti-capitalist values and relations 231

20 Mietshäuser Syndikat: collective ownership, the 'housing question' and degrowth 233
LINA HURLIN

21 Nonmonetary eco-collaborative living for degrowth 244
ANITRA NELSON

22 Summary and research futures for housing for degrowth 256
ANITRA NELSON AND FRANÇOIS SCHNEIDER

Index 265

Figures

2.1	RESPONDER project system map for housing for degrowth	17
2.2	A degrowth housing pathway (RESPONDER project)	18
2.3	A housing degrowth circular narrative	20
6.1	Exterior of April's tiny house	70
6.2	Partial interior of April's tiny house (I)	71
6.3	Partial interior of April's tiny house (II)	71
7.1	Taloa Village (Nguna Island) laneway leading to the seafront	81
7.2	The Taloa Farea on Nguna Island	82
7.3	Nguna Island dwellings made from sheet metal, bush timber and thatching	83
7.4	View to the main street in Port Vila and the harbour	84
7.5	The Chief's Nakamal in Port Vila, post-Tropical Cyclone Pam	86
7.6	A traditional house on Tanna Island	89
7.7	Example of built fabric found in suburban and peri-urban areas of Port Vila	90
7.8	A temporary 'pop-up' structure for the 2014 Independence Day Celebration (Tanoropo Village, Nguna Island)	92
11.1	Section of house with basement	138
11.2	Basement being constructed	139
11.3	A basement in use	141
11.4	Computer keyboards embedded in concrete roof	142
11.5	Smart roof functionality	143
12.1	The Undercroft, Lammas	148
12.2	The masterplan of the roundhouse, Holzen	152
12.3	Debarking day, March 2017	153
13.1	The micro-agro linked to the neighbourhood	159
13.2	Neighbourhoods in a borough	161
13.3	The microcenter, ground floor	163
13.4	A borough	165
13.5	A world map of possible territories	169
14.1	A theory of dwelling quality influencing subjective wellbeing	179
20.1	Roles and relations in the Mietshäuser Syndikat association	236

Tables

1.1	Average ratio of household debt to disposable income in select countries (1995 and 2015)	9
11.1	Soil quantity available from basements of various projects	140
11.2	Comparing various roof areas for their potential	143
13.1	Parachutes from capitalism = pillars of degrowth	157

Foreword

This is a splendid and entertaining book on housing and urban planning for degrowth. There are not only many chapters on types of degrowth housing but also discussions of top-down and bottom-up urban planning. The emphasis is on Europe, but there are also examples from the United States (US), Australia, the Pacific and India. Authors mentioned include, of course, Thoreau, Patrick Geddes, Lewis Mumford, Lefebvre's 'right to the city', David Harvey's 'rebel cities', Serge Latouche's 'décroissance' and Ted Trainer's 'Simpler Way' – with a chapter by him on his amazing house near Sydney, at Pigface Point. Another chapter summarises Hans Widmer's utopian book *bolo'bolo* (1983), emphasising the concept of neighbourhood.

It is easy to find – right around the globe – many cases of environmental conflicts over access to urban or peri-urban land, and over urban pollution and waste disposal in landfills or incinerators, cases related to growth and some mentioned in this book. Currently, for instance, between the airports of Roissy and Le Bourget near Paris, there is a major conflict on the proposed urban development of EuropaCity (listed in the online atlas of cases of environmental injustice, EJAtlas – www.ejatlas.org/). Farmers and environmentalists are against this megaproject driven by Auchan and Chinese investor Wanda.

On 6 March 2018, the administrative tribunal annulled authorisation for the immense 'greenfield' complex EuropaCity – proposed to house supermarkets, hotels and cultural facilities in the so-called 'zone d'aménagement concerté' in the 'Triangle of Gonesse', north of Paris. Their environmental impact assessment was considered to be insufficient. The administrative tribunal of Cergy-Pontoise considered that there was not enough information for a project that would eliminate 280 hectares of agricultural land and cost €3.1bn. Criticism has been in terms of 'gigantism' and loss of agricultural soils – an emblematic example of French conflicts between plans for large urbanisation and preservation of agricultural areas. It is likely to be another failed *'grand projet inutile imposé'* (large, useless and imposed project), like the airport in Nantes, which has been defeated by the *zadistes*.

These examples show how often urban planning for growth is linked to struggles for socio-environmental justice, and confronted by alliances of a variety of protagonists. There are different constellations of interests and values, and often the defence of peri-urban agriculture and water sources takes a prominent place, as shown in several chapters in this book. Other relevant contemporary cases in the EJAtlas include the fight against urban sprawl in Valle de Lurin (Lima), fights against pollution and inadequate housing in the Riachuelo-Matanzas river basin in Buenos Aires, and many cases of new infrastructure (such as motorways, airports and golf courses) sprawling outwards from Mexico City on land belonging to ancient *ejidos* (communal land collectively maintained). Thus, the filling in of lakes in Bangalore/Bengalura is explained in one chapter, which not only describes degrowth types of housing but also disasters of urban growth.

There is a scandalous coincidence, in many countries, between empty housing and increasing homelessness. New, unnecessary, housing is being promoted as an investment (asset). Mortgages force homeowners to give more of their income to the banks, which then offer even more mortgage credit. The ratio of household debt to disposable income has increased. In contrast, a degrowth perspective explores ways of responding to needs for shelter and security in a socially equitable and environmentally sustainable fashion. Thus, the resilience of local buildings in the face of a cyclone in Vanuatu, a Pacific nation, is carefully analysed in one of the chapters.

In Europe, we travel from cases of grassroots resistance and squatting in Barcelona (Claudio Cattaneo) to the 'right to the city and its social metabolism' in Rome (Elisabeth S. Olsen et al.) and on to the famous borough of Christiania in Copenhagen, where contributor Natasha Verco has lived. A methodology used in many chapters is described as 'auto-ethnography'. There are chapters on successful attempts at collectively self-built rural housing in Germany and at the Lammas ecovillage in Wales (Dale et al.), and 'tiny housing' in the US (April Anson). One chapter by Pernilla Hagbert (Stockholm) presents an ecofeminist viewpoint on housing. Lina Hurlin explains, with insider's knowledge, the work of the Mietshäuser Syndikat (an association of numerous collectively owned housing projects) in Germany. Similarly, Mara Ferreri discusses the refurbishment and demolition alternatives for social housing in London from an activist's point of view.

Several chapters analyse degrowth types of housing and varieties of living together, such as eco-collaborative housing in peri-urban Melbourne and Twin Oaks community (Virginia, US). Sharing housing in various forms should be allowed and even commonplace at national and local levels. Not only maximum rates of occupancy of houses and apartments should be prescribed, but also minimum rates of occupancy. There are far too many empty houses in Europe.

A debate draws several contributors into confrontation. Against urban growth, and for a 'localist' approach that does not imply chauvinism, is Andreas Exner who writes on the agricultural use of the Donaufeld (Vienna) and Karl Krähmer on rural markets (*genuino clandestino*) in Italy. On the 'open localism' side are also the very competent editors of the book, Anitra Nelson and François Schneider, both practising 'degrowers' and mature ecological economists and political ecologists. In favour of urban growth is Jin Xue, who knows about China but, here, writes as a top-down urban planner in Scandinavia, and Aaron Vansintjan, a follower of Murray Bookchin, who amusingly compares the bureaucratic difficulty with composting domestic waste in an urban park in London with the welcome he enjoyed from spontaneous urban agriculturalists in Hanoi.

Although the book has a very wide geographical range, Latin America, China and Africa are somewhat absent. The first two regions are fully urbanised while some countries in Africa are still suffering from very rapid rates of urban growth so it would be interesting – in further work in this area – to discuss alternatives to this trend. As Ignacy Sachs wrote decades ago about Brazil, 'it could be a rural Paradise but it is becoming an urban Hell'.

This book gives hope and inspiration beyond the fields of urban planning and sustainable housing. A degrowth perspective is based on decreasing social metabolism, while escaping from the market and the state into increasing communality and conviviality. This degrowth perspective opens up a very wide research agenda for a number of sectors of human activity, such as food and agriculture for degrowth ('food sovereignty') and energy for degrowth ('energy sovereignty'), concepts that inspired, in the present book, the idea of 'housing sovereignty'. Other books to follow in a degrowth series could focus on transport and degrowth; water and degrowth; health for, and because of, degrowth; informatics and degrowth; nature, conservation and biodiversity for degrowth; population growth versus degrowth; knowledge, education and degrowth. I wish that François Schneider and Anitra Nelson, so well-known already in degrowth studies, would become editors of such a series of books.

Joan Martinez-Alier

Acknowledgements

This collection evolved from a Housing for Degrowth session and papers on similar topics in other sessions of the 5th International Conference for Degrowth held in Budapest 30 August–3 September 2016, where we called for expressions of interest to contribute to such a collection. Therefore, we thank the organisers of that lively conference, which attracted more than 600 participants in a range of scholarly and activist events, and the networks that spread our call resulting in a range of submissions from which we made the current selection. In particular, we thank Joan Martinez-Alier, who was a keynote speaker at the conference and encouraged us in this enterprise; consequently we asked him to write the Foreword.

François Schneider (Chapter 2, especially) acknowledges the contribution of work completed within the RESPONDER, Knowledge Base: Sustainable Housing projects, specifically the first and second multinational knowledge brokerage events in Barcelona in 2012 and 2013 funded by the European Commission's FP7 under the Environment (including Climate Change) theme. This chapter has been possible thanks to the RESPONDER project. The ideas expressed are the authors, and, as usual, errors are ours.

April Anson gratefully acknowledges the photographer Jeremy Beasley for Figure 6.1 (Exterior of April's tiny house) and Olivia Clingman-White for Figure 6.2 (Partial interior of April's tiny house (I)) and for Figure 6.3 (Partial interior of April's tiny house (II)).

Mara Ferreri (Chapter 9) gratefully acknowledges that her project received funding from the European Union's Horizon 2020 research and innovation programme under Marie Skłodowska-Curie grant agreement No. 6655919.

Jasmine Dale et al. (Chapter 12) gratefully acknowledge Simon Dale (www.beingsomewhere.net), the photographer of Figure 12.1 (The Undercroft, Lammas).

Chapter 13 is a summary, by François Schneider, of P.M.'s (2014) work *The Power of Neighborhood and The Commons* published in Brooklyn by Autonomedia, whose permission we greatly appreciate to reproduce this version here, which includes five figures and a table from the original publication.

Chapter 15 by Jin Xue draws on, updates and revises a previously published article: 'Is eco-village/urban village the future of a degrowth society? An urban planner's perspective', *Ecological Economics* 105 (2014): 130–8, with permission from Elsevier.

All graphic contributions not otherwise credited are the work of the author/s of the chapter within which they appear. The co-editors gratefully acknowledge their creation of these images.

Abbreviations

£	British pound
€	Euro
A$	Australian dollar
ABC	Australian Broadcasting Commission
	Anti-Boredom-Centre/s (Widmer chapter)
aka	also known as
ASTRA	Alternative Science and Technology for Rural Areas (India), now the interdisciplinary Centre for Sustainable Technology
ATER	territorial agency for residential construction (Lazio, Italy)
AVEI	Auroville Earth Institute
BBC	British Broadcasting Commission
BDA	Bangalore Development Authority
BICA	Bend of Islands Conservation Association
CO_2	carbon dioxide (emissions)
CPO	compulsory purchase order
CSEB	Compressed Stabilised Earth Blocks
ELZ	environmental living zone
EU	European Union
FPÖ	Freedom Party of Austria
Gescal	Gestione Case per i Lavoratori
GFC	global financial crisis
GLA	Greater London Authority
Ha	hectare(s)
i.e.	that is
IMF	International Monetary Fund
IPCC	Intergovernmental Panel on Climate Change
IT	information technology
KDR	knock down and rebuild
kl/yr	kilolitre per year
km	kilometres
LBS	London Borough of Southwark
LID	low impact development

m²	square metre
m³	cubic metre
M5S	5 Stars Movement (*Movimento 5 Stelle*)
MJ	megajoule
NFS	National Forest System
OECD	Organisation for Economic Co-operation and Development
PAH	Plataforma de Afectados por la Hipoteca (Platform of People Affected by Mortgages)
RBA	Reserve Bank of Australia
RBCC	Round the Bend Conservation Co-operative
RV	recreational vehicle
SBCI	Sustainable Buildings and Construction Initiative
THOWs	tiny homes on wheels
TLIO	The Land Is Ours
UK	United Kingdom
UN	United Nations
UNISDR	United Nations Office for Disaster Risk Reduction
UNEP	United Nations Environment Programme
US	United States
US$	United States dollar
V	volt/s
W	watt/s
WWII	World War II

Contributors

Co-editors

Anitra Nelson is Associate Professor at the Centre for Urban Research, RMIT University (Melbourne, Australia). Research interests focus on housing and community-based sustainability, environmental justice, housing affordability and non-monetary futures. Nelson was a Carson Fellow at the Rachel Carson Centre for Environment and Society at the Ludwig Maximilian University of Munich (2017–2018) completing *Small Is Necessary: Shared Living on a Shared Planet* (2018). She has co-edited *Life Without Money: Building Fair and Sustainable Economies* (2011), *Planning After Petroleum: Preparing Cities for the Age Beyond Oil* (2016) and *Sustainability Citizenship in Cities: Theory and Practice* (2016) – https://anitranelson.info/

François Schneider has promoted degrowth, the degrowth movement and degrowth debate in France and Europe since 2001 (after initiating the Towards Carfree Cities Conference series in 1997). Schneider co-founded Research & Degrowth (2006) (http://degrowth.org/), initiated and co-organised the first two degrowth conferences, in Paris (2008) and Barcelona (2010) and has supported recent ones. He co-organised several seminars on housing for degrowth within the European Commission RESPONDER project and co-edited two degrowth special issues of the *Journal of Cleaner Production* (2010, 2013). He co-authored the influential French/Spanish *Degrowth: Ten Questions* (2010) and is (precarious) Associate Researcher at the Institute of Environmental Science and Technology (ICTA), Autonomous University of Barcelona. In 2012, he started the demonstration and experiential project Can Decreix (Cerbère, France), the 'house of degrowth', combining theory and practice – http://degrowth.org/can-decreix/

Foreword

Joan Martinez-Alier is Professor of Economics and Economic History, Institute of Environmental Science and Technology (ICTA), Autonomous University of Barcelona. Renowned author, including works such as *Ecological Economics: Energy, Environment and Society* (1987), *The Environmentalism of the Poor:*

A Study of Ecological Conflicts and Valuation (2002) and (co-ed.) *Handbook of Ecological Economics* (2015). Founding member and past-president of the International Society for Ecological Economics, a strong degrowth proponent, he advises Research & Degrowth (2009–) and was a key contributor to 'degrowth for housing' in the European Commission RESPONDER project.

Chapter contributors

April Anson is a doctoral candidate, Eric Englund Fellow in American Studies, and Jane Campbell Krohn Fellow in Literature and the Environment at University of Oregon (US). Her studies on indigenous, environmental and biopolitics in nineteenth-century American literatures have appeared in journals and books; her dissertation analyses literary genre for concepts of white possession, examining the implications of private property, sovereignty and settler colonialism for contemporary social and environmental justice movements.

Claudio Cattaneo gained his doctorate in Environmental Science from the Institute of Environmental Science and Technology (ICTA), Autonomous University of Barcelona, where he is Associate (= precarious) Professor. He has lectured in universities in Spain, Italy and Edinburgh. He practises and researches alternative, rural and urban squatting, and eco-communities – incorporating research on degrowth and agroecology. He co-edited a *Futures* special issue Politics, Democracy and Degrowth (2012) and *The Squatters' Movement in Europe: Commons and Autonomy as Alternative to Capitalism* (2014).

Wendy Christie is an Architect, currently practising in Australia, with several years' experience practising and teaching in remote tropical contexts. Wendy has expertise in disaster risk management as it relates to traditional architecture in Vanuatu and maintains an ongoing engagement with the University of Adelaide through its Master of Architecture international studio programme based in Vanuatu. While based in Vanuatu (2012–2015), Wendy worked in collaboration with the Vanuatu Cultural Centre on cultural heritage tourism projects, and completed an assessment of traditional architecture post-Tropical Cyclone Pam.

Jasmine Dale is a Permaculture Designer and Teacher, with 15 years' experience applying permaculture in 'low impact' settings. She lives at the Lammas eco-village in Wales where she has spent ten years designing and implementing an integrated landscape of natural homes, food growing, animal husbandry, fuel, energy and water systems with maximum regard for the environment. She has trained hundreds of people combining permaculture teaching with self-development, practical skills and playful creativity.

Andreas Exner studied Ecology at University of Vienna where he is completing his doctoral thesis in political science on 'Natural resources, green economy and ecological modernisation – the transformation of centre-periphery relations under conditions of multiple crises'. He has published widely on social ecological transformation, resource politics and urban development. He researches edible cities at Vienna University of Economics and Business, and is a Research Fellow at Catholic Social Academy (2018–2019), focusing on social ecological transformation and solidarity economy in a perspective of societal democratisation.

Mara Ferreri is Marie Curie Postdoctoral Research Fellow at the Autonomous University of Barcelona (Spain) on the Commoning Housing (2016–2019) project. In 2012 Ferreri – with Professor Loretta Lees, Southwark Notes Archives Group, the London Tenants Federation and Just Space – worked on the Challenging the 'New Urban Renewal' project, funded by the Antipode Foundation Scholar-Activist Award. In solidarity with organised residents, the project researched displacement caused by council housing demolitions, as recorded in *Staying Put: An Anti-Gentrification Handbook for Council Estates in London* (2014).

Pernilla Hagbert gained her doctorate in Architecture (Chalmers University of Technology) in 2016. Her thesis *Reconceptualising Home in a Low-Impact Society* examined socio-cultural aspects of home-related practises, norms and representations of 'sustainability' in Swedish housing developments. Currently, she is a Post-Doctoral Researcher in the division of Urban and Regional Studies, Department of Urban Planning and Environment, Royal Institute of Technology in Sweden, working on the Beyond GDP-Growth: Scenarios for Sustainable Building and Planning project – exploring alternative ways of building, living and residing as part of transitions to a low-impact society.

Anja Humburg and Robin Marwege designated all their energies, in 2017, to self-build a dwelling for low-impact living in northern Germany helped by volunteers and friends. As a freelance journalist for commons and degrowth, Anja has learned and written about ideas of low-impact living. Robin has worked as coordinator for study programmes on education for sustainable development at Leuphana University of Lüneburg, Germany. As builders, both Robin and Anja have participated in community building projects in Germany and Wales.

Lina Hurlin is an activist campaigning for 'the right to the city'. In 2013, she co-founded a housing project in Leipzig, Germany, following the model of the Mietshäuser-Syndikat. In recent years, she has supported new self-organised and anti-profit housing project groups to decide on their legal form, financial plan and communication structure. Her East of Leipzig neighbourhood work has included creating a social neighbourhood centre to confront gentrification processes. She studied Political Science and African Studies at Leipzig University and Addis Ababa University (Ethiopia), completing a thesis on Ethiopian social housing.

Karl Krähmer, an activist in the Italian Happy Degrowth Movement (Italian Movimento per la Decrescita Felice – www.decrescitafelice.it), completed his master's in Territorial, Urban, Landscape and Environmental Planning at the Polytechnic University of Turin (Italy). A Greenpeace volunteer for many years, when Krähmer discovered degrowth he decided it was an ideal framework for going beyond pure environmentalism to understand social, economic and environmental systems as an inseparable whole. Krähmer grew up in Munich (Germany) but has lived in Turin for several years where he finds fertile and active communities engaging on both degrowth and planning, though with few interlinkages.

Robin Marwege, see Anja Humburg.

Elisabeth Skarðhamar Olsen is a doctoral candidate in Human Geography at Lancaster University (UK) with a MSc. in Human Ecology from Lund University (Sweden). Her PhD focuses on food-political dynamics and visions in the Faroe Islands and in São Tomé e Príncipe. Elisabeth has experience of alternative housing strategies primarily from living in political house collectives in Copenhagen and in the Freetown Christiania, but also from periodic engagements with housing activism in Rome (Italy). As a scholar-activist, Elisabeth is interested in the diverse ways that people, movements and communities are forging post-development pathways.

Marco Orefice has experience of various alternative housing arrangements; in the past decade he has been active in Rome's housing movement and the occupied self-managed political laboratory space of Acrobax (ex-cinodromo). He has a BA in Philosophy and Cultural Encounters from Roskilde University (Denmark). In 2011, he participated as a researcher in a study of the living conditions in Rome's occupations. Marco participated in building community resilience through collective management, sharing and support systems within the last occupation/squat that he lived in (comprising up to 100 families).

Giovanni Pietrangeli has a doctoral degree in History from the University of Padova (Italy) with a MA in contemporary history from La Sapienza University of Rome. His doctoral research focused on the electronics business in Italy and connections between technology, labour, identity and culture. He currently works as a freelance consultant in the field of communication and the patrimonialisation of enterprises' cultural heritage. Since the early 2000s, Giovanni has been active in Rome's housing struggle and in other social movements.

John Salong is an Economist and Policy Adviser based in Port Vila. A consultant and adviser to the Vanuatu Government, particularly the Ministry of Internal Affairs and the Ministry of Lands, he is currently Chairman of the National Housing Corporation in Vanuatu.

Harpa Stefánsdóttir is Associate Professor in Urban Planning and Spatial Place-Making at the Norwegian University of Life Sciences (Ås, Norway) where she received her PhD in Urban Planning in 2014. As a member of the research group of Urban Sustainable Planning at the Faculty of Landscape and Society, her research focus is on sustainable urban travel, liveable urban environment and public spaces with a focus on perceptions of urban atmosphere and aesthetics. She holds a master's degree in Architecture (Oslo School of Architecture).

Ted Trainer is a retired Lecturer, School of Social Work, University of New South Wales, (Australia). His main interests have been global sustainability issues, radical critiques of the economy, alternative social forms and transitionary strategies to sustainable and just futures. He has written numerous books and articles on these topics – most notably *Abandon Affluence!* (1985), *The Conserver Society* (1995) and *The Transition to a Sustainable and Just World* (2010) – all the while developing Pigface Point, an alternative lifestyle educational site near Sydney, and a website for use by critical global educators – http://thesimplerway.info

Aaron Vansintjan is a doctoral candidate at Birkbeck, University of London, and co-supervised at the Institute of Environmental Science and Technology (ICTA), Autonomous University of Barcelona. His research investigates the effect of gentrification on marginalised communities' access to food, and how people may use food to resist or challenge development narratives. Vansintjan is interested in approaching urban issues from the fields of ecological economics, urban political ecology and urban geography. He co-edits the environmental politics website Uneven Earth and is a member of Research & Degrowth.

Natasha Verco did her honours degree focusing on social movements and collective action (University of Technology Sydney, Australia). She has participated in short- and long-term squatting defence actions for housing and social centres and in environmental justice mobilisations since 1997. Verco has lived in collective houses since 1999, many in Freetown Christiania on which she has spoken at many conferences. Natasha is a Seminar Leader for a course in Global Environmental Studies from a Political Ecology perspective, a vegan chef and an activist educator with a long-term focus on developing resilient communities of resistance.

Chitra Vishwanath is the Senior Architect and Managing Director of Biome Environmental Solutions in Bangalore (India), a multidisciplinary firm of around 30 people working on ecological architecture and intelligent water and waste design. Since graduating from the School of Architecture, CEPT India, Vishwanath has practiced in Bangalore – moving from designing economic buildings to an ecological approach so that the buildings she designs are not parasitic but rather positive additions in the Anthropocene environment. A visiting professor at Impact School of Architecture, she mentors at Laxmi Institute of Architecture.

Hans Widmer ('P.M.') was born in 1947, studied in Zurich, Paris and New York, then embarked on linguistic and literary novels *Weltgeist Superstar* (1980), *Die Schrecken des Jahres 1000* (1999), *AKIBA* (2008) and *Manetti Lesen* (2012); dramatic works (radio drama and documentary plays); and books and articles on urban, ecological and political topics, such as *bolo'bolo* (1993), *Subcoma* (2000), *Neustart Schweiz* (2009) and *The Power of Neighborhood and the Commons* (2014). He co-founded housing cooperatives (namely Karthago, Kraftwerk1 and NeNa1) and is a board member of the neighbourhood community network Neustart Schweiz (Restart Switzerland).

Jin Xue received her PhD in Urban Planning from Aalborg University, Denmark in 2012. She is currently Associate Professor at the Norwegian University of Life Sciences. Jin Xue has a research focus on environmental sustainability of housing development and limits to urban growth. She is actively engaged with the frontier of international degrowth debates to explore alternative sustainable urban futures. She has published widely on issues related to housing and urban sustainability, degrowth and ecocities in leading international scientific journals.

Part I
Simple living for all

1 Housing for growth narratives

Anitra Nelson

Our collection on housing for degrowth opens with this brief chapter on everyday narratives on mainstream housing for growth. Narrative inquiry focuses on subjective points of view and cultural paradigms for experiential understanding but here we are interested in mainstream aspirational narratives, narratives as they appear in the media, street and political discourses, both neatly reflecting and generating everyday practices and, by producing negative responses, even propelling counter-systemic change.

On the one hand, housing presumably intends to satisfy basic human needs, such as shelter, security and a context for sociability. On the other hand, it is a major sector of the economy. For instance, the construction sector accounts for around 9 percent of the gross domestic product (GDP) and 18 million jobs within European Union (EU) countries, with an internal market estimated at €13 trillion and clear significance for EU's Europe 2020 plans (EC 2016). Furthermore, the sheer amount of materials and energy used by the sector – indicated further below – is widely acknowledged. Indeed, the European Commission has specifically identified that: 'The great challenge faced by economies today is to integrate environmental sustainability with economic growth and welfare and "doing more with less"' (EC 2016, 6).

This chapter summarises key characteristics of mainstream housing and the general context within which degrowth theories and practices spelled out in later chapters develop as forms of resistance and creative construction of alternative housing futures. It suffices here to define 'degrowth' (one type of 'postgrowth') as a cultural, political and economic movement for societal transformation beyond capitalist growth and consumerism, aiming to achieve global ecological sustainability and satisfy everyone's basic needs. The chapter specifically introduces Chapter 2, which presents the umbrella narrative incorporating principles for creating homes, household practices, housing policies and planning strategies appropriate for degrowth housing futures. Chapter 2 also integrates how and where succeeding chapters fit in to address specific aspects of a holistic housing for degrowth trajectory.

The aspirational narrative: home ownership

The capitalist production of dwellings and residents buying and renting houses and apartments in the market are integral to the growth paradigm and growth narratives that dominate national politico-economic structures and global cultures in the early twenty-first century. The aspirational narrative of owning one's own home, private ownership, has grown over recent decades even in countries where rental and social housing had become primary norms during the twentieth century. In 2015, 69 percent of residents in the EU-28 member countries were in owner-occupied dwellings, 20 percent were in commercial tenancies and 11 percent were tenants in either free or 'reduced-rent' accommodation (Eurostat 2017).

The own-your-own-home narrative runs like this: save, buy your haven (your 'castle') and, as you pay it off, it becomes your 'nest egg', your asset. Parents, peers, builders, developers and financiers iterate this line; it is a dominant ideal powering the housing construction and real estate sectors and associated advertising. Likewise, governmental housing policies are structured around this narrative as it has become a self-fulfilling dynamic of preferred, indeed 'sensible', practice in the everyday world. Simultaneously, tenants become second-class citizens and homelessness even occurs in the wealthiest countries.

Housing for growth is newly constructed on either cleared land or as a redevelopment after demolition. Large industrial, financial and commercial players envisage more housing and larger houses built and sold as quickly as possible so they can make more money and remain competitive. As such, there is no incentive to build either more sustainably or for durability. In a complementary way, glossy housing and homemaker magazines, television programmes and Internet advertising promoting large, unsustainable, dwellings have multiplied, even as average household sizes shrink. The multi-award winning British television series, *Grand Designs*, presented by Kevin McCloud (BBC Channel 4 1999–) is exemplary of the narrative. The home is a status symbol and 'bigger', or simply more expensive, is 'better'.

Yet finding affordable, environmentally sustainable and well-located housing either to purchase or to rent has become increasingly difficult in many cities and towns, especially in growing 'global cities', such as most national and state (provincial) capitals. Strong markets for housing tend to drive up prices, as apparent in certain Organisation for Economic Co-operation and Development (OECD 2018a) countries over the last decade: the 2017 average price of Canadian dwellings rose to 153 percent on 2010 nominal prices (139 percent in real terms) and for Norway, over the same period, the rise was 147 percent in nominal prices (and 128 percent in real prices). Rising prices tend to favour homeowners, whose assets' worth increases but makes entry to home ownership difficult. As house prices escalate, flowing on to rental costs and charges, it becomes more difficult for renters to save for a deposit to purchase a home. In certain global cities such phenomena are widespread.

Tenancy, squatting and homelessness

The aspirational narrative denigrates renting as a waste of money. Moreover, poor rental conditions and regulations structurally support and drive people to home ownership. In the United Kingdom (UK) and Spain, for example, tenancy is not well regulated regarding key aspects of security and comfort such as length of tenancy, limits on rental charges and ability to alter dwellings. In 2017, four in every five tenants in Australia did not have a fixed-term lease or had a lease fewer than 12 months; 'thousands of tenants are being discriminated against and live in a climate of fear' (Kollmorgen 2017).

Many highly regard German rental regulations yet, in Berlin where renting is a well-established and culturally acceptable norm, by the mid-2010s rent had been rising around 4.6 percent per annum (Brady 2017) and tenant harassment is detailed in Chapter 20. Adding to the precariousness and cost of renting a dwelling in global cities, erstwhile rental properties re-purposed for tourists (say via Airbnb) have risen in number. Governments in Berlin, Amsterdam, Paris and Barcelona have moved to moderate the latter trend but covert rental continues, including through other platforms, and is not easily monitored (Gagnon 2018).

Late 2014, after squatting in, and being promptly evicted from, an abandoned bank premises in London, activist Clare Pauling (2014) ridiculed the legal system and police force who protected 1,500,000 vacant commercial and residential buildings while 110,000 people went homeless. That year a *Guardian* journalist also reviewed statistics across Europe to reveal 11,000,000 empty homes 'enough to house all of the continent's homeless twice over' (Neate 2014). Charity Shelter estimated that the rising number of UK homeless totalled one-quarter million by late 2016 (Butler 2017).

In short, secondary narratives on perceptions and experiences of renting, squatting and homelessness work to support the dominant one idealising home ownership.

The underbelly of the housing for growth narrative

Clearly, top-down housing for economic growth, does not produce housing that simply and universally meets the needs of people and the planet. The underbelly of the growth narrative is, perversely, insufficiency of housing for all, serious environmental impacts from housing developments and a political dynamic binding householders to growth capitalism.

Insufficiency: unaffordability

Home ownership comes with massive costs and risks. If you purchase an average-priced dwelling, say for £250,000 in an English city or £500,000 in London, you might well say 'I paid £250,000 (or £500,000) for it'. However, if you incurred an associated 25-year mortgage at a 5 percent interest rate for £200,000 or £450,000 respectively, think again: the cost over the life of such loans would be either more than £350,000 or close to £800,000, respectively. Adding in your deposit, as a mortgagor, your '£250,000' or '£500,000' dwelling will have cost you either more than £400,000 or more like £850,000. If interest rates rise, you pay out more. Meanwhile, if house prices fall, then selling the house – say to avoid defaulting because you have lost your job, need to move for employment or someone in the household suffers a serious illness, accident or death – could mean substantial loss of money or eviction and bankruptcy.

Indeed, household debt has risen during recent decades of neoliberal reforms that reduced social housing and other affordable housing policies, and increased private rental and home ownership in many countries. International Monetary Fund (IMF 2017) statistics for 2006–2016 show that housing price-to-income and price-to-rent ratios in many advanced capitalist countries of the Global North deteriorated. The average householder's capacity to comfortably afford either to buy or to rent housing that was convenient to work and basic services fell as wages in general failed to keep abreast of housing costs for either owner-occupiers with mortgages or tenants (IMF 2017, 1, 11). Accordingly, OECD (2015a) data shows widespread indebtedness with the average household debt in member countries varying between 51 and 292 percent of net disposable incomes.

In 2015, 11.3 percent of the populations of EU-28 countries lived in households that needed to reserve 40 percent or more of their equalised disposable income for housing. Those so affected included one in four tenants. While in certain countries, such as Ireland, Finland, Malta and Cyprus, fewer than one in 20 households had such onerous accommodation costs, two out of every five in Greece spent more than 40 percent of their equalised disposable income on housing. (Eurostat 2017.) Furthermore, with millions of homeless across Europe, reports from Spain, where mortgage terms and conditions have been particularly severe, show that in 2014 an average of close to 100 households were evicted each day as a prolonged recession had one in four unemployed (White 2015).

There is a distinct irony in current costs of housing when one compares the typical family household of half a century ago with one today: then, it had five members and one breadwinner, today it has four members and two income-earners, even if one works part-time. 'Home' is far from a haven, in fact a burden, for many households. Housing for growth is far from fulfilling all people's everyday needs for secure, modest and affordable shelter.

The environmental cost of dwellings

Capitalist production not only fails to fulfil human needs but also environmental efficiency. As with other commodities, the supply of housing is determined in quality and quantity by market producers, developers and builders in concert with investors and financial institutions. As these forces focus on opportunities to make money, dwellings are often made with newly extracted and manufactured materials using energy from non-renewable sources and tend to be as big in sheer size as the market, and banks providing the credit, can bear.

By the latter half of the twentieth century, larger homes – trending in the opposite direction to falling household sizes – have encouraged over-consumption. New housing incorporates storage and power points for appliances and even entire rooms for smart digital communication technologies, television screens and sound theatre systems. With housing for growth extending suburbs in newly cleared ex-agricultural lands, ostensibly affordable housing in outer suburbs of cities is generally in inconvenient locations, with poor local services and facilities, demanding higher environmental costs such as mandatory, excessive one-passenger private car use.

According to a study of building sector resource and material use and their environmental impacts, 75 percent of the total floor area of EU building stock is residential (Herczeg et al. 2014). Average newly built house sizes in specific European countries were reported in the early 2010s: France – 112m²; Denmark – 137m²; Germany – 109m²; and Spain – 97m² (with Australia, the United States (US) and Canada at 214m², 201m² and 181m² respectively!) (Wilson 2013). Environmental impacts of building sector resource and material use range from cradle to grave, i.e. related to extraction or harvesting, processing and production of building materials to activities of building and later the maintenance, renovation, demolition and final reuse of such material or their treatment as waste.

The Herczeg study estimated embodied energy in building products (2011) at around 1.9 million terajoules (one trillion joules), two-thirds accounted for by steel, aluminium and concrete. Comparing embodied energy in building products with the EU-27 industry's final energy consumption (2006), building products made up 20 percent (equivalent to Poland's total – or half of Italy's total – energy consumption). Moreover, the largest component in construction and demolition waste of around 850 million tonnes per annum, was concrete (Herczeg et al. 2014, 7–8, 36–7). Olivier et al. (2014, 31) have calculated that cement production was responsible for around 9.5 percent of global carbon emissions. Top-down and bottom-up observers note that residential building is 'low hanging fruit' for more sustainable building and home living practices, and that the mainstream housing sector is conservative (shy) with respect to using environmental designs, practices and materials (IPCC 2015).

Furthermore, clearing landscapes of vegetation for residential settlements eliminates habitat for native birds, wildlife and biodiversity, disrupting water systems, fragmenting and clearing forests, i.e. critical carbon sinks for absorbing emissions and ameliorating global warming. This is happening at a point in history when tens of thousands of species are being extinguished each year, thousands above the background ('normal') extinction rate. Between 1990 and 2015 an area equivalent to the size of South Africa was deforested (WWF n.d.). Bren d'Amour et al. (2017, 8941) have examined global patterns of urban expansion to estimate impacts on prime croplands; each year between 2000 and 2030, urban expansion globally has and will eradicate around one million hectares of cropland.

The National Forest System (NFS) incorporating forests and grasslands that cover 8.5 percent of the US is threatened by such residential developments. With land clearing, sealing and waterproofing areas, vegetation is destroyed, soil erodes, soil condition deteriorates and water tables rise, causing salinity – with social and environmental impacts. With 21.7 million acres of rural land close to NFS lands projected to succumb to housing development by 2030, Stein et al. (2007, 38) concluded that this would 'pose substantial challenges for the management and conservation of the ecosystem services provided by NFS lands and the critical ecosystem goods and services they provide'. Moreover, associated resource depletion (including land clearing for timber construction materials) was not accounted for in this study.

Housing for growth contravenes planetary limits of the regenerative capacity of ecosystems, even as it fails to meet everyone's basic need for housing.

The ties that bind

Whatever its tenure, a 'home' is central to our identities as residents, offering emotional and practical security, a place for children and adults to study and work, a haven from a cruel world and a status symbol for invited family and friends, visitors and guests to enjoy. For all such reasons, housing is of great mundane significance and, in turn, any housing crisis has widely felt implications for our everyday lives as well as for the economy. Nevertheless, most residential wealth across nations worldwide is held in the form of dwellings. Owner-occupiers are often attracted to purchasing a dwelling not only for long-term secure housing but also as a quasi-asset.

This home-cum-commodity, which is readily seen as a status symbol and asset, inveigles many owner-occupiers into mentalities and practices of the capitalist system. As home ownership has become the major form of tenure, most owner-occupiers are mortgagors. As mentioned, the quasi-ownership of a mortgagor is often achieved by way of a mortgage debt so onerous that it obliges the householder (or two) to a regular and substantial wage, to full-time and concentrated work, for decades in an onerous arrangement. The house as asset function often only appears on final sale as, for instance, the owner-occupier downsizes and keeps savings from the sale to fund their retirement.

While offering a significant use value as accommodation, owner-occupiers who work to repay large mortgage and other household debts associate their jobs with security of tenure in their homes, which can result in anxious and fearful conformity. They are less likely to leave a job or go on strike because the repercussions might immediately hurt their housing and 'savings'; an anti-growth or anti-capitalist stand is contradictory, even anathema to their everyday practices. Mortgage debt drives economic growth and home ownership as a crucial cog in the wheel of capitalism. Credit for mortgages is one of the safest forms of capital investment in countries where the mortgage contract obliges the mortgagor to repay the debt regardless of fluctuations in its market value. Furthermore, mortgagors' impacts on real estate markets, specifically their propensity to indebtedness, has a major influence on the level of house prices. Equally, high house prices magnify debt and risks for householders (and lenders).

By way of an indicator of the growth in housing costs, see Table 1.1, which shows how the average ratio of household debt to disposable income – a debt mainly attributable to home mortgages – has grown in select countries between 1995 and 2015 (OECD 2018b). Such burdens developed for various reasons, including: a slowdown in wage growth – affecting the disposable income

Table 1.1 Average ratio of household debt to disposable income in select countries (1995 and 2015)

Country	1995	2015
Australia	96	203
Canada	103	173
Denmark	193	293
France	66	109
Netherlands	148	276
Portugal	52	145
UK	102	150

Source: OECD (2018b)

denominator; growth in demand for scarce urban land, which increased real estate values; increasing construction costs due to size and more 'smart', sustainability measures, and convenience and leisure amenities; and rises in house prices out of proportion to their actual costs as access to increasing amounts of bank credit drove up demand. While foreign capital and 'baby boomers' have been blamed for high house prices, all the factors identified are attributable to ordinary everyday play of market forces relatively unconstrained in a neoliberal regulatory environment promoting economic growth.

Similarly, rent is likely to be the major factor in a renter's budget with associated housing costs, location and condition impacting on their energy, transport and water use. Following the owner-occupier, the renter is drawn into a growth dynamic of working to service their housing costs. With fewer housing advantages than owner-occupiers, tenants who are not passive can resist or protest but, arguably, risk losing their homes or experience the reverse effect of aspiring to be owner-occupants.

In short, capitalist economies and financial sectors rely heavily on construction and real estate sectors for the production of wealth. As the cost of housing and expenses of household energy and water services and household indebtedness have risen, many have experienced greater dependence on incomes from permanent and full-time work at a point in history when insecure and precarious work conditions have become the norm. Indebtedness binds, and tends to make people beholden to, economic growth narratives that make job maintenance and creation dependent on economic prosperity (more growth). Hefty mortgages and onerous levels of rental payments can make for more compliant workers who are subservient to growth narratives. However, resistance and rebellion can also ensue; the social and environmental burdens of growth have engendered degrowth thinking, strategies and actions.

Recession and degrowth

Demonstrating precisely how economically significant the housing sector is, the global financial crisis (GFC) of 2008 was triggered by inappropriate mortgage lending in the United States, leading to widespread defaults and serious instability in markets as house prices fell, financial institutions were shaken and key ones failed. Given that finance and trade connect all nations, repercussions were felt worldwide even if in distinctive ways from place to place at least as a recession, if not depression, that continues in certain places a decade later. OECD (2015b, 70) figures show that housing costs increased in more than half of its member countries 2009–2012 with the 'steepest rises . . . in Portugal, Italy, Spain and Greece, where household income fell further and more rapidly than housing costs'. Despite acknowledgements that pro-market neoliberalism contributed to the GFC, growth-oriented neoliberalism has endured in the forms of austerity and stimulus narratives both aimed to promote economic growth, despite adverse effects on workers and unemployment.

Pre-empting discussion in Chapter 2, it is crucial to point out here that degrowth is about 'a voluntary, smooth and equitable transition to re-localized and low-carbon livelihoods' not 'unplanned recession, imposed by economic crisis within a growth regime' (Jarvis 2017, 7). Growth is the key dynamic, the driver of capitalism, which is prone to crises mainly due to the fact that exchange values (money, prices and profits) dominate use values (the uses and qualities of goods and services for us) in both capitalist production and exchange. In contrast, the degrowth movement focuses on use values – especially social values and environmental use and abuse – to reframe social relations, production and exchange to fulfil human sufficiency and environmental efficiency. While capitalist growth is about money, prices and profits irrespective of social and environmental damage, degrowth is about a society in which human needs are satisfied while respecting finite planetary limits. It is of singular significance that degrowth narratives do not simply reverse growth narratives but, rather, turn growth narratives on their heads; degrowth is not a simple reversal of direction but, rather, offers an altogether different way of approaching the satisfaction of our needs.

System change not climate change

The challenges of unaffordable market-supplied housing have collided with rising concerns over climate change, with dangerous and increasing levels of carbon emissions from capitalist activities. Growth in production for the market uses a dizzying quantity of resources, polluting, wasting and intensifying damage to Earth. With respect to establishing more sustainable economies and lifestyles, the Intergovernmental Panel on Climate Change (IPCC 2015, 675ff) has singled out residential housing and householder practices as 'low hanging fruit' in cutting carbon emissions. Due to the durability and cost of housing, key strategies include regulating for more sustainable buildings; retrofitting for sustainability; conserving, reusing and efficiently using what we already have; and transferring to both renewable and sustainable sources and systems of energy and water supply.

During the last couple of decades, countries have brought in green building regulations and cities are being planned with environmental sustainability concerns in mind. However, such approaches to sustainability are framed within growth paradigms, say using 'innovative', 'smart' and 'green' technologies, materials and energy sources and devices in houses rather than simply working with householders to do 'more with less'. This prolongation of a growth mentality and practices – narratives that caused environmental crises in the first place, carbon emissions being just the tip of the environmental disaster iceberg – have, so far, resulted in unremarkable achievements in genuinely sustainable household practices. Such outcomes are not surprising from either systemic or temporal perspectives.

Regulations overwhelmingly centre on the small fraction of additional and replaced housing added to the stock of existing housing. Strategies have focused on encouraging the building of ostensibly more sustainable houses without sufficient account of householders continuing unsustainable practices within them. There has been little attention to the per capita space in new 'sustainable' homes; regulating for maximum sizes for residential dwellings is rare (Nelson 2018). Meanwhile householders' attention is directed to affordability concerns; the bottom line remains money. Increasing housing debt and rents drive economic growth as mortgagors and renters often rely on two incomes per household. Work has become more competitive and precarious with an especially high level of youth unemployment. Such vicious cycles turn worker-consumers into agents of growth that, in turn, use expanding quantities of resources and energy, with pollution and waste intensifying damage to Earth.

Such vicious cycles have led many environmentalists to campaign under the slogan 'system change not climate change'. Of course, 'system change' begs many questions about defining 'the system' and what's wrong with it, as well as what changes are necessary and how they might be achieved. Degrowth, as a movement, both internalises some of these quandaries and discursive conflicts over visions and strategies at the same time as creating a firm stand that the central challenge we need to address with the current system is the dynamic of 'growth', which has created intolerable anti-human and anti-environmental outcomes.

One concludes that it might be better not to refer to housing for degrowth as 'alternative housing' as is normally the case; contributors to this book indicate that housing for degrowth is the way of the future and work for strategic change to mainstream such housing. In a world where environmental limits are constantly breached, conserving and efficiently using environmental resources is crucial, pointing in a distinctly degrowth direction. Indeed, the next chapter offers a suite of housing for degrowth strategies that we might apply to create an environmentally and socially sustainable future for us all.

References

Brady, K. (2017) 'German art group "haunts" landlords with evicted-tenant horror stories', *Deutsche Welle*, 28 November – www.dw.com/en/german-art-group-haunts-landlords-with-evicted-tenant-horror-stories/a-41559862

Butler, P. (2017) 'Number of rough sleepers in England rises for sixth successive year', *The Guardian*, 25 January – www.theguardian.com/society/2017/jan/25/number-of-rough-sleepers-in-england-rises-for-sixth-successive-year

Bren d'Amour, C., Reitsma, F., Baiocchi, G., Barthel, S., Güneralp, B., Erb, K.-H., Haberl, H., Creutzig, F. and Seto, K.C. (2017) 'Future urban land expansion and implications for global croplands', *Proceedings of the National Academy of Sciences of the United States of America* 114(34): 8939–44.

EC. (2016) *The European Construction Sector: A Global Partner*. Ref. Ares (2016)1253962–11/03/2016. Brussels: European Commission.

Eurostat. (2017) *Housing Statistics*. Luxembourg: European Commission, February – http://ec.europa.eu/eurostat/statistics-explained/index.php/Housing_statistics

Gagnon, M. (2018) 'Berlin housing law replenishes housing stock for renters', *Deutsche Welle*, 30 January – www.dw.com/en/berlin-housing-law-replenishes-housing-stock-for-renters/a-42360345

Herczeg, M., McKinnon, D., Milios, L., Bakas, I., Klaassens, E., Svatikova, K. and Widerberg, O. (2014) *Resource Efficiency in the Building Sector: Final Report*. Rotterdam: ECORYS Nederland BV – http://ec.europa.eu/environment/eussd/pdf/Resource%20efficiency%20in%20the%20building%20sector.pdf

IMF. (2017) *Global Housing Watch*. (Data updated 3 May 2017) – www.imf.org/external/research/housing/

IPCC. (2015) *Climate Change 2014: Mitigation of Climate Change. Working Group III Contribution to the Fifth Assessment Report*. Cambridge and New York: Cambridge University Press.

Jarvis, H. (2017) 'Sharing, togetherness and intentional degrowth', *Progress in Human Geography* – https://doi.org/10.1177/0309132517746519

Kollmorgen, A. (2017) 'Rights are few, troubles are many', *Choice*, 15 February – www.choice.com.au/money/property/renting/articles/choice-rental-market-report

Neate, R. (2014) 'Scandal of Europe's 11m empty homes', *The Guardian*, 23 February – www.theguardian.com/society/2014/feb/23/europe-11m-empty-properties-enough-house-homeless-continent-twice

Nelson, A. (2018) *Small Is Necessary: Shared Living on a Shared Planet*. London: Pluto Press.

OECD. (2015a) 'Household debt', in *National Accounts at a Glance*. Paris: Organisation for Economic Co-operation and Development – https://data.oecd.org/hha/household-debt.htm

OECD. (2015b) 'How's life? In figures', in *How's Life? 2015: Measuring Well-Being*. Paris: OECD Publishing: 55–106 – http://dx.doi.org/10.1787/how_life-2015-en

OECD. (2018a) 'Housing real/nominal house prices, 2000–2017 (2010=100)', in *Housing Indicators: Organisation for Economic Co-operation and Development Data* – https://data.oecd.org/hha/housing.htm#indicator-chart

OECD. (2018b) 'Household debt', in *Housing Indicators: Organisation for Economic Co-Operation and Development Data* – https://data.oecd.org/hha/household-debt.htm#indicator-chart

Olivier, J., Janssens-Maenhout, G., Muntean, M. and Peters, J. (2014) *Trends in Global CO_2 Emissions: 2014 Report*. The Hague: PBL Netherlands Environmental Assessment Agency; Ispra: European Commission, Joint Research Centre.

Pauling, C. (2014) 'The scandal of empty buildings made us take direct action on homelessness', *The Guardian*, 26 December – www.theguardian.com/commentisfree/2014/dec/26/love-activists-empty-buildings-direct-action-homelessness

Stein, S., McRoberts, R., Alig, R. and Carr, M. (2007) 'Forests on the edge: Housing development on America's private forests', in Smith, W., Miles, P., Perry, C. and Pugh, S. (eds.) *Forest Resources of the United States, 2007*. Gen. Tech. Rep. WO-78. Washington, DC: US Department of Agriculture, Forest Service, Washington Office: 36–40.

White, S. (2015) 'Spanish housing foreclosures rise in 2014 even as crisis ebbs', *Reuters Business News*, 5 March – https://www.reuters.com/article/spain-economy-property/spanish-housing-foreclosures-rise-in-2014-even-as-crisis-ebbs-idUSL5N0W71S020150305

Wilson, L. (2013) 'How big is a house? Average house size by country', *RenewEconomy*, 17 July – http://reneweconomy.com.au/how-big-is-a-house-average-house-size-by-country-78685/

WWF. (n.d.) 'Deforestation/How many species are we losing?' *Our Earth (Forests/Biodiversity): WWF Global* – http://wwf.panda.org/about_our_earth

2 Housing for degrowth narratives

François Schneider

Housing for degrowth proposes reducing the total urban area; simplifying and redistributing access to housing; halting industrial urbanisation; deurbanising and renaturalising areas; renovating dwellings to improve living conditions; sharing dwellings more; and developing low-level, low-impact, small-scale, decentralised, compact settlements.

How might these processes of a degrowth transformation of housing arise? Certain aspects are already taking place; other aspects need to be invented. My objective in this chapter is to show how a variety of approaches detailed in all the remaining chapters of this book coalesce in a degrowth narrative, a narrative contra most current housing lobbies even from the Left. In this story, degrowth actors are part of a coherent coalition.

Narratives

A narrative gives a pattern and causal logic to events; such stories tend to fit within world views and values. Despite challenges to growth narratives, our society is still governed by them. As outlined in Chapter 1, in the sector of housing this translates to competition, individual success stories based on larger living areas per person, larger urban surfaces, so-called 'green' or 'ecological' housing incorporating advanced technical development ('smart' cities), powerful banks favouring 'safe (wealthy) borrowers', and the great significance of a dynamic housing sector for economic growth more generally. Those narratives colonise the minds of politicians. They include narratives presented as a conflict between 'bottom-up' (numerous individual consumers and entrepreneurs) and 'top-down' (large public and private powers) who, in reality, can work in somewhat complementary ways.

What is degrowth?

Degrowth challenges the hegemony of growth and calls for a democratically led proportional and redistributive downscaling of production and consumption as a means to achieve environmental sustainability, social justice and well-being (Demaria et al. 2013). A consensus for degrowth centres on reducing the exploitation of natural resources and humans, because 'planetary boundaries' and social limits to growth are being surpassed. Furthermore, degrowth implies other types of institutions and ethics, and an efficiency, which is frugal or based on reducing inputs and outputs.

Degrowth involves a multiplicity of actors working in complementary ways from the bottom-up (from the individual to the collective) and from the top-down (from the collective to the individual). These actors include, amongst others, practitioners, researchers, artists and activists. Degrowth involves a set of values typically encompassing the search for more justice, recuperation of ecosystems, care for future generations, preference for convivial, non-utilitarian human relations, the deepening of democracy, the importance of well-being and giving full meaning to our lives. Degrowth is about keeping the functional; a great deal of social and low-tech innovation, so-called 'frugal innovation' (Schneider 2006); a bottom-up refusal of certain technologies and reduction of others; the integration of limits; and the adjustment to a new systemic reality.

Degrowth narratives

The lack of storylines outside the growth paradigm impedes the possibility of alternative policies (Berg and Hukkinen 2011). Indeed, growth narratives are omnipresent, discarding degrowth policies by default. Currently degrowth is a 'non-story' and does not act as a policy motivator. The colonisation of the imaginary described by Latouche (2005) or existing mental infrastructure described by Welzer (2011) block the entry of degrowth into political and policy horizons. One way to break through such impasses is to better understand current narratives and identify alternative pathways.

Degrowth narratives combine principles of reduction with bottom-up and top-down actions and relate important values of degrowth. They convey visions of transforming society holistically embracing ecology, economy and well-being. Here people reduce their consumption and production, and share more; everybody can access resources they need, ecosystems flourish and the economy is sustained (Bayon et al. 2010).

Many local and global alternatives to the dominant growth narratives are emerging – creating solutions and giving birth to new systems. Creative unexpected processes emerge like brainstorms. Creative chaos means ideas emerge from complex systems through networks. We find a complementary process: a creative building of pathways within the self-constructing network, as described by Videira et al. (2014). Here we describe some types of 'circular narratives'; without start or finish points, circular narratives are reiterative. These 'spiralling narratives' and 'soft revolutions' are transformative revolutionary processes, sometimes incorporating key steps but mainly advancing in steady processes of change. From the complexity of network interrelations, soft revolutions can be identified and communicated as simple stories. For ethics, this process embodies a 'positive' loop. For cybernetics, it is a 'negative feedback loop', transforming towards sustainability.

Developing narratives demand convergence and alternatives; like anabolic processes where molecules are created from atoms, collectives are built from small groups. Narratives are built by active practitioners through divergences and oppositions; like catabolic processes that break down molecules into smaller units, collectives split into working groups, action (activist) groups. In addition, the process requires revolutionary reformists to transform institutions from the inside so, at some point, barriers to transformation are crossed.

Why do we need to support degrowth narratives? Politicians and citizens seem afraid that there is no societal alternative to the one we live in despite capitalism's multiple crises, so they stick to what they know, growth policies. When afraid, citizens sometimes end up voting extreme right. To open their minds and options, and to reduce their fears, they need to realise that alternative narratives outside the growth paradigm exist (Berg and Hukkinen 2011). Creating such narratives was the motive for the RESPONDER, Knowledge base: Sustainable Housing project, and the specific purpose of the first and second multinational knowledge brokerage events in Barcelona in 2012 and 2013 funded by the European Commission's FP7 under the Environment (including Climate Change) theme.

Consequently, Schneider et al. (2013) developed an approach for the collective design of transitionary pathways in the housing sector. They identified causal links and narratives on the basis of a literature review, then critically discerned the underlying narratives and proposals among the variables identified (as shown in Figure 2.1). Finally, pathways or storylines were constructed from the pool of inter-related proposals, collectively developing system maps, and narratives of growth and degrowth (Figure 2.2). This comprehensive process involved both anabolic and catabolic processes and revealed three representative types within Europe's housing sector. Both austerity and stimulus narratives have focused on fostering growth in housing capacity, considering it an important engine for the economy. Neither narrative addresses the challenges posed by ecological limits and the housing crises associated with affordability and sustainability. However, there is a third narrative – for housing for degrowth. This is the narrative that follows, binding the themes explored in chapters in this book.

Housing for degrowth

Degrowth advocates neither perceive dwellings as financial investments nor as objects of conspicuous consumption and status symbols but, rather, as places to fulfil important social needs and basic human rights, as recognised by the United Nations (UN 2014). Housing provides a public service, as do health and education sectors. Housing can be provided by owner builders, cooperatives and municipalities, understood as an element of social networking, conviviality, good universal accessibility and as a synergy of 'satisfiers' to use the terminology of Max-Neef et al. (1989). Housing satisfies the need for shelter, simultaneously contributing to the satisfaction of multiple human needs. A degrowth perspective explores ways of responding to needs, such as for shelter, recognition and security

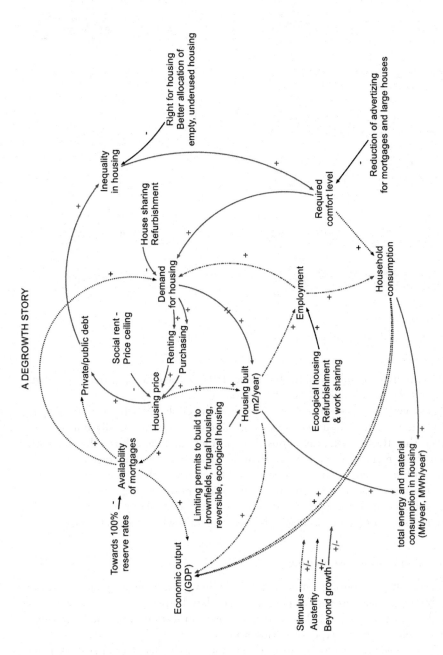

Figure 2.1 RESPONDER project system map for housing for degrowth

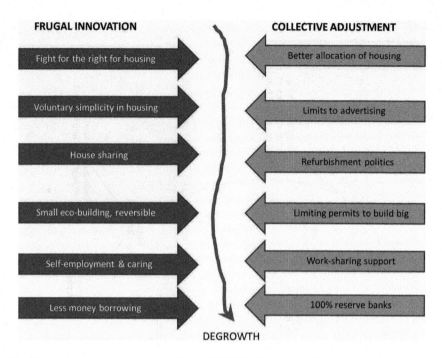

Figure 2.2 A degrowth housing pathway (RESPONDER project)

in a socially equitable fashion that leaves building new housing to a last resort. These are principles for housing for degrowth.

Degrowth and 'post-growth' supporters in the Global North most often argue that the growth of housing capacity in absolute terms is socially unnecessary given that there is excessive unused stock. Empirical data shows that for each household member there is more than 40 square metres of average useful floor area in Europe (Kees and Haffner 2010, 51) so, rather than more urbanisation, the housing crisis can be solved by re-allocating housing where people need it, or in protected areas through 'de-urbanisation', and redistributing empty or hardly used flats (the numerous secondary houses) to people who need a safe living space.

Frugal innovations in housing

The *first* frugal housing innovation is to refuse certain unacceptable housing technologies, such as sky scrapers and secondary houses only used a few weeks in the year (Schneider 2003). This is a strong innovation, from the bottom-up, saying 'No' to certain types of urbanisation.

The *second* frugal housing innovation is not a ban but a reduction, say reducing the urbanisation of the Mediterranean coast, urban sprawl, the number of swimming pools, the total area urbanised and housing under-used by the privileged.

The *third* frugal innovation is about transforming existing housing structures so that their functions drastically change to achieve better allocation and use of the available stock. This means preserving the compact city centre structure with its empty business flats or factories being re-purposed for housing and/or creating communal houses from previously individualised housing. This change of function might mean rezoning derelict urban and industrial areas, so-called 'brownfields' for collective land planning. This change of function expresses the principle of recognising limits.

The *fourth* frugal innovation is about developing alternatives, other types of urbanisation such as housing with low impacts on natural ecosystems and challenging urban sprawl. Unlike Le Corbusier and his followers, urban planning theorists, such as Patrick Geddes and Lewis Mumford, have offered guides. Here, housing efficiency is combined with frugality and conviviality. Divesting from housing projects with heavy environmental and social impacts could liberate resources for the creation of small-scale socio-ecological projects. Such practices could eliminate dependence on debt and economic growth, while generating meaningful jobs.

Finally, the *fifth* frugal innovation is frugal adjustment. Instead of a 'rebound effect' – where, say, monetary savings made through sharing are spent in a counter-productive (wasteful) manner – we have a 'debound effect' (Schneider 2003). Such frugal innovations result in an absolute reduction in the level (and, often, costs) of urbanisation, for instance, in terms of space that is sealed and covered in housing, reducing cement used and other materials extracted, reducing the flow of materials and energy use by the housing system. Last but not least, it is about a degrowth in terms of the imaginary so that a large house with swimming pool is no longer a status symbol. Overall, this adjustment enables a sufficient, even better, satisfaction of housing needs.

Developing housing for degrowth narratives

Housing is a fundamental economic sector and social need, and significant enough to indicate what we concretely envision for degrowth more generally. Degrowth housing narratives involve a sequence of small and large transformations in line with key degrowth values, namely social justice in housing, voluntary simplicity in living practices, reducing housing sector material and energy flows, reducing the ecological impacts of housing activities, encouraging housing settlement types favourable to deeper democracy, and changing how we perceive or use time and interrelate with one another.

Complementary bottom-up and top-down events can be identified in each step of the housing for degrowth narrative, i.e. in achieving social justice and housing sufficiency while reducing demand for newly built dwellings, shrinking cities, improving ecological integrity, deepening democracy, allowing more non-capitalist work time and delinking from the market (and money) more generally (see Figure 2.3). The following discussion shows how the topics and questions addressed in the chapters in this volume fit into this housing for degrowth narrative.

Figure 2.3 A housing degrowth circular narrative

Housing justice: the right to housing

Facing dramatic inequalities in housing and difficulty of access to basic housing by significant minorities, many movements defend the *right to housing*. Despite poor statistics and collection methods, it is generally acknowledged that there are more than 10 million 'empty' houses and over 4 million homeless people Europe-wide. In many countries, vigorous political movements challenge this situation. In Spain the Plataforma de Afectados por la Hipoteca (Mortgage Victims Lobby) focuses on direct action against evicting poor people who cannot afford to pay mortgages taken out towards the peak of the housing bubble in 2007. In France, there is a similar movement, Droit au Logement (Right to Housing).

There are countless bottom-up movements campaigning against gentrification and, instead, for de-urbanisation and more green spaces, for food gardening (in urban lots otherwise left vacant as the land appreciates in price), and for rehabilitating greenfields for food production. Bottom-up movements defending the right for housing include the movement in Rome (Italy) analysed by Elisabeth Skarðhamar Olsen, Marco Orefice and Giovanni Pietrangeli (Chapter 3), who raise questions about rights, distribution and justice in housing. In a complementary way, Claudio Cattaneo (Chapter 4) describes the squatters' movement in Barcelona, and associations between squatters' housing communities and the degrowth movement. Proposals along this line include strengthening squatters' rights and prohibiting house evictions, as accomplished in the cities of Grigny and Bobigny (France).

Justice is improved with social housing, where tenants pay no more than 30 percent of their incomes on rent irrespective of whether the house has a public, cooperative or private landlord. Social rent bears risks of promoting urban expansion and, perversely, pushing up average rental prices. However, social rent can promote degrowth when framed to avoid those problems, when it involves relatively low material and energy consumption, and it is most ecological when applied to existing housing infrastructure.

In most countries and cities today, access to social rent schemes is too limited to satisfy all those in need and waiting lists are very long. In some countries, like Spain or Greece, social housing is virtually non-existent, while in other countries, such as the Netherlands, it is still quite considerable, notwithstanding recent cuts. Some countries focus more on housing affordability, while others see social housing as a safety net for the poorest populations (Pittini 2013). Although there is no single European model for social housing and diversity in this field is high (Houard 2011), the stock of social housing in Europe tends to accommodate more and more vulnerable populations. Meanwhile, some prefer to self-organise housing in a social way. While social housing is increasingly seen as a neglected policy tool in European Union (EU) member states (Houard and Waine 2012), in a degrowth scenario such housing could be granted as a form of a basic income.

Renting is an obvious way to use erstwhile vacant houses, thus using existing capacity more efficiently. Transitionary policy supports could include a tax system penalising landlords of empty dwellings, favouring renting over buying and rent regulation to ensure accessibility of housing. Such regulations would need to include limits to sub-letting rooms at high nightly rates to tourists – such as with Airbnb, which is often misconceived as social sharing – because such practices disfavour permanent tenants paying inexpensive rental (Kallis 2014).

Another solution for housing justice is requisition, as demanded by many associations defending the right for housing, for example the 'DAL' (Droit au Logement) in France. A requisition law has existed in France since 1945 (Errard 2012) as applied in the 1960s – after the decolonisation of Algeria – with 120,000 requisitions under De Gaulle; in 1995, with 1000 requisitions, mainly of flats owned by banks and insurance companies, by Jacques Chirac; and, in 2001, with around 400 flats in the Paris area requisitioned by Marie-Noëlle Lienemann, state secretary of housing under Jospin. Requisition rights exist in France and Italy but could be under threat with free trade agreements like the Transatlantic Trade and Investment Partnership (IAI 2015). In the United Kingdom no such law has existed except in times of war, although British Labour Party leader Jeremy Corbyn has proposed requisitioning dwellings (BBC 2017). Housing for degrowth favours the right to fair requisition being extended and applied immediately. Olsen et al. and Cattaneo are clear: occupying and, as necessary, repairing appropriate buildings can adequately satisfy housing needs.

Sufficiency in housing

Sufficiency in housing requires an understanding of the basic needs fulfilled by housing, a process described in the chapter by Pernilla Hagbert (Chapter 5). Policies and actions that reduce advertising for cheap mortgages and luxury houses, and applying capital gain taxes on the sale of residential real estate both support viewing houses in terms of their use values rather than exchange values. Top-down limits to city branding and competition, as well as regulating advertisements for luxurious housing and mortgage schemes would dampen housing demand. Education about mortgage costs and risks, say showing the real (repayment) cost of loans over their full life, how costs vary according to different interest rates, and the costs of defaulting on a mortgage, would deconstruct housing dreams as nightmares (Berry et al. 2010).

The multi-faceted movement for simplicity in housing includes advocacy for tiny houses. Creating smaller but optimal dwellings is an innovation in the context of designs for so-called 'ecological' homes, which are most often relatively large. Recent light, reversible, renewable housing innovations revamp ideas pioneered in earlier mobile homes such as cabins, yurts, tents, tipis and caravans. Aspects of recent tiny houses are detailed by April Anson (Chapter 6) in her chapter speculating on their radical potential and limits as everyday homes. Simple and small houses are illegal under most current legislation in a range of countries but *mobile* homes escape normal minimum size regulations, which is why most 'tiny homes' are transportable (coming under mobile dwelling regulations). Reducing the size of apartments must be accompanied by the development of well-designed quality housing so dwellings fulfil sufficiency criteria – as detailed in the chapter by Harpa Stefánsdóttir and Jin Xue (Chapter 14).

Housing sufficiency must be understood in terms of the movement to voluntary simplicity, as shown in Ted Trainer's Simpler Way approach in Chapter 10 on making suburbs sustainable. Wendy Christie and John Salong (Chapter 7) offer a vivid description of how voluntary simplicity in housing contributes to resilience in the face of impacts of future climate changes by showing what happened to different types of housing when Vanuatu was struck by Tropical Cyclone Pam. Moreover, the chapter highlights how traditional practices of autonomy and collective self-help outstripped the delayed, centralised state and international aid in re-building. Extended to the Global North, if simplicity becomes a norm within perceived levels of comfort, the sufficiency of housing is more easily met and the demand for housing reduced.

Reducing housing demand

The demand for housing is reduced through the introduction and extension of efficiency, i.e. using each square metre of built space more efficiently, reusing urbanised land and reusing erstwhile construction 'waste'.

This can be achieved through sharing living spaces. During the twentieth century traditional family house sharing decreased as family sizes reduced. But recently it has become more widespread, say in Southern and Eastern Europe, for young adults to stay in their parents' homes longer. 'Shared/joint households' refers to cohabiting unrelated residents (Steinfuhrer and Haase 2009), typically at least two young adults, often without children. Sharing the associated costs of a dwelling is the basis of their relationship while convivially living with others can be an additional motivational factor.

Sharing challenges the norm of a private family home and such practices rise in times of economic crisis. He et al. (2010) have assessed the average cost per person of maintaining the same standard of living at around 40 percent less for a two-person household than in a one-person household. Research by Mayer et al. (1999) shows that the average single-person household uses 1.5 times as much water than a two-person household and twice as much per capita than a four-person household. Further economies of scale can be attained in larger dwellings with three or more people with reduced levels of resource use. Positive spill-over effects evolve from sharing electro-domestic appliances and various household tools.

A more complex level of sharing, 'cohousing' is a neighbourhood development where private dwellings and common facilities are combined to fulfil and balance collective and private needs. Many cohousing communities average between 15 and 35 families and 50–100 people. Lietaert (2010) identifies six fundamental characteristics of cohousing: participatory processes, intentional neighbourhood design, extensive common facilities, collective self-management, absence of hierarchy and separation of incomes. Like house sharing, cohousing communities enable and encourage efficient sharing habits. Cars, tools, toys and clothes for children are reused and services are offered between residents of the cohousing community and its neighbours.

Cohousing models are often set in urban or peri-urban areas whereas rural areas are more likely to support ecovillages. Nelson describes two collaborative housing models, one peri-urban quasi-cohousing and the other a rural ecovillage, in Chapter 21, which interrogates the roles of monetary and non-monetary exchange in degrowth futures. Cohousing communities are a constructive alternative to the growing atomisation and loneliness of single-person households in large cities. Natasha Verco (Chapter 8) describes the particular distribution of housing in the remarkable urban enclave ecovillage of Christiania, Copenhagen. Other types of house sharing are casual or occasional sharing associated with slowly spreading initiatives such as couch surfing and house swaps. They represent efficient improvements of the use of the housing infrastructure while building conviviality and trust.

Unfortunately, most national and city legislation does not account for communal ownership. Housing for degrowth implies that sharing is allowed and even commonplace in national and local jurisdictions. House sharing might be encouraged by progressively taxing dwelling space per capita above a maximum (Fack et al. 2011). Current laws usually specify a maximum rate of occupancy, whereas degrowth policies would apply a minimum rate of occupancy. Another policy proposal is to subsidise or offer tax reductions for house and goods sharing and to offer hospitality to homeless people (Vestbro 2013).

What is more inefficient than an empty building? The efficiency of existing buildings can be improved through refurbishment or renovation, thus avoiding the need for new constructions. However, many buildings which have not reached their use-by date are demolished instead of being renovated, an issue analysed by Mara Ferreri in Chapter 9 on a high-profile campaign against the demolition of a social housing estate in London.

Cuchi and Sweatman (2011) identify three objectives of refurbishments, first, increasing resource efficiency through productive investments to reduce the environmental impact of buildings; second, improving the habitability and technical facilities of buildings in terms of access to work, health, education, culture, sports and leisure; and, third, improving access to housing, defined as the right to a decent and adequate dwelling. They estimate that refurbishment policies could beneficially target the deep retrofit of 10 million primary Spanish residences built prior to 2001, transforming them into low-energy, low emissions, comfortable housing creating 110,000–130,000 stable, long-term jobs (2012–2050). Moreover, this initiative could reduce energy needs by up to 80 percent and hot water energy requirements by 60 percent by 2050. Refurbishment can take the form of collaborative design so that gentrification and 'renoviction' (eviction through renovation) are avoided (Anguelovski 2013). A first step would be to make an inventory of empty buildings and brownfields.

Reducing urbanisation

There are urban bottom-up movements which, in practice, are already attuned to post-growth, for instance the European Grands Projets Inutiles et

Imposés – campaigning against massive, redundant and imposed projects that highlight unnecessary infrastructures duplicating existing ones – as can be applied to housing. Urban shrinkage is a new path that is spreading widely across the world although the ways of making socially sustainable shrinking cities needs to be carefully studied (Haase et al. 2012).

Urban areas can be limited and managed in more socially and ecologically beneficial ways: reversing urbanisation of farming and wildlife zones that occurs with urban sprawl; rezoning urbanised (and 'urbanisable') land to agricultural or natural zones to support more compact ways of residing (distinct from 'mass-housing'); and sustainable transportation schemes. Land use planning can restrict urbanisation outside public transport nodes, bring back nature into the city and keep neighbourhoods compact (Register 1987). Not extending road, energy or water infrastructure is another approach. Reducing urbanisation reduces ecological impacts of housing.

Reducing ecological impacts of housing

The criteria for 'sustainable' housing within a degrowth scenario must fit neatly into a transition towards ecological and highly self-sufficient cities: converting car-based infrastructure into walking, cycling and open common spaces; relocating urban activities; developing multi-functionality and public spaces. Proximity of relationships can be fostered through urban redesign and reorganisation at small scales and distances, using regional materials and bioclimatic design and, within technical limits, tending towards water and (solar) electricity self-provision. Chitra Vishwanath (Chapter 11) highlights ways of recycling and bio-construction adapted in a city of the Global South in her chapter on design and practice for urban mud and brick dwellings in Bengaluru (South India). Furthermore, ecological cities need to be understood as all-inclusive, rather than accommodating a gentrified minority.

Urbanising wild areas is a constant risk. However, the worst aspects of sprawl can be avoided, argues Jin Xue – in Chapter 15 on compact development – if settlements are based on compact urbanisation, combining innovations in size with land planning that integrates natural ecosystems. A critic of top-down approaches, Aaron Vansintjan (Chapter 16) puts a strong case for the city including arguments involving governance and democracy.

The questions of housing at different scales, spatial relations, democratic impacts and closure raised by Xue and Vansintjan can be compared and contrasted with the multi-scale utopian vision in Chapter 13 by Hans Widmer ('P.M.'), who emphasises 'neighbourhoods as the basic module of the global commons'. Degrowth suggests that economic shrinking is not necessarily a recession. Similarly, localism is not necessarily related to closure and conservatism. Therefore, we editors, in an additional commentary, directed our attention to a clearer notion of 'open-localism' as initiated within the grass roots degrowth movement but surprisingly neglected by theoreticians of degrowth.

The two contributions by Xue and Vansintjan are enriched by three subsequent commentaries – Andreas Exner (Chapter 17), Karl Krähmer (Chapter 18) and François Schneider and Anitra Nelson (Chapter 19) – to comprise Part VI. This part displays, and allows interrogations of, the various heterogeneous views that have proliferated in the degrowth movement over urbanisation, decentralisation and associated strategies for achieving otherwise shared principles and values of degrowth.

A grassroots approach to reducing the ecological impacts of housing is by building eco-homes (Pickerill 2016) as described by Jasmine Dale, Robin Marwege and Anja Humburg in Chapter 12 on modest ecologically sound self-builds in Wales and Germany. Such housing challenges industrial housing development and brings conviviality along with new relations associated with the slow movement and work-life balance.

Housing and monetary relationships

Refurbishment could represent an important source of employment, substituting for investment and employment in 'greenfields', while leading to energy efficiency, improved design and local closed-loop business. Less production required in a degrowth scenario allows for reducing formal working hours, say to a four-day (30-hour) and, then, three-day (20-hour) working week. Work sharing, at the core of degrowth, would allow for personalisation of living spaces, neighbourhoods and general living environments, as meaningful and fulfilling individual and collective activities. Greater non-work time also means more time for deeper democracy and local planning, design and application of degrowth measures.

Claudio Cattaneo (Chapter 4) argues that reduced urbanisation implies less monetary flows and reduced demand implies less debt. A reform of the banking system, with higher reserve rates would support lower credit. Limiting the capacity of banks to create money (as debts) would likely lower the burden on natural resources and nature's sinks, as well as the overall debt burden on households. Systems of mutual financial support and alternative banks and credit cooperatives could replace commercial ones when it comes to simple small-scale housing developments, as with Cigales in France, or Fiare in Spain. Structural degrowth measures targeting housing bubbles have been suggested, including a capital gains tax on all housing. Price hikes would have to be justified by improvements in housing quality (McKim 2012).

Indicating transitionary, or hybrid, models Lina Hurlin (Chapter 20) describes a different way of investing, collectively, in modest housing through the successful model of the Mietshäuser Syndikat in Germany. In contrast, Nelson (Chapter 21) questions the role of money in a degrowth transition or vision, advocating for non-monetary avenues to institute degrowth, say through collective living where the level of collective sufficiency of communities in neighbourhoods even opens the possibility of a new mode of production.

Conclusion

This chapter has presented an approach to achieving degrowth that evolved from using system maps to deconstruct housing narratives and search for new storylines, or pathways. I argued that decolonisation of our imaginary is impeded by the absence of a degrowth narrative to exit our economic, social and ecological crises. The degrowth pathway presented was neither universal nor unique but should be read as an attempt to strike a balance between individual and collective actions along different dimensions, with everybody contributing to realising degrowth. The rest of the chapters in this book show a plethora of cases and activities that are demonstrating degrowth in practice as well as display the theoretical and political debates that degrowth has raised.

The degrowth pathway means drastic reductions of social inequality in housing, and deconstructing aspirations for luxury housing based on social comparison or financial investments, both supported by societal and individual acknowledgements that needs are best served when houses are perceived as places fulfilling important social functions, as elements of social networks and nests of conviviality. Frugal efficiencies based on better utilisation of existing housing capacity by means of sharing and a more efficient use of built space have been discussed. Alternative banking policies, such as higher reserve rates, might limit banks' capacity to offer mortgages and negatively impact on demand to increase the availability of housing through re-purposing, reusing erstwhile vacant houses and refurbishing urbanised land. In short, both social inequity and negative ecological impacts of housing reduce with economic degrowth.

References

Anguelovski, I. (2013) 'New directions in urban environmental justice: Rebuilding community, addressing trauma and remaking place', *Journal of Planning Education and Research* 33(2): 160–75.

Bayon, D., Flipo, F. and Schneider, F. (2010) *La Décroissance: 10 Questions pour Comprendre et Débattre*. Paris: La Découverte.

BBC. (2017) 'Reality check: Can the government requisition homes?' *British Broadcasting Commission News*, 16 June – www.bbc.com/news/uk-politics-40303142

Berg, A. and Hukkinen, J. (2011) 'The paradox of growth critique: Narrative analysis of the Finnish sustainable consumption and production debate', *Ecological Economics* 72: 151–60.

Berry, M., Dalton, T. and Nelson, A. (2010) *The Great Australian Nightmare: Mortgage Default and Repossession*. AHURI Research & Policy Bulletin #128. Melbourne: Australian Housing and Urban Research Institute.

Cuchi, A. and Sweatman, P. (2011) 'A national perspective on Spain's buildings sector: A roadmap for a new housing sector', *Working Group for Rehabilitation (GTR)* – www.gbce.es/archivos/ckfinderfiles/Investigacion/libro_GTR_engl_postimprenta.pdf

Demaria, F., Schneider, F., Sekulova, F. and Martinez-Alier, J. (2013) 'What is degrowth? From an activist slogan to a social movement', *Environmental Values* 22: 191–215.

Errard, G. (2012) *Quand Chirac, en 1995, réquisitionnait 1000 logements*. Paris: Figaro, 28 October – http://immobilier.lefigaro.fr/article/quand-chirac-en-1995-requisitionnait-1000-logements_badba004-2110-11e2-a06f-42da40fa6ca4/

Fack, G., Friggit, J., Geerolf, F., Gobillon, L., Laferrère, A., Ortalo-Magné, F., Renard, V., Schaff, C., Trannoy, A. and Wasmer, E. (2011) 'Pour sortir de la crise du logement, Regards croisés sur l'économie', *La Découverte* 9.

Haase, D., Haase, A., Kabisch, N., Kabisch, S., and Rink, D. (2012) 'Actors and factors in land-use simulation: The challenge of urban shrinkage', *Journal of Environmental Modelling & Software* 35(July): 92–103.

He, Y., O'Flaherty, B. and Rosenheck, R.A. (2010) 'Is shared housing a way to reduce homelessness? The effect of household arrangements on formerly homeless people', *Journal of Housing Economics* 19(1): 1–12.

Houard, N. (ed.) (2011) *Loger l'Europe. Le Logement Social dans tous ses États*. Paris: La Documentation Française, MEDDTL – DiHAL.

Houard, N. and Waine, O. (2012) 'Social housing in Europe: The end of an era?' *Metropolitics: An Online Journal of Public Scholarship about Cities and Urban Politics* – www.metropolitiques.eu/Social-housing-in-Europe-the-end.html

IAI. (2015) 'Housing action groups against TTIP, TTIP: A threat to social housing, land rights and democratic cities', *International Alliance of Inhabitants*, 17 April – www.habitants.org/news/inhabitants_of_europe/housing_action_groups_against_ttip_ttip_a_threat_to_social_housing_land_rights_and_democratic_cities

Kallis, G. (2014) 'AirBnb is a rental economy, not a sharing economy', *ThePressProject* – www.thepressproject.gr/article/68073/AirBnb-is-a-rental-economy-not-a-sharing-economy

Kees, D. and Haffner, M. (2010) *Housing Statistics in the European Union*. September. OTB Research Institute for the Built Environment, Delft University of Technology. The Hague: Ministry of the Interior and Kingdom Relations.

Latouche, S. (2005) *Décoloniser l'Imaginaire: La Pensée Créative Contre l'Économie de l'Absurde*. Lyon: Edition Parangon.

Lietaert, M. (2010) 'Cohousing's relevance to degrowth theories', *Journal of Cleaner Production* 18(6): 576–80.

Max-Neef, M.A., Elizalde, A. and Hopenhayn, M. (1989) 'Development and human needs', in *Human Scale Development: Conception, Application and Further Reflections*. New York: Apex.

Mayer, P.W., DeOreo, W.B., Kiefer, J., Opitz, E., Dziegieliewski, B. and Nelson, J.O. (1999) *Residential End Uses of Water*. Denver: American Water Works Association.

McKim, B. (2012) *Understanding Housing Bubbles*. San Bernardino: San Bernardino Pilot Project.

Pickerill, J. (2016) *Eco-Homes: People Places and Politics*. London: Zed Books.

Pittini, A. (2013) 'Social housing in the EU', Knowledge Unit, Responder Project, 2nd Multinational Knowledge Brokerage Event 'Sustainable housing in a post-growth Europe', Barcelona, 6–7 June.

Register, R. (1987) *Ecocity Berkeley: Building Cities for a Healthy Future*. Berkeley: North Atlantic Books.

Schneider, F. (2003) *Mieux Vaut Débondir que Rebondir*. Objectif Décroissance. Lyon: Ed Parangon – and in *Silence* 280, 2002 – www.decroissance.org/francois/recherche/articles/efficacite.pdf

Schneider, F. (2006) 'Dossier spécial "Pour des innovations frugales"', *Silence* 340: 4–19.

Schneider, F., Asara, V., Sekulova, F. and Martinez-Alier, J. (2013) 'Sustainable housing in a post-growth Europe', for the Responder Project, 2nd Multinational Knowledge Brokerage Event 'Sustainable housing in a post-growth Europe', Barcelona, 6–7 June.

Steinfuhrer, A. and Haase, A. (2009) 'Flexible–inflexible: Socio-demographic, spatial and temporal dimensions of flat sharing in Leipzig (Germany)', *GeoJournal* 74: 567–87.

UN. (2014) 'Special Rapporteur on adequate housing as a component of the right to an adequate standard of living, and on the right to non-discrimination in this context', *United Nations Human Rights Office of the High Commissioner* – www.ohchr.org/en/issues/housing/pages/housingindex.aspx

Vestbro, U. (2013) 'Saving by sharing cohousing for sustainable lifestyles', for the Responder Project, 2nd Multinational Knowledge Brokerage Event 'Sustainable housing in a post-growth Europe', Barcelona, 6–7 June.

Videira, N., Schneider, F., Sekulova, F. and Kallis, G. (2014) 'Degrowth narratives: A workshop', *Futures* 55: 58–77.

Welzer, H. (2011) *Mental Infrastructures: How Growth Entered the World and Our Souls*. Vol. 14. Publication Series on Ecology. Berlin: Heinrich Böll Foundation.

Part II
Housing justice

Part II
Housing justice

3 From the 'right to the city' to the 'right to metabolism'

Elisabeth Skarðhamar Olsen, Marco Orefice and Giovanni Pietrangeli

This chapter places a 'degrowth' lens on Rome's housing movement, its practice of occupying empty buildings and, particularly, the movement's claim for *diritto all'abitare* (the right to inhabit). The phenomenon of movements, collectives and trade unions occupying abandoned buildings in response to housing precarity is not new. In Italy *la lotta per la casa* (the struggle for housing) dates back to the 1960s. However, during the past two decades, especially after launching the nationwide movement platform *Abitare nella crisi* (Living in the crisis) in 2010, the movement has developed into a complex network of groups and alliances spanning major Italian cities such as Milan, Rome and Naples. Similar examples in Europe include the French *Droit au Logement*, organised as a national federation in 1998, and the Spanish squatters' movement.

With the Italian economy in a recession lasting almost two decades – arguably entering postgrowth – it is timely to begin a conversation on articulating the politics of urban housing rights within a degrowth framework. Literature engaging with both squatting and degrowth, such as Cattaneo and Gavaldà (2010), Cattaneo and Engel-Di Mauro (2015) and Cattaneo (2016), focuses on the complementarities between squatting and degrowth in practical terms (such as less resource use and convivial relations between squatters). Moreover, Martínez and Cattaneo (2014, 28) have noted that 'it is not the right to private property that is reclaimed by most squatters, but the right to a more just and equal distribution of the resources that allow a decent life'. This chapter elaborates on this point by exploring the potential of certain practices, principles and claims of Rome's mobilisation for the right to inhabit (*diritto all abitare*) to inform a sustainable degrowth of the city metabolism.

Theoretically, we draw from extensions of Lefebvre's concept of the 'right to the city' to a 'right to metabolism' (Heynen et al. 2006, 12) and the concept of 'sustainable degrowth', understood as 'an equitable downscaling of production and consumption that increases human wellbeing and enhances ecological conditions' (Schneider et al. 2010, 512). We argue that the politics of downscaling flows of matter and energy that comprise the urban metabolism raises questions about rights, distribution and justice. We suggest that movements of marginalised and precarious urban dwellers who resist pressures to move further and further away from the city centre and, instead, claim the right to inhabit the city, may be conceptualised as protagonists of a struggle for the right to metabolism, bearing the potential to advance a sustainable degrowth of Rome's metabolism.

Our methodology has taken an engaged, reflexive and ethnographic (including auto-ethnographic) approach. The analysis and questions explored are generated from direct experience in Rome's housing movement and a curiosity to engage with degrowth theory. Moreover, we interviewed four residents from two occupations, each inhabited by 70–80 families (circa 150 individuals), and three members of the youth squat project Lab Puzzle (15 inhabitants). All names have been pseudonymised.

Finally, a note on terminology: we avoid using the terms 'squatter', 'squatting' and 'squat' except following their particular usage in Italy, where such activity refers to anti-capitalist occupations, usually by anarchist and leftist youth. Since we discuss the realities of broader segments of society (such as low-income families, migrants and students) in Rome, we adopt their definitions of themselves as 'occupiers' (*occupanti*), 'occupying' (*occupare*), 'occupations' (*occupazioni*).

Housing welfare and housing movements in Rome

Significant connections and tensions characterise housing welfare and housing movements in Rome.

Housing welfare in Rome

After World War II, when the urban centres in the European continent underwent restoration and re-construction, housing became a cornerstone of most European public welfare systems (Scanlon et al. 2015). In Italy, the demand for low-budget housing was addressed through public housing (*case popolari*), i.e. low-income neighbourhood planning programmes carried out by the Autonomous Institute of Public Housing (Villani 2012) and a 'rent-to-buy' scheme introduced by the state-funded programme of INA Casa (Sotgia 2010; Nicoloso 2001).

After a decade in which the proportion of *case popolari* in Rome fell, in the early 1970s growth occurred. This was mainly due to the establishment of the *Gescal* fund (Gestione Case per i Lavoratori), the role of which became the construction of housing for workers, financed by deductions from Italian workers' salaries (Bonomo 2007; Imbesi and Scandurra 1978). Eventually however, the 1970s European trend to privatise publicly owned buildings (Houard 2012; Scanlon et al. 2015) influenced Italian housing policy. As a result, thousands of buildings across the country stood empty, although hundreds of thousands people in the major cities lacked decent housing (Emiliani 2008).

In Rome, in the early 2000s, this process culminated in what has become known as the 'the great expulsion'; residential numbers diminished circa 70 percent in historic central neighbourhoods in Rome as speculation forced real estate values to levels similar to New York's Manhattan (Berdini 2008). Residents who had traditionally inhabited and worked in the city had to relocate increasingly further away from the centre to the outskirts of Rome.

Moreover, with the 2008 Global Financial Crisis, Italy's unemployment rates became the highest in the European Union and, combined with high house prices, a 'grey zone' of residents without access to the private housing market or public housing programmes became an increasingly apparent and critical problem (Pietrangeli 2015). In Rome those most affected were low middle-class households, young people, students and migrants (Di Feliciantonio 2016a; Grazioli 2017).

Both centre-left and right political administrations have addressed this 'grey zone' housing crisis through encouraging the construction industry and intervening in real estate market mechanisms (Roma Capitale 2015a) such as the agreement made with private enterprises to construct *case popolari* under regulated prices (Roma Capitale 2015b). The former commissioner of the territorial agency for residential construction in Lazio (ATER) points out that this policy – in Italian confusingly referred to as 'social housing' (*housing sociale*) – is, in fact, an example of a neoliberal housing welfare policy. In practice, it functions as 'a price regulation policy supporting the private market' and forcing agencies like ATER to act as 'entrepreneurs and enter a competitive market which they are unable to survive' (Daniel Modigliani, interviewed 6 November 2015).

Rome's housing movement

Although housing welfare schemes operated during the Italian post-war period, the 'struggle for housing' has been a key theme throughout Rome's social movement genealogy since the 1960s. However, with the neoliberalisation of Italian housing welfare, and an increasingly critical housing emergency in Italy's urban centres, a new era of grassroots political mobilisations around housing emerged in the early 2000s. The struggle for housing had, up until then, mainly been supported by social groups such as the Italian lower classes, trade unions, autonomist and other leftist groups carrying out housing occupations for residential purposes, as well as squat projects and social centres (*Centri Sociali*, CSOA). However, in the twenty-first century, other precarious agents became key protagonists in the housing movement, such as non-Italian migrants (Nur and Sethman 2016; Mudu 2014), youths and student migrants from other parts of Italy (Di Feliciantonio 2016b).

With the neoliberal turn and new actors in the housing movement scene, the political analyses changed, as did the movement's claims and strategies. Consequently, the diverse actors involved in the movement all articulate their politics within the wider perspective and more complex claim for the 'right to inhabit', a concept closely linked to Lefebvre's 'right to the city' (Grazioli 2017; Sethman 2016). Mudu (2014) and Sethman (2016) have explored some of the approaches, strategies and various alliances and platforms characterising the right-to-inhabit movement. However, more recently, a new network called *Decide Roma* ('Rome Decides') entered the scene. This network consists of groups working on housing and other social issues, such as access to social services, and emphasises the integration of housing questions within broader social analyses and strategies.

As Sethman (2016) has highlighted, the right-to-inhabit mobilisation has experienced remarkable success in their general strategy to, on the one hand, occupy buildings and militantly resist evictions while, on the other hand, simultaneously negotiating with political institutions and obtaining public recognition for solving housing problems in Rome. It is, in fact, a prevalent understanding in Rome that the housing movement has been more capable than the political administration in solving Rome's housing emergency. For instance, a resident of the occupation *Laurentina* pointed out that:

> The municipality has to recognise the legitimacy of the movements because of their social role, solving problems that the city administration is unable to solve. That is a matter of fact: grassroots occupations of empty buildings have given people a roof over their head, and a legal address, instead of leaving them on the streets.
>
> (Diana, interviewed 7 April 2017)

One of the right-to-inhabit mobilisation's proposals for solving the housing emergency is *autorecupero* (literally self-recuperation). The struggle for *autorecupero* is, in many ways, exemplary of both the success and limits that the movement constantly faces when negotiating with political institutions. In Rome, *autorecupero* originated from meetings and debates emerging in the 1990s about alternative housing solutions, which led to the 55/1998 regional law of Lazio stating citizens' rights to propose rehabilitating a building by a shared cost agreement between a municipality and an association of future inhabitants. After a period of strong movement mobilisation – two coordinated days of eight and ten simultaneous occupations (the 'Tsunami Tours') – in January 2014 the regional administration agreed to implement projects of *autorecupero*, financed by remaining *Gescal* funds.

However, a few months later, the Italian government approved the so-called *Piano Casa* (Housing Plan), the decree n. 47/2014, proposed by the right-wing Minister of Infrastructures Maurizio Lupi, which completely overturned the *autorecupero* policy endorsed by the regional government of Lazio. *Piano Casa* is designed to strengthen the private real-estate market. Most significantly, one article (*Articolo 5*) stipulates that those occupying buildings cannot claim official residence (Grazioli 2017).

Ironically, the movement has faced intensified challenges to institutional recognition after *Movimento 5 Stelle* (M5S, the '5 Stars Movement') came to power in Rome's political administration in 2016. A political party, M5S promotes itself as a grassroots movement with five constituent claims: anti-privatisation of water supplies, free universal internet connectivity, green transportation, environmentalism and a radical development model with a degrowth framework. However, there has been an enormous gap between the radical pre-election claims and post-election performance. Current mayor Virginia Raggi has completely by-passed many pre-election promises on urban development issues, following, instead, a neoliberal approach to the municipality's real estate sector.

By way of an example, while supporting private investment in the AS Roma football club stadium to construct a 500,000 cubic metre luxury housing and business park, there has been no budget for housing welfare (Settis 2017; Favale 2017). Instead, the M5S administration has endorsed mass evictions of occupations, justified through 'legality' and 'security' discourses. This, the criminalisation of people living in occupations, and growing xenophobic and fascist tendencies in Europe have all contributed to media and public discourse representations of occupations as places of criminal activity and potential terrorist refuges.

'Right to inhabit' as 'right to metabolism'

> Reuse of empty space would also mean to create a city, which is not only a postcard city, where in down-town Rome you would find not only B&B, tourists and houses rented for thousands and thousands of Euros a month, but a city that belonged to those living and working in it, a city for those who inhabit it.
>
> (Diana, interviewed 7 April 2017)

Lefebvre and Rome's housing movement

The idea of the right to live in a dignified way inside the city, (re)claiming access and the right to animate Rome's urban spaces and services from processes of speculation and gentrification, is at the core of the political claim for the right to inhabit and distinguish Rome's current movement from the historical struggle for housing. Many scholars, such as Grazioli (2017) and Sethman (2016), have noted that Rome's contemporary housing movement frames the struggle for the right to inhabit more broadly than a struggle for a roof over one's head, instead, resonating with Lefebvre's articulation of the right to the city, as a refusal 'to be removed from urban reality' (Lefebvre 2006 [1973], 195).

Arguably, what makes Rome's right-to-inhabit mobilisation such a good example of Lefebvre's theorisation is found in the concept of *autogestione* ('self-management', in French autogestion). Lefebvre has emphasised *autogestion* as an essential element of the struggle for the right to the city. *Autogestion* is a key principle embedded in the political praxis of the actors animating Rome's right-to-inhabit mobilisation, manifesting in the way that meetings are organised and in a diversity of autonomous and self-managed initiatives, from sport centres to kindergartens. Lefebvre drew inspiration from the French non-communist and anarchist left of the 1960s and 1970s (Brenner and Elden 2009). In Italy *autogestione* is ingrained in the cultural and political methods of organisation and management of most non-parliamentary leftist groups – a legacy of the Italian *autonomia operaia* (workers' autonomy) movement, also of the 1960s and 1970s.

To Lefebvre (2009 [1966]), 150) *autogestion* was the 'essential element' of a political strategy 'giving value to the rest, and without which the rest would be worth nothing':

> It is both the way forward and the endpoint, the force that can bear the colossal load weighing on society, and which can overcome it. It shows the

practical way to change life, which remains the watchword, the goal, and the meaning of a revolution.

Thus, *autogestione* is key to the practical, process dimension of the right to the city. Harvey (2012, 5) elaborates on this pre-figurative dimension of the *process of claiming* the 'right to the city' as a form of 'shaping power over the processes of urbanisation, over the ways in which our cities are made and remade'.

Adding an environmental justice perspective (Martinez-Alier 2012) to this, we might fruitfully draw from Heynen et al. (2006) and translate the claim for the 'right to inhabit' to a claim for the 'right to metabolism', i.e. a struggle for access and control of the urban metabolism. Urban metabolism is understood as the 'global circulatory process of socio-natural relations that transforms and (re) creates urban ecosystems through the exchange of resources, capital, human and non-humans into and out of the spaces of global urbanization' (Newell and Cousins 2015, 721). As such, some of the principles and concrete proposals of Rome's right-to-inhabit mobilisation embody macro-political objectives resonating with a sustainable degrowth of the urban metabolism.

Degrowth justice?

Although degrowth – and environmental concerns more generally – have not been integrated into the analysis and politics of the right-to-inhabit mobilisation, we can observe that some of the movement's principles and proposals resonate with a degrowth approach to housing, such as the idea of *zero cemento* (zero cement) and the proposals for *bene comune urbano* (urban commons) and *autorecupero* (self-recuperation).

The complementarities of *zero cemento* with degrowth probably stems from the former concept's original evolution from struggles against the implementation of construction projects related to the '2008 Master Plan for Rome'. The Italian public research institute for environmental protection ISPRA (2015) has underscored that soil consumption is a critical aspect of urban development, with Rome's metropolitan area being one of the most intensively anthropised in the country. Thus, in relation to the '2008 Master Plan', housing activists began to link with groups such as the 'Stop I-60 committee', a civil society group criticising and mobilising against a 400,000 cubic metre construction project in Rome's south-western suburbs. Subsequently, the slogan '*zero cemento*' became a central principle of the housing movement's discourse. The claim to *autorecupero* stresses that there is neither a need for further cement nor further construction beyond the city centre, given existing unused and underused urban buildings. All our informants expressed this principle; Diana (interviewed 7 April 2017) argued that 'Rome is full of apartments and buildings which are empty . . . I don't think Rome needs more cement, the one we have is more than enough!'

This point stresses the key role of the concept of *autorecupero* for many occupations. The implementation of *autorecupero* would prevent the expulsion of citizens from the city centre, is a much less resource-intensive process and would likely lead to an increase in wellbeing (Agostini et al. 2008). According to Ricardo (18 April 2017) from Porto Fluviale, an occupation claiming recognition as a possible *autorecupero*:

> *Autorecupero* should be a cardinal and permanent policy. It is like a circular track. Family life is also a function of the city: if you like it in liberal terms, it is an 'efficiency'. People could give back to society and be more creative, do other things that would benefit the whole society. In my opinion, I do not see it as a benefit that a person should move 40–50 km from the city due to their economic condition . . . the opportunities of those living outside the city are not the same of those living in it. . . . If you spend half a day travelling, it takes a lot of your time. It seems banal but it is not.
>
> The only way to fight this is to allow people to liberate precious time for their life. I need a world which allows me a life-style that leaves me time to do the things I wish to give back to the community.

In theorising about bottom-up urban housing rights within a degrowth framework, the *zero cemento* principle and the *autorecupero* proposal are interesting, in that they act as strategies for solving housing rights and injustices with favourable impacts on Rome's urban metabolism. In fact, we would argue that this dynamic adds nuance to the debate and theorisation on relations between degrowth and environmental justice, prompting us to think beyond cases where these are two struggles in alliance with each other (Martínez-Alier 2012) to cases where the two struggles merge into one struggle for 'degrowth justice'.

However, if the claim for the right to inhabit implies a struggle for access and control of the urban metabolism, this begs the question of how access and control of the urban metabolism would be governed and managed if neither by the public administration nor market mechanisms? Answers to these questions can be deduced from the *bene comune urbano* (urban commons) concept and claim proliferating among some actors in the right-to-inhabit scene. This approach to urban property relations emphasises the right of communities to self-manage and self-govern the spaces that they inhabit as urban commons.

The concept *bene comune urbano* has existed in Naples' institutional statute since 2011, and has been extended to more than 20 medium and small municipalities in Italy to become a fundamental element of debate in the *Decide Roma* (Rome Decides) network, of which the youth squat project Lab Puzzle is a part. Sonia (interviewed 8 April 2017) from Lab Puzzle explains the urban common as 'a new institution', one that:

> goes beyond the public and beyond the private, because we do not feel comfortable in those two categories . . . but instead is embedded in the concept of community . . . understood as an actor which proposes itself as authoritative towards the political institutions.

The proposal of *bene comune urbano* is based on an analysis and critique of private property relations and speculation, while simultaneously rejecting public institutions as legitimate actors to govern urban space. Instead proponents of *bene comune urbano* propose enhancing more direct and participatory democracy through the notion of the urban space as a common.

Going back to the 'right to inhabit' and, ultimately, the 'right to metabolism' as a claim for access and control of the urban metabolism, we might characterise this notion of *bene comune urbano* as a proposed framework for managing and governing the urban metabolism – one that takes us beyond the state and the market.

An urban degrowth utopia?

So far we have looked at some macro-political claims proposed by Rome's right-to-inhabit mobilisation. We have suggested an elaboration of the right to inhabit as a claim for the right to metabolism in order to illuminate the socio-ecological dimension of the claim. In this last part we shift our attention to the dynamics that exist within 'the everyday life' of occupations. To do so, we found it fruitful to draw inspiration from Paulson's (2017) emphasis on habitual practices and cultural systems as key components for theorising about degrowth and pathways for social change in general. We also drew again from two interrelated Lefebvrian ideas: his dialectical approach to 'utopia' as a search for the possible (realistic) in relation to the impossible (idealistic) (Pinder 2013; Purcell 2014), and his point about everyday life as 'the inevitable starting point for the realization of the possible' (Lefebvre 2009 [1968], 14). The combination of these ideas allows us to articulate a thesis about the political claims and practices of Rome's housing movement resulting from debates and analyses based on lived realities, desires, perspectives, cultural systems and the micro-politics of the agents animating the movement.

We would like to suggest that the analyses and macro-political claims of the movement actors, such as *autorecupero* and *bene comune urbano*, come from debates, cultural encounters and tensions between those engaging in occupations, perceived in realist terms as coping strategies by actors and conceived of as pre-figurative practices in idealist terms. It is important to clarify that this analytical distinction between what is coping/realist/possible and prefiguration/idealist/impossible is not meant to simplify and separate, say as between 'social' (needs-based) and 'political' (ideology-based) occupations. Like Martínez and Cattaneo (2014), we recognise the complexity and problematics such separations entail; occupying with the purpose of solving an individual need can be a highly political endeavour, just as an anti-capitalist ideological stance might also solve an individual socio-economic necessity.

Nevertheless, maintaining an analytical distinction between coping and prefiguration allows us to shed light on some challenges that exist internally in occupations as a result of the diversity of motivations to occupy, right across the 'spectrum' from coping to prefiguration and prevents a conflation of this diversity, which all our informants mentioned. In the words of Davide (4 April 2017) from Porto Fluviale:

> my concept of *abitare* (to inhabit) – European, Italian with a particular history related to my particular personal biography – often conflicts with other cultural subjective biographies . . . I'm, for instance, thinking about the 'right to inhabit' and that nine out of every ten people in my occupation only think about the roof over the head.

Staying true to these kinds of nuances also prevents us from romanticising and idealising life as a housing occupant, which, in addition to the internal challenges within the occupations, is a life in constant precarity. Diana (7 April 2017) reminded us that even after eight years: 'you always have the feeling that one morning someone could come and evict you, kicking you out of the place where you have built a family, a life'.

Finally, on the positive dimensions of living in occupations, Diana (7 April 2017) stated it 'makes you more open-minded' and 'opens up a new world . . . many new worlds'. Moreover, in our experience, and confirmed by our interviewees, there are also a number of practical benefits of living in an occupation: exchange of goods such as clothes, children's toys and trolleys; the sharing of appliances; the sense of community and mutual aid, of helping each other with services such as child care and home repairs.

Conclusion

In addition to drawing attention to those aspects of sharing skills and conviviality that are characteristics of degrowth, this chapter aimed to demonstrate in this that both the micro-politics of many occupations and some macro-political claims forwarded by actors in the movement embody characteristics relevant to what we might tentatively conceptualise as an urban movement for the 'right to metabolism' and 'degrowth justice'.

We have sought to emphasise the importance of not romanticising the living conditions in occupations, but to recognise the challenges of such forced encounters between cultures, positionalities and intentions. At the same time, we have suggested that it is exactly such tensions that lead to utopian projects which 'reconstitute the possible', exemplified in Rome with macro-political claims for the right to inhabit, *zero cemento*, *autorecupero* and *bene commune urbano*. Although co-living arrangements have challenges, we expect that if the agents animating Rome's right-to-inhabit mobilisation were allowed to 'self-recuperate' urban space and freely develop their own strategies of living, this would potentially lead to sustainable degrowth futures that would embody the same micro-political elements of mutual aid, sharing, conviviality and *autogestione* that already exist in occupations.

References

Agostini, G., Bucalossi, G., Orefice, M., Palladini, C. and Pietrangeli, G. (2008) 'Inventare l'abitare', *Ass. Ideallab_06 and Coop. Inventare l'Abitare* (financier, Regione Lazio).

Berdini, P. (2008) *La città in vendita: Centri storici e mercato senza regole*. Rome: Donzelli.

Bonomo, B. (2007) *Il quartiere Delle Valli. Costruire Roma nel secondo dopoguerra*. Milan: Franco Angeli.

Brenner, N. and Elden, S. (2009) 'State, space, world: Henri Lefebvre and the survival of capitalism', in Lefebvre, H., Brenner, N. and Elden, S. (eds.) *State, Space, World: Selected Essays*. Minneapolis: University of Minnesota Press: 1–48.

Cattaneo, C. (2016) 'Natural resource scarcity, degrowth scenarios and national borders: The role of migrant squats', in Mudu, P. and Chattopadhyay, S. (eds.) *Migration, Squatting and Radical Autonomy: Resistance and Destabilization of Racist Regulatory Policies and B/Ordering Mechanisms*. London and New York: Routledge: 257–71.

Cattaneo, C. and Engel-Di Mauro, S. (2015) 'Urban squats as eco-social resistance to and resilience in the face of capitalist relations: Case studies from Barcelona and Rome', *Partecipazione e Conflitto* 8(2): 343–66.

Cattaneo, C. and Gavaldà, M. (2010) 'The experience of rurban squats in Collserola, Barcelona: What kind of degrowth?' *Journal of Cleaner Production* 18(6): 581–9.

Di Feliciantonio, C. (2016a) 'Subjectification in times of indebtedness and neoliberal/austerity urbanism', *Antipode* 48(5): 1206–27.

——— (2016b) 'Student migrants and squatting in Rome at times of austerity', in Mudu, P. and Chattopadhyay, S. (eds.) *Migration, Squatting and Radical Autonomy: Resistance and Destabilization of Racist Regulatory Policies and B/ordering Mechanisms*. London and New York: Routledge: 93–8.

Emiliani, V. (2008) 'Prefazione', in Berdini, P. (ed.) *La città in vendita. Centri storici e mercato senza regole*. Rome: Donzelli.

Favale, M. (2017) 'Stadio: Prima pietra nel 2017 ma la Regione avvisa Raggi "Serve una nuova delibera"', *La Repubblica.it* (Archives), 26 February – www.eddyburg.it/2017/02/accordo-stadio.html

Grazioli, M. (2017) 'From citizens to citadins? Rethinking right to the city inside housing squats in Rome, Italy', *Citizenship Studies* 21: 393–408.

Harvey, D. (2012) *Rebel Cities: From the Right to the City to Urban Revolution*. London and New York: Verso.

Heynen, N.C., Kaika, M. and Swyngedouw, E. (2006) 'Urban political ecology: Politicizing the production of urban natures', in Heynen, N.C., Kaika, M. and Swyngedouw, E. (eds.) *In the Nature of Cities: Urban Political Ecology and the Politics of Urban Metabolism*. London and New York: Routledge.

Houard, N. (2012) *Social housing in Europe: The end of an era? Metropolitics*, 29 September – www.metropolitiques.eu/Social-housing-in-Europe-the-end.html

Imbesi, G. and Scandurra, E. (1978) *La Produzione Edilizia Gescal: Aspetti Ttipologici e Costo del "Programma Decennale"*. Rome: Leberint.

ISPRA. (2015) *Il consumo di suolo in Italia*, Report 2015 – http://www.isprambiente.gov.it/files/pubblicazioni/rapporti/Rapporto_218_15.pdf

Lefebvre, H. (2006 [1973]) 'Space and politics', in Kofman, E. and Lebas, E. (eds.) *Writings on Cities*. Oxford: Blackwell Publishing: 185–202.

——— (2009 [1966]) 'Theoretical problems of autogestion', in Lefebvre, H., Brenner, N. and Elden, S. (eds.) *State, Space, World: Selected Essays*. Minneapolis: University of Minnesota Press: 138–52.

―――― (2009 [1968]) *Everyday Life in the Modern World*. New Brunswick and London: Transaction Publishers.

Martínez, M. and Cattaneo, C. (2014) 'Squatting as a response to social needs, the housing question and the crisis of capitalism', in Squatting Europe Kollective, Cattaneo, C. and Martinez, M. (eds.) *The Squatters' Movement in Europe*. London: Pluto Press: 26–58.

Martínez-Alier, J. (2012) 'Environmental justice and economic degrowth: An alliance between two movements', *Capitalism Nature Socialism* 23(1): 51–73.

Mudu, P. (2014) 'Ogni sfratto sarà una barricata: Squatting for housing and social conflict in Rome', in Squatting Europe Kollective, Cattaneo, C. and Martinez, M. (eds.) *The Squatters' Movement in Europe*. London: Pluto Press: 136–64.

Newell, J.P. and Cousins, J.J. (2015) 'The boundaries of urban metabolism: Towards a political–industrial ecology', *Progress in Human Geography* 39(6): 702–28.

Nicoloso, P. (2001) 'Genealogie del piano fanfani. 1939–1950', in Di Biagi, P. (ed.) *La grande Ricostruzione. Il Piano Ina Casa e l'Italia Degli Anni '50*. Rome: Donzelli: 31–63.

Nur, N. and Sethman, A. (2016) 'Migration and mobilization for the right to housing in Rome', in Mudu, P. and Chattopadhyay, S. (eds.) *Migration, Squatting and Radical Autonomy: Resistance and Destabilization of Racist Regulatory Policies and B/ordering Mechanisms*. London/New York: Routledge: 79–92.

Paulson, S. (2017) 'Degrowth: Culture, power and change', *Journal of Political Ecology* 24: 425–48.

Pietrangeli, G. (2015) 'Come cambia la domanda di case in Italia', *Civiltà di Cantiere* 5: 65–7.

Pinder, D. (2013) 'Reconstituting the possible: Lefebvre, utopia and the urban question', *International Journal of Urban and Regional Research* 39(1): 28–45.

Purcell, M. (2014) 'Possible worlds: Henri Lefebvre and the right to the city', *Journal of Urban Affairs* 36(1): 141–54.

Roma Capitale. (2015a) 'Una risposta alla questione abitativa a Roma: l'abitare non solo case', 27 April, PowerPoint presentation – www.corviale.com/wp-content/uploads/2015/04/Roma_Housingsociale_slide.pdf

―――― (2015b) 'Housing sociale, nel 2015 interventi per 2200 alloggi', 27 April, Roma (site) – www.comune.roma.it/pcr/it/newsview.page?contentId=NEW853986

Scanlon, K., Fernández Arrigoitia, M. and Whitehead, C.M.E. (2015) 'Social housing in Europe', *European Policy Analysis* 17: 1–12.

Schneider, F., Kallis, G., and Martinez-Alier, J. (2010) 'Crisis or opportunity? Economic degrowth for social equity and ecological sustainability: Introduction to this special issue', *Journal of Cleaner Production* 18(6): 511–18.

Sethman, A. (2016) 'From contention to co-governance: The case of the right to inhabit movement in Rome (2000–2013)', *Antipode* 50(2): 456–77.

Settis, S. (2017) 'All'ultimo stadio', *Eddyburg*, 3 March – www.eddyburg.it/2017/03/allultimo-stadio.html

Sotgia, A. (2010) *Ina Casa Tuscolano. Biografia di un quartiere romano*. Milan: Franco Angeli.

Villani, L. (2012) *Le Borgate del Fascismo. Storia Urbana, Politica e Sociale delle Periferie Romane*. Milan: Ledizioni.

4 How can squatting contribute to degrowth?

Claudio Cattaneo

Studies of both degrowth and squatters' movements are emerging fields of research. In the crisis of capitalism that post-industrial societies are now experiencing, proposals for degrowth and squatters' activism offer viable solutions and alternatives. In this chapter, I focus on the intersection between the two. I expand on those degrowth proposals that dealt with the strategy of 're-using empty housing and cohousing', as debated at the Second International Degrowth Conference (Barcelona 2010). The optimal use and maximum occupation of the building stock constitutes a comprehensive measure and new left policy proposal for 'prosperity without growth' (Kallis 2015). Moreover, I draw on squatters' movement studies that have dealt specifically with the housing issue (Mudu 2014; Dee 2014), enriched by my own research and personal experience as a participant in the Barcelona squatters' movement.

The chapter is organised in the following way. First, I present a definition of squatting and brief overview of relevant squatting studies that relate to degrowth. Second, I outline relevant aspects of squatting movement politics and of my experience of squatting. Third, I consider how squatting empty houses contributes to degrowth through less material consumption, and identify some drawbacks, mainly related to the uncertainty of the duration of a squat that contributes to more material consumption than otherwise necessary. Fourth, I present the case for how squatting contributes to financial and monetary degrowth, including the relevance of housing issues, namely unaffordable housing and the mortgage crisis, both of which relate to the political dimension, which is treated in the fifth section.

Squatting

Squatting can be defined as the illegal occupation of unused or abandoned private or public space in order to create a home, to provide autonomous space for personal development or to open a 'social centre', i.e. where popular activities are provided to the public by the squatting group who manage the place organised horizontally in an assembly. As such, squatting is often referred to as 'occupying' and a property that is squatted as 'occupied' or as a 'squat'.

Organised and visible squatting originated at different times across different European cities (Van Der Steen et al. 2014) – from as early as the post-war period in both England (Reeve 2005; Watson 2016) and France (Nasiali 2014). The Netherlands followed in the 1960s (Prujit 2014), along with developments in Italy referred to as the 'housing struggle' (Tozzetti 1989). In the 1970s, the *centri sociali* evolved (Mudu 2004) and, in the 1980s, squatting became prominent across several cities in Spain (Martínez-Lopez 2002) and Germany (Holm and Kuhn 2010). Such cases since the 1960s were often not as related to the basic need for accessible or affordable housing as to the need for visible spaces for autonomous political organisation. However, as rents grew steadily up to and beyond the turn of the century, housing has become unaffordable for a growing number of the population. Consequently, the number of squatting actions oriented to providing a roof over one's head has increased dramatically.

Needs motivating squatting range from practical needs to political or social needs, typically opening up a social centre. There is an important distinction between squatting that fulfils private needs (for accommodation or personal development) and squatting that fulfils social and political needs, as in the cases of social centres and where squatting for housing is part of a broader political campaign related to universal housing rights, the right to the city, or against gentrification. Very often occupiers of squats have both private and socio-political motivations.

A squat might serve as a social centre and have some housing in it, or a housing squat might constitute activities and relationships that make it a visible part of a social movement. In Spain, activists in the well-known Plataforma de Afectados por la Hipoteca (PAH, Platform of People Affected by Mortgages) squat buildings to rehouse people evicted from their previous homes, which constitutes one of the strategies PAH adopts to denounce the commodification of housing. Squatting to fulfil a basic housing need is easier for the rest of civil society to understand than the social need for self-organisation that motivates activists agitating for radical social change to address issues such as economic inequalities and environmental unsustainability.

While 'the housing question' (see Chapter 20) is more broadly understood in society than the socio-political needs of the autonomous movement, there are certain signs of a process that integrate the two. Social movements close to squat communities – but not entirely by, of and for them – have emerged to focus on the provision of dignified housing and against speculative interests over housing. For example, twenty-first century Spain is an exemplary case of speculation and growth in the real-estate sector alongside a serious lack of social housing or any rent control measures. This resulted in the rise of the PAH around 2010, following the Taller Contra la Violencia Inmobiliaria e Urbanistica (2006) (Workshop Against Real Estate and Urban Violence) and the subsequent rise in occupations of empty buildings not so much to create active social centres as to respond to the need for affordable and accessible social housing.

Throughout this chapter I focus on a type of squatting that is very common, particularly among the most politicised activists. It centres on community and living collectively in large groups. In short, this type of squatting resembles housing communes, including cohousing initiatives (Lietaert 2010), and can contribute to degrowth through living less individualistic lifestyles. Not all housing squats are like this, but 'community squat' types are prevalent and most relevant to degrowth prerogatives so they make a natural focus for this chapter.

It is important to clarify the distinction between squatting for personal needs versus squatting for social and political reasons because of their very different implications with respect to the meaning and understanding of degrowth and the various facets that these understandings can imply. I argue that the most significant contributions that the practice of squatting offers degrowth relates to material consumption; to the monetary dimension of decreased real estate business, speculation and commodification; and, when squatting for housing forms part of a social movement, to the political and democratic dimensions of degrowth, for instance, by exemplifying an institution that is neither private nor public.

The broad understanding of squatting is as a social and political action, i.e. the phenomenon of squatting social centres, and relates to the understanding of degrowth as a radical societal transformation enhanced by a change of (the decolonisation of) the imaginary, citizenship re-politicisation, democratisation of decision-making via non-hierarchical assemblies and consensus decision-making, and the enhancement of bottom-up processes stemming from grassroots movements. While these very relevant governance and cultural practices are foci for degrowth studies and deserve mention, they go beyond the scope of this particular chapter.

Certain relationships between squatting and degrowth have been raised in analyses concentrating on the specific case of rurban squats in Barcelona, such as Cattaneo and Gavaldà (2010); exploring Spanish squatters' capacity to live with much less money (Cattaneo (2011); and assessing the contribution of squats set up by urban waste pickers to manifesting left-wing degrowth ideals (Cattaneo 2017). However, I focus on the specific relationships between squatted housing and degrowth – analysing in concrete terms how this relationship has been realised by drawing from my experience as a squatter for nearly two decades. In a critical way, I assess the ways, and extent to which, squatters contribute to (and detract from) degrowth. In doing so, I operationalise the multi-faceted aspects of degrowth triply from material, monetary and political perspectives.

Experiencing squatting as a political act

I have been familiar with the squatters' movement, mainly as a user of social centres in Italy, since the 1990s. But, it was not until I moved to Barcelona to study ecological economics and learn about the existence of social centres in the hills of the Collserola Natural Park that I started to look at the phenomenon of squatting from material and ecological perspectives. Emphasising the material dimension, through the ecological economics lens (Bayon et al. 2010; Demaria et al. 2013), I began to understand the act of squatting not only as a political act against property laws but also, and primarily, as an example of ecological activism – analysed in detail in the next section. From a theoretical perspective, the material dimension of squatting relates to ecological economics literature on the biophysical 'limits to growth', the entropic dimension of societies and natural resource scarcity. Schneider et al. (2010), D'Alisa et al. (2013) and Bonaiuti (2014) have offered a thorough analysis of the material dimension of degrowth directly relating to my experience as a squatter.

Along similar ecological economics lines – and knowing experientially how a squatters' lifestyle allows one to live decently and happily with very little money – early on as an activist, I appreciated the economy in a totally new light, not reduced to the monetary dimension but, instead, understood in Aristotelian terms or *oikonomia*, i.e. as 'the art of living well'. In oikonomic terms, the monetary perspective is not of primary importance, nor is economic growth desirable. Freed from economic formulations, the squatters' oikonomy relates to the substantivist economic approach that Karl Polanyi described (1944) in his attempt to dismiss the supposed natural origin of the market economy. The squatters' oikonomy is a real and material economy that fits well within the anti-utilitarian discourse of certain French intellectual inspirers of degrowth (Latouche 2005; Kallis et al. 2013).

The political perspective is most relevant among the squatters' movement, and to a lesser extent to the movement of squatting for housing. Going against the law, risking punishment and social stigmatisation, implies *per se* a political choice. Moreover, if squatting actions and squatted projects become visible and make public declarations of the intent to reclaim a different approach to housing, say denouncing real estate speculation and gentrification, and promoting the right to use public spaces and alternative lifestyles, then the political dimensions of squatting assumes an even more prominent role. Degrowth relates to political and democratic debate (Cattaneo et al. 2012), especially in discussions of how degrowth might be achieved (Kallis 2017), the empowerment required for living according to degrowth principles and the implications of those basic principles of most squatting projects – a shift from the dominant growth-based imaginary towards notions of autonomy, conviviality direct democracy and communalism (Castoriardis 1975; Illich 1973, 1978).

Squatting and communal living contribute to material degrowth

The building sector has made a significant contribution to the deterioration of natural resources and rising carbon emissions, which constitute the exploitative ecological crisis in which we now all live. Large amounts of construction materials and energy are required to create new buildings, from the production of cement and transport of building material to the site to the ecological impacts on land cleared for buildings, as is evident in source-points of depleted mining and forested landscapes to the end-points, predominantly urban sprawls.

In comparison, the material costs of rehabilitating masses of empty or abandoned housing stock can be relatively small. This is especially so in the case of abandoned buildings. The costs might even be negligible in the case of squatting a fully furnished unsold dwelling. Empty houses and other abandoned properties are likely to be recycled and fixed up using low cost materials and low technology (i.e. expending little energy) by squatters. Developers, in contrast, destroy older buildings to build completely new dwellings.

The net material costs of squatting an unsold and uninhabited home can even be negative. Buildings left unused usually slowly deteriorate and can be denuded of electric, sanitary and heating installations by house scavengers searching to recycle materials such as copper (in electric wiring and heating systems) and aluminium (in doors and windows) or to reuse kitchen and bath furniture (such as sinks, marble tiles, toilets and shower bases). If, instead, the building is inhabited by squatters, such fittings are conserved and used in situ to secure the comfort of dwellers.

However, the illegality of squatting has drawbacks that can contribute to a higher material consumption than if the occupation was regarded legal, for temporary use. Commonly, when a building is squatted, the duration of the project is uncertain. The first stage of repair is considered temporary, in order to avoid the higher investment of fixing a building properly and then losing it in an almost immediate eviction. When recycled materials are employed, minimal consumption is associated with this early stage but, often, the energy-intensive material of cement is used. As a minority of squatting projects make it through the initial phase, and secure more or less temporary legal agreements offering certainty of a mid-term duration of occupation, then more repair and maintenance works are done and more materials employed. For instance, new glass, and even new frames for windows and doors, might be installed and electric, sanitary and heating appliances and infrastructure upgraded. Finally, as a few projects gain long-term leases or as-good-as permanent arrangements, further work and materials will be used. If these projects had initially been clearly of long-term duration, then the material consumption of the early stage of repair would have been avoided.

In the case of scaling up this model of recycling empty houses, under the most favourable circumstance of immediately securing legal permanence, minimal material use would be achieved with lower material and energetic impacts and a near to zero land-use cost. Furthermore, from a material degrowth perspective, if squatting and recycling empty houses incorporate setting up intentional communities or cohousing projects, then there are likely to be further savings, in terms of economies of scale, although the total requirements might not be very different to the case of certain typologies of individual dwellings. For instance, refurbishing one large apartment or house for one dozen inhabitants would (other things being equal) imply less material per capita than refurbishing six smaller apartments with two persons inhabiting each unit.

Squatting and communal living contribute to monetary degrowth

In terms of financial and monetary degrowth, not paying for rent constitutes a major item because the proportion of rent can be as high as 50 percent or more of a minimum income. There are two points worth considering in terms of redistributive justice. First, as rent is not paid, there can be re-allocation of wealth among different social classes because a financial transfer is not made from non-owners (likely to be less well-off than home owners) to wealthy landlords. In turn, landlords will be forced to lower rents because of a fall in demand so squatting empty and abandoned houses has positive repercussions for the entire housing market with respect to redistributing resources.

Moreover, for owners of erstwhile empty homes now in use there should be no financial loss. Occupiers are interested in looking after their living space and contribute to repair and maintenance. There can be alternatives for the medium to long term that go beyond squatting to legal occupation; squatting can be a useful strategy to start a housing project. Agreements can be reached between squatters and property owners, such as being responsible for maintenance rather than paying rent or a scheme can be devised to improve the condition of a building over a period of occupation while no rent is paid. Such agreements over maintaining the building involve no third parties (namely credit providers, such as banks) who require remuneration for their support, so this can further contribute to degrowth in monetary flows.

However, the consequences of illegal squatting can increase monetary flows, such as paying for hiring lawyers, conducting legal trials and performing the many evictions involving sheriffs and police forces. Legal costs are only minor compared to decreased demand for rent and not all squatting results in a court case that might take several months to conclude. Rental payments avoided can be higher than legal costs. However, if costly police evictions are performed without going to court and occur immediately after a squatting action is made public, the rent avoided is insignificant. In summary, the balance between rent saved and legal or eviction costs will depend on several factors. Such factors can be country- or city- and time-specific, depending on how likely a court case and eviction might be avoided, say by squatters and owners entering into negotiations, how easily a police eviction can be performed without a court case, and by how long a court case might take.

Finally, in the case of setting up a communal or cohousing project, there are monetary benefits to living together, including:

- benefitting from economies of scale, such as buying food and other basic necessities in bulk or directly from the producer
- collectively organising so that the communal household performs more productive functions than an individual household, as in the concept of the 'domestic mode of production' (Sahlins 1977), in contrast to the consumptive household of neoclassical economics
- optimising the use of space (such as kitchens, bathrooms and living spaces) and the monetary costs of maintaining them
- sharing tools and infrastructure, such as car-sharing, household appliances, garage or other household workshop tools.

The degree of monetary degrowth experienced in these situations depends on the degree of communality and sharing that each community practices and the boundaries set between individual and communal spheres. The greater communal sharing that participants can achieve, the lower the monetary spending that will be required. Larger and more diversified communities have access to more knowledge and skills and, therefore, lower monetary costs. Clearly, plumbing, electrical, cooking, carpentry, welding and gardening skills are all more likely to be found in a community rather than in one or two individuals (Cattaneo 2008).

In summary, collective housing can amplify the monetary savings of simply avoiding rent.

Squatting and communal living contribute to political dimensions of degrowth

Degrowth not only centres on shrinking the material and monetary size of economies, but the political dimension is, in my opinion, the most significant although least easily quantifiable aspect of squatting and cohousing for degrowth. The political dimension is associated, in part, with the dimensions of material and monetary degrowth already discussed but, most importantly, goes well beyond both.

In as much as squatters are relieved of paying rent they have reduced need to work in capitalist enterprises for an income. Therefore, much time erstwhile spent in the labour market can be devoted to the defence, management and organisation of the occupied house, partly for the satisfaction of other needs and partly for personal growth. 'Free' time can be spent on hobbies or creative leisure (Cattaneo 2008). The 'amateur economy' as defined by Norgard (2013) or the 'B economy' as defined by Trainer (2012) represent other interpretations of such alternative economies, outlining how time can be used differently when it is not paid work time. Having less income means starkly different outcomes for those on high disposable incomes who tend to consume more in the market.

In short, squatting offers three major forms of potential, or strategies, for moving towards a degrowth society:

- Saving time from the labour market for the capitalist economy contributes to time dedicated to a variety of political activities that can contribute to a degrowth society.
- Living in a collective allows for a wealth of experience of self-organisation and collective empowerment, embodying how degrowth societies can overcome the usual dichotomies of citizen–state and consumer–market, the communal dimension expanding and developing on the individual – mass and public – private dimensions.
- Illegal actions prompt a new political subject, the squatters' community being a powerful political subject capable of impacting on politics and institutions, particularly at the city level (Martinez 2012) and for citizens in general (for instance, members of PAH were politicised as a result of illegal squatting

developing an understanding that collective action is the way forward in struggling for housing).

Residents with aspirations to become private property owners, who proceed to act collectively to solve their financial problems, often begin to feel more empowered, identifying as, and with, a new political subject (Garcia-Lamarca 2017).

Because many squatters end up occupying houses where former residents were evicted because they could not pay their mortgages, the housing crisis and responses of occupation have contributed to shaping these new degrowth subjects, who become more inspired by collective action and aspire less to owning private property. This consciousness raising and commitment to the degrowth movement makes squatting such a good partner movement.

Conclusion

The objective of occupying empty houses combined with the creation of resident groups of wishful cohousers is a strategy with varying degrees of potential for degrowth. The illegality of squatting prevents many urban residents from pursuing occupations. However, legal variants can be constituted by the re-occupation of empty buildings, either via prior negotiation with owners or through successful negotiations once a building is occupied. This approach could be scaled up until, ideally, the total stock of vacant homes was inhabited. Thus, although initially the idea of squatting houses might seem to have limited potential, its use as a tool for entering into negotiations with owners or the proposal of setting up cohousing communities and collective living with experiences and skills development in self-organisation and self-determination could be broadly applied by the population at large.

The proposal here is to start movements devoted to high-level radicalism that cannot be confused with the heterogeneous squatting movement because they explicitly identify with the possibility of a wide-spread urban movement. Such a broad movement could be oriented to providing inexpensive dignified housing, at stopping real-estate speculation and, as a consequence, at redistributing property rights and achieving degrowth in material and monetary terms but, most significantly, towards creating politically emancipated degrowth agents.

References

Barcelona. (2010) 'Reusing empty houses and co-housing', paper at the Second Conference on Economic Degrowth for Ecological Sustainability and Social Equity, 26–29 March, University of Barcelona – http://barcelona.degrowth.org/Reusing-empty-houses-and-co-housing.89.0.html

Bayon, D., Flipo, F. and Schneider, F. (2010) *La décroissance, 10 questions pour comprendre et en débattre*. Paris: Éditions La Découverte.

Bonaiuti, M. (2014) *The Great Transition*. London: Routledge.

Castoriardis, C. (1987 [1975]) *The Imaginary Institution of Society*. Cambridge/London: MIT Press.

Cattaneo, C. (2008) *The Ecological Economics of Urban Squatters*. Doctoral thesis submitted to the Institute of Environmental Science and Technology University Autonomous Barcelona, Bellaterra.

—— (2011) 'The money free autonomy of Spanish squatters', in Nelson, A. and Timmerman, F. (eds.) *Life Without Money: Building Fair and Sustainable Economies*. London: Pluto Press.

—— (2017) 'Natural resource scarity, degrowth scenarios and national borders: The role of migrant squats', in Mudu, P. and Chattopadhyay, S. (eds.) *Migration, Squatting and Radical Autonomy*. London: Routledge.

Cattaneo, C., D'Alisa, G., Kallis, G. and Zografos, C. (2012) 'Degrowth futures and democracy', *Futures* 44: 515–23.

Cattaneo, C. and Gavaldà, M. (2010) 'The experience of rurban squats in Collserola, Barcelona: What kind of degrowth?' *Journal of Cleaner Production* 18: 581–9.

D'Alisa, G., Demaria, F. and Kallis, G. (2013) *Degrowth: A Vocabulary for a New Era*. London: Routledge.

Dee, E.T.C. (2014) 'The right to a decent housing and a lot more besides: Examining the modern English squatters movement', in Squatting Europe Kollective, Cattaneo, C. and Martinez, M. (eds.) *The Squatters Movement in Europe*. London: Pluto Press.

Demaria, F., Schneider, F., Sekulova, F., and Martinez-Alier, J., (2013) 'What is degrowth? From an activist slogan to a social movement', *Environmental Values* 22: 191–215.

Garcia-Lamarca, M. (2017) 'Creating political subjects: Collective knowledge and action to enact housing rights in Spain', *Community Development Journal* 52(3): 421–35.

Holm, A. and Kuhn, A. (2010) 'Squatting and urban renewal: The interaction of squatter movements and strategies of urban restructuring in Berlin', *International Journal of Urban and Regional Research* 35(3): 644–58.

Illich, I. (1973) *Tools for Conviviality*. London: Calder and Boyars.

—— (1978) *Toward a History of Needs*. New York: Pantheon Books.

Kallis, G. (2015) 'Yes, we can prosper without growth: 10 policy proposals for the New Left', *The Leap: System Change on a Deadline*, 23 January – https://theleapblog.org/yes-we-can-prosper-without-growth-10-policy-proposals-for-the-new-left/

—— (2017) *In Defence of Degrowth: 27 Essays and Thoughts on Degrowth* – https://indefenseofdegrowth.com/

Kallis, G., Kerschner, C. and Martinez-Alier, J. (2013) 'The economics of degrowth', *Ecological Economics* 84: 172–80.

Latouche, S. (2005) *L'invention De L'économie*. Paris: Albin Michel.

Lietaert, M. (2010) 'Cohousing's relevance to degrowth theories', *Journal of Cleaner Production* 18: 590–5.

Martinez, M.A. (2002) *Okupaciones de Viviendas y de Centros Sociales*. Barcelona: Virus.

—— (2012) 'The squatters' movement in Europe: A durable struggle for social autonomy in urban politics', *Antipode* 45(4): 866–87.

Mudu, P. (2004) 'Resisting and challenging neoliberalism: The development of Italian social centers', *Antipode* 36(5): 917–41.

—— (2014) 'Ogni sfratto sarà una barricata', in Squatting Europe Kollective, Cattaneo, C. and Martinez, M. (eds.) *The Squatters Movement in Europe*. London: Pluto Press.

Nasiali, M. (2014) 'Citizens, squatters and a-socials: The right to housing and the politics of difference in post-liberation France', *The American Historical Review* 119: 434–59.

Norgard, J. (2013) 'Happy degrowth through more amateur economy', *Journal of Cleaner Production* 38: 61–70.

Prujit, H. (2014) 'The power of the magic key: Scalability of squatting in the Netherlands and the United States', in Squatting Europe Kollective, Cattaneo, C. and Martinez, M. (eds.) *The Squatters Movement in Europe*. London: Pluto Press.

Reeve, K. (2005) 'Squatting since 1945: The enduring relevance of material need', in Somerville, P. and Springings, N. (eds.) *Housing and Social Policy: Contemporary Themes and Critical Perspectives*. London: Routledge.

Sahlins, M. (1977) *Stone Age Economics*. London: Tavistock.

Schneider, F., Kallis, G. and Martinez-Alier, J. (2010) 'Crisis or opportunity? Economic degrowth for social equity and ecological sustainability. Introduction to this special issue', *Journal of Cleaner Production* 18: 511–18.

Taller Contra la Violencia Inmobiliaria y Urbanisitca. (2006) *El Cielo está Enladrillado*. Barcelona: Edicions Bellaterra.

Tozzetti, A. (1989) *La Casa e Non Solo: Lotte Popolari a Roma e in Italia dal Dopoguerra a Oggi [Housing and Not Only It: People's Struggles in Rome and in Italy from 1945 till Today]*. Rome: Editori Riuniti.

Trainer, T. (2012) 'De-growth: Do you realise what it means?' *Futures* 44(6): 590–9.

Van der Steen, B., Katzeff, A., and van Hoogenhuijze, L. (2014) *The City is Ours: Squatting and Autonomous Movements in Europe from the 1970s to the Present*. Oakland: PM Press.

Watson, D. (2016) *Squatting in Britain 1945–1955: Housing, Politics and Direct Action*. London: Merlin Press.

Part III
Housing sufficiency

5 Rethinking home as a node for transition

Pernilla Hagbert

'Home' constitutes a key part of the everyday, the mundane and familiar, but also provides a basis for our aspirations and visions of what kind of life we wish to lead and, by extension, what kind of society we construct. How we physically, socially and cognitively construct our home as an aspect of how we conceive our relation to society and the planet, has significant implications for the social and environmental impact of residential development.

A critical understanding of the domestic, and the potential of the everyday, has been recognised in calls for both local and society-wide transitions from a 'home front' perspective (Gibson-Graham 1993; Astyk 2013), and proposes going beyond the four walls of the private dwelling to acknowledge the diverse transformative practices needed to challenge dominant norms and lock-ins. The perspective in this chapter emphasises housing for degrowth as rejecting Western bourgeois and consumerist representations of home and, instead, presents alternative housing practices, with examples from Sweden that challenge a high-consuming culture of indebtedness and neoliberalisation of housing, reimagining home as a collaborative, decommodified and feminist engagement with people and place, and a node for transitions to a low-impact society.

Finding home

The notion of home has been well-explored in Western poetry, music and literature throughout recent centuries. One of many examples is the stanza from the early nineteenth-century song 'Home, Sweet Home' by American lyricist John Howard Payne: 'Mid pleasures and palaces though we may roam, be it ever so humble, there's no place like home'.

This type of romantic depiction of home as a geographical, but also spiritual, resting place is, perhaps, one of the most common associations and conceptualisations of home in Western popular culture. Yet this concept of home is neither unproblematic in its bourgeois assumption and imperialist heritage nor is it necessarily the dominant framing in today's representation of home as embedded in consumer society. So, how could the very idea of home be critically examined, and reconceptualised – as a way of approaching the inherent proposition of immaterial values and humbleness expressed in the lyrics above – challenging the material-intense manifestations of modern ways of living?

While a deeper etymological inquiry is not the primary focus here, the terms used to define home over the centuries are relevant to address in trying to examine current conceptualisations. The English word 'home' can be traced back through early Germanic forms, where Brink (1995) connects it to meanings such as world, country, farm, village, camp, resting place and lair (signifying a connection to place and settlement) and to notions of family, household servants, love and marriage (in terms of affection and practical arrangements of everyday life). Semantic connections to fire – illustrated in the mythology of Hestia, the Greek goddess of home, hearth, family, domesticity and architecture (Moore 2000) – further underline home as connected to place and the need for shelter, but also encompass the social codifications and community constructed around the hearth.

With Western imperialism and industrialisation – particularly the rise of coal combustion and steam power – localisation of production became less bounded by local natural landscape prerequisites, instead lending itself to a rationality of market exchange and centralising labour in urban settlements (Malm 2014). Moore (2000) notes a 'domestication' of the word 'home' during urbanisation, as pre-industrial meanings signifying birthplace or native environment shift to refer more narrowly to family dwelling or house. The home came to represent new economic and socio-technical ideals of an emerging middle class, with bourgeois notions of home and domesticity associated with aspects of intimacy, privacy, seclusion and the sanctity of property. These normative understandings have shaped how Western urban residential environments developed, yet were far from the reality of overcrowded working class life, whether in nineteenth-century industrialised England, early twentieth-century Sweden or twenty-first-century marginalised communities across the globe.

Home as a political agenda

As industrialisation moved most economic (male) interests from the home to the industrial sphere, the home has tended to be less explicitly on the political agenda, instead, invoked as an aggregated 'housing issue'. Mixing politics and home life has been cautiously regarded as a private affair rather than a matter of public policy. Yet normative assumptions of what constitutes good or poor morals, a good or poor home and home life, nonetheless, have abounded, shaping policies and ideological framings of residential culture, household configurations and meanings of home as a structure of society. In the portrayal of women as harbingers of 'homeliness', the home is seen as both restrictive and empowering (Rybczynski 1986), reproducing social norms of what it means to be a good home-maker, providing a (private) domain for women and imbued with social hierarchies and patriarchal oppression.

The more direct political potential of the home was actualised in understandings of modernity and democracy during the late nineteenth and early twentieth centuries, not the least in shaping the modern Western welfare state, exemplified in the Swedish Social Democratic notion of a 'People's Home'. Within this framing, the private was made into public policy, with 'good housing for all' underlined by the ideological premise of a good resident as a productive citizen, ensuring personal freedom through collaboration in developing the country (Hård 2010).

In the era of individualisation and globalisation since, the debate regarding the extent to which home can be considered a private or public political matter echoes the same issues of a century ago. Since the deregulation of the Swedish housing sector during the 1980s and 1990s (Hedin et al. 2011), the market has steered housing development to a greater extent. In a results-oriented neoliberal view, the perceived subjectivism of home is reduced to individual preferences assumed met through the market, yet the associated concept of home tends to be streamlined and prescriptive in its market framing towards a target group, the urban 'creative' middle class.

The commodification of home

Entangled with normative ideas of what constitutes a 'good life', underlying assumptions of modernity, comfort and control in conceptualising home must be examined in the resource-intensity of mainstream residential development and the consumerist framing of what it means to live well within capitalism. The commodification of home as a product purchased and sold should be understood as an aspect of the increased speculative financialisation of housing and continued emphasis on home-ownership (Forrest 2015), but also relates to the 'lifestylification' of home and everyday life.

The framing of housing as a commodity is underlined by interlinking mortgage systems and speculative global finance. Fostering an unsustainable debt culture, the home is framed as an investment which, in turn, relies on and reproduces dominant economic and social structures that tie people to growth dogma. The ideal of home-ownership is an aspect of social, political and economic norms surrounding control over one's private domain, defining and validating you and your accomplishments as a 'responsible citizen' (Smith 2015). Within this logic, the notion of a 'housing career', as making a profit from living, is lauded as smart and responsible. Similarly, the dominating private right to property over the human right to housing reduces residents to either owners or tenants. Moreover, the idea of home as linked to private ownership perpetuated in popular media and political rhetoric supposes that people not personally invested (with a financial stake) in their residence are less attached and engaged as residents or neighbours. Yet the relation between home-ownership and place attachment (or feelings of 'at-homeness') is weak (Windsong 2010).

Furthermore, the commodification of home prescribes certain patterns of living, underlining a capitalist valuation of time and space. Beyond a shelter over one's head, there are socialisation and self-expressive needs for a home (Lawrence 1987), the latter increasingly co-opted in the equation of home, lifestyle and consumerism. From the housing sector's perspective, residents are assessed based on their willingness-to-pay and segmented into specific market groups. As an emotional, social or restorative product, the home comes to serve as a marker of social status and identity – a symbol of the cultural or financial capital associated with particular neighbourhoods and housing typologies (Gram-Hanssen and Bech-Danielsen 2004; Hauge and Kolstad 2007). In this rationale, home becomes an object of accumulation of stuff, an aspect of the technological development of domestic environments and artefacts.

The modernist idea of the home as a machine continues to influence a now increasingly globalised residential development and reduces the relation between notions of home and the productive and reproductive nature of household work to a techno-centric focus on the ability to manage household tasks as swiftly and conveniently as possible. Still, the gender divide in time spent on household work underlines a patriarchal and imperialist approach to the Western domestic ideal, where the resource and labour intensity of a comfortable home is an externality. In this view, a 'greener' way of living translates into consuming more efficient products or services (shifting domestic work further away from home), rather than fundamentally challenging the conceptualisation of home and socio-ecological implications of contemporary housing practices.

Reconceptualising home as part of degrowth transitions

Acknowledging the notion of home as an aspect shaping our connection with people and place, and organisation of everyday practices, means that we need to recognise the role home might play in transitions to a low-impact society (Hagbert 2016a). With the failure of mainstream, growth-oriented housing development to provide healthy, affordable and meaningful living environments, more and more people are seeking ways of living that are less resource intensive and more diverse – including living smaller, simpler and sharing spaces and resources. In conceptualising a more sustainable manifestation of home, a key aspect is seeing the dynamic of 'degrowing home', beyond a neoliberal view based on individual residential preferences and commodification. The home encompasses cognitive aspects of what constitutes a good life, which will need to be re-imagined, and a practical reality of being a central node for daily life, where alternative patterns of practices need to be enabled. Thus, the possibility of conceptualising home as a node for more radical societal transformations must embrace both the built environment and the mind.

Here, the home is placed as a crucible between society and individual, demanding a critical framing of agency and structural changes in the provision of housing (as a commodity and/or building) and of living environments. As a platform for engaging in low-impact degrowth practices, the home is a starting point for change bridging the segmentation of home life from other societal areas. Here, the metaphor of node proposes a shift in mind-set from what is commonly portrayed as delimited policy arenas to more useful ways of imagining everyday life as interconnected in socio-spatial terms. Situating home as an aspect of constructing alternative social and feminist ecologies, rather than relying on mainstream stories of growth and technological innovation, means considering 'doing home' in different ways.

By exploring attitudes towards and engagements in alternative housing practices – explored by Hagbert (2016b) and Hagbert and Bradley (2017) – other ways of conceptualising home that challenge current housing market logics emerge. This can be seen as 're-politicising' home, beyond any blanket solution to 'housing issues' suggested by market or standardised state-driven housing provision and, instead, emphasises a diversity in approaches, situated in the everyday. By putting other aspects into practice, the focus is shifted from the intertwined economic interests of urban and residential development, to potentially new ways of organising life, and what one can do in, and from, the home base. The following sections examine practical examples of what home could mean in a degrowth, low-impact future, based in empirical insights from alternative housing practices and projects in Sweden that explore collaborative, self-sufficient and convivial home practices.

Autonomy through collaboration

One key aspect in formulating alternative, low-impact conceptualisations of home is to critically examine an individualistic neoliberal urban development and reliance on large-scale technical systems that alienate residents from each other – paradoxically, often within an increasingly densified urban environment – and from ecological systems. Indeed, several examples of housing ideas and projects, such as eco-villages and cohousing initiatives, seek development characterised by self-management and re-connection with people and place (Chapter 21 this volume; Chatterton 2013; Vestbro and Horelli 2012), or various self-sufficiency and self-build initiatives (Hagbert and Bradley 2017; Seyfang 2010).

These approaches often acknowledge the agency of residents not as consumer or 'end users' but as actors in their own right, altogether creating the premise for a resilient local community. Particularly in countries such as Sweden, with high household indebtedness, a large number of single-person households and an ageing population, the potential of organising alternatives to increasingly isolating urban experiences within a diminishingly attainable housing market is being recognised in initiatives to create diverse living environments that enable sharing (rather than competition for) spaces, knowledge and resources.

Calls for re-ruralisation and re-localised production challenge an eco-modernist approach of further centralisation and densification and are aspects of striving for independence from an urban growth economy. Here, home is not seen primarily as a financial investment in a speculative market but as the basis for community-building that invests in another type of growth altogether. As expressed by a woman who left suburban life to transition to a post-carbon way of living in a semi-rural municipality in western Sweden, the potential in community goes beyond simply 'waving to the neighbours' over a suburban fence, keeping jobs just to pay a mortgage and purchasing everything needed for one's sustenance. A key motivation emerging in empirical studies of Swedish households engaging in transitions (Hagbert and Bradley 2017) is self-management, underlined by a desire to self-provision. Their approach to building a sustainable future is based in understanding the inter-dependency and need for neighbourly collaboration.

While the notion of home as a 'man's castle' is a prevalent analogy to signify control (and patriarchal reign), a more collaborative view of the home means embracing the struggles of negotiating shared practices and spaces. Sandstedt and Westin (2015) describe Swedish cohousing life as going beyond the dichotomy of Gesellschaft and Gemeinshaft to mediate between striving for personal independence and reciprocity in cohousing communities. However, cohousing projects have been criticised because they risk self-segregation and tend to social and ethnic homogeneity among residents (Chiodelli and Baglione 2014) – pointing to needs for inclusionary practices in who gets to take part in shared activities and spaces, and appropriate scales for collaborative efforts. For instance, a young female housing activist and resident in a newly built co-house in the Swedish city of Malmö described the use of a shared kitchen and dining space beyond serving the direct cohousing community (where residents take turns cooking communal meals twice a week), to provide a platform for urban activism and opening up the space for neighbourhood social or cultural activities.

Handling conflicts that inevitably emerge in living with others demands daring to see home as a conflicted experience, and acknowledging the voices of others. For instance, an old retrofitted Swedish co-house in Stockholm, where informal forums for discussion (outside of the regular house meetings) take place on the couch as a democratic gathering point offers opportunities for exploring 'new' forms of collective decision-making that challenge a top-down authoritarianism of the home as being ruled by a (male) 'head of the household'. Issues that arise in everyday life are brought up as 'couches' – a literal meeting on one of the couches in the shared spaces of the house where everyone in attendance is free to say whatever they want and not be judged. By negotiating individual positions in relation to the collective, compromises are made involving the benefits and limits of collaboration, and there are resources and labour available to satiate different needs at different times.

The formulation of home as both autonomous, self-sufficient and a shared experience of everyday life challenges conventional representations of home as an individualistic (nevertheless conformist) endeavour within a consumerist frame and follows understandings of autonomy as a collective project (Deriu 2014), valuing the care of people and place not as a service to be purchased, but as commonly created.

Conviviality and self-sufficiency

Rather than seeing the dwelling as an object, a commodity, in alternative housing practices the home is framed as a convivial space. As both an arena and a tool for transitions, the relationship between residents and their home environments emphasise lay (or situated) knowledge and interpretations rather than expert top-down planning. Employing a transformative understanding of housing for degrowth positions residents as co-creators of their homes and as agents of change, potentially challenging mainstream processes of housing development altogether through practices that entail reskilling and shared learning in aspects of design, construction and maintenance. By redistributing the role and power of the landlord or property owner, residents are finding different ways to re-engage with the ongoing process of making home as not only a cognitive or consumerist act, but also as a bodily, physical experience.

Within the completely ordinary but abundant existing residential stock that will have to be reinvented in a low-impact future, people are forming their lives and communities in spite of current structures, for example, reinvigorating both rural villages and large-scale modernist multi-family suburbs – both having been left to their demise in an urbanised economy – into transition hubs. As an example of the former, over the last decade, the small village of Uddebo in Western Sweden has seen an influx of people seeking affordable, low-impact or even off-grid housing solutions (Uddebo 2018). Based in a vision of 'play, experimentation and community', projects range from refurbishing an old weaving factory into workshops, art studios and meeting places, creating space for musical venues in old abandoned buildings, to forming a local co-op, building a village sauna, a bike kitchen and a community garden. Through low land costs, and housing experiments such as tiny houses, people can significantly lower their cost of living and downshift from the formal economy to further engage in the variety of activities surrounding music, theatre, art, politics, crafts and agriculture being developed. While there is a risk that such 'back-to-the-land' initiatives often consist of creatives and people with cultural (if not necessarily financial) capital, the convivial premise of these types of communities often provides an open pluralism in cultural expression and experimentation as 'trying by doing' rather than prescribing certain forms and frameworks of living, as in both conventional suburbia.

These types of practical, alternative examples propose a different way of structuring housing development, often driven by residents in either co-building or retrofitting older buildings to enable functions lost in new market-driven housing and providing opportunities to re-evaluate the very understandings of everyday life and practices in which one can engage in the existing environment. In the project HOPP in the area of Hökarängen, south of Stockholm, local residents reclaimed the story of the stereotypically marginalised suburb to, instead, co-create a vision for a post-carbon, post-growth future, 'inspiring action', for example, through integrating urban agriculture (based in permaculture principles) in, and adjacent to, modernist housing so often set in natural landscapes deemed unproductive or as potential places for further urban densification (Hoppbloggen 2018). By challenging both the functionalist segmentation of these types of housing areas as passive 'bedroom suburbs' and the current prevailing neoliberal commercialist notion of the 'mixed attractive city', residential environments are re-imagined as spaces for production in building local resilience and self-sufficiency.

Conceptualising home as a site for re-localised production, integrating multiple functions rather than the spatial and social segmentation of everyday life, means challenging both the dwelling as set functionally and the layout of the living environment prescribing certain practices. In placing the home as a node for transition, the very organisation of the home will need to facilitate experimentation, reskilling and conviviality. This, in turn, demands space that is both accessible (non-commercial) and available to change (not already scripted or spatially organised only allowing for certain operations). Open-floor plan apartments built in new urban developments within a consumerist 'lifestylification' approach do not offer the supposed flexibility as activities imagined to take place are limited to dinner parties and television-watching, rather than being seen as spaces for experimenting. Enabling self-expression through meaningful practices entails breaking with normative residential design ideas. In examples from both cohousing and other alternative housing developments, negotiation of space for activities such as woodworking, sewing, childcare and decision-making, political discussions and activism are integrated into the home environment at different scales. Instead of a clear delimitation of spaces, as in the bourgeois urban home – controlling a series of thresholds, from the neighbourhood to the entrance gate to the apartment door – the everyday practices of degrowth are not so spatially bound and open the home up for collaboration rather than enclosure.

Feminist re-imaginations of everyday life

Work-centric growth societies – where work is understood as external to and separate from home – tend to supress time for family, community and political activities (Schor 2014). In the striving for a simpler, more convivial and self-sufficient way of life, the role of 'work' in relation to home is being reassessed, whether through reducing the number of work hours per day, or working from one's kitchen, living room or neighbourhood spaces to provide goods and services that offer alternatives to mass-production and consumption. In challenging the privatised dwelling, a more participatory approach to housing also suggests cultivating 'public time', sharing spaces, time and the work involved in upholding home and daily life as a collective engagement (Jarvis 2011). More collaborative forms of living might also challenge traditional household configurations and gender norms (Vestbro and Horelli 2012) with the potential to renegotiate social relations and aspects of child-rearing as part of a common undertaking (Wasshede 2017).

Currently, largely replaced by simplistic market surveys conducted by private developers, the rigorous domestic research of the twentieth century focused on gaining understandings of the everyday and built upon the rich, situated female knowledges and experiences embedded within the practices and (re)productive work of home life (Åkerman 1984). The formulation of cohousing manifestos and programmes during the 1970s and 1980s (such as the 'live in community' idea, [bo i gemenskap], 'BIG' for short, proposed by a group of women as a model for organising housing communities through activities such as self-work) rejected the separation of productive and reproductive work, and the modernist idea of minimising and rationalising household tasks (Vestbro and Horelli 2012). Acknowledging that women's often un- or undervalued work within the home provides a valuable contribution to society demands a different valuation of knowledge associated with these types of practices. Rather than being tedious and mindless, the skills and know-how involved in what was traditionally gendered as 'female' tasks (Darke 1994) instead emphasise *other* ways of knowing and doing.

In this perspective, beyond assuming and searching for universal theories or systems for radical transformation, the home can provide a basis for feminist re-imaginations of everyday life, for example, drawing upon Haraway (1988) and Gibson-Graham (2008) to consider situated knowledge among diverse groups (women and non-Western 'others') in the mediation of home and home-making. Conventional notions of home practices are challenged by both the myriad of ongoing local transitions that make home the centre for societal transformations (Astyk 2013) and communities all over the world already engaging in non-consumerist practices and connection to place (Gibson-Graham 2008, 2011). Here, the 'mundane' is made political, where mending socks or making jam is (often tongue-in-cheek) framed as acts of non-consumerist resistance, and where cooking communal dinners or inviting strangers to dine transforms a kitchen table into a platform for cultural exchange, as in the case of the Swedish 'Invitational Department' connecting fluent Swedish-speakers with newly arrived immigrants to promote a 'society where we meet as people, talk and build relationships', from the humble basis of one's home (Invitationsdepartementet 2018).

Conclusion

This chapter explored concepts of home as a mediation between the individual and society, between the everyday and aspirations for what kind of life we want to live. Such concepts need to be critically examined for understanding the assumptions and norms inherent in a contemporary unsustainable housing development and to formulate degrowth futures. By rejecting a Western (but increasingly globalised) bourgeois and consumerist representation of home, housing for degrowth will need to explore alternative conceptualisations and practices of 'doing home'. Exploring the ways in which home is implicitly and explicitly political, might provide a different starting point in thinking about transitions to low-impact societies as situated in the everyday, where home is an ongoing process and not a product or simply a showcase for an individualised lifestyle. Re-politicising home means embracing the messiness of this process, where new forms of collective decision-making among people as interdependent neighbours and communities, who are acknowledged as actors in their own right, replace the top-down relationship between landlord and tenant, or speculative transaction between housing developer and home-buyer.

This chapter has offered certain examples from housing practices and projects in Sweden that reimagine a decommodified, collaborative and feminist conceptualisation of home. Discussing key degrowth ideas being explored in practice, the different perspectives described here emphasised only some of a diverse range of transformative practices that cut across any single concept or solution and propose alternatives to a mainstream growth-oriented urban development. This includes seeing home both as a basis for autonomy and self-management, and for inclusion, a space for experimentation and reskilling, and for sharing both spaces and knowledge, a place for embracing the everyday as convivial and collaborative rather than segmented, gendered and hierarchic. The humble potential of home lies precisely in the cross-section between physical, social and cognitive constructs of 'the good life'. Enabling a more sustainable housing development cannot simply be a question of providing more of the same – generic residential developments that lock people into inherently unsustainable structures – but underlines the need to rethink home as an evolution of our connection to people and to place, providing sustenance rather than demanding it, and as a node for transition to a low-impact society.

References

Åkerman, B. (1984) *Kunskap för Vår Vardag: Forskning och Utbildning för Hemmen.* Stockholm: Akademilitteratur.
Astyk, S. (2013) *Depletion and Abundance: Life on the New Home Front.* Gabriola Island, BC: New Society Publishers.
Brink, S. (1995) 'Home: The term and the concept from a linguistic and settlement-historical viewpoint', in Benjamin, D. and Stea, D. (eds.) *The Home: Words, Interpretations, Meanings and Environments.* Aldershot: Avebury: 17–24.
Chatterton, P. (2013) 'Towards an agenda for post-carbon cities: Lessons from Lilac, the UK's first ecological, affordable cohousing community', *International Journal of Urban and Regional Research* 37(5): 1654–74.
Chiodelli, F. and Baglione, V. (2014) 'Living together privately: For a cautious reading of cohousing', *Urban Research & Practice* 7(1): 20–34.
Darke, J. (1994) 'Women and the meaning of home', in Gilroy, R. and Woods, R. (eds.) *Housing Women.* London: Routledge: 11–30.
Deriu, M. (2014) 'Autonomy', in D'Alisa, G., Demaria, F. and Kallis, G. (eds.) *Degrowth: A Vocabulary for a New Era.* New York: Routledge: 55–8.
Forrest, R. (2015) 'The ongoing financialisation of home ownership – new times, new contexts', *International Journal of Housing Policy* 15(1): 1–5.
Gibson-Graham, J.K. (1993) 'Waiting for the revolution, or how to smash capitalism while working at home in your spare time', *Rethinking Marxism* 6(2): 10–24.
―――― (2008) 'Diverse economies: Performative practices for "other worlds"', *Progress in Human Geography* 32(5): 613–32.
―――― (2011) 'A feminist project of belonging for the anthropocene', *Gender, Place and Culture* 18(1): 1–21.
Gram-Hanssen, K. and Bech-Danielsen, C. (2004) 'House, home and identity from a consumption perspective', *Housing, Theory and Society* 21(1): 17–26.
Hagbert, P. (2016a) *A Sustainable Home? Reconceptualizing Home in a Low-Impact Society.* Doctoral thesis submitted to the Department of Architecture, Chalmers University of Technology, Göteborg, Sweden.
―――― (2016b) '"It's just a matter of adjustment": Residents' perceptions and the potential for low-impact home practices', *Housing, Theory and Society* 33(3): 288–304.

Hagbert, P. and Bradley, K. (2017) 'Transitions on the home front: A story of sustainable living beyond eco-efficiency', *Energy Research & Social Science* 31: 240–8.

Haraway, D. (1988) 'Situated knowledges: The science question in feminism and the privilege of partial perspective', *Feminist Studies* 14(3), 575–99.

Hård, M. (2010) 'The good apartment: The social (Democratic) construction of Swedish homes', *Home Cultures* 7(2): 117–33.

Hauge, Å.L. and Kolstad, A. (2007) 'Dwelling as an expression of identity: A comparative study among residents in high-priced and low-priced neighbourhoods in Norway', *Housing, Theory and Society* 24(4): 272–92.

Hedin, K., Clark, E., Lundholm, E. and Malmberg, G. (2011) 'Neoliberalization of housing in Sweden: Gentrification, filtering, and social polarization', *Annals of the Association of American Geographers* 102(2): 443–63.

Hoppbloggen. (2018) *Home* – https://hoppbloggen.wordpress.com/

Invitationsdepartementet. (2018) *Home* – http://invitationsdepartementet.se/

Jarvis, H. (2011) 'Saving space, sharing time: Integrated infrastructures of daily life in cohousing', *Environment and Planning A* 43(3): 560–77.

Lawrence, R. (1987) *Housing, Dwellings and Homes: Design Theory, Research and Practice*. Chichester: John Wiley & Sons.

Malm, A. (2014) *Fossil Capital: The Rise of Steam-Power in the British Cotton Industry, c. 1825–1848, and the Roots of Global Warming*. Doctoral thesis submitted to the Department of Human Ecology, Lund University, Lund, Sweden.

Moore, J. (2000) 'Placing home in context', *Journal of Environmental Psychology* 20(3): 207–17.

Rybczynski, W. (1986) *Home: A Short History of an Idea*. New York: Penguin.

Sandstedt, E. and Westin, S. (2015) 'Beyond Gemeinschaft and Gesellschaft: Cohousing life in contemporary Sweden', *Housing, Theory and Society* 32(2): 131–50.

Schor, J.B. (2014) 'Work sharing', in D'Alisa, G., Demaria, F. and Kallis, G. (eds.) *Degrowth: A Vocabulary for a New Era*. New York: Routledge: 195–8.

Seyfang, G. (2010) 'Community action for sustainable housing: Building a low-carbon future', *Energy Policy* 38(12): 7624–33.

Smith, S.J. (2015) 'Owner occupation: At home in a spatial, financial paradox', *International Journal of Housing Policy* 15(1): 61–83.

Vestbro, D.U. and Horelli, L. (2012) 'Design for gender equality: The history of co-housing ideas and realities', *Built Environment* 38(3): 315–35.

Wasshede, C. (2017) 'The child of the common: Governing children in the Freetown Christiania, Denmark', *Children & Society* 31(5): 403–13.

Windsong, E.A. (2010) 'There is no place like home: Complexities in exploring home and place attachment', *Social Science Journal* 47(1): 205–14.

Uddebo. (2018) *Udebbo* – http://uddebo.se/

6 Framing degrowth

The radical potential of tiny house mobility

April Anson

The phenomenon of mobile 'tiny houses' has gained popularity across the United States (US). Although tiny houses can designate any structure smaller than 800 square feet (75m²), the term is generally associated with homes on wheels that average 140 square feet (13m²) and promise distance from the toxicity of accumulation-driven consumerism. In the last few years, the US has witnessed a surge in interest in these small structures. However, recent attention given to the movement by reality television, popular magazines and various news outlets belies the complex realities of the tiny house trend.

Through a critical examination of tiny houses and their relationship to global movements like degrowth, we can articulate a more just and systems-oriented sustainability. My perspective on the tiny house movement evolved with my experience as a tiny house builder, inhabitant and landlord. I have come to believe that contemporary tiny homes on wheels (THOWs) can articulate with the principles of degrowth to expose neocolonial paradoxes imbedded in the architectural and social aesthetics of sustainability. Together, these movements converge to offer transformative environmental and social justice models that rupture the settler colonial and neoliberal logics of America and Europe.

As a scholar working in environmental politics, I became interested in the tiny house movement as an everyday application of my academic and political interests. With the help of friends and family, I built a mobile tiny home to reside in while completing my studies. What initially seemed a straightforward building and living project quickly became entangled with philosophical and material contradictions: the tiny house movement ostensibly emerges out of desire to consume *less* and contribute to community *more*, yet it has been validly critiqued for bolstering economic accumulation and preserving individualistic fictions of 'free land', or *terra nullis*, property frameworks used to justify colonialism and settler colonialism (Anson 2014; Milkman 2016).

The recent popularity of the movement exemplifies how the commodification of environmental sustainability continues to shelter economic and class privilege. This chapter explores how the tiny house movement can benefit from sustained engagement with sustainability-driven movements like degrowth, with their refusals of these capitalist, colonial and settler-colonial practices. The chapter shows that tiny houses offer some degrowth potential but also entail limitations as a simple anti-capitalist and anti-colonialist strategy for achieving degrowth.

Romance and reality

Beginnings are often romantic. My own experience with the tiny house movement is no exception. In fact, the romanticism of my tiny house initiation may be the rule. Even though the term 'tiny house' is flexible enough to refer to any range of small sized dwellings with foundations or built on trailers, the structures at the heart of the tiny house movement in North America appear like miniaturised middle-class American houses secured to mobile trailers. THOWs captured my imagination with their charming promises of simple living. Additionally, as their wheels make them unable to be classified as permanent living space, THOWs skirt building codes. I was compelled by the ways these homes and the larger movement were challenging us to reimagine space and relationships to commodities, community and building codes. Seeing the tiny house as a way to incorporate my scholarly work into my everyday life, I quickly moved to deepen my intimacy with tiny houses from mere admirer to builder and dweller.

Soon after starting the build, I began seeing the seeming simplicity of the small structures to conceal the difficult realties of tiny house life. I was first wooed by their modest aesthetics and self-contained promises. THOWs seemed like a perfect fusion of the tree house I wanted as a child and the simplification that I longed for as an adult. This was 2010, a time when there were no more than a handful of US companies building tiny houses. Despite having very few accessible real-life models, my building partner and I began construction, equipped with a minimal building plan and the kindness of many people who donated time, tools and materials. Even with such generosity, construction of the tiny house was much more labour intensive and expensive than expected, despite *and* because of using reclaimed and recycled materials. Even more troubling, as we were hammering on the last of the outer shingles – (see Figure 6.1) – my tiny house began to take shape as a somewhat new and charming exterior for an old politics of class identity.

I began to realise that what distinguished the tiny house on wheels from other mobile structures like a mobile home or recreational vehicle (often referred to simply as a 'RV') were aesthetic differences based on class associations. These class distinctions have been astutely appraised by Milkman (2016) in 'The Tiny House Fantasy' article in the socialist magazine *Jacobin* and my earlier work (Anson 2014). A more recent iteration of the desire for simple living as a classist form of life-style branding can be found in the bohemian #vanlife movement, somewhat romantically explored in *The New Yorker*, a publication arguably with bourgeoisie class associations (Monroe 2017). The increasing popularity of simplicity movements led publications such as *Outside* magazine to feature an exposé on mass-manufactured luxury tiny houses, exposing some to be ironically marketed as meagre-living for the low cost of $100,000 (Sundeen 2016). I have written at length about my own tiny house experiences, the interior of which is

Figure 6.1 Exterior of April's tiny house
Source: Jeremy Beasley (photographer)

shown at reverse angles in Figure 6.2 and Figure 6.3. I conclude that images of modest life in a miniature house often hide difficult realities of building, living in and owning one (Anson 2014, 2017).

Once built, living in the tiny house brought more frustrations – with land use laws, insurance bureaucracy, seclusion and the hypocrisies that regularly accompany tiny house living. First, land use laws around the country vary widely but most do not recognise tiny houses as permanent, legal dwellings (American Tiny House Association 2017). However, I was able to take advantage of the lenient land-use laws of Lane County, which allow for indefinite camping on family land – I was fortunate enough to have family with land in the city where I was going to graduate school. Beyond this rare initial fortune, I share a more common experience with other tiny homeowners regarding the difficulty of insuring the structure. I secured insurance only to have the coverage revoked, re-categorised and revoked again as companies were unsure of how to classify the home. Once

Figure 6.2 Partial interior of April's tiny house (I)
Source: Olivia Clingman-White (photographer)

Figure 6.3 Partial interior of April's tiny house (II)
Source: Olivia Clingman-White (photographer)

I had the assurance of an insured tiny house, I was limited by the fact that the only legal place for me to park was a substantial distance from my university and the town centre. After three years of driving an hour every day and feeling increasingly isolated, I looked for a location closer to my work and leisure communities. I learned that even with such uniquely tolerant policies as Lane County provides, I could not move without risking fines or eviction.

After years of thinking about the ways the tiny house movement's rhetoric was at odds with its realities, the difficulties of tiny house living had 'hit home'. I relocated to the east coast and, because of the high cost to move the tiny house and the parking difficulties once moved, I had to leave the house in Oregon. There, I have been unable to locate a semi-permanent parking site that will permit someone else to live in the house in my absence. Outside of Lane County, tiny house living is mostly illegal in Oregon. In Lane County, parking is restricted to family land, which inevitably affects who can live in the house. I am unable to donate the house without first paying off the loans required to build it. The only options left are both rather bleak. I can either leave the house vacant or find a buyer. These complex realities are not unique to me, or my house. Many experience THOW life as a journey in search of romantic landscapes but regularly constricted by austere bureaucratic and economic horizons.

Building settler capital

The arc of my experience within the tiny house movement has taught me much about the logics embedded in some of the architectural and social aesthetics of 'green' movements. Over the three-and-a-half years that I built and lived in my tiny house, I watched popular interest and media attention in the US grow around the phenomenon. I became more aware of, and wrote about, how the realities of tiny house living frequently contradicted the romantic rhetoric circulating about the homes (Anson 2014). This rhetoric regularly echoed the language of American romanticism and national identity formation that belong to histories of human and environmental exploitation.

Recently, such well-known US publications as *The New Yorker*, *Architectural Digest* and *National Geographic* have run stories about the movement, its history and its contemporary consumer appeal. Additionally, a few reality television series have capitalised on the concept of small living, and the satirical series *Portlandia* has even taken up the tiny house as a subject of parody. The story generally told about the US tiny house movement shares some troublesome characteristics associated with American national identity formation, such as its consumer present and heroically individualised past. Most journalistic treatments of the movement trace the beginning of the contemporary phenomenon to Lloyd Kahn's 1973 *Shelter*, Les Walker's 1987 *Tiny, Tiny Houses* or Sarah Susanka's 1997 *The Not So Big House*. Jay Shafer, founder of the Tumbleweed Tiny House Company, is frequently depicted a visionary initiator of the current phenomenon in articles revealingly titled with slogans like 'Green Empire' (Terdiman 2010). Henry David Thoreau's experiment in living at Walden Pond is frequently cited as an early formative inspiration for alternative living choices in America (Anson 2017).

Too often tiny house narratives are accompanied by a myth of freedom that reduces the diverse history of minimal living from communities across time and across the globe. A historical corollary to mobile tiny houses is the house-truck phenomenon emerging almost simultaneously with the modern symbol of America, the automobile. One photo, dated 6 September 1929, shows Charles Miller of Ogden (Oregon) standing proudly alongside his mobile masterpiece – a colonial tree house set on a truck bed, complete with porch railings and grass lawn seeded along each running board (Greenless 2011).

By ignoring the long and diverse histories of living with less by choice and by circumstance, tiny house rhetoric is positioned on the side of elitist impulses to flee to the woods in order to forget the troubles of 'modern life'. The aesthetics of romanticism's flight to the country has a distinctly political undercurrent, according to William Cronon and Roderick Nash. Romanticising nature invokes an Edenic ideology that, in its denial of human relationality, invents an ideal refuge in the 'wilderness', a sanctuary in service of the human. Tiny house rhetoric at times repeats Arcadian claims of sanctuary by hallowing the tiny house as a back-to-the-land project. As Nash's famous *Wilderness and the American Mind* astutely traces, this Edenic compulsion can be linked to issues of appropriation, empire building, boundary creation and, too often, bad environmental policy – all of which thwart the tiny house movement's ostensible goals of increased access and environmental responsibility. When articles envision tiny houses as the new American Dream, we have to wonder if that dream diverges much from irresponsible idealism used to justify and mask the multi-various violence of American colonisation (Andrews 2014).

Indeed, the romantic rhetoric often surrounding the tiny house movement is closely linked with elite environmentalism, transcendentalism and Western expansion. I have written at length about the complexity of the movement's use of Henry David Thoreau (Anson 2014, 2017), but the tiny house movement's recourse to romantic tropes extends beyond that figure associated with a small one-room cabin on Walden Pond. The movement's celebration of individual self-reliance, its invocations of pioneering rhetoric and accompanying images of vacant and free land all represent a particular notion of the environment that has justified conquest, racialised violence and reinforced white capitalist patriarchy in the US (Anson 2017). Based on European ideologies, white settlers in North America justified their occupation of land inhabited by Indigenous cultures by declaring Indigenous lifestyles antithetical to land ownership. Settler-colonial logic defined Indigenous relationships to land as *occupation* but not *ownership*.

Unfortunately, many tiny house companies promote their THOWs through images rife with the deceits of settler colonial imaginaries: visions of a lone house travelling down an empty freeway, its owner anticipating the freedom found through moving through, and claiming, unoccupied land. However, the connections between tiny houses and settler capital are more than just imagistic. In a legislative continuation of this settler-private property marriage, most land use laws force THOWs to capitulate to the same owner-occupied land logics first used to dispossess Indigenous peoples. While the THOWs are promoted as mobile and free – free to continue to occupy stolen land – tiny houses are almost as dependent on private property laws as houses with foundations. THOW rhetoric tends to truck in the centuries-old yet still vibrant settler colonial myths of unoccupied, free land used to reinforce the logic of private property justifying westward settler expansion.

The tiny house movement's recycling of well-worn settler-colonial capitalist notions of individual autonomy and pioneering spirit reinforces existing conditions of economic and political inequality. While seeking to disrupt compulsory and conspicuous consumption, the movement often exemplifies what Heather Rogers (2010) sees as tailoring environmental crisis to be less threatening to existing social relations. Indeed, the movement's use of tropes associated with settler colonialism and westward expansion continues to buttress the 'possessive individualism' at the heart of much of the American environmental imagination. Macpherson (1962) describes possessive individualism as a notion of the individual as sole owner of their destiny, driven by the principle duty of safeguarding property. What Fred Magdoff and John Bellamy Foster (2011, 105) call the 'corporate green movement' profits by feeding into this possessive individualism; in *What Every Environmentalist Needs to Know about Capitalism* they expose the ways capitalism cultivates individual self-interest. They warn of popular hype that emphasises sustainable consumption to create 'would-be green consumers, who feel that by purchasing "sustainable" commodities they can pursue their same consumerist lifestyles and feel virtuous at the same time' (ibid.).

Through these reality television shows, DIY books, car commercials and countless specialty companies, tiny houses prove emblematic of Magdoff's and Bellamy Foster's analysis, thoroughly accepted in the corporate green movement. However, despite the increased visibility and interest in THOWs, there has been very little accommodation for tiny houses in municipal infrastructure. Infrastructure, land use laws and economic realities of most places in the US make the idea of the egalitarian tiny house community only viable in so far as it is useful to market the structures. In this way, tiny houses are frequently indistinguishable from other green-consumer products, non-threatening to current political and social realities.

No matter how well intentioned, the movement's ethos too frequently represents settler capitalism where landscapes of the American dream, and even American nature conservation, continue to mask systems of white privilege (Anson 2014). By using frontier rhetoric of pioneering, homesteading and individual freedom tied to histories of class and racial violence, the tiny house miniaturises instead of challenges class distinctions: Milkman (2016) suggests that the tiny house phenomenon took off after the 2008 housing market crash when people's 'yearning for autonomy aligned with their desire to continue owning property'. In this correlation, the tiny house functions as a mode of accumulation that benefits the already upwardly mobile in the US, a generally white propertied class (Desmond 2017). Thus, the American tiny house movement offers another version of an aesthetics and property-driven elite environmentalism that reveals the inverse of Cheryl Harris's (1993) notion of 'whiteness as property' to be true. The movement adds the 'property value of whiteness' to Harris's original formulation, as property ownership reinforces already existing class inequalities along racial lines. Moreover, this white privilege is often re-presented as a lack of diversity within the movement (Pera 2017). Thus, the 'simple life in a tiny house' slogan frequently signals a (white) short-term experiment motivated by a type of poverty tourism or fetishisation of asceticism – a 'playing at poverty' that China Miéville (2015) sees as indicative of the social sadism that sustains class privilege. Of course, in a culture with disproportionally enormous carbon emissions like the US, self-denial and downsizing can be very good. Self-denial is just not a choice everyone is fortunate enough to make.

The obsession with growth that tiny-housers often wish to criticise is more explicitly articulated by the global campaign known as degrowth.

Framing (with) degrowth

In its promotion of simpler living, less consumption and increased engagement with the stuff that money cannot buy, the tiny house phenomenon shares anti-consumerist and anti-capitalist philosophies with the degrowth movement. Both the tiny house movement and degrowth are opposed to the notion that economic productivity and growth are the highest purpose of human organisation. Moreover, degrowth explicitly rejects the idea of sustainable development as an oxymoron, a position that offers a much-needed correction to some of the more commodified versions of the American tiny house phenomenon. By correlating certain principles of the American tiny house movement with the ethos of degrowth, both movements' colonial and neoliberal entanglements can be disarticulated from, and thus emphasise, their radical potential.

Degrowth and the tiny house movement share some complicated histories. Degrowth can trace its beginnings back to some of the anti-industrialist figures typically cited as both the origins of American environmentalism and early progenitors of the tiny house movement. Moreover, the movements share affinities with Thoreau's anti-consumerist sentiments, the Arts and Crafts movement's interest in social reform as a critique of industrialist methods and an ongoing intellectual tradition that investigates the limited carrying capacity of the earth. This lineage also belongs to colonial and settler colonial history: Thoreau's oft-critiqued ambivalence toward Native peoples and his own privilege as an antebellum white male (Anson 2017), the Arts and Crafts movement's links to pastoral escapism (Lears 1994) and the scarcity model that frequently interprets finite resources through a reprise of the Lockean private property refrains which justified colonisation.

Degrowth and tiny house movements unofficially began in the same era that marks the rise of neoliberalism. Degrowth's unofficial founding text, *The Limits to Growth*, was published in 1972, an age known also for its dramatic increase in the popularity of house-trucks, an early inspiration for the contemporary American THOWs. Many environmental historians and ecologists know this era by Garrett Hardin's influential 1968 article 'The Tragedy of the Commons', which assumes overuse of resources as inevitable, and thus continues to define a certain ecological scarcity model used to justify privatisation of resources. Hardin's concept, though influential, has been substantively and thoroughly critiqued for assuming a universally selfish and unchanging human nature whose sociality is made up of self-interested individuals acting independently of the common good (Angus 2008). The simultaneity of degrowth, tiny houses and the privatisation apologia of neoliberalism provides an invitation to critically think about how the colonial logic of 'proper use' hides in claims of resource scarcity. Scarcity can easily function as an updated Lockean justification for resource, and land, privatisation as well as a call to further infinitesimal units of 'nature' to be properly managed by neoliberal markets.

Ultimately, this correlative history is meant to expose the potentially perilous political positions in each movement in order to, ultimately, assist in strengthening them. In truth, degrowth principles can help the tiny house movement to articulate a more radical environmental ethics – one that rejects systems of private property, wealth accumulation and limitless growth in favour of relations of responsibility instead of scarcity. Indeed, though the tiny house movement has been traced to the 2008 recession, it is just as viable to mark the real tipping point in the popularity of the North American tiny house movement in 2011, in concert with the Occupy movement and its global resonances in degrowth projects. Although the rhetoric of 'occupation' that circulates in degrowth, tiny house projects and even Occupy Wall Street sometimes regard occupation an unqualified good, connecting these movements helps us scrutinise the 'occupation' concept as inextricable from the ongoing dispossession of Indigenous peoples and systems of colonialism and capital accumulation. This single example shows how connecting the principles of degrowth and the US tiny house movement unsettles settler colonial and capitalist logics that perpetuate racial, class and environmental violence.

By placing these movements in conversation and in historical and philosophical contexts we can more clearly identify the ways elite environmentalism cloaks colonial and neoliberal logics. Taken together, both movements avoid the dystopian 'tragedy' of Hardin's scarcity model and evade the impractical utopianism of which Samuel Alexander (2015) has warned. The explicitly anti-development principles of degrowth help correct the trend toward commodification of the tiny house movement. Moreover, the tiny house movement's 'pioneer' rhetoric acts as a warning to any de-historicised use of 'occupation' as an unproblematic good. Both movements reject capitalism's creed of never-ending accumulation, making them well positioned to denounce the individual property owner as primary devotee and beneficiary of the free market orthodoxy on which neoliberalism structures its ceremonies. Placed alongside each other, these movements better enable us to identify radically engaged political models outside of neocolonial and neoliberal markets.

Ecological revolution

Together, the degrowth movement and the tiny house phenomenon can offer versions of ecological revolution through radical social transformation. Contemporary critics of neoliberalism, such as David Harvey, cite radical social transformation as critical to contemporary social, environmental and climate justice. In concert with Harvey (2005), Magdoff and Bellamy Foster (2011, 122) call for an 'ecological revolution' consisting of 'a transformation in social relations: in community, culture and economy, in how we relate to each other as human beings, and how we relate to the planet'. Degrowth and tiny house movements can answer these critics' calls by helping us imagine such transformative social relations. Together, they suggest a notion of the commons not as a place to be exploited for personal gain but instead as a transformative *activity* that reinforces the mutual dependence of humans and nature. By providing explicitly political visions of anti-capitalist daily practice, both movements can help disprove Fredric Jameson's (2003) notorious claim that it is easier to imagine the end of the world than the end of capitalism. Thinking of the tiny house movement and degrowth together, we can articulate projects that exemplify this radical ecological revolution.

Examples of such transformative social relations can be found in ways of living inspired by or affiliated with the degrowth movement, such as squatting and autonomous movements that gave rise to the Bauwagenplatz in Germany and elsewhere. The Bauwagenplatz is an urban settlement consisting mainly of trailers and cars illegally occupying land, renting their parking space or exchanging services with the community for land use. The Bauwagenplatz exemplifies the assertion that how and where one lives is a political act and, in some cases, offers resistance and counterculture alternatives to capitalism through everyday actions such as offering community meals and household duties, and shared property. They are also known for active struggles against fascism, private property, gentrification and racism as in the detailed historical accounts in Squatting Europe Kollective (2013) and Van der Steen et al. (2014). Outside of Europe, Kothari et al. (2014) locate other radical living models in Brazil's favelas, the Latin American Buen Vivir movement and Indian Ecological Swaraj, all of which regard justice as inextricable from environmental concerns. Radical alternative living models exist across the globe, suggesting an exciting transnational trend of transformative social relations.

On the North American continent tiny houses are being used to build more just and sustainable futures. First Nations peoples in Yorkton (Canada) are teaching students to build THOWs while the Idle No More movement turned to tiny houses as a way to sustainably address the housing crisis. The Secwepemc people are building ten tiny houses in the pathway of Kinder Morgan's Transmountain pipeline to block the illegal route through Secwepemc territory (*Secwepemcul'ecw Assembly* 2017). In the US, there are a number of cities that are embracing tiny houses as a way to envision sustainable housing justice. Examples include a tiny house 'OM village' founded and run by Occupy Madison in Wisconsin that provides tiny houses for the homeless. There are more examples at Tiny Houses Greensboro (North Carolina), Resurrection Village (Colorado), Community First! (Texas), Othello and Quixote Villages (Washington) and SquareOne and Opportunity Villages in Oregon, all which offer tiny home communities for people in need. Such projects use tiny houses to address both economic and environmental justice and help us to imagine how to live not just more simply but more justly. They put pressure on municipalities, make legal code and infrastructure changes vital to the long term viability of tiny house living – revising land use laws to allow for more than one structure on a property and adjusting minimum building size standards to accept smaller and alternative dwellings. The more that tiny house communities are built, the more likely that infrastructure changes will follow to challenge the growth-model status quo.

Life in a tiny house magnifies the discrepancies between the popular rhetoric of environmental sustainability and the realities of privilege and elitism in much environmentally conscious consumption, such as the ability to build or buy a tiny house and the logic of private property that dominate where tiny houses can or cannot be. It is precisely this sort of confrontation that invites the social imaginaries necessary for radical degrowth. In conversation with one another, the tiny house movement and degrowth can help us imagine otherwise. We must increase the visibility of these global trends and support those championing the use of tiny houses to frustrate systems of inequality and resource extraction. Together, the North American tiny house phenomenon and the global degrowth movement can radically fortify one another, working in concert to reimagine abundant collectives. Jointly, these movements articulate small-scale models of the larger social transformations urgently needed to address social injustice, corporate violence and environmental crises.

References

Alexander, S. (2015) 'What Is Degrowth? Envisioning a Prosperous Descent', *Permaculture Research Institute*, 17 November – https://permaculturenews.org/2015/11/17/what-is-degrowth-envisioning-a-prosperous-descent/

American Tiny House Association. (2017) 'Zoning', *American Tiny House Association*, 5 September – http://americantinyhouseassociation.org/zoning/

Andrews, E. (2014) 'Cabin fever: Are tiny houses the new American dream?', *Grist*, 4 March – https://grist.org/living/cabin-fever-are-tiny-houses-the-new-american-dream/

Angus, I. (2008) 'The myth of the tragedy of the commons', *Climate and Capitalism*, 25 August – http://climateandcapitalism.com/2008/08/25/debunking-the-tragedy-of-the-commons/

Anson, A. (2014) '"The world is my backyard": Romanticization, Thoreauvian rhetoric, and constructive confrontation in the tiny house movement', in Holt, W. (ed.) *From Sustainable to Resilient Cities: Global Concerns and Urban Efforts*. Research in Urban Sociology 14. Bingley: Emerald Insight: 289–313.

—— (2017) 'The patron saint of tiny houses', in Finley, J. (ed.) *Henry David Thoreau in Context*. Cambridge: Cambridge University Press: 331–41.

Desmond, M. (2017) 'How homeownership became the engine of American inequality', *The New York Times*, 9 May – www.nytimes.com/2017/05/09/magazine/how-homeownership-became-the-engine-of-american-inequality.html

Greenless, D. (2011) 'A twenties motor home complete with a lawn', *The Old Motor*, 18 October – http://theoldmotor.com/?p=31758#comment-39813

Hardin, G. (1968) 'The tragedy of the commons', *Science* 162(3859): 1243–8.

Harris, C. I. (1993) 'Whiteness as property', *Harvard Law Review* 106(8): 1707–91.

Harvey, D. (2005) *A Brief History of Neoliberalism*. Oxford: Oxford University Press.

Jameson, F. (2003) 'Future city', *New Left Review* 21: 65–79 – https://newleftreview.org/II/21/fredric-jameson-future-city

Khan, L. (1973) *Shelter*. Bolinas: Shelter Publications.

Kothari, A., Federico, D. and Acosta, A. (2014) 'Buen vivir, degrowth, and ecological swaraj: Alternatives to sustainable development and the green economy', *Development* 57(3–4): 362–75.

Lears, T.J. (1994) *No Place of Grace: Antimodernism and the Transformation of American Culture, 1880–1920*. Chicago: University of Chicago Press.

Macpherson, C.B. (1962) *The Political Theory of Possessive Individualism*. Oxford: Oxford University Press.

Magdoff, F. and Bellamy Foster, J. (2011) *What Every Environmentalist Needs to Know about Capitalism: A Citizen's Guide to Capitalism and the Environment*. New York: Monthly Review Press.

Miéville, C. (2015) 'On social sadism', *Salvage*, 17 December – http://salvage.zone/in print/on-social-sadism/

Milkman, A. (2016) 'The tiny house fantasy: The tiny house movement embraces individualistic visions of property while ignoring the real causes of housing insecurity', *Jacobin*, 19 January – www.jacobinmag.com/2016/01/tiny-house-movement-nation-tumbleweed-environment-consumerism/

Monroe, R. (2017) '#Vanlife, the bohemian social-media movement: What began as an attempt at a simpler life quickly became a life-style brand', *The New Yorker*, 24 April, 2017 – www.newyorker.com/magazine/2017/04/24/vanlife-the-bohemian-social-media-%20movement

Pera, L. (2017) '"Everyone's welcome": The façade of the tiny house movement', *Medium*, 22 September – https://medium.com/@leepera/everyones-welcome-the-facade-of-the-tiny-house-movement-936d56d2dbb8

Rogers, H. (2010) *Green Gone Wrong: How Our Economy Is Undermining the Environmental Revolution*. New York: Scribner.

Secwepemcul'ecw Assembly (2017) 'Tiny house warriors: Our land is home', *Secwepemcul'ecw Assembly*, 6 September – www.secwepemculecw.org/tiny-house-warriors

Squatting Europe Kollective. (2013) *Squatting in Europe: Radical Spaces, Urban Struggles*. New York: Minor Compositions/Autonomedia.

Sundeen, M. (2016) 'The tiny-house revolution goes huge', *Outside*, 27 December – www.outsideonline.com/2144261/tiny-house-revolution-goes-huge

Susanka, S (1997) *The Not So Big House*. Newtown: The Taunton Press.

Terdiman, D. (2010) 'Building a green empire, one tiny house at a time', *CNET News*, CBS, 10 November – www.cnet.com/news/building-a-green-empire-one-tiny-house-at-a-time/

Van der Steen, B., Katzeff, A. and van Hoogenhuijze, L. (2014) *The City Is Ours: Squatting and Autonomous Movements in Europe from the 1970s to the Present*. Oakland: PM Press.

Walker, L. (1987) *Tiny, Tiny Houses*. New York: Overlook Press.

7 Housing and climate change resilience
Vanuatu

Wendy Christie and John Salong

While the degrowth movement is widespread in the Global North, in particular in Europe, it is still burgeoning as a movement in the Global South. In Vanuatu, an independent nation spread across an 83-island archipelago in the South Pacific Ocean, there is no consciously labelled degrowth movement. The typical way of life for most people, however, is very compatible with grassroots concepts of degrowth. Rather than a collective decision to consume and produce less, people do so as a continuation of their self-sufficient, agricultural-based economies.

Degrowth projects in the Global North, such as cooperatives, community gardening and coliving (Ciobanu 2012) are not projects but, rather, are standard living practices in Vanuatu. Ni-Vanuatu (the people of Vanuatu) living outside the main urban centres typically rely on subsistence agriculture, often with little or no access to any formal income. In the city, many people maintain urban market gardens to supplement their diet and income. Produce markets flourish in both the outer islands and urban environments, and local currencies still circulate in the form of *kastom* (custom) payments, which are based on food production and crafts. Households typically consist of extended families living collectively in self-built dwellings, usually made from locally sourced or recycled materials.

When Tropical Cyclone Pam – a Category 5 cyclone on both Australian and Saffir-Simpson scales, with winds exceeding 280 km per hour – devastated many parts of Vanuatu on 13 March 2015, the resilience of communities was demonstrated in the rebuilding phase, which was overwhelmingly autonomous and independent of centralised services. The concept of housing in Vanuatu is pertinent for degrowth advocates in the Global North, as it presents a modality of housing that is resilient, self-reliant and, in many instances, environmentally sustainable. House building actively engages communities during construction processes and creates convivial community environments through vernacular spatial configurations.

In this chapter, the reader embarks for the islands, taking a narrative journey through to Vanuatu's capital city Port Vila. Along the way, different housing typologies will be identified, leading to a broad discussion that includes the rebuilding response to Tropical Cyclone Pam and the way in which it unconsciously paralleled degrowth concepts. Unless referenced otherwise, much of the material related to traditional *nakamals* draws from Vanuatu Cultural Centre and

Christie (2017), where more detail about Vanuatu's *nakamals* and how they performed during Tropical Cyclone can be found.

Island dwelling

Let's start on one of the islands (as in Figure 7.1). Peering down the narrow pathway we catch a glimpse of turquoise ocean framed by the distant escarpment. The modest dwellings lining either side of the path have been built using a variety of forms from an eclectic material palette comprised of metal, timber, concrete and thatch. Some forms are contemporary, with flat or shallow gabled roofs. Others are reminiscent of the past with steep, triangular roofs and deep, low eaves that almost reach the ground. Pawpaw, banana, cassava and taro are cultivated in gardens nestled against the lee of the hill while colourful flourishes of bougainvillaea and hibiscus, maintained as low hedges, demarcate household boundaries.

We are in Taloa Village, located on the southern tip of Nguna Island. Towards the eastern end of the village a small timber bridge crossing a dry creek bed leads to an open clearing where stands a vast concrete-block Presbyterian church – replacing the original weatherboard building – with an historic missionary cemetery beyond. A crushed coral pathway along the seafront leads back to the centre of the village. Heading around the point, a large thatched structure appears

Figure 7.1 Taloa Village (Nguna Island) laneway leading to the seafront
Source: Wendy Christie (September 2015)

from behind the trees (Figure 7.2). On moving closer, the structure is revealed as a unique ovoid form of the village *farea*, a traditional chiefs' meetinghouse, commonly known throughout Vanuatu as a *nakamal*. The *farea* has been built and rebuilt over centuries utilising traditional building techniques passed down through intergenerational knowledge from materials that are predominantly sourced from Nguna Island.

The Taloa Farea has an elongated oval-shaped floor plan, with a large entrance facing away from the sea and a long, low opening along the western side. The structure is made from hardwood timber framing, thatched with wild cane and tied together with plaited pandanus ropes. The form of the structure, revealed through the exposed timber framing, resembles an upturned boat, or the carcass of a whale.

While the Taloa Farea is regularly renovated, and re-thatched approximately every 15 years, the whole structure will be rebuilt when it reaches the end of its life span. The entire community is involved in the construction, including children who take part in an apprentice-type system whereby master-builders pass traditional building knowledge onto the next generation. Men cut the timber and erect the main structure, while women prepare and weave thatching for the roof. The process involves *kastom* ceremonies that mark significant stages of the build.

Since European contact, contemporary building techniques, styles and materials have evolved to intermix with the local and traditional ones in Taloa. Significantly, the traditional *farea* endures in contrast to surrounding houses made from

Figure 7.2 The Taloa Farea on Nguna Island
Source: Wendy Christie (December 2012)

Figure 7.3 Nguna Island dwellings made from sheet metal, bush timber and thatching
Source: Wendy Christie (September 2015)

hybrid construction (Figure 7.3). Coiffier (1997, 1168), referring generally to the architecture of Vanuatu, notes that:

> Formerly, there were many different types of habitat which are now being replaced by standardized buildings. Colonization and Christianity brought new models which have come to correspond to new ways of living.

The Taloa Farea marks a significant space in the village, demonstrated in its size and function. Historically, its primary function has been to accommodate *kastom* governance, but now it is also a community centre for the entire village, hosting workshops, meetings, dances, weddings and funerals.

Urban dwelling

A 45-minute boat trip across the harbour introduces the picturesque tropical island landscape typical to Vanuatu. In the distance the large volcanic forms of the Shepherd Islands rise from the sea as the diesel-powered boat motors towards the island of Efate. Located away from the main urban centres of Port Vila and Luganville, where cars and concrete buildings proliferate, the typical dwellings in the villages further afield are typically constructed using traditional techniques and local materials. But, after landing, we must first travel by bus around the island before arriving in the city.

Moored along the edge of the wharf is a collection of fibreglass motorboats, while a small traditional outrigger canoe drifts along the horizon. While driving around the island we pass by small villages and roadside market garden stalls until the suburbs of Port Vila eventually creep into view. An assortment of functional building types lines the road into town: hardware stores, supermarkets, petrol stations, car dealerships, dwellings and pop-up market garden stalls. The vernacular architecture of the city is concrete and sheet metal. The vibrant main street, crowded with the mini-buses that make up the main form of transport, is lined with government and corporate offices, hotels, cafes and restaurants, new and second-hand clothing stores, banks and currency exchange outlets, and at the centre of town, the central fruit, vegetable and flower market (Figure 7.4).

As we venture into the suburbs spreading out from the centre of town, the built urban density decreases to an assortment of detached and semi-detached dwelling types that occupy residential neighbourhoods. While some houses are solidly constructed, most are self-built dwellings made from an assortment of home-made concrete blocks, timber framing, sheet metal cladding and the occasional thatched roof or wall. Many of these materials are likely to have been

Figure 7.4 View to the main street in Port Vila and the harbour
Source: Wendy Christie (November 2016)

recycled or salvaged, while others would have been purchased from one of the local hardware stores.

The impact of Tropical Cyclone Pam on the built landscape

The effects of Tropical Cyclone Pam on buildings in Vanuatu present a strong argument to support the proposals of European degrowth advocates and should temper concerns of planners, architects, engineers and builders about the use of traditional building materials and building techniques in residential construction (see Chapter 10 and Chapter 12). In addition, a comparison of the recovery processes led by both formal organisations and the grassroots mutual support exercised by residents shows the strength of autonomous and convivial activities advocated by the degrowth movement.

It is estimated that Tropical Cyclone Pam affected approximately 188,000 people, destroying or damaging in excess of 20,000 homes (Vanuatu Shelter Cluster 2015). The majority of buildings in Vanuatu had not been built to a standard appropriate to withstand the forces of such a strong cyclone. Most dwellings in Port Vila, for example, are built by skilful homeowners, rather than trained builders. Remarkably, however, there were relatively few confirmed fatalities (11) directly resulting from the cyclone (Government of Vanuatu 2015, ix) – partly attributable to lightweight construction materials. 'What contributes to the low death toll is the fact that the materials are not so heavy', noted anthropologist Margaret Rodman (cited in Bolitho 2015): 'So you're not dealing with masonry falling on people'. Buildings made from heavier building materials, if not properly constructed, create a higher risk of personal injury when they collapse (Christie and Laboukly 2015).

While most buildings in the path of the cyclone were destroyed or damaged, several traditionally constructed Chiefs' meetinghouses, *nakamals*, withstood its forces. The Post Disaster Needs Report delivered by the Government of Vanuatu (2015, 51) in the wake of Tropical Cyclone Pam concluded:

> The performance of *nakamals* during Tropical Cyclone Pam demonstrates why traditional knowledge remains relevant and must be preserved as part of living heritage and culture.

The Taloa Farea, for example, was barely damaged, while an adjacent community centre of similar scale made from imported materials was completely destroyed.

Several *nakamals*, which are historically and anecdotally known to have been built as cyclone shelters, provided protection to people during the cyclone, thus illustrating the value of the intergenerational building knowledge in Vanuatu that has evolved over centuries to suit the local climatic conditions. Coiffier (1997, 1168) has noted that the oblong-shaped buildings of the central and southern islands 'resist the strongest cyclones and represent one of the most judicious technical inventions of the Vanuatu peoples'. As Figure 7.5 shows, the Chief's Nakamal in Port Vila – meetinghouse for the Malvatumauri (National Council

Figure 7.5 The Chief's Nakamal in Port Vila, post-Tropical Cyclone Pam
Source: Wendy Christie (October 2015)

of Chiefs) – suffered extensive damage to its thatched roof and wall cladding, yet the primary structure maintained its integrity.

The formal rebuilding response

After Tropical Cyclone Pam there was an influx of people and organisations to assist with rebuilding. The Vanuatu Shelter Cluster, led by the Government of Vanuatu Public Works Department (2015), became the central point for the emergency shelter and rebuilding response. Its goal was 'to provide people affected by Tropical Cyclone Pam with the means to live in safe, dignified and appropriate shelter'. The Vanuatu Shelter Cluster did not provide shelters or building materials but assisted with the coordination of partner and stakeholder organisations by providing information, including technical expertise and funding advice, and advocating for the shelter sector. 'Building Back Safer' and 'Disaster Risk Reduction' strategies were at the core of its response (Government of Vanuatu Public Works Department 2015.)

The initial emergency response included delivering shelter packages containing tarpaulins, blankets and basic tools. Unfortunately, the recovery phase that followed coincided with El Niño and the worst drought experienced in Vanuatu for several years, hindering the re-establishment of food crops and building material plantations. During the recovery phase, the Vanuatu Shelter Cluster and more than 35 partner organisations supported self-recovery by providing tools, materials and technical assistance, and organising early recovery activities, emphasising making dwellings stronger, safer and more resilient (Shelter Cluster Vanuatu 2015).

The two main strategies put forward to strengthen buildings of any construction type were to use cross-bracing and binding connections. Several organisations promoted the use of these two techniques across the provinces. Several groups focused on 'hybrid' structures using both imported and traditional materials and construction techniques. Many advocated a role for traditional architecture through their shelter programmes. In addition, immediately after the cyclone there was an influx of international companies promoting and testing prefabricated housing modules.

The grassroots rebuilding response

While the Shelter Cluster played an important role in recovery, particularly in advice and coordination, general rebuilding of dwellings was neither organised nor regulated centrally. The main grassroots response was organic, evolving intuitively as people rebuilt immediately from whatever materials they could find, without relying on or waiting for assistance. Relatively few visual reminders of Tropical Cyclone Pam remain in the built environment, arguably because communities rebuilt independently and immediately after the cyclone. The destruction of so many dwellings indicates room for vast improvement of building standards, particularly with regards to the strength of buildings. Such improvements, however, need to take into account the self-build modality shown to be critical to the resilience of the people in the aftermath of the cyclone.

Writing in mid-2017, there is no building control in Vanuatu. While a National Building Code for Vanuatu, written in 1990, and the Republic of Vanuatu (2014) Building Act of 2013 do exist, there is still no mandated requirement for building to a specified standard. There is a general lack of compliance with local planning schemes in Port Vila, and no operating national housing policy in Vanuatu. With population growth and an urban drift, urban planning will become more pressing, especially for managing traffic, settling rural-urban migrants and maintaining protection for existing neighbourhoods.

Appropriately integrated building regulation is critical to protecting lives and property, and has the potential to minimise requirements for disaster responses. Building code compliance potentially reduces the loss of lives and protects investments and household assets (World Bank Group 2016). Natural catastrophes in Vanuatu are not only limited to cyclones: earthquakes, volcanic eruptions and tsunamis are also threats to communities and their built environment. The *Sendai Framework for Disaster Risk Reduction 2015–2030*, endorsed by United Nation

General Assembly mid-2015 shifted the focus from managing disasters to managing the risk of disasters (UNISDR 2015).

Vanuatu is made up of over 100 Indigenous cultures speaking their own distinct languages. Each autonomous cultural group formed its rules based on decisions made in its *nakamal*. While today the Parliament of Vanuatu is the primary law-making body, *kastom* law maintains some constitutional and judicial recognition (Forsyth 2009). Vanuatu society is still largely based on these autonomous cultures: a visitor to an island must subscribe to the rules of the Chiefs of that island. Even today in Port Vila, which is co-habited by people from all of the six provinces, this mentality prevails.

How might building controls apply efficiently across the approximately 65 inhabited islands of Vanuatu – given the persistent paradigm of autonomy whereby people do not traditionally accept centralised authority, including (presumably) regulators? The enforcement of any kind of building code would be very difficult to implement across the dispersed archipelago, particularly where rules conflict with social, habitual and cultural norms.

In the suburban capitalist environments of the Global North people do not generally have the skills to build a house. Contractors are hired to build according to permits and plans, processes requiring significant amounts of time and money to comply with regulations. In most households in Vanuatu people have retained the skills required to build their own dwellings and they typically self-build. The absence of regulations means that people can build quickly without having to conform to potentially cost-prohibitive regulated processes. This approach extends to government and commercial organisations, where staff members might assist in renovating or extending their workplaces when more space is required.

If a highly prescribed notion of regulated housing had been followed, Vanuatu's built landscape may still not have recovered after Tropical Cyclone Pam. Because the recovery was based on independence and autonomy, people rebuilt their houses using whatever materials were available to them. There was no requirement to comply with systems that underlie a regulated built environment, such as waiting for engineered building plans, agreements with financiers or land registration. The current system in Vanuatu relies on the autonomy of the community, which creates a sustainable and resilient society. However, there are concerns that this autonomy comes at a cost in the face of future cyclonic events, if dwellings have been rebuilt only to a similar standard as existed prior to Tropical Cyclone Pam.

There is no welfare in Vanuatu, and survival is based on independence. The 2009 Vanuatu Census showed that most people still cook by wood fire and rely on sources other than the electricity grid for household lighting (Vanuatu National Statistics Office 2009). Pre-Tropical Cyclone Pam it is estimated that 43 percent of dwellings were 'traditional housing' (as in Figure 7.6), 30 percent 'semi-permanent housing' and 27 percent 'permanent housing' (Government of Vanuatu 2015). Outside Port Vila, a significant proportion of dwellings are made from local

Figure 7.6 A traditional house on Tanna Island
Source: Wendy Christie (September 2013)

materials, while urban centres and growing peri-urban areas include many semi-permanent dwellings.

For the current generation of ni-Vanuatu, the notion of dwelling does not necessarily align with the concept of housing as imagined by engineers and town planners. As with degrowth practices in the Global North, ni-Vanuatu living in the islands generally construct their houses from what can be sourced from the local environment. Each island has its own vernacular architecture, utilising different materials and forms in response to the local context. Dwellings are designed in response to the cultural context, environment and climate. A house located in an exposed location will be oriented to deflect the wind. Without access to contemporary engineered materials, a house positioned on a steep site will be designed to accommodate the gradient of the land. Dwellings are designed to create spatial arrangements that are culturally appropriate and comfortable for those who will live in them. These principals are transported and adapted to urban centres. Local materials are replaced with what can be found at the local hardware store or salvaged second hand (Figure 7.7). All these techniques are similar to evolving degrowth housing practices of the Global North.

While there is a limited supply of government-owned housing in Vanuatu, broadly accessible affordable public housing in Vanuatu is still burgeoning as a concept. Many matters need to be resolved prior to any kind of public housing movement, including financial and management aspects related to payments of rent, land use planning and access to infrastructure and services.

Figure 7.7 Example of built fabric found in suburban and peri-urban areas of Port Vila
Source: Wendy Christie (November 2016)

An aerial view of the lot divisions of Port Vila presents typical suburban layouts with minimum plots of 600 square metres. A different situation is revealed on the ground: one plot is likely to accommodate several families, potentially comprising up to 20 to 30 adults and children. Amenities on the site might be limited to one toilet and one shower shared by the entire household. Most urban areas of Port Vila have been leased, leaving little room for rural-urban migrants who are forced to share lots and services.

In addition to other reasons for overcrowding, extended family relationships are intrinsic to ni-Vanuatu society whereby people generally do not follow a nuclear family household model. A typical household in Port Vila might include: parents and their children; uncles and aunts from the islands generating income for their families; cousins in town to access education; grandfathers and grandmothers in Port Vila to access services. Households are busy, fluid and dynamic. Any future urban planning will need to find a strategy that simultaneously improves living conditions and reduces overcrowding whilst supporting this modality of dwelling.

In 2016, the government launched a plan for national sustainable development through to 2030: *Vanuatu 2030: The People's Plan* (Republic of Vanuatu 2016). The three pillared sustainability vision follows the 'triple-bottom-line' approach of society, environment and economy, with 'Vibrant Cultural Identity' objectives to enhance traditional and cultural knowledge. Movements to forward housing policy will need to acknowledge that current building technology incorporates both traditional and contemporary knowledge and materials. It will be important to maintain housing traditions, strengthening *kastom* through utilising local materials and techniques, and recognising cultural spatial planning. It will be critical to adapt the centuries-old building knowledge to contemporary systems in order to marry the benefits of the old with the new, and maintain an awareness of degrowth principles by recognising that growth has environmental limits.

Contexts: Global South and Global North

The 2008 global financial crisis began with a crisis in the subprime mortgage market in the United States, where household debt was being repackaged, and on-sold, ultimately defaulting and contributing to the financial crisis. Ni-Vanuatu do not usually borrow money for housing: there is little access to debt or lending, and interest payments are beyond the reach of most families. Most people do not use credit, including credit cards. Consequently, they build within their financial means, with materials that they can readily access. It is far more affordable to build a house without having to pay design, engineering or regulatory fees, using materials sourced or salvaged cheaply from the environment and with households providing the labour.

This approach extends to communal activities requiring temporary buildings, where 'pop-up' structures are constructed for events such as public holiday celebrations (Figure 7.8). Built over only a few days, communities come together to collaborate on their construction using affordable materials such as bush timbers, thatching, fabric and sheet metal roofing. Once the event has finished, the structures are taken down.

Suburban houses in neighbouring countries such as Australia – where houses have more than doubled in size in the last 60 years while the average size of households has been declining (Stephan and Crawford 2016) – belong in a culture of the Global North, where homes are status symbols, associated with conspicuous consumption and treated as financial 'assets'. There, multiple living areas, media rooms and ensuites are commonplace requirements to residential architects' briefs. While housing aspiration in Vanuatu does not exist to the same extent, the cost of housing is still likely to be the main family financial outlay, along with children's education, micro-enterprise schemes and the fulfilment of social obligations such as weddings. Ni-Vanuatu houses are typically built to the size required to accommodate the household size, and extended as required to accommodate growing households. These dwellings stand in stark contrast to proliferating, gated, ex-patriot housing enclaves in Port Vila, with their imposing footprints and imported housing attitudes.

Today, many ni-Vanuatu might aspire to have a concrete block house with a sheet metal roof. A sheet metal roof lasts longer, requires less maintenance, allows for water collection and is, arguably, a status symbol. However, it is still

Figure 7.8 A temporary 'pop-up' structure for the 2014 Independence Day Celebration (Tanoropo Village, Nguna Island)

Source: Wendy Christie (July 2014)

quite common to see a thatched veranda roof incorporated into the design of these contemporary dwellings.

Pescomaggiore ecovillage

The resilience shown by ni-Vanuatu communities after Tropical Cyclone Pam has parallels with a self-built ecovillage in Pescomaggiore following the L'Aquila earthquake (6 April 2009) as described by Fois and Forino (2015) and on which the following comparison draws. This 6.3 magnitude earthquake affected the Abruzzo region in Italy, in particular L'Aquila city and its surrounding villages. More than 60,000 buildings were damaged and 18,000 left unsafe for occupancy. The emergency response led by the Italian Civil Protection Department, with support from the Italian state, included placing survivors in tent camps and tourist accommodation, then instituting relocation strategies, including prefabricated housing and new earthquake-proof housing complexes.

Accordingly, residents of the small historic town of Pescomaggiore were to be relocated to a new housing complex more than 8 kilometres away. Protesting this centralised directive, which some inhabitants felt compromised their identity and would fragment their community, a group of residents using participatory decision-making processes created near Pescomaggiore an autonomous ecovillage, primarily constructed from timber and straw bales. A straw bale system is suitable for use in earthquake prone areas, and considered an affordable, environmentally sustainable, safe natural building system proving good insulation.

There are obvious differences in contexts, circumstances and responses between Pescomaggiore after the earthquake and Vanuatu post-Tropical Cyclone Pam. In particular, in Vanuatu, there were no government-provided prefabricated housing solutions or new cyclone-proof housing complexes, and no architects or planners involved in resident-led rebuilds or requirements for authorised building plans or permits. In Vanuatu, people rebuilt immediately out of necessity, without having any other options for their survival. However, the many similarities include strong participation of residents and their retention to place and neighbourhood communities. In both, people took responsibility for post-disaster actions autonomously and collaboratively, without relying on centralised or organised emergency services, and they demonstrated strong community resilience.

Conclusion

As a small island developing state of the Global South, Vanuatu is yet to experience significant growth, let alone a counter movement of degrowth. However, it does serve as a relevant model for the predominantly European degrowth movement. Its traditional and collaborative housing approaches reflect arguments made by degrowth advocates: using community-collaborative processes to self-build simple, appropriate and affordable dwellings that embody low energy through the use of natural local and recycled building materials. The housing outcomes and achievements post-cyclone illustrated the advantages of this modality.

Examples of housing in Vanuatu exemplify the merits of frugal living that sit in contrast to mainstream living in the Global North, where many houses are now far larger than necessary for their number of inhabitants and epitomise conspicuous consumption. These houses often waste resources and energy both during construction and throughout their lifetime. Housing in Vanuatu is typically based on community living and convivial environments, in contrast with suburban capitalist housing that often prioritises security and privacy, which can alienate inhabitants from their communities.

Climate change brings with it the increasing risk of stronger cyclones and the very real potential for future cyclonic events that threaten to decimate built environments across Vanuatu. As the population of Vanuatu grows and urban areas are expanded, planning and regulation of the built environment will become more critical. Regulation will need to include building control that strengthens buildings to minimise destruction of the built environment in the face of natural disasters. In line with the Sendai Framework for Disaster Risk Reduction, such regulation would assist in managing the risk of disaster to mitigate emergency disaster response action.

Nevertheless, a balance needs to be found between, on the one hand, regulation and planning, and, on the other hand, autonomy and independence. Positive aspects of planning and regulation might be better appreciated if introduced within a model of participatory democracy and, if accepted, would encourage the appropriate construction of buildings and dwellings to withstand cyclones, whilst maintaining the autonomy, strength and resilience of the people.

This discussion shows that degrowth principles are compatible with existing approaches to building in Vanuatu that encourage appropriate and sustainable practices in contrast to pressures for growth measured by consumption or even notions of sustainable growth. Future development and regulations that support traditional construction techniques, encourage environmentally sensitive housing design and promote building to appropriate standards will lead to a more sustainable built environment. Simultaneously, this will allow people to maintain their independence in the face of natural disasters, and will have great potential to support sustained resilience and better future outcomes for the people of Vanuatu.

References

Bolitho, S. (2015) 'Tropical cyclone Pam: Why the Vanuatu death toll was so low', *ABC News* – www.abc.net.au/news/2015-04-01/explainer3a-why-was-the-vanuatu-death-toll-from-cyclone-pam-so/6363970

Christie, W. and Laboukly, B. (2015) 'Rebuilding a safer and stronger Vanuatu after cyclone Pam', *The Conversation*, 18 June – http://theconversation.com/rebuilding-a-safer-and-stronger-vanuatu-after-cyclone-pam-42181

Ciobanu, C. (2012) 'South invited to de-grow', *Inter Press Service News Agency*, 25 September – www.ipsnews.net/2012/09/south-invited-to-de-grow/

Coiffier, C. (1997) 'Vanuatuan (2.II.5.q)', in Oliver, P. (ed.) *Encyclopedia of Vernacular Architecture of the World*. Cambridge: Cambridge University Press: 1168–9.

Fois, F. and Forino, G. (2015) 'The self-built ecovillage in L'Aquila, Italy: Community resilience as a grassroots response to environmental shock', *Disasters* 38(4): 719–39.

Forsyth, M. (2009) 'The relationship between the state and kastom systems', in Forsyth, M. (ed.) *A Bird That Flies with Two Wings: The Kastom and State Justice Systems in Vanuatu*. Canberra: ANU Press.

Government of Vanuatu. (2015) *Vanuatu Post Disaster Needs Assessment, Tropical Cyclone Pam*, March – https://reliefweb.int/sites/reliefweb.int/files/resources/vanuatu_pdna_cyclone_pam_2015.pdf

Government of Vanuatu Public Works Department. (2015) *About the Vanuatu Shelter Cluster*, GVPWD with International Federation of Red Cross and Red Crescent Societies and Shelter Cluster Vanuatu – www.sheltercluster.org/sites/default/files/docs/about_the_shelter_cluster_bbs_twig_v2.pdf

Republic of Vanuatu. (2014) *Building Act 2013*, Vanuatu Sessional Legislation – www.paclii.org/vu/legis/num_act/ba201391/

––––––– (2016) *Vanuatu 2030: The People's Plan – National Sustainable Development Plan 2016–2030*. Port Vila: Department of Strategic Policy, Planning and Aid Coordination – www.nab.vu/document/national-sustainable-development-plan

Shelter Cluster Vanuatu. (2015) *Tropical Cyclone Pam Response: Shelter Cluster Strategic Framework – Executive Summary V2.2 15 September 2015*. Vanuatu – www.sheltercluster.org/vanuatu-cyclone-pam-2015/documents/150915-scv-strategic-framework-executive-summary-v22

Stephan, A. and Crawford, R. (2016) 'Size does matter: Australia's addiction to big houses is blowing the energy budget', *The Conversation* – http://theconversation.com/size-does-matter-australias-addiction-to-big-houses-is-blowing-the-energy-budget-70271

UNISDR. (2015) *The Sendai Framework for Disaster Risk Reduction 2015–2030*. Geneva: United Nations Office for Disaster Risk Reduction.

Vanuatu Cultural Centre and Christie, W. (2017) *Safeguarding Indigenous Architecture in Vanuatu*. Paris/Apia: United Nations Educational, Scientific and Cultural Organization.

Vanuatu National Statistics Office. (2009) *2009 National Population and Housing Census: Executive Summary*. Port Vila: Ministry of Finance and Economic Management.

Vanuatu Shelter Cluster. (2015) *Tropical Cyclone Pam Response Lessons Learned*, May. Port Vila: Government of Vanuatu Public Works Department, International Federation of Red Cross and Red Crescent Societies, and the Shelter Cluster.

World Bank Group. (2016) *Building Regulation for Resilience: Managing Risk for Safer Cities*, Summary. WBG with Global Facility for Disaster Reduction and Recovery – www.gfdrr.org/sites/default/files/publication/Building_Regulation_for_Resilience_Managing_Risks_for_Safer_Cities.pdf

Part IV
Reducing demand

Part IV
Reducing demand

8 Christiania
A poster child for degrowth?
Natasha Verco

The Freetown Christiania is a long-standing oppositional community of around 900 residents that occupies 85 acres of inner city space in Northern Europe's Copenhagen, the capital of the small state of Denmark. Squatters used the abandoned Bådsmandsstræde barracks that has been home to the community from 1969, but the entity 'Christiania' did not come into being until it was declared a 'Freetown', two years later. The community arguably shares many values with the degrowth movement and may offer insights into some current debates about housing for degrowth. The definition of degrowth orienting this chapter follows Schneider et al. (2010, 512): 'an equitable downscaling of production and consumption that increases human wellbeing and enhances ecological conditions at the local and global level, in the short and long term'. While degrowth is difficult to pin down to a few simple characteristics or descriptors, D'Alisa et al. (2015) identify a number of core concepts and practices associated with degrowth, many of which can be found in Christiania.

Christiania and degrowth

Christiania began on 26 September 1971 with a staged symbolic re-breaking of the fence, a birthday party and declaration of intent, the Freetown manifesto (Thomassen 2013):

> Christiana's objective is to create a self-governing society, whereby each and every individual can thrive under the responsibility for the entire community. This society must economically rest in itself, and the joint efforts must continue to be about showing that psychological and physical destitution/pollution can be diverted/prevented. This is how it was formulated by Sven, Kim, Ole and Jacob with the right to improvements. 13.11.1971

Christiana (2005) reports its birth story as a confluence of persistent re-squatting of the former military area by local residents to start a playground for local children, a squatter's movement searching for a place to 'realise their dreams', and a pivotal alternative newspaper article 'Emigrate on bus number 8' inviting people to join the new community.

The official visitors guide of Christiania (2005) summarises the rest of its history as a 'long and tangled tale of struggles, victories and defeats' with crucial elements of un-governability and creative resistance. Key moments in this history include acceptance as a 'social experiment' in the 1972 agreement, the 1989 Christiania Law effectively legalising the squat, and the abandonment of this law in 2004 in favour of 'normalisation' by a new conservative government (Christiania 2005). The most significant recent change in Christiania's relationship with the Danish State was in 2011, almost a decade into the most right-wing government in Christiania's history (Karpantschof 2011). The Freetown made an agreement with the state to form a collective foundation that bought, at 'symbolic value', a portion of its space and signed a 30-year lease for the rest of the area (Coppola and Vanolo 2015).

Even with its recent compromises, Christiania could offer some prominent degrowth theorists a messy colourful 'poster child' of their ideals. The declared goals of economic self-sufficiency and avoidance of environmental pollution are evident materially and structurally in the community, in sharp conflict with the social norms of growth-based mainstream society. Indeed, Jarvis (2011, 2013) highlights potential connections between predominant lifestyles in Christiania and 'down-shifting', 'compacting', 'voluntary simplicity' and 'slow living agendas', all referenced as examples of degrowth living practices (Demaria et al. 2013). Christiania has been claimed as an alternative to neoliberal development, a refuge from capitalism, an alternative urban imaginary, an adaptive reuse laboratory and an alternative to top-down sustainability. It has its own local currency, around 90 businesses and institutions, many of which are workers' cooperatives, and impressive structures to support less materially intensive living. Nowtopias, squatting, eco-communities and disobedience are all practices identified with Christiania and with degrowth activities (Thorn 2011; D'Alisa et al. 2015).

Christiania's original manifesto also claimed autonomy from the legal power and authority of the state (Karpantschof 2011). While there is debate about the extent to which Christiania is autonomous, and indeed the extent to which autonomy is possible within the current dominant social structure, autonomy is a key concept, particularly for French degrowth theorists (Martinez-Allier et al. 2010). Furthermore, an important element of naming the community a freetown was to constitute Christiania as a public urban space open to everyone, in direct conflict with processes of enclosure that have increasingly defined urban space in recent decades (Thorn 2011). Commoning and resistance to enclosures are a key goal and strategy, respectively, of degrowth (Helfrich and Bollier 2015). Finally, residents of the Freetown have low incomes compared to other Danes, and only one-third of the community is in the labour market, yet Christiania is extensively referenced as supporting a higher-than-average quality of life (Jarvis and Autogena 2014) – intersecting with degrowth theorising 'the good life' separate from income or material wealth (Nierling 2012).

Despite these significant overlaps, little explicit connection has been drawn between degrowth and Christiania to date, perhaps not so surprising given the similarly small amount of work discussing housing and degrowth. More surprising is how little detailed exploration of the Christiania housing model there is beyond the incidental reflections on housing found in most studies of it. Literature specifically on housing in Christiania has mainly been written from an architectural or urban planning standpoint (Hvilsby and Skov 2005; Vanolo 2013; Knutz et al. 2014). This chapter draws on this literature, and experiential observations from a decade of living periodically in Christiania, to describe features of its housing model and explore their potential contribution to current discussions on degrowth housing. In particular, I focus on insights relevant to degrowth debates on housing in either compact cities or decentralised settlements, and the importance of local self-management for degrowth housing.

Degrowth and housing Christiania-style

There is debate in the degrowth literature about the ideal form of housing for degrowth (see Part IV). Scholars investigating housing models for degrowth have proposed that decentralised communities, such as ecovillages and bioregional developments, are useful models for locally embedded sustainable housing (Latouche 2009; Trainer 2012). Other theorists have drawn on urban village ideas to imagine urban transformation for degrowth (Homs 2007). Yet Stefánsdóttir and Xue (Chapter 14) have raised possible negative effects of adopting either ecovillage or urban villages as templates for degrowth – critiquing what they characterise as the anti-urban orientation embedded in the idea of a degrowth model of decentralised and small-scale human settlements. Instead, Xue (2014) presents a considered, if contentious, argument for including compact cities in potential degrowth futures based on their expected social and environmental sustainability.

Since the implementation of compact city models in various locations worldwide from the early 1990s, sustained criticisms of their failure to deliver promised sustainability outcomes have emerged (Mindali et al. 2004). For instance, evidence from compact city developments suggests that many residents have not oriented their lives around their locality, so the anticipated energy saving from mixed zoning has not materialised (Mindali et al. 2004). Amongst other scholars, Daneshpour and Shakibamanesh (2011) and Neuman (2005) suggest that this evidence indicates that a focus on urban form is counter-productive. Instead, they argue for shifting focus to the process of urban development and to community control of that process. The Christiania case supports this contention.

Community control of development in Christiania takes the form of collective self-management and entails rejection of decisions made by external authorities about the community. Instead, the community holds common meetings, which any resident of Christiania is free to participate in, to manage housing and other issues. Self-management extends within 14 self-defined areas, the largest housing more than 80 residents, the smallest just ten, all making relatively autonomous localised decisions (Christiania 2016). Many of the houses or apartment blocks in larger areas have collective meetings to manage decisions pertaining to just that house or apartment block. Although this structure is often articulated as a model where the highest decision-making body is the common meeting, operating practices and principles demonstrate governance at the lowest level possible.

Prominent Danish architect Steen Rasmusen (in Bøggild 2011) has argued that Christiania's self-management – rather than mixed zoning – has increased its integration of work, living and leisure spaces. Rasmusen contrasted Christiania to his flagship New Town development Tingbjerg. Tingbjerg was designed to mix home, work and leisure facilities – as in recent compact city initiatives – but, instead, failed to foster social cohesion and a sense of place amongst residents. Rasmusen observed that, without the latter, people failed to orientate their lives locally, choosing to commute and 'escape' elsewhere for leisure and work. By contrast, argued Rasmusen, residents in Christiania develop and maintain a sense of place through self-management, and choose to orientate various aspects of their lives around the community. This analysis is supported by many residents whose sense of place and connectedness is fostered by the community's collective self-management. Christiania's experience in this regard suggests that self-management may be required for mixed zoning to deliver more sustainable outcomes in urban development.

Furthermore, the Christiania case suggests that it may be more useful for degrowth proponents to focus on supporting local community self-management of housing developments for degrowth rather than on new compact city developments or urban villages that are produced for communities. This point resonates with Nelson (Chapter 21) and housing and degrowth work by Cattaneo and Gavaldà (2010) who offer examples of the low ecological impacts of squatting communities that they live in and study, to argue that collective self-management enables less energy intensive living, even in communities without declared ecological commitment.

Nonetheless, to attribute Christiania's sustainability or even Christiania's social cohesion to self-management alone would be overly reductive. For example, Christianittes (permanent residents of the community) contend that the particular form of their decision-making processes is also significant for social cohesion. Since its start, Christiania used direct participatory democracy based on consensus decision-making in all community meetings (Hellström 2006). Early scholars investigating Christiania argued that this form of decision-making was an expression of how authority was structured in the community and constituted the main difference between Christiania and mainstream society (Løvetand 1978).

The ideal of Christiania's consensus decision-making is that everyone can participate equally (Winter 2016). Unlike majority rule or other voting systems, no individual or group has the right to impose their will on any individual or group. No one has the authority, or can be vested with the authority, to tell another resident of the community what they must do, and everyone sharing in making a decision must consent to its implementation (Starcheski 2011). Christiania (2016) describes one of the reasons for its self-managed consensus democracy as directly related to social cohesion: 'the structure has spaciousness and prevents the social marginalising and expulsion that we usually see in the rest of the Danish society' and participating in decision-making reduces marginalisation and 'the risk of "falling out" of other society [community] functions'.

Another significant feature of housing in Christiania, arguably significant in fostering social cohesion, is the commitment to partially collectivising some of the costs of living. Residents, and guests that stay for more than three months, pay a monthly contribution to the Christiania economy called a *'brugslej'* (i.e. 'use-rent'). In 2017, the *brugslej* was the equivalent of about one-third to one-half the average cost for accommodation outside the community. The *brugslej* is quite different from *'huslej'* (regular Danish rental payments) so including rent in the name is somewhat misleading (Holmstead Larsen 2007). In contrast to regular Danish *huslej*, failure to pay *brugslej* does not lead to eviction. Although failure to pay has contributed to pressure for people to leave the community, it is somewhat common for residents to delay payment sometimes depending on their circumstances. If a Christianitter is unable to pay *brugslej*, say because of health or social issues, they can access a system of social assistance from community funds to pay for them (Jarvis 2011).

Instead of being private profit for a landlord, the remainder is divided between the local area and the Christiania common fund serving to support residents in other various ways. The part that goes to the house or area supports its maintenance and development. The part that goes to the common purse funds infrastructure institutions, including the garbage and machine maintenance collective, gardening group, economy group and building office, collective bathhouse, health house, four different childcare and youth-related collectives, and Christiania's social help office, all of which helps to foster a sense of community in the Freetown. Since 1989, a proportion of the brugslej income contributes to the collective land tax that Christiania negotiated to pay in response to government pressure.

A wide range of factors beyond self-management have been posited as significant in developing cohesion in Christiania, from joint ritual development to collective identity forged by the shared experience of police violence (see Løvetand 1978; Lund Hansen 2006; Biddault Waddington 2006; Vanolo 2013; Jarvis and Autogena 2014; Winter 2016; Bandyopadhyay 2014). Similarly, many scholars have explored the reasons for Christiania's sustainability and attributed this to factors beyond the effect of social cohesion on residents' lifeworld orientation. Arguably, factors as broad as the temporal rhythms of squatting, extensive communal facilities and the freedoms that come with resistance to planning permission have contributed to the community's less materially intense living (Winter 2016; Wendler 2014).

Moreover, in contrast to Cattaneo and Gavaldà's (2010) study of squatter communities, and indeed many existing European squatter communities, Christiania had a clear ecological foundational intention (Jarvis 2013). This intention was explicitly expressed in the original manifesto, becoming a very publicly discussed distinguishing feature of Christiania in earlier years (Jarvis 2013). Similar to the squats chronicled by Cattaneo and Gavaldà (2010), there is little enforcing of a sustainable approach within the community except that residents maintain Christiania as a car-free town, with transportation inside limited to trolleys and cargo bikes. Instead of enforcement, there is a network of infrastructural support that embeds such values in the processes of the Freetown (Lund-Hansen 2006). This infrastructure is socially supported by an internal community norm, 'the Christiania way', which Jarvis (2013) describes as a collection of values to support low consumption and low-impact living. While perhaps less prominent or noticeable today, the Freetown's ecological foundation commitment is still an important contributor to Christiania's sustainability as a community (Winter 2016).

Yet, Christiania is far from a typically imagined eco-community. Although part of both the Danish and global ecovillages networks, Christiania is much less focused on long-term sustainability than planned ecovillages, reflecting much more closely the shorter-term temporal rhythms of squatting (Winter 2016). It was not purposefully developed and planned, instead developing organically through reuse and elaboration of existing building stock (Winter 2016). Rather than one dominant form of housing, Christiania contains a mix of housing collectives with spaces organised more like cohousing areas and individual dwellings (Jarvis 2013). It is only the collective in Christiania that organises common meals and there is no required minimum contribution of time or work to the community. Unlike many other eco-communities, Christiania doesn't strive towards self-sufficiency in food production. More significantly however, Christiania's housing model is more oppositional than typical eco-communities.

Cristiania's housing: outside the market

In contrast to mainstream capitalist housing norms, in the Freetown, housing is not treated as a commodity. There is no buying, selling or trading of homes or land (Christiania 2016). Accumulation of housing or land for profit making is not possible. When a resident leaves the community, they do not get any compensation for the investment or work done on a house (Christiania 2016). Nor is there a right to inheritance; if someone dies or moves out, family members get no compensation for the property and are only be able to claim their family member's personal belongings (Svolkinas 2010). This approach to property is fundamental to the community. The Danish Government proposed in 2006 that Christiania retain their collective decision-making and residency rights but introduce private ownership and the possibility for profit making on homes. Christiania replied that the Government's proposal would effectively destroy the Freetown by turning it into 'nothing more than a self-administered housing experiment' (Karpantschof 2011). So, rather than an optional addition to self-management, opposition to marketisation and ownership of homes must be understood as a core value in Christiania's housing practice.

Opposition to marketisation and ownership of homes is also significant in fostering Christiania's less materially intensive living. For example, the integration of work, leisure and home life in the community must be partially attributed to residents not having to pay large amounts to secure, keep or maintain dwellings.

Without the obligation to engage in full-time work to afford housing, residents are then more free to choose to orientate their life around the community. Additionally, as Cattaneo and Gavaldà (2010) highlight, being freed from full-time work can virtuously reduce consumption and needed energy use. Even the community's prioritisation of reuse of building materials is partly a product of being developed in a context that rejects private ownership of homes (Mollerup 2005).

The importance of opposition to commodification of housing, the commitment to partially collectivising the costs of living, and the base ecological commitment all contribute to the sustainability of Christiania. This suggests that, while self-management may be necessary for sustainability, a model of degrowth housing based on self-management alone may be overly reductive. Acknowledging the complex bundle of contributing factors in Christiania's experience, at the very least, an ecological commitment and rejection of ownership or commodification of homes should be added to self-management as the basis of any Christiania-style housing model for degrowth.

However, this raises the question of whether it would even be possible to establish more Christiania-style housing projects. Some theorists argue that Christiania's development and continued existence relies on a specific permissiveness of Danish culture or the Danish state. While potentially politically useful, this argument is a significant warping of the historical mirror as it fails to take into account the extent to which Christiania is a product of struggle, the vicissitudes of Danish public opinion, or how persistently the Danish state has attempted to shut down the Freetown (Karpantschof 2011). Yet, few comparable squatter communities exist in European capital cities and certainly none covering as large an area, that are home to close to a thousand people. Indeed, there is no doubt that Christiania's development and experience is specific to the particular spatial location and socio-historical context it inhabits (Thorn 2011). This uniqueness and the significance of context to its development and persistence, signal potent limits to its usefulness in imagining degrowth housing futures.

Nonetheless, authors, particularly in the field of urban planning, have argued that Christiania is an important model for alternative urban practices (see for example Hvilsby and Skov 2005; Bøggild 2011) Many focus on the importance of community self-management in urban design based on Christiania's experience. The more oppositional aspects of Christiania's housing model have received far less attention in this literature. Given that Christiania's more oppositional model also prevents the sort of housing speculation fundamental to a growth economy (Amouroux 2011), discussions of housing in the degrowth literature should not make the same mistake.

Conclusion

This chapter offered a short historical accounting of Christiania and briefly outlined some of the potential overlaps between degrowth desires and the Freetown. In terms of housing and degrowth debates, I have argued that focusing on the form of housing is not as useful as focusing on the process and, especially, a commitment to local self-management in degrowth housing. Moreover, I have highlighted how a focus on self-management alone may be overly reductive. An elaborated model of housing for degrowth that encompasses self-management, rejection of ownership and commodification of homes, and a declared principle of striving towards less materially intense living has been suggested. Yet the question remains: Would a model encompassing a more confrontational approach be embraced by the degrowth community?

Many degrowth proponents currently focus on individualised change in consumption patterns rather than collective or oppositional action for degrowth (Correia 2012). Moreover, a substantial body of degrowth theorists resist more radical positioning in order to appeal to a broader audience (Andreucci and McDonough 2015). This last cohort of degrowthers, preoccupied with widening degrowth's appeal, may well reject Christiania as their poster child. This would be a mistake.

Christiania holds enormous appeal to a much broader audience than those already committed to degrowth. It is one of the most widely used public spaces in Copenhagen and one of the top three tourist attractions in the Danish capital city (Vanolo 2013). Christiania's ongoing appeal is intimately tied to its more confrontational opposition to the mainstream and the resultant highly symbolic value that the community has for those working towards alternatives to mainstream consumer capitalism (Thorn 2011). Becoming more mainstream, more normal – say, in order to relate to the mainstream – would make it much less interesting. More cautious degrowth proponents could well learn from this outstanding and long-standing oppositional case.

References

Amouroux, C.S. (2011) 'Normalisation within Christiania', in Thorn, H., Wasshede, C. and Nilson, T. (eds.) *Space for Urban Alternatives? Christiania 1971–2011*. Stockholm: Gidlunds: 235–62.

Andreucci, D. and McDonough, T. (2015) 'Capitalism', in D'Alisa, G., Demaria, F. and Kallis, G. (eds.) *Degrowth: A Vocabulary for a New Era*. Oxon: Routledge: 59–62.

Bandyopadhyay, M. (2014) *Property and Publics Negotiating State – Citizen Relationships in Christiania*. CAS Working Paper Series 14–8. New Delhi: Centre for the Study of Social Systems Jawaharlal, Nehru University.

Biddault-Waddington, R. (2006) 'An experimental aesthetic audit of a city within a city: The case of Christiania', in Carrillo, F. (ed.) *Knowledge Cities: Approaches, Experiences and Perspectives*. New York: Butterworth-Heinemann: 177–87.

Bøggild, S.S. (2011) 'Happy ever after? The welfare city in between the Freetown and the New Town', in Thorn, H., Wasshede, C. and Nilson, T. (eds.) *Space for Urban Alternatives? Christiania 1971–2011*. Stockholm: Gidlunds: 98–131.

Cattaneo, C. and Gavaldà, M. (2010) 'The experience of rurban squats in Collserola, Barcelona, what kind of degrowth?' *Journal of Cleaner Production* 18: 581–9.

Christiania. (2005) *Christiania Guide*, Christiania – www.christiania.org/wp-content/uploads/2013/02/Guideeng2.pdf

―――― (2016) *This Is How Christiania's Self-Management Works*, Christiania – www.christiania.org/info/pages-in-english/paper
Coppola, A. and Vanolo, A. (2015) 'Normalising autonomous spaces: Ongoing transformations in Christiania, Copenhagen', *Urban Studies* 52(6): 1152–68.
Correia, D. (2012) 'Degrowth, American style: No impact man and bourgeois primitivism', *Capitalism Nature Socialism* 23(1): 105–18.
D'Alisa, G., Demaria, F. and Kallis, G. (eds.) (2015) *Degrowth: A Vocabulary for a New Era*. Oxon: Routledge.
Daneshpour, A. and Shakibamanesh, A. (2011) 'Compact city: Does it create an obligatory context for urban sustainability?' *International Journal of Architectural Engineering and Urban Planning* 21(2): 110–18.
Demaria, F., Schneider, F., Sekulova, F. and Martinez-Alier, J. (2013) 'What is degrowth? From an activist slogan to a social movement', *Environmental Values* 22: 191–215.
Helfrich, S. and Bollier, D. (2015) 'Commons', in D'Alisa, G., Demaria, F. and Kallis, G. (eds.) *Degrowth: A Vocabulary for a New Era*. Oxon: Routledge: 75–8.
Hellström, M. (2006) *Steal this Place – The Aesthetics of Tactical Formlessness and the Free Town of Christiania*. Doctoral thesis, Swedish University of Agricultural Sciences, SLU Reproenheten, Alnarp.
Holmstead Larsen, C. (2007) 'Christiania: Eine Geschichte zwischen Utopie und "Normalisierung" (1971–2007)', in Birke, P. and Holmsted Larsen, C. (eds.) *Besetze Deine Stadt! – BZ Din By! Häuserkämpfe und Stadtentwicklung in Kopenhagen*. Berlin: Azzoziation A: 159–70.
Homs, C. (2007) 'Localism and the city: The example of "urban village"', *International Journal of Inclusive Democracy* 3(1): 1–8.
Hvilsby, S.H. and Skov, P. (2005) 'Fra Idealrum til Hverdagsrum – Utopi eller Virkelighed? Et rids gennem Christianias udviklingshistorie', *Nordisk Arkitekturforskning* 2: 45–53.
Jarvis, H. (2011) 'Alternative visions of home and family life in Christiania: Lessons for the mainstream', in Thorn, H., Wasshede, C. and Nilson, T. (eds.) *Space for Urban Alternatives? Christiania 1971–2011*. Stockholm: Gidlunds: 156–80.
―――― (2013) 'Against the "tyranny" of single-family dwelling: Insights from Christiania at 40', *Gender, Place & Culture* 20(8): 939–59.
Jarvis, H. and Autogena, L. (2014) 'Christiania's place in the world of travelling ideas: Sharing informal liveability', in *Nordic Encounters: Travelling Ideas of Open Space Design and Planning at the 10th International World in Denmark Conference, 2014*. Copenhagen, Denmark, 12–14 June 2014.
Karpantschof, R. (2011) 'Bargaining and barricades – The political struggle over the Freetown Christiania 1971–2011', in Thorn, H., Wasshede, C. and Nilson, T. (eds.) *Space for Urban Alternatives? Christiania 1971–2011*. Stockholm: Gidlunds: 38–68.
Knutz, E., Markussen, T. and Christiansen, P.R. (2014) 'The role of fiction in experiments within design, art and architecture: Towards a new typology of design fiction', *Artifact* III(2): 8.1–13.
Latouche, S. (2009) *Farewell to Growth*. Cambridge: Polity Press.
Løvetand, P. (1978) 'The Freetown of Christiania', in Lemberg, K., Løvetand, P., Juhler, S., Falkentorp, J., Kløvedal, M. and Hansen, D.R. (eds.) *Dominant Ways of Life in Denmark/Alternative Ways of Life in Denmark*. Paper presented at first meeting of the Alternative Ways of Life Sub-Project of the GPID Project, Cartigny, Switzerland 21–24 April 1978.
Lund Hansen, A. (2006) *Space Wars and the New Urban Imperialism*. Lund: Department of Social and Economic Geography, Lund University.

Martinez-Alier, J., Pascual, U., Vivien, F. and Zaccai, E. (2010) 'Sustainable de-growth: Mapping the context, criticisms and future prospects of an emergent paradigm', *Ecological Economics* 69(9): 1741–7.

Mindali, O., Ravey, A. and Salomon, I. (2004) 'Urban density and energy consumption: A new look at old statistics', *Transportation Research* Part A 38: 143–62.

Mollerup, M.A. (2005) 'Christiania's aesthetics – You can't kill us/we are a part of you', in Mollerup, M.A., Dirckinck-Holmfeld, M., Keiding, M. and Reddersen, J. (eds.) *Learnings from Christiania*. Hørsholm: Arkitektens Forlag.

Neuman, M. (2005) 'The compact city fallacy', *Journal of Planning Education and Research* 25: 11–26.

Nierling, L. (2012) '"This is a bit of the good life": Recognition of unpaid work from the perspective of degrowth', *Ecological Economics* 84: 240–64.

Schneider, F., Kallis, G. and Martinez-Alier, J. (2010) 'Crisis or opportunity? Economic degrowth for social equity and economic sustainability. Introduction to this special issue', *Journal of Cleaner Production* 18: 511–18.

Starcheski, A. (2011) 'Consensus and strategy: Narratives of naysaying and yeasaying in Christiania's struggles over legalisation', in Thorn, H., Wasshede, C. and Nilson, T. (eds.) *Space for Urban Alternatives? Christiania 1971–2011*. Stockholm: Gidlunds: 263–87.

Svolkinas, L. (2010) '"On the precipice of a volcano": Negotiating continuity and change in the Danish alternative community Christiania', *Identity Politics: Migration, Communities, and Multilingualism. Acta Historica Universitatis Klaipedensis* XX (Studia Anthropologica IV): 87–98.

Thomassen, S. (2013) *History of the Christiania Area*. Bygningssyrelsen – www.bygst.dk/(X(1)S(4kekvhldfiaqds5dma2xwqws))/english/knowledge/christiania/history-of-the-christiania-area/?AspxAutoDetectCookieSupport=1

Thorn, H. (2011) 'Governing freedom – Debating Christiania in the Danish Parliament', in Thorn, H., Wasshede, C. and Nilson, T. (eds.) *Space for Urban Alternatives? Christiania 1971–2011*. Stockholm: Gidlunds: 68–97.

Trainer, T. (2012) 'De-growth: Do you realize what it means?' *Futures* 44(6): 590–9.

Vanolo, A. (2013) 'Alternative capitalism and creative economy: The case of Christiania', *International Journal of Urban and Regional Research* 37(5): 1785–98.

Wendler, J. (2014) *Experimental Urbanism: Grassroots Alternatives as Spaces of Learning and Innovation in the City*. PhD Thesis submitted to the University of Manchester – www.research.manchester.ac.uk/portal/files/54558825/FULL_TEXT.PDF

Winter, A.K. (2016) '"Environmental Sustainability? We don't have that here" Freetown Christiania as an unintentional eco-village', *ACME: An International E-Journal for Critical Geographies* 15(1): 129–49.

Xue, J. (2014) 'Is eco-village/urban village the future of a degrowth society? An urban planner's perspective', *Ecological Economics* 105: 130–8.

9 Refurbishment vs demolition?
Social housing campaigning for degrowth

Mara Ferreri

The global financial crisis has stimulated a renewed interest in the growth-versus-environment debate. Ecological economics proposes 'a-growth' (van den Bergh 2011) and 'degrowth' (Schneider et al. 2010; Kallis 2011) to challenge orthodox growth measures such as gross domestic product that do not account for a wide range of environmental and social costs and benefits and to discuss multiple alternative scenarios to the imperative of compound growth in local, national and transnational political agendas (van den Bergh and Kallis 2012). In post-crisis Europe, the notion of degrowth has begun to gain traction as a potential opportunity for rethinking the economy in terms of social equity and ecological sustainability, as 'an equitable downscaling of production and consumption that increases human wellbeing and enhances ecological conditions at the local and global' levels, in both the short and long terms (Schneider et al. 2010, 512).

Moreover, as a 'deliberately subversive slogan' that aims to challenge a political imaginary dominated by growth and development, degrowth has offered an expanded vocabulary (D'Alisa et al. 2015) and an interpretative frame not only for interdisciplinary debates within academia but also for discussions in the arenas of policy-making, civil society organising and social movements (Demaria et al. 2013). Within these discussions, housing provision has remained a comparatively under-investigated issue, often addressed in terms of new housebuilding models or small-scale living experiments.

In this chapter, I argue the need to examine the potential role of existing dwellings for a wide-reaching housing degrowth agenda. Combining environmental and social concerns, I engage with the ideas and proposals of residents about the future of low-income social housing – a significant non-market sector now under threat in many cities across the globe – in the context of pro-growth urban development agendas (Porter and Shaw 2009; Smets and Watt 2017). Drawing on the analysis of a high-profile campaign against the demolition of a social housing estate in London, United Kingdom (UK), I discuss the centrality of the politics of valuation in the wider 'demolition versus refurbishment' debate.

Housing and degrowth

Perhaps surprisingly, housing has remained a relatively under-explored theme in debates about imaginaries and prefigurative practices for a degrowth urban society. The literature on housing and degrowth to date appears to be focused on small-scale examples that provide various degrees of social, economic, environmental and technical innovation. Many involve the analysis of relatively marginal, if growing, alternatives to mainstream building and residential typologies, such as low-impact collective living and co-housing (Lietaert 2010; Pickerill 2011) and intentional communities in rural or semi-rural settings (Pickerill and Maxey 2009; Cattaneo and Gavaldà 2010). Combining environmental and social concerns, these studies share thematic insights with literature on community-controlled and democratically managed models of housing provision in the search for housing *commons*, a key term in the degrowth vocabulary (Helfrich and Bollier 2015). Similarly, cooperative housing for rent (Johanisova et al. 2015; Larsen and Lund Hansen 2015) and community land trusts (Thompson 2015) have been proposed as tenures and mechanisms for producing and maintaining housing outside the logic of growth and mainstream urban development.

Such a small-scale approach risks limiting research into housing for degrowth in two significant ways. First, by focusing on marginal experiences that are numerically, socially and geographically insignificant, it reproduces imaginaries of exclusivity in which innovative housing options exist only under rare conditions and are accessible only to those who have specific sets of resources, whether economic, cultural, social or political (Thompson 2015). Studies in alternative housing models, such as community land trusts (Bunce 2016) and refurbished senior cohousing (Scanlon and Fernández Arrigoitia 2015) in metropolitan cores such as London, have drawn attention to the political economy of land ownership and the financing of construction as significant barriers to self-organised forms of more socially and environmentally just housing provision. Such barriers need addressing.

Second, by neglecting already existing housing provision, small-scale approaches disregard the vast multiplicity of housing models that co-exist alongside market housing, some with the potential for important large-scale social or environmental responses. If existing market conditions engender very high entry costs for new 'alternative' housing, the wider transformative potential of a housing degrowth agenda should be tested against its capacity for transforming *existing* housing towards greater social and environmental justice.

Reflecting this perspective, this chapter argues that a truly 'subversive' degrowth housing agenda pays great attention to urban material conditions and addresses the challenge of reimagining and transforming existing housing, particularly housing that is at the margins of the housing market. Therefore, I consider housing degrowth in the context of the experiences and demands of residents and local communities working towards the transformation of existing low-income municipal housing provision. Specifically, I draw on an extended case study approach to review plans to demolish a social housing complex, the Heygate Estate, and to discuss the social and environmental alternatives proposed by residents and campaigners within a wider 'demolition versus refurbishment' debate on the future of municipal housing in London. Critically examining the efforts of residents and campaigners can offer important insights into the political, legal and institutional barriers to challenging the dominance of an urban growth agenda on housing in cities today.

The question of municipal housing in London

Greater London was transformed by the construction of a high number of municipal housing for social rent, from London County Council construction pre-World War II (WWII) to the vast and rapid developments from the late 1940s through to the mid-1970s (Cole and Furbey 1994). By the late 1970s, public housing represented 31 percent of total dwellings and reached nearly half in some inner London boroughs (Forrest and Murie 1988, 116). The British model of public housing was characterised by municipal production, management, maintenance and financing of public housing stock – supported by a central state subsidy – with the tenure of choice being social rent.

Since this peak, an estimated 1.9 million social rented homes have been lost through demolition and privatisation (Hodkinson 2012, 510) in what Hodkinson and Essen (2015) – quoting Peck and Tickell (2002) – have described as an example of 'roll-back neoliberalism'. By 2014, public housing in Greater London had dwindled to 12 percent of all total dwellings, although inner city boroughs still retained a high proportion (Mayor of London Office 2014). Alongside disposal, public housing stock was affected by a policy of residualisation (Cole and Furbey 1994), produced by reductions in central government subsidies for building new public housing, and diminishing repair and maintenance budgets for existing housing which, by 1997, had left an estimated £19 billion disrepair backlog (Hodkinson and Essen 2015).

The withdrawal of political and financial support for existing public housing, combined with the deterioration of the housing stock, offered fertile ground for New Labour's urban regeneration discourse and policy programme, which targeted disinvested urban areas with large proportions of public housing (Imrie et al. 2009). In addition to long-term shifts in central government housing policies, urban regeneration housing programmes were majorly impacted by shifts from municipal housing to other social housing providers (Social Registered Landlords), from direct public investment to private-public partnerships and financial initiatives (Hodkinson and Essen 2015), and by practices of demolition and rebuilding in 'mixed-community' neighbourhoods (Bridge et al. 2012).

The Mayor of London Office (2014) acknowledged that, with the deterioration of the municipal stock, 'programmes to demolish or refurbish estates have divided opinion amongst communities, social landlords and developers'. The replacement of social rented units with private homes and less affordable rental on offer was interpreted by critical commentators as encouraging gentrification de facto (Lees 2014; Watt 2009a). Such socially disruptive urban policies have promoted and naturalised the demolition of council-built housing undertaken 'often without adequate consultation, and involving disruption and some degree of dispersal of established communities' (Edwards 2016, 233). The Heygate Estate, in Southwark, became an emblematic case (Lees and Ferreri 2016).

The Heygate Estate in Southwark

After WWII, inner London boroughs had higher percentages of public dwellings under local government's ownership and management than outer areas. The London Borough of Southwark (LBS) is a key inner city borough of over 300,000 inhabitants where, until the late 1990s, nearly half of all housing stock was publicly owned and managed (Watt 2009b, 221). In the mid-1990s, LBS embarked on a strategy to redevelop the northern parts of the borough through investment in infrastructures and the built environment, stretching from the riverbank to the Elephant & Castle, where the Heygate Estate was located. Plans were made to demolish and redevelop the 1974 medium-sized purpose-built estate housing around 1,200 households (social tenants and leaseholders), as part of a comprehensive council-led urban regeneration programme.

The deteriorated state of the physical fabric of the buildings was an important component of the argument in favour of its demolition and redevelopment but needs contextualising. As with many other municipalities across England facing dwindling central government budgets for maintaining existing municipal dwellings, in 1998 the *Southwark Housing Stock Condition Survey* calculated the estimated cost of maintaining its more than 40,000 public housing units over a 30-year period as £23,363 per dwelling on average (London Borough of Southwark 1999). Over the same period, maintenance costs for the Heygate Estate were lower, at £21,742 per dwelling. Around the same time, the council commissioned a comprehensive Option Appraisal Study of the Heygate Estate to establish and evaluate cost estimates for repair and refurbishment versus demolition. The survey, presented in September 1998 by engineering firm Allott and Lomax Consulting (1998), found the buildings structurally sound and recommended refurbishing the maisonette blocks whilst redeveloping the perimeter blocks on the North and Western end of the estate. Despite these independent recommendations and the council cost assessment, a Strategic Committee report – not made public until the late 2000s – revealed that the decision to demolish was taken in 1998. In January 2001, the council stopped issuing new secure tenancies and only minimally maintained the site, further exacerbating the building's state.

In the late 1990s, in the context of the regeneration, estate residents and community groups began organising for more democratic decision-making processes. Initial proposals revolved around re-housing Heygate Estate residents on site. Later, the demand was for re-housing in nearby early housing sites and on site 'like-for-like' replacement homes (DeFilippis and North 2004), a key demand that Bloom et al. (2015) point out is seldom found in processes of social housing redevelopment. As tenants began to be re-housed elsewhere in the borough and leaseholders received compensation for the early termination of their leases, local organising shifted to trying to influence redevelopment plans after demolition. Activities of a key local organisation, the Elephant Amenity Network, promoted open master planning, affordable housing and 'regeneration that benefits all'. Mapping Heygate's social facilities included calculating the social and environmental value of its trees and green areas, to counter its image of an inhuman 'concrete jungle'. A range of alternative proposals collected through a public conference were published in the *Imagining the Elephant* report (Elephant Amenity Network 2011).

Socially and environmentally just alternatives to demolition

A less well-known aspect of opposition to the regeneration plans was the attempt to reshape debate towards more socially and environmentally just solutions than those in the redevelopment master plan. In May 2012, local residents and groups started the '35% campaign', referring to the then current percentage of social rented housing required by local planning policy (35percent 2013). The campaign questioned local benefits brought by the regeneration plans and critiqued the proposed development scheme on the basis that it generated a net loss of genuinely affordable housing in the area, entailed the destruction of existing open green amenities (including over 400 mature trees) and their replacement by a privately managed park and, finally, offered negligible renewable energy provision in a development that originally strived to be 100 percent. Additionally, research undertaken by community groups unearthed the already-mentioned 1998 Option Appraisal Study and raised public awareness of the option of refurbishment.

The option of refurbishment for high rise council dwelling began gaining traction, particularly due to cases such as the £16.13 million regeneration of the Edward Woods Estate in the London Borough of Hammersmith and Fulham – built between 1966 and 1971, slightly earlier than the Heygate Estate, and containing fewer units (854 in total), but with a similar mix of high rise towers and walk-up blocks. The case for retrofit combined environmental rationales, such as reducing energy consumption and social benefits, including improving the estate's attractiveness and decreasing risks of fuel poverty for existing low-income residents who remained in situ while works took place (Bates et al. 2012). Importantly, the Edward Woods Estate showed that retrofitting social housing does not need to lead to 'renoviction' (displacement or displacement pressure due to rent increases for low-income households), a risk recently debated by Baeten et al. (2016) and Thörn et al. (2016).

Moreover, the idea that the Heygate Estate could be refurbished gained citywide attention due to a published proposal by multinational architecture firm Gensler and constructing consultancy Baqus to the 2012 Building Trust International's HOME competition (Building Trust International 2012). The call was for a design and costing exercise to create decent urban housing for less than £20,000 outlay per dwelling. Gensler's team showed that it was possible to refurbish the entire 1,200 Heygate Estate units for an estimated £35 million. The refurbishment was presented as feasible and the estimated unit cost of £14,000 was close to a £13,000 grant available to local authorities under the Homes and Communities Agency's Grants Programme (2012). Furthermore, this refurbishment would save up to 40,000 tons of embodied carbon dioxide emissions per square metre, and retain the canopy and biodiversity of the 40+ year-old open access green areas of the estate (Southwark Notes 2013). The Gensler proposal provided not only an important case study to challenge current development plans but also the possibility to discuss different scenarios for the Heygate and other large-scale dilapidated estates across London. For example, the HOME competitions' winner proposed converting council estate's garages into homes without any structural modifications, at the same time giving impetus to car-free developments and providing more housing on site.

Building on the attention generated, the community-led campaign group Better Elephant (n.d.) formed to explore and divulge 'proposals for an alternative and more sustainable regeneration of the Elephant & Castle' in environmental, social and economic ways. Exposing that alternatives to complete demolition were discarded without proper consultation highlighted the high social costs of displacing residents and supported those leaseholders still living on the estate awaiting the expropriation of their homes by the government through a Compulsory Purchase Order (CPO). The Better Elephant campaign contrasted the estimated cost of £35 million of the Gensler proposal with the £65.4 million that LBS had already spent on emptying the Heygate Estate by 2014. Not only was the LBS's decision exposed as counter to the independent surveyors' recommendation, but also its socially and environmentally disruptive strategy of long drawn out re-housing and demolition had been much costlier than the refurbishment alternative that would have enabled residents to stay put. An example of the gagging of alternatives to hegemonic pro-development and pro-growth agendas, shortly after publication, Better Elephant received a request to remove the Gensler's presentation slides from its blog and the slides were removed from the official competition website.

Making the case for refurbishment versus demolition

The activities promoting refurbishment versus demolition centred on the Heygate CPO Public Inquiry, the results of which spread to campaigns outside their immediate area.

The Heygate CPO public inquiry

Organising to give visibility to the refurbishment option was not limited to the level of campaigning. Local community groups used the formal and public planning inquiry into the Heygate CPO as a platform to challenge and dissect the decision-making process that favoured demolition and challenged the master plan planning application being approved at the time. They argued that alternatives to wholesale demolition and displacement had not been given due consideration. The original architect of the Heygate Estate was an expert witness during the inquiry and questioned the evidence and rationale behind LBS's decision: although the estate had been poorly maintained over the years, no structural assessment of the building had been carried out to justify demolishing it. Additionally, no assessment had been made to evaluate, architecturally and financially, a potential retrofit.

In their rebuttal, LBS conceded that independent consultants had recommended partial demolition and refurbishment in 1998 but that other considerations prevailed. As explained in the written testimony by the Elephant & Castle project director:

> the option to repair and refurbish was the minimum option and had the lowest capital cost but it did not represent best value for money when taken into account whole life costs and social viability.
> (London Borough of Southwark 2013, 12)

A formulation of 'whole life costs and social viability' points towards a wider political agenda of dismantling the edifice of municipal social rented housing in the medium to long term. It became clear that the objective of 'realis[ing] the value of this strategically placed site' (ibid.) was given priority over an option that was, from the onset, considered less environmentally and socially disruptive, as well as less costly.

The dispute clearly reveals a conflict of valuation between the rationales of an ideology of urban growth and alternative imaginaries of municipal housing futures. In this case, objectors to the demolition sought to make a persuasive argument by appealing to cost-benefit analysis and 'the common language of economic valuation' (Martinez-Alier 2009, 86). The response of the local government demonstrated a wider shift in how local authorities in London have become 'constrained to think of their land and social housing as "assets", not use values' (Edwards 2016, 223), leading to a dismissal of the social and environmental costs of demolition and displacement.

Beyond the Heygate

While the CPO was confirmed and the estate ultimately demolished in late 2013, the case of the Heygate gained public notoriety, laying the basis for campaigns in other municipal estates threatened with demolition. To support the argument for refurbishment, a review of evidence of demolition versus refurbishment was commissioned by the community planning network Just Space and the London Tenants Federation. The 2013 report, jointly produced by UCL Urban Lab and Engineering Exchange, noted that existing technical studies rarely measured the embodied carbon of municipal housing estates while the construction and demolition sectors contribute up to 47 percent of all waste in London every year. Taking a holistic approach to social housing improvement, it noted that promoting refurbishment would enable 'the creation of jobs requiring a new set of skills that will be in demand if the UK is to meet its carbon emission reduction targets' (UCL Urban Lab and Engineering Exchange 2014). Consequently, at a London Assembly Hearing in June 2014, Just Space demanded that the Mayor of London make a strategic requirement for reports on embodied carbon emission for future public housing, as raised in the *Knock It Down or Do*

It Up report on the future of public housing in the city by the London Assembly Housing Committee (2015).

A similar argument over the methods and politics of valuation was made in 2015, during the Public Inquiry into the CPO of a bloc of leaseholder flats that were part of the large-scale regeneration by demolition of the Aylesbury Estate in Southwark (Lees 2014). As with Heygate opposition, the objectors demanded 'a full independent cost/benefit analysis, which includes not only an economic but also environmental and social analysis of the benefits of demolition versus refurbishment' (Aylesbury Leaseholders Group 2015, 7). They cited the Doddington Estate in Wandsworth and the Six Acres Estate in Islington as successful cases of recently refurbished council estates (Aylesbury Leaseholders Group 2015). The argument for different forms of accounting for the social and environmental costs of demolition was not even considered in the Inspector's judgement revealing further difficulties in pressuring elites to measure the full costs of economic growth in a scenario dominated by the urban growth agenda at local and metropolitan levels (Greater London Authority 2016).

Refurbishment as degrowth? Some final reflections

One of the aims of the 'deliberately subversive slogan' of degrowth is to decolonise an imaginary dominated by a one-way future expressed in terms such as 'growth' and 'development' (D'Alisa et al. 2015, 5). Further work is needed for such decolonising to occur in the housing sector, particularly in core cities where making decisions is dominated by growth-seeking policy orthodoxies. In this chapter, I have proposed to expand the degrowth debate by addressing one of the casualties of this colonised urban imaginary: the withdrawal of state support and the dominance of the demolition-to-redevelop agenda for ageing low-income housing across Europe and beyond (Smets and Watt 2017).

Taking on the challenge of rethinking the future of low-income housing through a degrowth perspective means expanding its research agenda to include the transformation of existing stock through retrofitting. The argument for refurbishing the Heygate Estate was not explicitly framed through degrowth slogans but the strategy of challenging the imperative of urban growth through a demand for different languages of valuation echoes degrowth insights into environmental disputes of the poor (Martinez-Alier 2009). The in-depth analysis of campaigning strategies has outlined the multiple institutional and political challenges faced by residents and community groups resisting demolition and displacement, and has shown the ways in which political power was expressed 'as the power to impose one particular decision-procedure and a standard of valuation' (ibid., 87).

To conclude, conflicts of valuation are embedded in the balance of priorities that motivate decision-making processes around the future of social housing both within the 'refurbishment versus demolition' debate and within the rationale for refurbishment. To iterate, in some cases privileging environmental over social issues risks supporting processes of gentrification and displacement, making retrofitting a double-edged demand for low-income residents (Baeten et al. 2016).

In other contexts, monetary logics of cost-benefit analysis have led to complex structures of subcontracting and a diminished accountability to residents in key phases of refurbishment processes. In London, June 2017, the tragic consequences of the latter came to international attention when a fire devastated the newly refurbished Grenfell Tower and led to the death of over 60 residents of the low-income Lancaster West Estate in the Royal Borough of Kensington and Chelsea (Architects for Social Housing 2017). Beyond a demand to account for the social and environmental costs of demolition, a degrowth agenda for decolonising the imaginary of social housing through retrofitting requires a fundamental reassertion of the value of human life above urban growth and economic profit, and of low-income residents' right to re-imagine and decide the future of their homes.

References

35percent. (2013) *E&C Regeneration Timeline* – http://35percent.org/
Allott and Lomax Consulting. (1998) *Heygate Estate Option Appraisal Study*. London: London Borough of Southwark.
Architects for Social Housing. (2017) *The Truth about Grenfell Tower*, 21 July 2017 – https://architectsforsocialhousing.wordpress.com/2017/07/21/the-truth-about-grenfell-tower-a-report-by-architects-for-social-housing/
Aylesbury Leaseholders Group. (2015) *Compulsory Purchase Order 2014*. London: Aylesbury Leaseholders Group Statement of Case.
Baeten, G., Westin, S., Pull, E. and Molina, I. (2016) 'Pressure and violence: Housing renovation and displacement in Sweden', *Environment and Planning A* 49(3): 631–51.
Bates, K., Lane, L. and Power, A. (2012) *High Rise Hope: The Social Implications of Energy Efficiency Retrofit in Large Multi-Storey Tower Blocks*. London: LSE Housing and Communities.
Better Elephant (n.d.) 'Creating a more sustainable Elephant', *Better Elephant* — http://betterelephant.github.io/
Bloom, N.D., Umbach, F. and Vale, L.J. (eds.) (2015) *Public Housing Myths: Perception, Reality, and Social Policy*. Cornell: Cornell University Press.
Bridge, G., Butler, T. and Lees, L. (eds.) (2012) *Mixed Communities: Gentrification by Stealth?* Bristol: Policy Press.
Building Trust International. (2012) *£20K House [aka HOME] Competition (2012)* – www.buildingtrustinternational.org/homecompetition.html
Bunce, S. (2016) 'Pursuing urban commons: Politics and alliances in community land trust activism in East London', *Antipode* 48: 134–50.
Cattaneo, C. and Gavaldà, M. (2010) 'The experience of rurban squats in Collserola, Barcelona: What kind of degrowth?' *Journal of Cleaner Production* 18: 581–9.
Cole, I. and Furbey, R. (1994) *The Eclipse of Council Housing*. London and New York: Routledge.
D'Alisa, G., Demaria, F. and Kallis, G. (eds.) (2015) *Degrowth: A Vocabulary for a New Era*. London and New York: Routledge.
DeFilippis, J. and North, P. (2004) 'The emancipatory community? Place, politics and collective action in cities', in Lees, L. (ed.) *The Emancipatory City? Paradoxes and Possibilities*. London: Sage: 72–88.
Demaria, F., Schneider, F., Sekulova, F. and Martinez-Alier, J. (2013) 'What is degrowth? From an activist slogan to a social movement', *Environmental Values* 22: 191–215.

Edwards, M. (2016) 'The housing crisis and London', *City* 20(2): 222–37.

Elephant Amenity Network. (2011) *Imagining the Elephant: Summary Report* – https://elephantamenity.files.wordpress.com/2011/06/imagining-the-elephant-elephant-amenity-network-report-v1-final-lores4.pdf

Forrest, R. and Murie, A. (1988) *Selling the Welfare State: The Privatisation of Public Housing*. London/New York: Routledge.

Greater London Authority. (2016) *Up or Out: A False Choice. Options for London's Growth*. London: GLA.

Helfrich, S. and Bollier, D. (2015) 'Commons', in D'Alisa, G., Demaria, F. and Kallis, G. (eds.) *Degrowth: A Vocabulary for a New Era*. London and New York: Routledge: 75–8.

Hodkinson, S. (2012) 'The new urban enclosures', *City* 16(5): 500–18.

Hodkinson, S. and Essen, C. (2015) 'Grounding accumulation by dispossession in everyday life: The unjust geographies of urban regeneration under the private finance initiative', *International Journal of Law in the Built Environment* 7: 72–91.

Imrie, R., Lees, L. and Raco, M. (eds.) (2009) *Regenerating London: Governance, Sustainability and Community in a Global City*. London and New York: Routledge.

Johanisova, N., Suriñach Padilla, D. and Parry, P. (2015) 'Co-operatives', in D'Alisa, G., Demaria, F. and Kallis, G. (eds.) *Degrowth: A Vocabulary for a New Era*. London and New York: Routledge: 152–5.

Kallis, G. (2011) 'In defence of degrowth', *Ecological Economics* 70: 873–80.

Larsen, H.G. and Lund Hansen, A. (2015) 'Commodifying Danish housing commons', *Geografiska Annaler: Series B, Human Geography* 97: 263–74.

Lees, L. (2014) 'The urban injustices of new labour's "New Urban Renewal": The case of the Aylesbury estate in London', *Antipode* 46: 921–47.

Lees, L. and Ferreri, M. (2016) 'Resisting gentrification on its final frontiers: Learning from the Heygate estate in London (1974–2013)', *Cities* 57: 14–24.

Lietaert, M. (2010) 'Cohousing's relevance to degrowth theories', *Journal of Cleaner Production* 18: 576–80.

London Assembly Housing Committee. (2015) *Knock It Down or Do It Up? The Challenge of Estate Regeneration*. London: London Assembly.

London Borough of Southwark. (2013) 'Proof of evidence of Jon Abbot', extract from the *Inquiry into the London Borough of Southwark (Heygate) Compulsory Purchase Order 2012*. PINS Reference NPCU/CPO/APP/NPCU/CPO/A5840/70937. 11 January 2013 – www.southwark.gov.uk

Martinez-Alier, J. (2009) 'Social metabolism, ecological distribution conflicts, and languages of valuation', *Capitalism Nature Socialism* 20(1): 58–87.

Mayor of London Office. (2014) 'To renovate or demolish? The social housing estate debate', 16 June – www.london.gov.uk/press-releases/assembly/to-renovate-or-demolish

Peck, J. and Tickell, A. (2002) 'Neoliberalizing space', *Antipode* 34(3): 380–404.

Pickerill, J. (2011) 'Building liveable cities: Urban low impact developments as low carbon solutions', in Bulkeley, H., Castan Broto, V. and Hodson, M. (eds.) *Cities and Low Carbon Transitions*. London: Routledge: 178–97.

Pickerill, J. and Maxey, L. (2009) 'Geographies of sustainability: Low impact developments and radical spaces of innovation', *Geography Compass* 3: 1515–39.

Porter, L. and Shaw, K. (eds.) (2009) *Whose Urban Renaissance? An International Comparison of Urban Regeneration Strategies*. London and New York: Routledge.

Scanlon, K. and Fernández Arrigoitia, M. (2015) 'Development of new cohousing: Lessons from a London scheme for the over-50s', *Urban Research and Practice* 8: 106–21.

Schneider, F., Kallis, G. and Martinez-Alier, J. (2010) 'Crisis or opportunity? Economic degrowth for social equity and ecological sustainability', *Journal of Cleaner Production* 18: 511–18.

Smets, P. and Watt, P. (2017) *Social Housing and Urban Renewal: A Cross-National Perspective*. Bingley: Emerald Publishing Limited.

Southwark Notes. (2013) *The Siege of the Elephant Report*. London: Southwark Notes.

Thompson, M. (2015) 'Between boundaries: From commoning and guerrilla gardening to community land trust development in Liverpool', *Antipode* 47: 1021–42.

Thörn, C., Krusell, M. and Widehammar, M. (2016) *Rätt att bokvar. En handbok i organisering mot hyreshöjningar och gentrifiering*. [The right to stay put. A handbook on how to organize against rent increases and gentrification] – https://koloni.info/Ratt_att_bo_kvar_2016.pdf

UCL Urban Lab and Engineering Exchange. (2014) *Demolition or Refurbishment of Social Housing? A Review of the Evidence*. London: UCL Urban Lab.

van den Bergh, J.C.J.M. (2011) 'Environment versus growth – A criticism of "degrowth" and a plea for "a-growth"', *Ecological Economics* 70: 881–90.

van den Bergh, J.C.J.M. and Kallis, G. (2012) 'Growth, a-growth or degrowth to stay within planetary boundaries?' *Journal of Economic Issues* 46: 909–20.

Watt, P. (2009a) 'Housing stock transfers, regeneration and state-led gentrification in London', *Urban Policy Research* 27: 229–42.

——— (2009b) 'Social housing and regeneration in London', in Imrie, R., Lees, L. and Raco, M. (eds.) *Regenerating London: Governance, Sustainability and Community in a Global City*. London/New York: Routledge: 212–33.

10 The Simpler Way

Housing, living and settlements

Ted Trainer

My perspective on alternative housing grew out of my upbringing on a bush homestead in rather impoverished circumstances. This necessarily involved a lot of do-it-yourself, self-sufficiency and living frugally, although that was not experienced as a deprivation or problem. It built a sense of the normality of looking for resource-cheap ways of living and being content to live without unnecessary expenditure or 'standards'.

Our house was built in 1946, from an army storage Nissan igloo. I have added bits and pieces since then, and built a two-bedroom caretaker's cottage, along with various huts and sheds, some out of earth. This experience puts me in a good position to assert that housing is one of the most absurd aspects of consumer-capitalist society, and that perfectly adequate, extremely cheap and, indeed, beautiful dwellings could easily be available to everyone.

Simpler Way centre

Around 1980, we began to bring groups of students to our 50-acre Pigface Point homestead site to introduce them to limits to growth, sustainability and alternative society themes. It is close to Sydney but within 250ha of environmentally protected bushland in wilderness condition. Recently, we have had about 1000 visitors each year. We meet all costs and do not charge visiting groups taken on our two-hour explanatory tour. This outlines a very broad and radical perspective on the global resource, economic and environmental crisis. It begins with an indication of the seriousness of the global predicament and explains the case that the problems cannot be solved in or by this system; only transition to a very different combination of settlement, economic, political and cultural ways can enable a sustainable and just world (Trainer 2018). The central concern, however, is to convince visiting groups that there are very satisfactory and workable alternatives, a Simpler Way, and that it would enable a higher quality of life.

The tour includes illustrations of many alternative technologies, including building using earth, solar panels, two windmills, garbage gas, water wheels (one 4.5 metres tall), a run of river tidal turbine, a pelton wheel, teaspoon turbine, 12-volt electrical circuits and machinery, solar thermal technologies, distilling, blacksmithing, metal casting and stem power. We walk through forest and wetlands containing castles, caves, pagodas, a flying fox, a 6-metre (concrete) crocodile, ponds, 13 little bridges and sculptures. In addition, we practice many arts and crafts including sculpture, painting, model making, blacksmithing, wood turning, bush carpentry, pottery, stone work, candle making, paper making, leather work, spinning, rush and basket work and garden pot making. Add the concept of settlements full of little firms and farms, and commons crammed with forests, edible landscapes and ponds and it is evident how leisure-rich community working bees could make future settlements.

Housing: an indication of our approach

I briefly explain some aspects of housing at Pigface Point before going on to a theoretical discussion of how alternative housing might fit into a wider vision of the kind of restructured settlements that would enable a sustainable society. Our caretaker's cottage illustrates some of these ways and ideas (although much more impressive examples could be given).

The approximately 50-square-metre, two-bedroom fibro house was completed in 1989 for A$8,000. It was built to council standards, meaning expenditure on some unnecessary requirements. It was an enjoyable project, taking me about 6 months, working in my spare time using only hand tools. Neither this nor the main house is connected to the urban grid for electricity, water, garbage collection, postal or sewer services. Water is collected from roofs and space heating comes from firewood gathered on leisure rambles. Had the house been built from earth it could have cost far less. (On the miracles of cob building, see Bee 1997.)

The main house – more than 70 years old – has never been connected to the grid and for decades we used only kerosene lamps, but now we have a solar photo-voltaic system. Per capita consumption in the main house averages fewer than 10W compared with the national average of around 230W. For decades we cooked on a wood stove and heated shower water in a tin 'chip heater'. Without a fridge, cooling was via a Coolgardie safe (Smith 2005), a hessian-covered evaporating box. Since getting a fridge, we have purchased bottled gas. The house isn't well insulated but I have cobbled together a very effective firebox from tin, with a brazed copper pipe grid inside taking hot water around the house in winter. In addition, there is a tiny fan drawing hot air from a sleave around the chimney in the attic and pushing it to the cold parts of the house.

Washing is done by a home-made rattle-trap device powered by a 70W car fan motor, which also drives some pumps. Soon, it will be connected to the world's slowest firewood saw. Collecting and cutting firewood is a valued leisure activity, justifying bushwalks. I have made a 12V drill, grinder and metal turning lather, but all other tools are hand operated. We grow vegetables. Repairing broken things and sewing up worn out clothes are valued hobbies. All kitchen, animal and garden wastes go to compost heaps or the garbage gas unit. Water is our biggest problem so every drop gets recycled to the garden.

When I was young, our bedding was sewn up from the bags that the chaff and chicken feed came in. (I still prefer heavy blankets.) The pillows were stuffed with feathers from the poultry. To keep our feet warm in bed at night, a house brick would be placed beside the open fire and then wrapped in a feed bag. Primitive? Who cares? Not just sufficient, but the way I prefer. I don't live *in* the house; I spend all day going in and out to the garden, workshop, windmills, pumps, bush, swampland and animals. I live *in* my patch, my landscape.

It is full of problems: animals that get out, gates to fix, pumps that clog, systems that need redesigning, firebreaks to clear. But, mostly, they are good problems providing endless variety and purpose, using many skills and demanding exercise. When the original water tanks became rusted, I converted the tank stand into a veranda where I practice a sacred 'cuppa tea' ritual, sitting and gazing at our forest, including the more than 200 big trees I planted (in the wrong places) decades ago.

Perhaps 'normal' people would be borderline disgusted at my house or, if polite, would say it is much too scruffy and primitive. Some of our tour visitors have classified it as a 'KDR' (knock down and rebuild) proposition. But it is much too big and luxurious for me, far more than sufficient. How many of the world's people don't have a house? Nothing makes me feel more privileged and guilty than taking a warm shower. I could live happily in the kitchen space, although I use lots of workspace and storage in simple sheds out the back. It's the best house in the world and, even if a dollar price could be put on it – it was once valued at A$20,000 – that would have nothing to do with its real value.

My point here is that I have personal credentials for pronouncing on housing and sustainability. A glance at the environmental state of the over-consuming world shows that we must move to a far less affluent house and settlement pattern than is the norm and my experience leaves me in no doubt that we could very easily adopt housing designs that are very resource cheap, sustainable *and* beautiful.

There is a vast 'limits to growth' literature showing that the levels of resource consumption, production, consumption and gross domestic product (GDP) in rich countries is probably ten times over those that could be sustained or spread to all people on the planet (World Atlas 2016). This is increasingly recognised, as is evident in the emergence of the degrowth, ecovillage and transition towns movements. But there has been insufficient thought given to the general form that a sustainable society must take so I have been offering such ideas which I refer to as the 'Simpler Way'. The Simpler Way must be an integrated vision, including and connecting elements from the household level, through to neighbourhood, town and regional levels and then to the national level, and incorporating the design and remaking of housing, settlements, the economy, political and, especially, cultural systems. Housing must take a form determined by its role in the holistic interconnected social system and delivering global sustainability and justice. A sketch of the kind of overall pattern envisaged as the Simpler Way follows.

The Simpler Way

Because of the magnitude of the reductions required, the general model for sustainable settlements must be mostly *small* and highly *self-sufficient local economies*, *self-governing*, under *social control* (i.e. not determined by market forces and profit), in which non-material pursuits deliver rich life satisfaction. This means maximising use of household and settlement space for production of food and other socially beneficial items and linking individual households into networks for running, maintaining and benefiting from community production. Thus, there must be many cooperatives, commons, committees and informal arrangements. For instance, rather than every house trying to produce its own honey, a network of hobby bee keepers, small businesses and cooperatives could look after this realm. Similarly, town industries (such as poultry, fishing, aquaponics, forestry and orchard) can be integrated arrangements, incorporating households – fish could come from small intensive backyard ponds – commons, small firms and cooperatives.

Houses would be surrounded by dense 'edible landscape' commons – enabled, for instance, by digging up most roads not needed when settlements become highly self-sufficient and require less transportation of goods. This will be accompanied by dramatically reduced work time and, thus, vehicles or roads to get people to distant employment every day. The many commons would provide *free* goods such as fruit, nuts, timber, herbs and fish; we would 'pay' for them by contributing to voluntary and enjoyable working bees.

These integrated economies would enable thorough recycling and the elimination of all erstwhile waste. For instance, all food and garden scraps would go directly to animal pens, fish ponds and compost heaps, more or less eliminating the need for a global fertiliser industry and trucks and ships to transport fertilisers, as well as eliminating the energy and environmental costs of throwing away nutrient rich animal manures. All household water, namely grey and black (toilet) water, would be recycled to gardens via methane digesters.

These settlements would follow basic permaculture principles, especially designed for multiple and overlapping functions. For instance, forests provide timber, fruit, nuts, honey, mulch, firewood, grazing, wind breaks, coolness and leisure resources. Working bees get the orchards pruned and the windmills painted, but also produce conversation, leisure activity, ideas for community improvement and social bonding. Ducks produce eggs, meat, feathers, fertiliser, ducklings and entertainment. In consumer society animal manure is a waste challenge, requiring trucking, and often dumping, and transnational corporations ship in more artificial fertiliser, which damages soils. Massive complex chains from iron ore and phosphate mines through to global shipping lanes to steel works and factories and trucks contribute to producing an industrial egg, but a backyard egg has almost no resource or dollar cost, and comes from happy chickens. Moreover, the industrial product, such as the tasteless supermarket tomato, is often inferior.

Permaculture designers look for ways that nature might do most of the work for us. Grazing on the fire-danger side of town or land mean that animals reduce bushfire risks, chickens free ranging in orchards eat fallen fruit and break the fruit fly breeding cycle. Ducks eliminate slugs and snails and their ponds produce nutrient rich water. Gravity delivers clean water from slopes to houses and takes the waste water down to gardens, eliminating the need for pumping. Locating aged care facilities in the town's centre, next to workshops and community gardens automatically enriches seniors' experiences. Thus localism, integration, complexity and smallness of scale enable overlaps, immediate and easy recycling, and resilience and synergism. Agribusiness has broken up all these automatic and mutually beneficial processes presenting demand for energy, machinery, computers and expensive professionals. Now that the feedlot waste is on the other side of the continent to the fields, nutrients cannot be recycled, and the resulting depletion of soils requires a vast intercontinental fertiliser industry.

Almost all the clothes we wear could be simple, tough, cheap and durable, old and heavily mended. Few, if any, would need to work in a suit or tie, let alone new clothes. (I never wear either.) Much clothing and footwear could be made at home as a hobby. Some people could specialise in small business dress making and tailoring. There would be a great deal of that miraculous art form, knitting, using wool spun from local sheep. Many other products would be much more enjoyably made at the hobby or household firm level, such as furniture and carpentry, pottery, preserves, footwear and baskets.

'Remaking Settlements' (Trainer 2016) estimated the possible effects of applying such design ideas to an outer suburban area of the Australian capital city of Sydney. Use of fairly detailed data, especially on potential food production areas and yields, indicated that perhaps a 90 percent reduction could be made in numerous key sustainability indices. Similarly, Dancing Rabbit Ecovillage in Missouri (United States) achieves reductions of this order (Lockyer 2017). This assumes conversion of many little-used roads to community space, creation of edible landscapes and other commons, water recycling and setting up committees, working bees and cooperatives. A notable benefit is 3000 person hours per week that could be applied to community enrichment if 3000 locals spent just one hour on a working bee each week.

The social, political and cultural aspects of such new settlements is taken up further, below.

Housing design

In the context of the Simpler Way approach, housing design, especially location and functions, must maximise the community's material, social and spiritual 'productivity' in ways that all the world's people could share. The need for large-scale degrowth obviously implies a shift to housing that is as small, cheap and humble as is reasonably possible. This would strike most people in consumer society as totally unacceptable. Thus the task for us is to show that sustainable housing for all the world's people does not have to involve deprivation or hardship, indeed that it can be delightful. For a start, it makes housing possible for all, whereas currently housing is a commodity enabling wealth-seeking speculators to get richer without having to work while, even in the richest countries, large numbers of people cannot afford a house.

In a sustainable settlement, most new housing, work places and community buildings would be made from earth, along with locally produced stone and timber. Houses would be very small by present standards, with low ceilings. In my view, tiny houses are beautiful and big houses are aesthetically and morally ugly. The general building height limit would be four stories, eliminating the need for mechanical lifts. Most floors of single-storied buildings would be made from earth, hardened by, for instance, linseed oil, turpentine and beeswax. Some roofs would be earth (sod) over timber supports, and many would be domes and vaults made from mud bricks (as in the Middle East) surfaced, where necessary, by a thin layer of cement.

The cheapest form of earth building is cob, a mixture of earth, clay and straw dumped on walls and shaped by a shovel as it dries out. Bee (1997) explains how cob enables strong and space-saving curved walls that can be easily modified, say, to add another window; provides sound insulation and thermal mass; and, is both fire and termite proof. Many cob houses in Europe are centuries old. In the near future roofing might best be made from corrugated iron, ideally eventually replaced by ceramic tiles made from local clay and wood-fuelled kilns. We would create durable sealers and paints from plant and animal sources, such as white-wash (lime and milk) for earth brick walls.

Consider my estimated energy and dollar costs for a quite small house that I would be happy living in, and that I think would be ideal for a young couple. The walls would be cob, mud brick or rammed earth, and the floor surfaced earth. The ground floor would have a living-bedroom (8m by 3m), a toilet, and a clothes washing and shower room, without a bath (3m by 3m), plus storage space. The main room would have a kitchen area at one end, a wood-fuelled stove, and a large table at the other end for dining, writing and art and craft. In the middle of the long wall would be an open fire, an easy chair and a reading light.

The solar passive design would provide most heating and cooling. A water jacket around the fire would syphon hot water to an insulated tank. Wood boxes could be built into the walls outside. Ceilings would be low with a tiny stairway to the sleeping area in the triangular attic and more storage space. A mini-veranda would catch morning sun in winter. Tanks to store rainwater would be home-made from cement plastered over chicken wire against a form. (The per litre cost of bought tanks is about six times that of mine, exclusive of labour costs.)

The internal walls would be cob, mud brick, rammed earth or straw bale with rammed earth floors (over a plastic membrane) incorporating pipes for circulating hot water. Roof frames would be made from sawn timber but ceiling beams adzed from rough saplings. Most fittings, cupboards, window frames and furniture could be home-made at a relaxed pace from wood, with minimal use of metals and plastic. No wall-to-wall carpets, just rugs to take out and shake, eliminating need for a vacuum cleaner. Many households might not need a fridge given refrigeration units close by in the neighbourhood centre and readily available fresh food.

My detailed estimate in 2017 Australian dollars (A$), assuming new materials, is that such a house (including most fittings and furniture) might cost around A$6,000. Use of recycled materials would lower this figure. Dollar costs for labour are excluded because the house would be home-made using hand tools, an enjoyable creative activity partly assisted by local friends and expert small builders repaid by assisting them on their projects. Building at a leisurely pace, one could move in once the roof was on and fit it out slowly. Space for storage, hobbies, crafts and a workshop could be provided in simple sheds, with their roofs expanding rainwater collection. Off-grid electricity supply would add, say A$2000, for two panels, a battery and a regulator.

Lifetime repair, maintenance and insurance costs would be very low, given the small scale and simplicity of the dwelling, and minimal need for tradesmen to fix anything. If it became necessary, additional rooms could be added later. In short, you need not be anxious about eviction due to defaulting on a daunting decades-long mortgage. Compare this with the typically astronomical cost of mainstream housing. An average new Australian house is amongst the biggest in the world, over 230 square metres in area, and probably obliging you to earn close to A$1,000,000 just to pay for the building (land costing extra) because, for each dollar borrowed, at least two would have to be paid back to the bank and, for each three dollars, four must be earned because the tax man will take one of them (see Chapter 1).

Necessary economic and social restructuring

Given the need for large-scale degrowth, the implications for sustainable social design go far beyond the mentioned changes in physical aspects of housing and settlements. Glaringly obvious is that degrowth is utterly incompatible with the present kind of economic system driven by market forces, the quest for limitless GDP growth and 'freedom' for those few who own most capital to maximise profits. Because we have far exceeded the limits to growth already, a sustainable economy means all the world's people sharing a stable level of GDP, far less production and consumption than at present, and social – not free market – control.

However, there could be a large sector of a satisfactory economy left to market forces and private firms, so long as it was under the control of local assemblies, thus ensuring that it was geared to the welfare of the town. The guarantee for a sensible needs-oriented economy must come from a conscientious citizenry, highly aware of the need to minimise restrictions on freedom, to look after everyone and prioritise town solidarity. As this atmosphere develops, pressure to reorient state-level functions under control of local assemblies will increase (see further details below).

This means there must be a very different political practice. Most of the issues that affect daily life would be handled at the local level, by committees, town assemblies and referenda. In the long run, relatively little would be left for state-level agencies to deal with, just areas such as national railway and electronic systems. In fact, many issues and problems would be resolved informally and without bureaucracy by the spontaneous action of ordinary people who spot problems and immediately get together to attend to them. In stable communities not focused on competing for scarce jobs and wealth, acutely aware that their personal welfare depends on whether the town thrives, political wrangling over things like zero-sum struggles for development approvals would be minimal.

Small regional factories located within 5–10km would produce many basic items that villages could not produce for themselves, such as bicycles, cutlery, pots and pans, roof tiles and hardware. Only small quantities of more elaborate items, such as electronic devices, would need to be imported from the national economy and fewer still from overseas. The few specialised or large-scale factories needed to produce equipment such as lathes and drill presses, cloth, cement and steel, would be distributed throughout the nation so that all towns could produce some items for export and, thus, contribute to meeting national needs while earning the small amount of income needed to import basic necessities from other regions. Little international trade would be required, just, for instance, for high-tech medical equipment. Very few ships, large trucks or aircraft would be needed.

Most production would not require highly specialised skills. The most valuable 'worker' would be the 'Jack/Jill-of-all-trades', able to make and fix many things. People would be able to move between several quite different tasks each week, in their garden, hobby and craft groups and on working bees and committees. They could volunteer at schools and hospitals or on committees organising concerts, leisure activities and festivals. Older, experienced people would be highly valued contributors to production and, more importantly, to social functioning, given their wisdom and their knowledge of local people, conditions and history. There would be no compulsory retirement age, so people could slowly phase down their level of activity as they wished. Most would want to remain active contributors.

Community members spending little time working for money would spontaneously take over much of the care and social needs of those with disabilities and older people. Old people would be able to remain in their homes longer; there would be little need for retirement 'homes' and their specialised staff. There would be small local hospitals and nursing facilities close to where people lived, located in the busiest parts of settlements, so that people could drop in and residents could see and be involved in activities around them.

It is important to stress that there need be no reduction in resources for socially useful technological development, higher education, research or high-tech areas such as medicine. In fact, we could greatly increase these if we phased out the enormous amount of currently unnecessary production.

The psychological, social and 'spiritual' benefits

Possibly the biggest health problem in the rich world now is depression, along with stress, anxiety, loneliness, alienation, with associated indices of social breakdown, including drug and alcohol abuse, smoking, domestic violence, family breakdown and suicide. If we moved to the kind of communities sketched out here, these problems would be largely reduced. They are less frequent in ecovillages where high subjective quality of life is reported (Grinde et al. 2018; Duckworth 2005;

Mulder et al. 2006). A Simpler Way community would eliminate any concern about unemployment or poverty, because the provision of a worthwhile and valued *livelihood* for all would be a top priority. Community engagement and support would be readily available, if only because it is obvious to all that one's own welfare depends on making sure everyone else is in good shape. If town morale is poor, the working bees will not be well attended.

Because people would derive life satisfaction mostly from non-material pursuits, meaning far less production, people would only need to work for money about two days a week, leaving abundant time for home-making, community activities, arts and crafts, gardening and studying. Thus, The Simpler Way is about liberation from the rat race of consumer society where we must be working at least three times as long as would be necessary!

In addition, the work-leisure distinction would disappear. We would enjoy producing things, mostly by hand tools, while sharing any boring tasks, such as keeping the few mass production factories going. Cooperatives would produce many of the things we need, ensuring efficient and enjoyable conditions. In addition, we would do away with the 'alienated' nature of work in capitalist society. Most might 'work' in their own little firms and farms, in control of their situation and seeing familiar local people appreciate their products.

Committees would monitor many factors, including how older people, adolescents and invalids are getting along, what new fruit varieties might be tried, what tasks should go on the working bee list, and especially general indices of quality of life, including town morale and cohesion. People living in ecovillages know that the greatest benefits of these ways are 'spiritual' – freedom from the burdens imposed by the individualistic, competitive and acquisitive culture of consumer-capitalist society (Trainer 2015.) But would the Simpler Way only work if we all became 'saints'? Obviously, it requires a very different mind-set and values to those currently dominant, but the abundant rewards would provide strong incentives for change.

I have argued that we have to think about matters such as housing in the context of the big and very radical change required before a sustainable and just world can be built. The kinds of shelter must be designed in terms of the roles they play in settlements that are highly self-sufficient, self-governing, environmentally benign, frugal and socially synergistic. I hoped to show that these new ways would be, in principle, attractive and very easy to implement *if* enough of us wanted to do that. They are technically simple. Little or no need for bulldozers, ships, high-tech or professionals. We ordinary people in ordinary suburbs can do most of what needs to be built.

How might we get there?

The key element in the Simper Way approach to the transition is the notion of slowly building a new economy underneath the existing one to deal with neglected community needs in cooperative ways without attention to profit or market considerations. Many groups are already coming together to form community ventures enabling participants to cooperatively provide for themselves and disadvantaged groups with low cost or free food, shelter, clothing, repairs and so on. 'Do we have bored youth around here, unemployed people, lonely aged people, homeless people? Well let's just figure out what we can get together to do!' The goal is to gradually take on more initiatives and attract more participants in the process of building up our cooperative needs-oriented 'Economy B' (outlined above), towards the day when we are in control of the provision of what everyone in our town needs for a satisfactory life.

Of course, none of this can happen unless there is a huge change in culture, i.e. in the ideas and goals most people have about progress and the desirability of growth and the affluent consumer way. At present such change seems unimaginable but we will be greatly assisted by the accelerating deterioration in the mainstream economy. This will jolt many of those it is trashing into realising the need to shift to the emerging Economy B. Many in the Transition Towns and related movements are pioneering these new ways.

The hope must be that this growth of localism and these increasingly bold community initiatives will, in time, lead to powerful grassroots demand for the radical reorientation of state and national economies. Thus the profound global political and economic change required will grow out of localism. It will not, and cannot be, initiated from the top in a system dominated by the transnational super-rich elite. As resource scarcity and the contradictions within capitalism intensify, it will become clearer to ordinary people that state-level capacities must be directed at ensuring a national economy geared to providing the basic inputs the towns need (Trainer 2017).

Conclusion

I have given reasons for believing that Simpler Way communities enabling a high level of provision of basic necessities could be developed relatively quickly by ordinary people using local resources, with very little need for capital or for engagement with national or international economies. This basic form of sustainable development is the only viable model for defusing global problems. Only by shifting to ways that enable enormous reduction in per capita resource consumption, i.e. radical degrowth, can we eliminate resource depletion, deprivation of the Third World, ecological destruction and conflicts over access to oil and other resources.

Obviously, Simpler Way alternative development clashes head on with the interests of global corporations, banks and elites. Simpler Way communal and self-sufficient development is a mortal threat to those who possess most of the capital and want to retain a system driven by their freedom to maximise business turnover. The chances of us making this transition are not good, but I argue that there is no other ultimate goal to work for, that we can draw inspiration from the vision sketched above, and that many are now pioneering such new ways.

References

Bee, B. (1997) *The Cob Builders Handbook*. Murphy (Oregon): Groundworks.

Duckworth, N. (2005) *Quality of Life and Social Capital in Intentional Communities*. BA Thesis submitted to the University of Lethbridge, Alberta, Canada.

Grinde, B., Nes, R.B., MacDonald, I.F. and Wilson, D.S. (2018) 'Quality of life in intentional communities', *Social Indicators Research* 137(2): 625–40.

Lockyer, J. (2017) 'Community, commons, and degrowth at Dancing Rabbit Ecovillage', *Political Ecology* 24: 519–42.

Mulder, K., Costanza, R. and Erickson, J. (2006) 'The contribution of built, human, social and natural capital to quality of life in intentional and unintentional communities', *Ecological Economics*, 59: 13–23.

Smith, C. (2005) *Coolgardie Safe*. Museums Victoria Collections – https://collections.museumvictoria.com.au/articles/709

Trainer, T. (2015) *The Case for Simplicity* – thesimplerway.info/SIMPLICITY.htm

——— (2016) 'Remaking settlements', *The Simple Way* – thesimplerway.info/Remaking Settlements.htm

——— (2017) 'The transition process: The Simpler Way perspective', *The Simpler Way* – http://thesimplerway.info/TRANSITION.htm

——— (2018) 'The global situation, the sustainable alternative society, and the transition to it . . . we must move to the Simpler Way', *The Simpler Way* – http://thesimplerway.info/TSWMain.htm

World Atlas. (2016) 'Countries with the largest ecological footprints' – www.worldatlas.com/articles/countries-with-the-largest-ecological-footprints.html

Part V
Ecological housing and planning

11 Degrowth

A perspective from Bengaluru, South India

Chitra K. Vishwanath

At the heart of degrowth is the concept of reduction to the minimum for survival and the celebration of the ability to survive with the minimum. While this concept is being explored and developed, the world moves headlong into the depletion of resources through excessive consumption in certain regions while there is a somewhat contradictory need to develop better life conditions in others. Is there a degrowth path that can ameliorate the depletion of resources, satisfy our needs and be environmentally positive? This chapter discusses housing design initiatives using degrowth ecological and social principles in a subtle manner, engaging professional architects in changing building practices and processes, specifically in Bengaluru (South India).

Bengaluru – prior to late 2014 known as Bangalore and capital of the state Karnataka – has seen massive growth in its population and economy over the last 25 years. It is the very epitome of the Indian model of economic growth – aiming to 'catch up' with the rest of the world. The increasing population has forced the city to grow three times its size in the last 25 years, with increases in housing demand and services that have not been met, especially in terms of affordability. This growth has strained services, particularly in the water and sanitation sector. Moreover, the ecological limits with respect to water resources and the incapacity of ecosystems to absorb urban waste had become evident by early this century.

Resources and techniques for construction have become very important for making housing affordable and ecological to live in – homes replete with ecological services, giving them a positive ecological imprint, not a parasitical one. In contrast, the conventional mode of construction in Bengaluru has been resource consumptive, creating a large ecological footprint and debasing construction and trade skills to a repetitive machinist mode – all of which has eroded resilience. This chapter explores the alternative of building affordably and creating resilient futures by examining various resources and techniques of construction based on our experience in a well-established architectural practice in Bengaluru.

Political background to environmentally unsustainable development

In the last 25 years, after economic liberalisation, there have been massive changes in Indian cities like Bangalura, most clearly visible in land-use. Agriculture and other green areas have given way to urban built form, negatively affecting the ecological services that originally endowed Bengaluru, making the city a preferred destination for entrepreneurs and companies. With the myopic vision of economic growth as the driver, and without checks and balances placed on the use and abuse of ecological services, the city's ecosystem now verges on collapse: lakes are used as landfills and trees are felled to make way for residential and commercial developments. The effects do not remain within the boundaries of the city. The ecological footprint of Bengaluru is large, negatively affecting its hinterland.

The builder and developer lobby anticipates urban growth patterns and influence it. Developers speculatively purchase land before planned development is realised or land released, and they encourage government investments in infrastructure, such as roads, water and electricity, close to such assets. They wield considerable influence in the design of building by-laws and allowable floor space indexes (i.e. the size of the building in relation to the plot size). Due to their speculative early purchases, the developers' investment in land is minimal and allows for maximum permissible profits once the land has been built on.

This approach worked for some years, since housing demand was always high and supply was short. As long as such developments were within the range and carrying capacity of the infrastructure provided by the city government, it seemed like a 'win-win' situation. However, changes within the central business group – as motivated entrepreneurs and lobby groups influenced policies of the development bodies of the state and the city – made certain residential areas into commercial ones, the city grew more vertically, floor to space indexes increased and green and open space reduced commensurately. The character of the city in such growth areas changed from bungalow houses to apartments and then to gated communities, such as Malleswaram and Whitefied.

Jayaraj Sundaresan (2016) has called this type of planning governance 'political participatory planning':

> A large number of people from inside and outside the government and various social groups participate at different levels in decisions about planning outcomes and land-use changes, which then are accommodated by the formal land-use categorisation, and from that perspective, then, there is no planning in Bangalore but only participation. Simply put, the challenge becomes to distinguish who participates in which land-use decisions and how. Individuals, government and non-government entities violate, ignore, or modify the land-use plan and building regulations to suit their interests. Politicians, policy elites, administrators, local councillors, engineers, and everyday citizens are active participants in this mode of planning. This is exemplified by the many exceptional clause amendments to the planning law, on-demand back-door changes to the master plan, elite advisor-led projects deviating from plan, hundreds of thousands of violations routinely regularised, political interference, multiple interventions by political brokers, policy elites, and so on.

The development lobby's approach was to create profit as quickly as possible without long-term vision. To be fair to this lobby and government satraps who took the decisions to change land-use around Bengaluru, they did not have the knowledge or the wherewithal to understand the future implications of their actions. Developments created to maximise profit, in turn, boosted a speculative economy. Land which had been cheaper than the costs of construction before 1990, depending on its location, often became some five times the cost of construction 25 years later. The developer lobby used the lacunae in the system of governance in Indian cities to its maximum, aligning themselves with politicians without allegiance to the city because their voting base was predominantly rural. This political situation has been excellently described by Patrick Heller et al. (2016), showing how the city is a 'growth cabal' reliant on a hybrid of rule- and deal-based systems.

As the development hype grew, nearby agriculture lands were acquired and water bodies filled with the individual intent of profit and general intent of satisfying the market. At no time were the negative environmental externalities of this kind of growth questioned except by certain protesting citizen groups. The spiralling cost of land demanded increased extraction because it resulted in larger and taller developments which, in turn, required more space for roads and other services. Without a democratic and inclusive system in place the state was no longer a player in housing provision and lack of, or adherence to, planning norms made for ad hoc and 'firefighting' responses to the problems. Pollution of air and water, and loss of biodiversity are the result of such developments. Designs of mass housing leave much to be desired; they are ill-conceived with respect to climatic conditions, making them resource intensive to maintain. Large-scale developments have arisen on lands without amenities. Marginalised groups and eroded ecological systems pay the price.

Due to the costs of construction, processes for sourcing material resources and associated damage to ecological services, this paradigm of development implies a large ecological footprint. In most cases, ecological and locally sourced materials are limited in quantity and may require specialised local, relatively scarce and costly skills for use in construction. Large-scale manufacturing is cheaper due to various subsidies and cheaper labour.

Twenty-first century changes in economic and building practices

In short, economic liberalisation has been solely responsible for privatised activity in the housing sector in India. After 1990, it became possible for employed middle-class people to take out housing loans to buy already built homes. At the same time, Bengaluru saw an enormous influx of educated young professionals from all over the country joining its information technology (IT) industries. The salubrious climate and the cosmopolitan nature attracted many to settle in the city. Furthermore, up until 2000, the Bangalore Development Authority (BDA) had been actively engaged in bringing land banks into the fold of the city and making them available for people to construct their own homes.

In the twenty-first century all this has changed. The government is no longer in a position to provide much land in the market. Private developers manage the partitioning of land into smaller parcels and create 'plotted' (planned) residential developments. When the plotting was done within BDA limits, connection to water, sanitation and electricity were ensured. In contrast, in the case of plotted land or apartments developed by a private developer, water might be supplied simply from a borehole and there might only be a modicum of sewerage treatment, or even none. Even though this situation is now changing, due to demand from buyers and city officials creating laws for approvals based on onsite sewage treatment, there do still exist many, especially plotted, developments which have neither water supply nor sewage treatment and residents have to manage with systems of their own. In most cases, electricity supply is assured, though the quality and quantity of electricity might well be variable and unreliable.

Almost three decades after liberalisation, agriculture remains the highest employer, with the construction sector the second highest employer. Indian agriculture is highly monsoon-dependent so, in the drier months, many people from rural areas migrate to cities in search of work. This kind of short-term migration has been very common (Chandrasekhar and Shama 2014), for a plethora of reasons (Kumari 2014), and the construction industry has assimilated the migrants as unskilled labourers. Some members of a family stay in the city, acquire skills and make the city their home, to move up the income ladder. They, in turn, train other migrants coming from their hometowns. They remit part of their income to their village home. Many build themselves a home in their village to which they expect to retire.

Mahadevia (2012) has elaborated on the construction sector as an industry which provides decent work for migrants from rural areas. However, in the 2010s, the construction sector has been undergoing rapid change due to financial demands placed on builders and developers to make greater gains on their investments. There is, therefore, an entrepreneurial push towards mechanisation and pre-cast systems, which provide jobs reliant on lower investments. The results are loss of jobs, because less labour is required at a construction site when such technologies are used, and loss of worker skills and training in traditional construction.

In terms of the city more generally, Bangalura's salubrious climate has been changing due to increased urban density, loss of tree cover and higher levels of pollution. The nature of urban work and transportation is changing. Work spaces are increasingly air-conditioned, especially in the IT sector, and the air-conditioned car has become a preferred mode of travel. Affluence, access and affordability concerns mean that residents opt for air conditioners in their homes. Meanwhile, nationally, residential and commercial energy use has risen circa 8 percent per annum in the last few decades: 'Building energy consumption has seen an increase from 14% in the 1970s to nearly 33% in 2004–05' (UNEP SBCI 2009, 2).

In short, in the twenty-first century, Bengulura's model of growth, both in the building and construction sector and beyond, is environmentally unsustainable and demands rethinking and re-planning for a sustainable future.

Could Bangalura create a different model closer to degrowth?

While the dominating trend is for faster and more expansive ways of building, Bangalura has fostered many out-of-the-box ideas and has developed a culture of trialling and executing innovation involving many practitioners and institutions. To be environmentally positive, new construction practices must involve lower embodied energy, emit less carbon, incorporate waste as a resource and integrate respect for biodiversity. Adopting the perspectives of both designers of homes and degrowth advocates, the key question is: Can new construction focus on designing for climate resilient features and allow, even encourage, convivial living? A sketch of existing alternatives, which have the potential for wide application in similar urban contexts, follows.

Bangalura's soil is lateritic, most of it is red earth, as found on site. This soil, which is a mix of sand, silt and clay, can be made suitable for creating Compressed Stabilised Earth Blocks (CSEB) through the addition of sand or quarry dust and admixtures for stabilisation, such as cement or lime. In general, the composition of Bengaluru's CSEBs is half-earth and half-sand or quarry dust with between 5 and 8 percent cement used as a stabiliser (Nagaraja et al. 2014). The addition of lime as a stabiliser improves the block quality but, in Bangalura, lime is not readily available so most blocks use cement stabilisation.

In 1974, the Civil Engineering department of the Indian Institute of Science fostered an innovation cell, 'ASTRA' (Alternative Science and Technology for Rural Areas, now known as the interdisciplinary Centre for Sustainable Technology), where extensive experiments were done on compressed earth technology and pre-cast roofing systems. Innovations were communicated to architects and engineers in the city and country via building workshops, and the home built by Professor Yogananda, one of the senior scientists working with this technology, was a showcase for use of these possibilities in an urban scenario. Yogananda built his home in 1987–8 and later, in 1995, established a testing and dissemination facility, Mrinmayee, in Bangalore. Since then this consultancy firm specialising in stabilised mud blocks and building alternatives has offered many workshops and consulted with many architects. The similarly active Auroville Earth Institute (AVEI n.d.) has favourably compared the embodied energy and carbon emission of CSEBs with conventional country-fired bricks in India, to find that a CSEB created on site with 5 percent cement is likely to consume 11 times less energy than a country-fired brick and the CSEB produces circa one-thirteenth the carbon emissions of a country-fired brick.

Applying this knowledge, Biome Environmental Solutions designs buildings with a preference for making blocks from earth sourced from space made for the basement (see Figure 11.1 and Figure 11.2). In terms of the quantity of earth sourced from basements, our team did a comparative study of homes designed

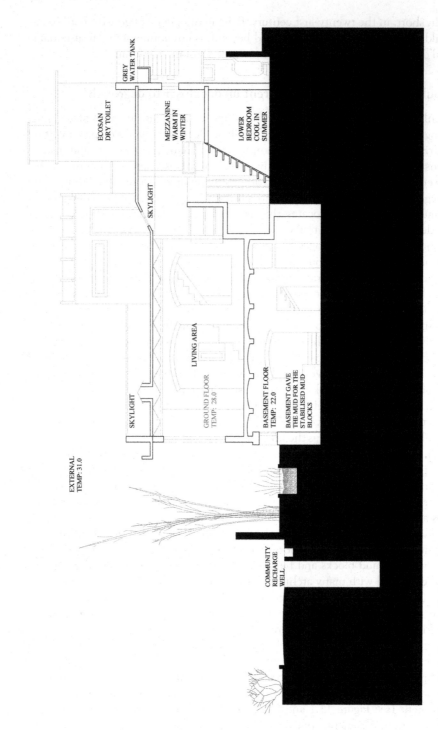

Figure 11.1 Section of house with basement

Figure 11.2 Basement being constructed

with and without basements. Table 11.1 shows that the soil available from one basement is almost double the quantity required for making blocks for an average structure for that site. Due to site and budget constraints certain homes are designed without basements. By applying a collaborative and co-operative process, excess earth from houses with basements can be used in the homes without such a resource. In this manner, the city itself can provide the material resources to build the walls and roofs of its residents' homes. Such an approach opens opportunities for the foundations of self-built homes applying a culture of sharing in production.

The earth sourced from making room for the basement is used for making foundations, walls, floors and roofs. Various kinds of walling techniques are adopted for 230mm thick load-bearing CSEB block masonry, adobe, rammed earth and cob. The techniques, requiring various levels of skills and materials, allow for versatility. By altering stabilisation levels, walls can be designed for taking various kinds of loads as well as spans. This is not possible in other conventional materials in use in India. Structural designs need to be supplemented with reinforced concrete framed structures to adapt to the differences from conventional material. Furthermore, the CSEB blocks are versatile in terms of their sizes, therefore they can be incorporated as thinner and lighter infill walls in framed reinforced cement concrete constructions.

Table 11.1 Soil quantity available from basements of various projects

	Units	Mini	Mukherjee	Ramadurai	Uma Devi	Ghosh	Sheeba
Plot area	m²	368.0	218.5	220.8	147.2	346.7	220.8
Plot coverage	m²	104.9	132.5	116.0	75.2	87.8	127.7
Built up area	m²	290.9	272.0	389.6	175.5	151.4	225.0
Occupants	no.	6.0	4.0	4.0	4.0	3.0	3.0
Roof area	m²	104.9	132.5	143.2	63.5	62.9	91.7
Basement area	m²	80.9	64.7	126.0	0.0	0.0	0.0
Soil available	m³	149.3	116.7	263.8	0.0	0.0	0.0
Soil required for earth blocks*	m³	55.2	55.6	38.8	43.9	27.1	47.0
Embodied energy for earth walls	MJ	406,658	412,794	290,438	333,916.0	270,267	348,791
Embodied energy for burnt brick*	MJ	1,027,921	1,043,430	734,149	844,048	683,120	881,649

* A cubic metre of wall contains 175 CSEBs, and 530 burnt bricks. Burnt bricks are roughly half the volume of CSEBs.

The earth used for construction is sourced from 300 mm below the upper layer so it is devoid of any organic content. Earth for construction can also be sourced from, and used to create, landscape features like ponds and water harvesting structures. During the excavation the upper layer of earth is saved for use in landscaping and terrace gardening, which might be used to produce food for the household or to enhance local ecological diversity.

In a study done on ambient temperature inside the basements created in these buildings in Bangalura, the Biome Environmental Solutions team found that indoor temperatures tend to be around 22°C throughout the year, making them multi-functional spaces (Figure 11.3). With improvement in design, by incorporating skylights and gardens, we have made basements an integral part of the homes. Therefore, basements can be seen as an important climate resilience strategy in home design.

Earth or soil is half of the material required for the making of CSEBs. At present, in order to reduce the clay content, sand or quarry dust is added. Typically, such sand is sourced from the rivers, hampering river flows as well as biodiversity. Quarry dust is sourced from the granite quarries around Bangalura and entire hills have been lost, physical assets and visual heritage in the process. However, a viable alternative to sand and quarry dust, is crushed sand from building debris generated in the city, where buildings are being demolished to make way for larger constructions. Neither the demolished building debris nor the waste generated in new construction is being processed in an efficient manner. Both could be processed to the grain sizes needed and used as replacement for sand to avoid quarrying hills around Bangalura. But, as of 2017, one entrepreneur is converting construction and demolition waste to manufactured sand and Bangalura municipality is proposing three more.

Figure 11.3 A basement in use

By emphasising the use of earth from site and waste materials, the home becomes a waste sink to offset further ecological debts in construction. Figure 11.4 shows a roof with computer keyboards as filler material. The keyboards reduce the weight of the reinforced cement concrete structure by substituting for concrete below the neutral axis and endure through the building's life. It is hoped that advances in waste recycling systems might mean that keyboards can be recycled like this, as an advance on current practices of landfill.

Such ecological buildings incorporate the services required for healthy living. Rain water is harvested, used and recharged. The wastewater is treated on the site and used as nutrient rich additive for landscaping and growing food. The terrace accommodates panels for water heating as well as photovoltaics for generating energy. Being small, the homes use horizontal site surfaces to the maximum, leaving very little ground space and making terraces and roofs very important functional spaces. In Bangalura culture, the terrace is not used much by inhabitants even if it gets the best of the rain and the sun. The roof can be used in smart ways to catch water, to collect solar power for electricity and to passively assist with thermal needs, and as space to grow food. Figure 11.5 is a graphic depiction of a smart roof functioning on the terrace of my home. Additionally, the terrace can provide space for treating the grey water generated in a residence, using a specially designed plant-based filtration system. Afterwards, such treated water can be used for toilet flushing and landscape purposes. Table 11.2 shows a clear relationship between water harvested and occupancy below a certain area of

Figure 11.4 Computer keyboards embedded in concrete roof

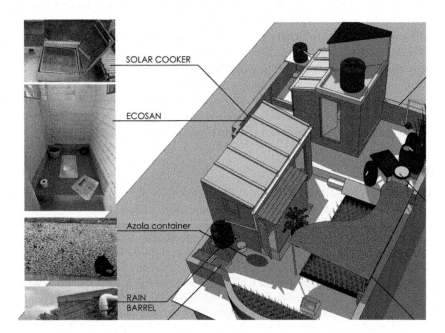

Figure 11.5 Smart roof functionality

Table 11.2 Comparing various roof areas for their potential

	Units	Mini	Amit	Vasanthi	Uma Devi	Ghosh	Sheeba
Plot area	m²	368.0	218.5	220.8	147.2	346.7	220.8
Plot coverage	m²	104.9	132.5	116.0	75.2	87.8	127.7
Occupants	number	6.0	4.0	4.0	4.0	3.0	3.0
Roof area	m²	104.9	132.5	143.2	63.5	62.9	91.7
Fresh water requirement	KL/yr	295.7	197.1	197.1	197.1	147.8	147.8
Rain water harvested	KL/yr	83.9	106.0	114.6	50.8	50.3	73.4
Grey water treatment	KL/yr	197.1	131.4	131.4	131.4	98.6	98.6
Black water treatment	KL/yr	87.6	58.4	58.4	58.4	43.8	43.8
Fresh water from outside	KL/yr	124.1	32.7	24.1	87.9	53.7	30.6

roof, providing a matrix to assist in understanding and designing for the carrying capacity of the land.

Conclusion

Ecological ways of designing homes can play an important part in providing viable resources for building and spaces for conviviality; the examples in this chapter are plots that exist as their own quarry to save the hinterland and reuse of erstwhile waste generated in the city. In such ways they can provide resources, connect other users and people in need, and create a more collaborative society.

There is potential for such production to transform social relationships from a vendor and consumer monetary exchange to a relationship of sharing and respectful connectedness. Furthermore, through constructing ecologically sensitive buildings for convivial living, the house building process fosters a sense of social and environmental worth. In this way designers can take an active role in promoting housing for degrowth in those types of urban areas prevalent in the Global South with challenges and potential similar to Bengaluru.

References

AVEI. (n.d.) 'Compressed stabilised earth block', Auroville Earth Institute – www.earth-auroville.com/compressed_stabilised_earth_block_en.php

Chandrasekhar, S. and Shama, A. (2014) *Urbanization and Spatial Patterns of Internal Migration in India*. WP-2014-016. Mumbai: Indira Gandhi Institute of Development Research.

Heller, P., Mukhopadhyay, P. and Walton, M. (2016) *Cabal City: Regime Theory and Indian Urbanization*. The Watson Institute for International and Public Affairs Research Working Paper 2016-32. Providence (Rhode Island): Brown University.

Kumari, S. (2014) 'Rural urban migration in India: Determinants and factors', *International Journal of Humanities and Social Science* 3(2): 161–80.

Mahadevia, D. (2012) *Decent Work in Ahmedabad: An Integrated Approach*. International Labour Organisation, Asia-Pacific Working Paper. Bangkok: International Labour Office DWT for South Asia and Country Office for India.

Nagaraj, H.B., Sravana, M.V., Aruna, T.G. and Jagadishb, K.S. (2014) 'Role of lime with cement in long-term strength of compressed stabilized earth blocks', *International Journal of Sustainable Built Environment* 3(1): 54–61.

Sundaresan, J. (2016) 'Politics of land use planning in Bangalore', in Beebeejuan, Y. (ed.) *The Participant City*. Berlin: Jovis.

UNEP SBCI. (2009) *Background Paper for Sustainable Buildings and Construction for India: Policies, Practices and Performance* [Round table 4 February 2009, New Dehli]. Working Paper, United Nations Environment Programme, Sustainable Buildings and Construction Initiative – www.teriin.org/eventdocs/files/sus_bldg_paper_1342567768.pdf

12 Low impact living
More than a house

Jasmine Dale, Robin Marwege and Anja Humburg

A small, yet growing, number of people are reclaiming the birth right of all species to live lightly in a place of their choosing. It is a response to our deep need for connection with nature and impulse to design and evolve a method of meeting our basic needs as an individuated expression of life. The outward manifestation of this is the emergence of small self-built homes that respond to their landscape settings and the personal needs of the occupants. These 'low impact' approaches embody a practice and process that converges with a degrowth approach to housing by looking beyond the confines of manufactured materials and industry standardisation. In an era where urbanisation is increasing and regulation is tightening around all aspects of life, low impact living has re-emerged to create breathing space. This chapter outlines some key principles of low impact living and offers two examples of establishing housing for low impact living in distinctly different contexts. The case studies link the principles of the process to degrowth homes through our personal journeys.

Low impact development: a response to urbanism

Low impact living was originally defined by Simon Fairlie (1996, xiv), as 'development that through its low impact either enhances or does not significantly diminish environmental quality'. He later elaborated in his Foreword to Pickerill and Macey (2009, 1) that:

> Neither the term nor the concept was new. People have been living low impact lifestyles in low impact buildings for centuries; indeed, until very recently the majority of people in the world lived that way.

This means, in practice, that low impact living matches reclaimed and natural resources to meet basic needs on a small scale and in response to landscape factors, individuals' expertise and local opportunity. In this context, a low impact shelter is relatively independent of fossil-fuel based infrastructures and demonstrates potential for how housing might evolve in a degrowth world.

The Land Is Ours (TLIO) and its planning consultancy 'Chapter 7' is based in the United Kingdom (UK) and campaigns for the right to access land and its resources in order to live a low impact lifestyle. TLIO has been a major contributor to defining the parameters of low impact development (LID) and the creation of the One Planet Development policy in Wales. TLIO (n.d.) define low impact homes as 'varying greatly' as 'characterised by being very discreet, requiring next to no infrastructure and being built from environmentally friendly materials' and most significant because 'they reintegrate people into the landscape'.

Currently, access to housing and employment, and the costs of energy and food, are intrinsically linked to the oscillations of international finance and economic growth. Thus, the provision of basic needs is skewed and interpreted through complex and vast regulatory and industrial frameworks (Fleming 2016). Building materials must comply to regulations that often respond to manufacturing trends rather than the direct needs of the occupants, environmental imperatives or the landscapes prioritised for housing. This creates a fundamental inefficiency in terms of energy use and misses the opportunity to harness energy inputs inherent in the landscape that can be substituted for fossil fuel inputs.

In contrast, a low impact response to housing starts with a survey of the proposed site, the materials available locally and the dreams and desires of the likely residents. Traditionally, low impact shelters have been self-built by the people who will live in them, and this introduces diverse potential outcomes depending on their prior experience, aptitude for developing new skills and their personal propensity for innovation and exercising judgement in the design process. Usually they have built in a rural context while, say living in a tent, according to need and availability of resources (Spero 2017).

In the hierarchy of human needs, shelter comes before food and water. In our current growth-orientated world, the legacy of housing primarily in urban centres would leave us with shelters co-dependent on the infrastructures of a fossil fuel economy. Without sewage systems, mains-supplied electricity, gas and water, these houses are potentially poor places to live. It remains to be seen how well conventional housing might function in a degrowth world without access to services linked into growth economies. However, in towns and cities, manufactured materials are often so abundant that what we currently view as waste could become vital resources to transition to a degrowth home.

In Britain, low impact housing has developed in rural areas, where there is less competition for space, and natural materials are generally more readily available. Combined with a general desire to be closer to nature and less dependent on conventional, unsustainable infrastructures, this has led to an emergent culture of self-built houses, self-reliance for the provision of services and food and innovation in design.

Permaculture: a tool for transition to a degrowth world

Strongly associated with low impact development is 'permaculture' (Welsh Government 2012). This is a design process in which unsustainable energy and ecological impacts are replaced by using the human imagination to harness landscape factors and natural flows of resources. A house becomes one element (Zone 0) in an integrated network of beneficial relationships, drawing resilience and efficiency from the connections with other elements, such as energy and food production, biodiversity habitat, water provision and 'waste' recycling (Mollison 1988).

Permaculture solutions arise from applying principles and patterns that are observable in thriving wild ecosystems and associated communities (usually of Indigenous people) that are living in balance with their resources. There is no need for energy inputs from outside and no waste outputs are created. This immediately introduces a holistic systems approach, where inputs and outputs are linked and no unsustainable energy source is required. A shelter, thus, becomes more than a house. Rather, it is an element in a system of beneficial relationships with other elements, such as social recreation, food cultivation, fuel, energy and water, with reuse and recycling of materials.

Permaculture is a 'pattern language', a way-marker on the journey towards re-centring human activity in harmony with natural systems. It is a method to meet all our needs through nature, combined with our awareness, as the ultimate provider – rather than state and industrial provision. To draw on the resilience and efficiency embodied in natural systems and awaken our intuition is a significant 'magic key' to unlock our potential and provide the upskilling required to provide for our own shelter sustainably like every other creature on earth and as known by our ancestors for millennia before us.

The application of permaculture is a road map to degrowth housing and relies on observation of the actual territory where a house will be planted. A transition to a degrowth world may be abrupt and this is a limiting factor for sound observation. Similarly, when applying for permission for a low impact development under the Welsh One Planet Development regulations, there are often serious constraints on observing the site before building, specifically, the need to set up shelter and energy systems and prove viability of food growing, small businesses and fuel provision within five years. However, without the choices and constraints of our current 'growth' world, the immediacy of our basic needs and the viability of what is feasible create conditions for an observation feedback cycle and a quick learning curve. For example, if no central heating is available, the wind direction and its effect on the warmth of your shelter become quickly apparent and you are self-motivated to do something about it.

The Undercroft: a low impact shelter

The example of the Undercroft at the Lammas eco-village in West Wales, illustrates the possibility of non-professionals making simple shelters from locally available resources. It is a small house of 45 square metres, about half the UK average area per person. The surrounding landscape and materials express our current resource base and manufacturing economies; suspending these factors allows us insight into what is possible in a degrowth scenario. A house basically needs to be structurally sound, warm and allow for adequate air flow. This protects us from the weather, injury, pests such as rodents, and maintains a healthy interior environment.

Using a permaculture approach, the house is sited to maximise water catchment from its landscape, its roof and any nearby springs, ponds or rivers. Sector analyses of soils, predominant wind and rain, shade and frost, all led us to site the Undercroft (seen in Figure 12.1) in relation to the surrounding landform, slope and conifer plantation to the south. These design decisions were informed by a two-year process of observation, surveying and mapping, combined with our prior experience of building simple shelters.

With sensitivity to landscape factors, such as the slope, orientating the windows to the sun, siting firewood trees in relation to the house as a windbreak, and collecting roof and glasshouse water for ourselves and food growing, we can see the house as part of a network of beneficial relationships. Each element supports the function of another. For example, people need food, food needs heat and attention and the house needs warmth. A glasshouse on the south side of the house meets these needs with no fossil fuel energy provision. The Undercroft took a few months' work and a few thousand pounds and provides a feasible solution in a transition to a degrowth world.

The local authority prosecuted the initial low impact builders at the Lammas eco-village for failing to meet building regulations. Eventually, the court case was dropped, because Simon Dale painstakingly showed that our approaches and materials were safe and fit-for-purpose. The main constraint for low impact housing emerged as a lack of understanding of using recycled and natural materials, rather than their fundamental unsuitability for modern living standards. This

Figure 12.1 The Undercroft, Lammas

Source: Simon Dale – www.beingsomewhere.net

case-by-case, step-by-step building of understanding and expertise between regulators and low impact builders seemed to work, albeit at great personal effort.

Subsequent low impact developments in the region have reverted to more conventional and less ecological materials in order to save their energy for land-based activities and establishing sustainable livelihoods. Our current regulatory frameworks of building regulations and planning permission are in place to protect householders from dangerous buildings and from untrammelled development in the open countryside. These are uniform standards to meet all situations and require an industrial level of global standardisation. This results in house construction and design being limited to materials that can be bought from a retailer so that standards can be enforced and a lowest common denominator of safety and reliability is achieved (Alexander 1979).

To create conditions for a genuine culture of low impact shelter making, more room for innovation needs to emerge all over the UK. Appropriate regulations tailored to a low impact home are viewed as desirable in a context where the builders have no prior relationship to the materials and processes. Many low impact builders would welcome this for their peace of mind. In our own experience, learning and adapting from other low impact homes the imperative of making a structure safe for your family and a commitment to observation and small and slow solutions is an adequate self-regulatory framework.

Housing sovereignty: a self-built roundhouse in Germany?

Another example of a low impact building, in progress, is located in Holzen (Lower Saxony, Germany). Co-authors of this chapter, Anja and Robin, never wanted to own a house before or would have thought it even worse to build a new one – there were so many houses that could be ecologically renovated and urban sprawl was continuously degrading landscapes. Yet their curiosity for ways to live sustainably led them to Lammas Eco-Village in Wales. There they learned about building a low impact house from scratch. From hereon in, until the conclusion, co-authors Anja and Robin write in the first person.

Everything started with an article about roundhouses in Wales and the One Planet Policy that has allowed building off-grid in open land, only if a certain degree of self-sufficiency is realised. Subsequently, we were able to take a tailored two-week course about permaculture and help build a roundhouse with Simon Dale and our co-author Jasmine Dale. This course was like putting the pieces together for us: our vision for living with others, but in a defined private space, and living in closer connection with nature seemed wonderfully balanced in Lammas.

Building in a village: Holzen

Holzen, the place of our roundhouse project, is in a very different kind of location than the rural landscape surrounding Lammas in Wales. Holzen is an ordinary German village of 300 people, 15km east of Lüneburg, which is the regional centre with 70,000 inhabitants. Large-scale conventional agriculture surrounds the village. The landscape is spotted with wind turbines. Vast forests are close by and the Elbe river biosphere reserve can be reached by bike within an hour. The residents are a mix of old people, farmers, commuters and families from different social milieu. In 2013, eight young friends started a shared-living project in a rented 250 square metre house, so Holzen became home for us and our daughter.

On the one hand, the roundhouse project is our step to root ourselves here permanently, to live in community with others and, at the same time, to be able to define a clear space for family life – in contrast to the shared house where we have been living when writing this chapter in mid-2017. On the other hand, the building site is an experiment to realise housing sovereignty with our own hands within the boundaries of German planning legislation. 'Housing sovereignty' means to be independent of unsustainable building practices that harm our planet. Concrete, for example, is one of the most obvious problems in modern building and architecture: carbon dioxide emissions from the concrete industry make up to approximately 5 percent of all global emissions – way more than total aeroplane flights (KIT 2009).

But, beyond reducing emissions, our aim is to decolonise housing from 'megamachine' capitalism, where the infrastructures of a growth economy lock in unsustainable housing and people are distracted from taking responsible actions for themselves, others and the ecosystem. Housing sovereignty, as a new term, aligns with 'food sovereignty', which means the right of all people and countries, to define their agricultural and food practices autonomously from big enterprises or global politics. By sharing our experiences we want to encourage others who think about radical approaches to housing to start a roundhouse project in other countries and in different settings.

Permaculture principles and an openness to observe and work with what is given in a specific environment can enable people, even academics like us, to embed a house within the landscape as a connected element rather than it appear as a concrete alien. That is the point: everyone with a functioning body and mind should be able to fulfil the basic need for shelter, at least partly, by themselves to be a bit more independent from industrial processes and standards that might be good for making money, but are much less good for the earth. Reading *A Simple Roundhouse Manual* by Tony Wrench (2015) was very helpful for us to believe in our abilities and our potential.

The practical process

One of our first practical steps towards the roundhouse was to produce and store approximately 500 straw bales, on a hot day in August 2016, with the help of family and friends and two old tractors. Luckily, a family member is a sparetime farmer who knows everything about old machines and even owns a lot of useful equipment. The way we produced the bales shows our general approach:

arrange a huge picnic, send an email to thirty friends, and get in contact with some experts and your neighbour who has a big barn. The old tractor and straw baler were run with fuel, but the rest was done by hand. A self-built sledge carried the bales upstairs into the barn, pulled by cheering people who enjoyed both the exercise and the simple, convenient technique.

Another early, and most important, step was to find an architect or construction engineer to help us with the documents for planning permission. In Germany, planning documents can only be handed in by approved engineers or architects. Who would be able to calculate the technical details of round wood carpentry, and a round roof with a skylight in the middle without a central post, using methods that would convince German planning officials that our roundhouse would be safe and sound?

We found a person who had done technical analyses for an outdoor museum – a Bronze Age theme park, where they had built round wood houses – so we tried to contact the responsible engineer. He was an interesting combination of a conservative local politician, a passionate hunter, a classical and experienced construction engineer, and he was open to eco-friendly ideas and our building project. The masterplan of our 70 square metre roundhouse is shown in Figure 12.2.

This was our opportunity to work with a classical, but open-to-new-ideas engineer who could fit our vision into German planning regulations. Of course, it also meant compromise, for instance, the timber ended up being specified a little thicker than we would have liked – because the officials were not experienced with round wood and, therefore, took a very precautionary approach. Consequently, we might not be able to lift our wooden rafters manually and might end up having to use an expensive crane. Another trade-off is that we must be grid-connected, especially in regard to waste water. We will have to gradually disconnect afterwards and experiment with the different solutions for off-grid systems for warmth, electricity and water, systems that focus on reduction and reuse of resources as well as on renewable sources.

Planning

We had some good advice from Lammas, which went something like this: talk to officials personally and explain that you need their help to safely and correctly build something that is good for the environment and its inhabitants. We handed in our application for building permission personally, but received only a short comment: 'Ah yes, it's round. And how will your waste water be treated? Regularly? All right, we will pass it on'.

Our application was passed on through numerous offices. We found out too late which of the other officials we should have informed personally about our project. If we had talked to two specific officials, and explained better what we as a family had planned, we could have saved at least two months in which simply nothing happened at the building regulation office. We learned afterwards that the officials were delaying because they were unsure about whether the building

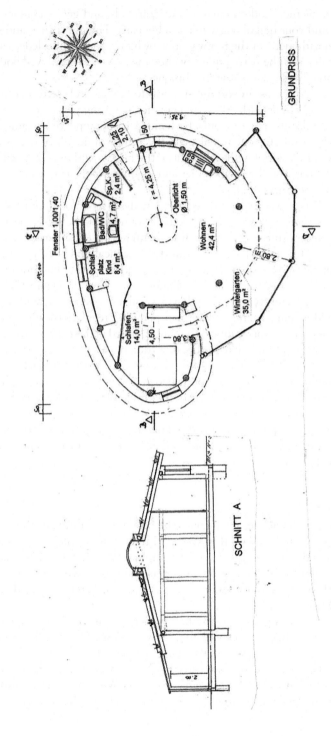

Figure 12.2 The masterplan of the roundhouse, Holzen

might affect the business of the slaughterhouse next door – not because we were using straw bales and round wood timber for building!

The owner of the slaughterhouse was afraid that we might end up complaining about noise or smells from the slaughterhouse and, therefore, constrain his work processes. Ultimately, we were simply asked to report to the planning office how many animals were normally killed and processed per year. The short answer was that the slaughtering is so little that the business could even expand without contravening noise and smell emission regulations. But we waited too long to talk in detail to the owner of the slaughterhouse and the officials because we did not want to stir things up. Unfortunately, we tried too hard not to be annoying or 'super special' with respect to our roundhouse project.

Conviviality

Another practical example illustrates the core of what we intended with the building project: building together can create a sense of connectedness with each other and to nature, forms of connectedness that are deeply satisfying and generate happiness.

The setting was the day of debarking in March 2017, when eight people who only loosely knew each other, gathered on a windy and sunny field – see Figure 12.3. Several trestles were prepared, knifes sharpened and, of course, the picnic was laid out. The group became a true unity when altogether we carried the big logs around, acting out what we referred to as the 'wood caterpillar'. We worked joyfully together with a sensation of freedom and the feeling that we were taking a small step towards something that is globally relevant: personal growth and self-fulfilment without harming the planet, the opposite of paying for a house to be built by companies that are part of megamachine capitalism.

By including volunteers on our building project, we also partly give up control over the result. Instead, we trusted that every talent would bloom and that the

Figure 12.3 Debarking day, March 2017

house would, in the end, not only be a manifestation of individual needs and ideas but also bear the imprint of a common spirit. This spirit was so important for us, especially in times of doubt, when the already-mentioned obstacles tested our motivation to proceed with the planning and building.

An encouraging model: Heckenbeck

We looked at another case in Germany to strengthen our faith that it is possible to create islands of change in very ordinary places where wonderful developments can start. The village of Heckenbeck, also in Lower Saxony, is known for its alternative, self-run school (*Freie Schule*) and various sustainable activities that are accepted, and often supported, by local residents. Everything started with only a few friends who moved out into the countryside. Today, even other municipalities travel to Heckenbeck to learn more about the so-called *Mitfahrbänke* – roadside benches where you indicate, using a flag system, in which direction you would like to hitch-hike. Even grandmothers and grandfathers use it to do their shopping!

Of course, it was a process to get to this point. Half of the residents are 'new', having moved there within the last decade. Today, the village of Heckenbeck as a whole is on a flourishing degrowth path in experimenting with sustainable ways of living. This is our vision for Holzen, of which our roundhouse project is a part.

Conclusion

The principles and process of low impact living are concurrent with a degrowth world, yet naturally there are contradictions as we make the transition from a socio-economic hegemony dependent on fossil fuels. Whether it is dependence on transport, manufactured food or building materials, it is inevitable that greater concentrations of people taking up low impact lifestyles in rural or urban settings will facilitate more opportunities for local self-reliance. Limiting factors to LID, such as low rural population density, keep people yoked to travelling for education, leisure, income and purchasing food. More people living a low impact lifestyle is a positive driver for degrowth; a greater diversity of people and their livelihoods will create more goods and services and reduce patterns of unsustainable production and consumption.

Our visions, which propelled these housing projects, are based on a confidence that many people, maybe most people, would like to live more in harmony with other people and our planet, but many of us cannot see how to do that. However, practical, local and real examples connected to everyday life and ordinary places help us imagine our future better. These practical steps might not be totally radical, and will even be full of compromises, yet they have the potential to continuously change the system. Even if this is a slow process, at the beginning, the seed is then planted and such seeds are ready to multiply when the time is ripe.

References

Alexander, C. (1979) *The Timeless Way of Building*. Oxford: Oxford University Press.

Fairlie, S. (1996) *Low Impact Development: Planning and People in a Sustainable Countryside*. Charlbury: Jon Carpenter.

Fleming, D. (2016) *Surviving the Future: Culture, Carnival and Capital in the Aftermath of the Market Economy*. London: Chelsea Green.

KIT (Karlsruhe Institute for Technology). (2009) *Grüner Zement*. Presseinformation 143/2009 – www.kit.edu/kit/pi_2009_610.php

Mollison, B. (1988) *Permaculture: A Designers' Manual*. Tyalgum: Tagari Publications.

Pickerill, J. and Maxey, L. (eds) (2009) Low Impact Development: The Future in Our Hands. *Leeds: Footprint Workers Cooperative* – https://lowimpactdevelopment.files.wordpress.com/2008/11/low-impact-development-book2.pdf

Spero, D. (2017) *Settlements*. West Dorset: David Spero.

TLIO. (n.d.) 'Land for homes', *The Land Is Ours: A Landrights Campaign for Britain* – http://tlio.org.uk/aims-2/land-for-homes/

Welsh Government. (2012) *One Planet Development Practice Guide*, 19 October. Cardiff – http://gov.wales/topics/planning/policy/guidanceandleaflets/oneplanet/

Wrench, T. (2015) *A Simple Roundhouse Manual*. CreateSpace Independent Publishing Platform – www.createspace.com/

13 Neighbourhoods as the basic module of the global commons

Hans Widmer ('P.M.') with
François Schneider

Prefatory note

In the 1980s, 'P.M.' (Hans Widmer) was part of the European squatters' movement – intent on building an international movement. Strongly repressed and facing activists' despair, P.M. developed a pamphlet *'bolo'bolo'* (P.M. 1986), to convey a nonviolent optimist's vision of the possible future – a satisfying and ecologically sensible way of life. Significantly, he challenged the idea of economic growth and his work has inspired many hands-on neighbourhood projects. This summary by François Schneider of P.M.'s (2014) work on 'the power of neighbourhood' shows how his vision of degrowth is based on the principles of commons (as explored by Elinor Ostrom [1990]) and resilience (Zolli and Healy 2012; Hopkins 2011) and offers perspectives from neighbourhood to planetary scales. As P.M. (2014, 61) points out: 'having big schemes is not a vice, but a necessity'. His vision is neither a prescriptive model nor a comprehensive and finely detailed scenario to follow step by step. It may be criticised as 'unrealistic', or not radical enough; for instance it does not address the impacts of climate change and multiple wars and migrations. However, such symbolic proposals are useful to stir and organise people's imagination, contributing to discussions happening in many forms and places today.

* * *

Instead of waiting for – or speculating about – a collapse, we need to establish just and enjoyable systems. The best time to try out alternatives is, always, 'now'. Institutional experience and know-how is available and being tested. There is no single alternative model: it would be a fallacy to try replacing the present system with a single perfect system; systemic stability requires several independent metabolisms.

The first 'parachute' from disaster – or pillar of a degrowth society – relates to focus existing states on public services, increasing transparency and democratic participation (see Table 13.1). Successful action to reduce inequality and challenge oligarchic interests would reduce states' repressive and governing functions ('power over') to become cooperative administrations. The second pillar of

Table 13.1 Parachutes from capitalism = pillars of degrowth

Sphere of commons	1. Public services	2. Agricultural subsistence	3. Creative/cooperative projects
function	basic supplies, industries, banks, social services	food	crafts, light industries, arts, services
organisation	direct and indirect democracy	direct democracy	free association
size/number	600 territories 400,000 'branches' towns, boroughs	16 million neighbourhoods	unlimited

a degrowth society requires subsistence neighbourhood communities that, most importantly, assume most food production and supply. The third pillar is making the creative-cooperative sector flourish, with free associations that, nevertheless, are obliged to respect social and ecological guidelines.

Comparable forms and sizes of organisation are essential for global equality and fair exchange. The global household needs universal modules with clear boundaries. Most commons and activities can be distributed in five modules corresponding to different scales. To face the present ecological, economical and psycho-social challenges, we propose to organise the 3.5 billion households of the planet by means of five 'modules':

1   16 million neighbourhoods
2   400,000 boroughs or small towns
3   4,000 big cities and regions
4   600 territories
5   1 planet

Such emergent entities would enable general features of stable, resilient systems such as minimising transport, economies of scale, and integrating communicative and political functions. Modules would be applied according to local conditions. They are, simultaneously, open-spaces and meeting points.

Neighbourhoods

Neighbourhoods would be the most promising institutions for commons, their size determined according to the requirements of resilience (modularity, relocalisation, size and belonging), subsistence and all the principles for managing successful commons. Ostrom's (1990) rules of the commons, such as defined boundaries, monitoring and internal mediation, correspond with statutes of housing cooperatives and can be practically applied. Furthermore, logically, neighbourhoods linked to regional agricultural land are ideal subsistence communities. Transforming neighbourhoods into communities of subsistence, we clearly privilege reproduction over production. Making life possible and enjoyable is the main goal. Industrial and social production are simply means to achieve this goal. From a purely ecological point of view, neighbourhoods are an ideal starting point.

Cities are densely populated areas but a lot of space reserves remain that can be used to achieve higher density without creating 'ant heaps' and living with total strangers. The objective is strong social relations and communication, not density per se. Living in dense neighbourhoods saves on agriculturally useable land, and shortens transport and travel distances. A neighbourhood can take numerous shapes. As an example it might take the shape of a block, blocks of around 160 family dwellings occupying just over six hectares, exclusive of streets. Such more-or-less square blocks exist in many large cities, such as Barcelona, Paris, Vienna and New York, where they might be ecologically upgraded and re-established as the small urban microcosms that they assumed at the start of the twentieth century. Built in the era before the automobile, such neighbourhood blocks are best suited for pedestrians. High-rise buildings – expensive, unattractive and not conducive to community – are not necessary for density and could be transformed. Sprawling suburbs of the automobile age are more difficult to transform because they rarely represent real neighbourhoods. Existing neighbourhood-affine structures are of great importance, as it is difficult to re-build cities completely or to construct new ecological cities on a large scale (like Masdar in Abu Dhabi) without using huge amounts of resources and creating carbon emissions. So, we will have to improve the places we already live in.

The neighbourhoods proposed here are logistic terminals, modules of household economy, re-localised clusters of formerly scattered living functions. Within the blocks everything is within walking distance (circa 80 metres), a proximity conducive to a great number of synergies. You don't have to dress up; you can even move around in your bathrobe. Errands in this perimeter can be done on the spur of the moment – you can fetch an onion or an egg once you have started your cooking. You can interrupt a working-process without losing the context. It's a range that allows you to be very effective. Neighbourhood blocks help create lively street scenes: interchanges between quiet and private courts or courtyards and busy, public, mainly pedestrian streets make urban life more thrilling and varied, as in Arab cities such as Marrakesh.

Households are strictly private. They can take many forms: single-person dwellings, small flats for couples, family-flats or communal household dwellings for 10–30 people. In neighbourhoods the private, semi-public and the public are completely separate spheres. Neighbourhoods must be relatively large, approximately 500 inhabitants or, say, 200 medium-sized flats of some 100 square metres each. Their linkage with the surrounding 'micro-agro' – an agricultural surface area of about 80 hectares in a perimeter of 20 to 50 kilometres, depending on local conditions (see Figure 13.1) – is fundamental to achieve food subsistence.

A minimal and stable size of population is required to even out fluctuations due to mobility, birth and mortality. Stability is essential for cooperation to succeed,

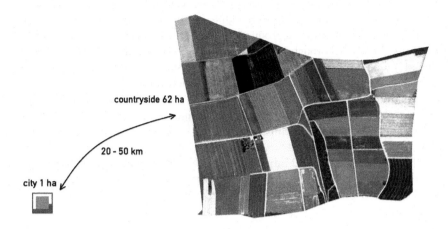

Figure 13.1 The micro-agro linked to the neighbourhood

since cooperation requires familiarity without too much intimacy. There must be room for internal sub-communities, communal and family households. A size of 450–600 people enables internal organisation to be transparent and non-intrusive while a larger size would risk anonymity, hinder cooperation and render higher administrative costs. According to Dunbar (1993) people are comfortable communicating informally with up to 150 in a group. Therefore, the ideal neighbourhood size must be larger, to create a systemic pressure for consciously designed formal communication avoiding buddy systems, favouritism or mafia-like forms of dominion. Neighbourhoods are neither clans nor tribes; they are cool social modules of common access with rules and formal institutions.

The ideal size proposed supports a feeling of neighbourhood 'belonging', which is important for resilient structures and to avoid unnecessary management. Too much neighbourhood interaction makes us nervous, too little renders us lonesome. We need communal spaces and well-protected private spheres. Neighbourhoods are 'nests', not prisons. Equilibrium between private and semi-public spheres can be defined in different ways appropriate to each neighbourhood, depending on cultural background, members' ages and other circumstances.

Size affects the resilience of 'household economics' and possibilities for division of labour. Collective cooperation can be organised flexibly, an appropriate occupation found for everyone, achieving diversity and security more easily. Multiple people have the same skills so the absence of one does not lead to disarray in producing and distributing goods and services. If a community is stable, diversified and large enough, this enhances the surplus and possibilities for sharing. Size has systemic, even political importance. Social modules of the commons that are too small tend to fail. An appropriate size allows age groups to interact effectively and heterogeneity to operate. Cooperation needs 'clusters' (Nowak and Highfield 2011).

Care work and housework (misnamed the 'care economy') is labour-saving and less tiring if groups are large enough to maintain a generous, accessible and sustainable infrastructure. Reproductive work can be shared more easily within neighbourhoods or boroughs – for special services and needs. The old system of dumping housework on women alone can be dispensed with by sharing housework in its manifold forms between genders, according to individuals' talents and inclinations. 'Material feminism' can also be good news for men. Elderly or sick people can stay in their neighbourhoods, improving health and well-being. Friendly neighbourhoods mean that children have diverse experiences, further developing their social skills.

The proposed size of 500 inhabitants or 200 flats permits cost-efficient building, reconstruction and renovation. Compact urban buildings have less costly, smaller façade surfaces and make for ecologically sound construction.

What about the rural areas?

The current crisis arises in the countryside through the industrialisation of agriculture, deforestation, mining, transport, land grabbing and contamination of the environment. Restructuring rural areas must go hand in hand with urban transformation. Protecting rural areas from grand real estate developments and establishing instead community-supported agriculture can revive countryside and cities together. Consolidating erstwhile suburbanites into newly revived central cities means gaining local agricultural land for the city. Agrocentres revive country villages and secure the exchange between rural and city lifestyles.

Not everybody wants to live in neighbourhoods. A substantial majority of people will be sufficient for a systemic reconfiguration of our lifestyle and will guarantee the 'power of neighbourhood'. In between and in remote locations there is space for hermits, introverts, small groups, families and all kinds of idiosyncratic communities. However, we want to show that a subsistent neighbourhood is a feasible model and to make variations on it measurable.

The neighbourhoods will have diverse degrees of communality: some will be more like apartment hotels, with great independence, others will embody intense collective living. Between the neighbourhoods all kinds of networks and cooperative enterprises exist, including care infrastructure. Together in a borough of neighbourhoods (see Figure 13.2), each neighbourhood represents a stable context of real social security without formal or administrative structures. Adjacent neighbourhoods guarantee each other a livelong right to stay in a community highly conducive to good health.

New food logistics will be essential to achieve an ecologically sustainable lifestyle. The 'reinterpretation of the cities from the countryside' (Shiva 2008) is the basis of all serious proposals for a degrowth society. According to our estimates, a neighbourhood would need around 6 tons of food per week. Land use can be reduced substantially by a mainly vegetarian diet, but even a moderate reduction in animal production (milk, eggs, meat) is compatible with a globally sustainable

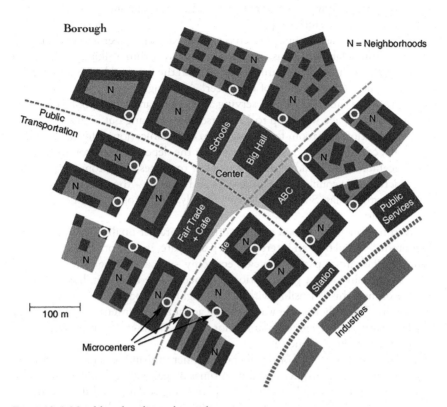

Figure 13.2 Neighbourhoods in a borough

lifestyle. Some products, such as potatoes and cereals, are delivered yearly transported in bulk by train.

Cooperation in deliveries between neighbourhoods would require a small 2-ton truck shared by the two neighbourhoods. The small food delivery truck could be fuelled by biogas generated by consumer waste or by other bio-mass. The simple logistics of moving from A to the close B replaces current food logistics responsible for immense environmental waste moving goods between distribution and shopping centres, supermarkets as well as consumers travelling backwards and forwards.

No single territory need achieve 100 percent autarchy on food. Most cities and nations were not conceived on ecological but, rather, historical grounds. Some continental, even global, food imports or exports can be fair and even necessary. A neighbourhood food depot-cum-kitchen of about 400 square metres on the ground floor would provide space for storing, processing, preparing, preserving and cooking. Instant, fresh and cooked takeaway meals would be available from the depot (80 metres or 1 minute away) for heating and/or seasoning in dwellings, or eaten in an adjacent dining space. Cooking and eating together is much fun and a great opportunity for informal and continuous communication. All kinds of dinner or gourmet clubs are possible.

This synergistic depot-cum-kitchen is embedded, like a supermarket every 100 metres, within neighbourhoods, open 24 hours a day within walking distance and accessible by elevators. This minimises storage in the flats and household fridges, even the time to fetch a glass of cool beer! A dining space of, say, 300 square metres would be multifunctional, serving as lounge, bar, library, pool room, café and/or working space where up to 150 persons could hang out at any one time. It would function as a room for spontaneous communication, information sharing, chats, confrontations and encounters. In the depot-kitchen you would find fresh vegetables and bread, dozens of types of tomatoes, eggs from happy hens, new quiches, new soufflés, pâtés, sausages and pastries – the perfect carrot will replace boring caviar. Sufficiency, done properly, can become the basis of a new form of luxury.

Given neighbourhood food supply, consumers are personally acquainted with their producers and take an interest, even participate, in food production. Appreciating agriculture as part of the care economy – as care of the soil, plants and animals – requires direct participation. We need to be more familiar with food production and this is feasible within the neighbourhood located close to food production. The only feasible way of doing agriculture is intensive, mixed-crop, largely organic production unprofitable for the mass market currently. What conditions might make it economic?

A core professional staff of members of the agro-urban cooperative will need to supply a number of workers, mainly in times of seasonal peaks. Not everybody needs to work in the fields, the general pool being so large and flexible that a wide choice of chores can be offered including cooking, tending to the depots, maintenance of buildings and childcare.

The ground floor of the microcenter (see Figure 13.3) might cover, say 1,300 square metres, divided into the depot-cum-kitchen, bakery, processing area, restaurant/bar/lounge and terrace, library, internal goods depot, area for clothing and other textiles, laundry, repair shop, tools, community bath, retreat, children's play room and administration centre. The microcenter with its many entrances and exits is multifunctional allowing for engagement with other people and for avoiding them. Not a collection of small businesses, the microcenter is an integral element of the neighbourhood cooperative, run by waged professionals and by unwaged members.

The neighbourhood as described could deliver one planet lifestyles with different climatic regions requiring different energy level but serviced by renewables. A reduction by a factor of six is feasible with respect to technological efficiency, renewable sources and a more luxurious, but more communal, lifestyle. I estimate that the features of an average sufficiency lifestyle would look like 20 square metres of heated or cooled private living space in an insulated building: no car, no plane flights, 10km per day of train travel, train trips totalling 2500km per year, a boat voyage of 12000km per year, 15kg of meat per year, 70 litres of water per day and one newspaper per ten inhabitants.

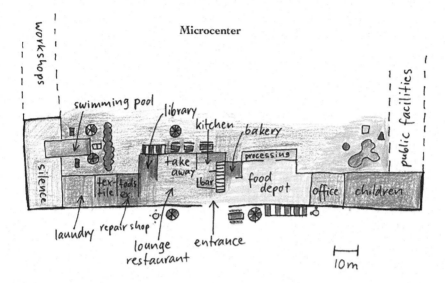

Figure 13.3 The microcenter, ground floor

This illustration just given is just an example of one possible mix of energy uses: vegans might take a plane. People who need more living space could cut down on train trips. We need to develop ecological boats and good sharing systems. Heating, car traffic and plane trips make massive environmental impacts. It is impossible to produce enough energy to replace non-renewable energy sources by renewable ones in our time limit. Stopping fossil fuel is necessary for our ecological systems and climate, and a low-energy lifestyle is slower, lighter, more personal and less worrisome. We will not be able to do without some form of rationing of natural resources. But, for reasons of justice, instead of 'cap and trade' we should try to 'cap and share'. Trying to regulate our use of resources through pricing means the rich in their Porsches will joyously overtake us while we pedal along on our bicycles. We're not that stupid.

Is it all about living more efficiently?

Neighbourhoods as described above are not only ecologically and economically effective units but also form the indispensable social basis of a new civilisation based on commons. They are resilient, stable, just, enduring, cooperative, commons-framed, energy-efficient units with fundamental social and political functions. Without a basic 'demos', a Greek word for the autarchic communities of citizens, there can be no real democracy, or inclusive, egalitarian participation. If each member of such a community is not aware that their personal involvement is vital, neighbourhoods will degenerate and become purely administrative units and eventually decay (De Angelis 2012). If the (micro-) centres cannot hold, the whole will fall apart.

It is not a coincidence that many organisations have their offices or meeting places in the liveliest urban neighbourhoods and are part of an informal global network of activists. 'Occupy your neighbourhood' is a logical consequence of 'Occupy Wall Street'. Since the 1980s, the 'space wars' in inner cities have been fought over the reanimation and defence of neighbourhoods against gentrification and attempts at turning them into quaint open-air shopping malls. The horizontal 'international of global neighbourhoods' will be an essential complement to the regionally and globally interlocked institutions of commoning with indirect, vertical and delegated responsibility. The global neighbourhood is a basis for all other spheres that depend on it.

These neighbourhoods in all their diversity, from African fisher-folk villages to urban high-rises in Hong Kong, can embody ways of living harmoniously together on this planet. Neighbourhoods will nurture the attitudes and rules we need to govern larger commons (such as lakes and rivers). If we do participate in governing our immediate social context, we think things will get out of hand. Trust, mutual support, responsibility, conflict-resolving skills and democratic participation are acquired and preserved in this local communal sphere. The 'power to do' is based there. As such multifunctional cooperative neighbourhoods cannot be created administratively but by future inhabitants who will be transformed in the process. Similarly, with cooperative housing projects, future tenants must have the means to determine the project, to create personal relationships and to identify with the nascent social unit. An authentic neighbourhood is the result of the story of commons (a 'realistic novel') so we need new nodes of citizen initiatives that can mobilise support from local administrations and know-how from universities and political parties.

Defending the waning qualities of existing neighbourhoods against real estate developers and short-sighted local authorities is not enough. We must move forward and posit our neighbourhoods as the global modules of a new civilisation, a universal project. Far from being hermetically defined spaces, neighbourhoods are like open crossroads, places to meet, arrive and depart. They need air to breathe, other neighbourhoods and cooperation on the level of boroughs or small towns (see Figure 13.4). They also relate to their larger urban context, to big cities like New York, Sao Paulo or Lagos, which follow their own logic and qualities.

A borough or town

The next unit is an urban area of 10,000–50,000 inhabitants, which might be part of a larger city, or constitutes a small town on its own in the country. A borough comprises 10–40 neighbourhoods, serving as a branch office for general services. Most everyday errands within a borough can be performed within a perimeter of 500 metres, or within 5 minutes. There is a clearly defined pedestrian centre, a link to the territorial, if not global, railroad or subway system, bus lines and industrial plants near the train tracks.

In the centre you would find a cooperatively run 'world' supermarket supplying those foods and other goods not produced – or produced in sufficient

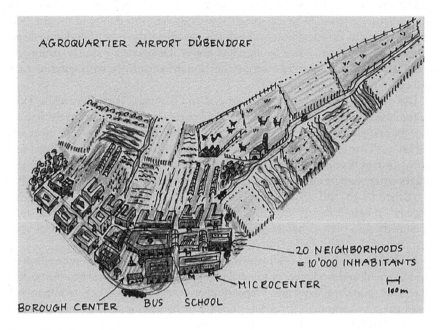

Figure 13.4 A borough

quantity – locally. Exchanges of goods also happen directly between neighbourhoods, as wine from a sister neighbourhood is exchanged for bacon or cheese from a distinct region but only exceptionally, as a form of cultural exchange and bonding. Global exchange of foods or other goods can be fair and sustainable if shipped in bulk, to make the handling and packaging more effective. Thus, autarchy is not an absolute principle but more a side effect of energy-efficiency and preference for familiarity. In the borough we find a small health centre and emergency clinic with a pharmacy, administrative offices, a police station, a big hall, various cinemas and coffee houses. A moderately large square with a band stand in its centre.

Such medium-sized urban units play an important part in the reorganisation and recentralisation of the sprawling megacities in the Global North and South and stop the flight from rural areas. Why not link via the Internet all the theoretically possible borough centres, setting up webcams, video walls, sound systems and ABC (Anti-Boredom Centres) around the bar areas to enhance these popular cultural and information spaces? This would allow live communication worldwide at any time, to watch other people play sport, follow discussions, readings, lectures, concerts and stay connected and up to date. This would maximise transparency, communication, well-being and minimise physical travelling. Schools, a hotel, a library and a museum of local history could complement the ABC and lodge occasional guests.

The size of this unit must be appropriate to the range of public services and infrastructure offered. Whereas neighbourhoods are semi-public units, the borough is a public, political unit and public stage. Here the private individual can appear as a citizen in a role as an equal player. Democracy requires aware and committed citizens, diversity means richer and dynamic lives, with self-advocacy and open, receptive engagement.

The differences between neighbourhood and borough centre depend on local cultural background. Perhaps, in your neighbourhood, you go down to the lounge in jeans and pullover but, if you go to the borough centre, you dress up, make up, put on a silk tie or wear perfume. The microcenter is a mostly de-sexualised territory for family and friends; the town centres have an erotic undertone. In the microcenter you relax on old sofas and listen to your favourite music. In the ABC you dance tango, and sip an aged Armagnac. The neighbourhood is the stage of tragedy – death, jealousy, love, divorce, hate, families – the borough is the stage of comedy. You play a character of your own choice, you can laugh about your destiny and the folly of your ambitions. It is Commedia dell'Arte!

A whole borough of 20 neighbourhoods would produce its food on its adjacent land. Agricultural work may be prescribed by physiotherapists and fitness coaches to replace sports and workouts. Depending on your personal fitness requirements you'd get a programme of weeding, hoeing or harvesting. Sometimes an agro-quartier would be created on a disused airport.

Boroughs are the sphere of the commons where embedded neighbourhoods receive support when difficulties, shortages or failures occur. Boroughs have an extra pool of resources to balance out unequal distribution of resources. The goal is not total equality, but the keeping of inequalities within limits. It would be disastrous if some sort of competition arose between poor and rich neighbourhoods, which effectively replaced the current one between rich and poor individuals. This function of embedding is relevant to subsequent spheres: regions, territories and globally, where conflict resolution is most urgent.

The region

The further away the unit is from immediate needs the more loosely defined is its size. The region is open to many different interpretations; comprising of dozens of boroughs or hundreds of neighbourhoods, it has an additional centre. The region includes most of the neighbourhoods' land with a perimeter of, say, up to 100 miles in the case of global cities like New York or Shanghai (which means it corresponds to metropolitan areas and a surrounding agricultural zone). The region's population is substantial, say varying between 200,000 and 20 million people. In Europe a 'typical' region might well encompass the 'hinterland' of a larger city of 500,000 inhabitants. The region functions to provide services such as universities, hospitals, power plants, industries, museums, public transport, opera, stadiums, banks and courts. Metropolitan-cum- regional services will be lighter than those in populous cities today, as a lot of services are effectively provided in boroughs or neighbourhoods.

The region integrates town and country, connected by public transportation with most places reached within half an hour by bus, train and tram, or within an hour on bicycle. Regions manage their natural environment, such as rivers, lakes, coasts, forests and moors. In scarcely populated areas with no large cities, public service centres would evolve in an appropriate geographic location without dense urban settlements. In some situations, regions and territories would fuse, such as the city-states of Singapore and island nations like Malta, Cyprus and Fiji.

The organisation of industrial subsistence, research and cooperation and the pooling and allocation of general resources are other important functions of regions in governing commons – almost like banking today. However, the necessity of democratic planning requires transparent public institutions that replace big business and opaque banking. Broad-scale cooperation has two main aspects: defining projects (including for research, innovation, 'ideas', inventions and technologies); and, pooling necessary resources (material, know-how and work effort). Big cities centres are the ideal location for both functions, which are technical and political. All stakeholders, entrepreneurs, investors and consumers should be able to participate.

The institution where these two elements are combined is called a 'cooperatory', a permanent fair, place of knowledge exchange and laboratory for the definition of projects of public interest and impact. They are the institutions of the global commons of know-how, technology and science. The cooperatory is a relatively large complex of exhibition halls, meeting rooms, lobbies, rooms with technical resources, laboratories for trials, tests, workshops for model-making and prototypes, cafés and restaurants. It's the place where 'things happen', a form of modern agora, where groups of citizens, researchers or individual inventors meet to develop their projects and present them to the public. Know-how, academic and practical, is mobilised here in a 'hands-on' and collaborative atmosphere with elected juries from members of universities and professional associations evaluating projects and ideas.

The cooperatory is where public discussions are held, the public utility of developing ideas or practical inventions are discussed in public media and decided upon through democratic institutions. Public resources are allocated via loans and project organisers use the cooperatory on-line and off-line to find cooperators with the appropriate training, sources of materials and so on. Banking will be a public service supplying water or providing education. 'Private business' can be done just as well with loans from a state bank. The cooperatories of various spheres, from the towns upwards, are linked (via Internet, conventions or fairs) across levels and territories to the global sphere to enhance the overall efficiency and progress.

Citizens' general education is acquired at formal schools or more informally at the ABC. Analogous to the ABC, every city of 200,000 inhabitants or more could establish what we call a 'metro foyer' to make the centre more civic, accessible and lively. This relatively large structure, say around 50,000 square metres and up to five floors, might well be constructed in the covered-market style of the nineteenth century. On the ground floor is a big hall connected with the main train station – the gate to global inter-metropolitan exchange, bringing the world into the city-centres and creating an off-line complement to the 'global city' of the Internet. On the upper floors are assembly halls for all kinds of occasions (parties, union activities, non-government organisations and citizens' initiatives), office space and facilities to organise social activities and interventions. Additional space is for cinemas, theatres, media depots, reading rooms and dance floors. Ideally, on the roof are several panoramic restaurants, for socialising and savouring the local cuisine. This metro foyer would be a relaxed meeting place for people from all generations, particularly younger generations making friends and finding partners.

Territories

There would be around 600 world territories, say the size of states in the United States and Mexico, the *régions* in France, provinces, and small countries like Costa Rica, Estonia, Scotland and Belgium. Most territories would be around 50,000 square kilometres, with a population of 10 million and geographically compact so residents can reach any point within 2 hours, which means no time away from home overnight to work.

Territories are a promising medium-size category with a lot of ecological, political and other advantages. Significantly, territories have the potential for ecological integration and national, i.e. political, neutrality (avoiding the development of real global superpowers through size). Giving more physical and political autonomy to territories seems a good way to reduce the impact of greater nations that are dysfunctional. To achieve a balanced global organisation of the commons, we need more evenly matched members, small enough to be dependent on each other, yet large enough to function independently for a certain time (see Figure 13.5). So a global cooperative of territories seems a good role model for such a democratically structured institution.

Planet

A global organisation of the commons must attract legitimacy and foster democracy. Existent organisations like the United Nations and International Monetary Fund are neither very democratic nor considered legitimate because its constituent members include undemocratic states and such institutions are dominated by a few big nations.

We can set up a Planetary Assembly of 600 representatives elected on the basis of the 600 territories which can substitute for organisations such as the Food and Agriculture Organisation. Subcontinental and global cooperation is particularly important for the just attribution of non-local, basic resources and for industrial subsistence. We neither own the resources, which we happen to sit on; nor do we own the air that flows across our territories. For ecological reasons it's best to

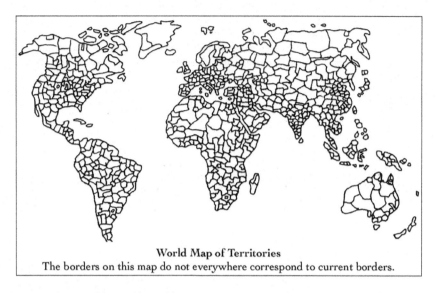

Figure 13.5 A world map of possible territories

leave many resources in the soil or use them on the spot and to share products where they are created.

We need large-scale cooperation so, say, transfers of resources go to emerging or needy existing institutions of the commons, to neighbourhoods, towns and territories. Food subsistence (micro-agro) can be realised almost everywhere. Moreover, a basic package of services and technical equipment must be made accessible for all inhabitants of the planet. This decent infrastructure must be defined in concrete technical, not financial terms. It can be instituted in the form of twinning between the towns in the over-equipped Global North and the towns or territories of the under-equipped Global South. This transfer should be seen as a reparation for colonial exploitation, slavery or more recent robberies like land grabbing and mining.

References

De Angelis, M. (2012) 'Crisis, Capital and Co-optation', in Bollier, D. and Helfrich, S. (eds.) *The Wealth of the Commons*. Amherst: Levellers Press.

Dunbar, R.I.M. (1993) 'Coevolution of neocortical size, group size and language in humans', *Behavioral and Brain Sciences* 16(4): 681–735.

Hopkins, R. (2011) *The Transition Companion, Making Your Community More Resilient in Uncertain Time*. Chelsea: Green Publishing.

Nowak, M. and Highfield, R. (2011) *SuperCooperators: Altruism, Evolution, and Why We Need Each Other to Succeed*. New York: Free Press.

Ostrom, E. (1990) *Governing the Commons: The Evolution of Institutions for Collective Action*. Cambridge/New York: Cambridge University Press.

P.M. (1986) *bolo'bolo: une utopie pour l'an 2000?* Lausanne: éditions d'en bas.

—— (2014) *'The Power of Neighborhood' and the Commons*. Brooklyn: Autonomedia.

Shiva, V. (2008) *Soil Not Oil: Environmental Justice in an Age of Climate Crisis*. Boston: South End Press.

Zolli, A. and Healy, A.M. (2012) *Resilience: Why Things Bounce Back*. London: Simon & Schuster.

14 The quality of small dwellings in a neighbourhood context

Harpa Stefánsdóttir and Jin Xue

Reducing the average size of floor space per capita is important to reduce the environmental impact of the housing sector and to support the densification of urban areas. Notably, residential buildings alone account for around 30 percent of carbon emissions worldwide (Swan and Ugursal 2009). Given that average household size is decreasing – the average household in Europe had 2.3 members in 2015 (Eurostat 2017) – one way to diminish floor area per capita is to build smaller private dwelling units than we now have. Controlling the average size of new dwellings has been proposed as the most effective way towards climate-friendly residential development in the future (Priemus 2005; Xue 2014; Næss and Xue 2016; Vestbro 2012; Aall 2013).

Controlling the average size of new dwellings draws on several arguments. Large dwellings require more construction materials than small ones, more furniture and appliances and more energy for space heating and cooling (Høyer and Holden 2001). Smaller dwellings may play an important role in urban densification, making cities more compact. Newly developed housing often requires clearing natural areas and agricultural land, decreasing erstwhile carbon sequestering areas. The extent of environmental impacts are highly affected by dwelling size and housing type. Compared to compact and smaller types of housing, detached single-family houses mean low-density urban development, contributing to increased traffic and higher proportions of motorised travel (Næss 2012). Internationally, density is considered very important for climate-friendly urban development (Newman and Kenworthy 1999; Jenks et al. 1996; Næss 2001; Jenks and Jones 2010; OECD 2012).

However, implementing a policy of small dwellings is challenging, not the least in relatively wealthy Western communities. Small dwellings are often seen as lacking adequate quality and as a temporary solution, say for young people in the beginning of their housing career. Prestige is regularly connected to greater dwelling sizes and smaller floor areas associated with, for example, less flexibility (Schmidt 2009). The current focus on the quality of small dwellings is mainly related to technical standards, number of rooms and layout (Manum 2005; Guttu 2003). Meanwhile, dwelling quality in terms of characteristics that influence happiness and subjective wellbeing beyond the size of the dwelling has received limited research attention. Moreover, a dwelling's quality in terms of liveability may depend on how it relates to its surroundings and opportunities in the neighbourhood. Urban densification could be better managed with more focus on the quality aspects of dwellings and their surroundings that support perceived living quality. In light of degrowth debates, living in a smaller space should not reduce possibilities for experiencing happiness.

In this chapter, we argue for the importance of approaching aspects of the quality of small dwellings in terms of liveability and broad contextual perspectives. Since there is little earlier research to build on, this study provides a theoretical perspective. Our aim is to identify and describe significant themes and concepts for studying the perception of dwelling quality in terms of liveability. This includes the broad implications smaller dwellings might have in terms of their immediate surroundings and neighbourhood. The concept 'liveability' is suitable in this context, because it combines measures of human needs and subjective wellbeing with opportunities provided by the built environment (Costanza et al. 2007; Mouratidis 2017). In order to identify relevant topics, we searched broad interdisciplinary fields of literature. Our contribution is a conceptual framework for further investigation. As will be shown, perceived dwelling quality involves various physical components of the dwelling and its surrounding, which all have roles in stimulating householders' quality of life and subjective wellbeing.

Topics for the framework: literature review

Themes of importance for the study of perceived dwelling qualities influencing subjective wellbeing of households are introduced in the following sub-sections.

Liveable dwellings

Sustainable development is increasingly linked to concepts of quality of life, subjective wellbeing and liveability (Godschalk 2004) where housing is an essential component. For example, quality of life depends on various aspects of the location of one's home, such as distance to daily destinations.

In degrowth theory, social relationships, environmental quality and health are significant factors impacting on human wellbeing while in neoclassical economy the focus is on the producer–consumer relationship (Andreoni and Galmarini 2014). In degrowth, wellbeing is both determined by the satisfaction of basic human needs (such as access to clean water, food, education and social security) generally quantified in objective indicators and by satisfaction of desires strictly related to individual preferences and largely influenced by subjective evaluation. In degrowth, the values, principles and priorities of the present society are questioned, based on qualitative aspects involving 'life choices' and personal perception of wellbeing (ibid.): living in a small dwelling should not require individual martyrdom or a decrease in subjective wellbeing. Our approach to wellbeing in dwellings and pleasurable opportunities provided by the built environment to increase happiness uses the 'liveability' concept. Wellbeing is a basic end goal in life, therefore liveability can be a powerful tool for urban planning (Veenhoven 2012).

Physical components of the dwelling and its surroundings

The physical components of the dwelling focus on the private dwelling unit, its immediate surroundings, neighbourhood and urban density. The arrangement of these physical components is the task of disciplines working on designing the built environment.

Private dwelling unit

Changes in society and new knowledge about the sustainability of various living habits require reconsideration of which physical components of dwellings are most important. Downsizing a dwelling requires in-depth study of the most significant functions of the dwelling unit and the degree of separation needed between different activities, say requiring separate rooms. In addition, there is a need to identify which activities involve the 'togetherness' of the household and how different functions and activities interact internally as well as with their external surroundings. Such interactions might have different possibilities within different kinds of housing types. This programming is the first stage of the architectural design process of the dwelling and should represent relevant values, goals, facts and facility needs of the household and society (Hershberger 2015).

The minimum housing size standard requirements for the Norwegian State Housing Bank to provide loans was around 55m^2 for a two-room apartment in the years 1992–2005. The municipality of Oslo had a minimum requirement of 40m^2, which was reduced to 35m^2 in 2005 (Schmidt 2009). In this chapter, we refer to small dwellings as a maximum of 55m^2.

Neighbourhood

One way to reduce the average size of new dwellings is by limiting the number of private functions of one dwelling and sharing some with other households – either in the same building, the immediate surrounds of the building or in the neighbourhood. Reducing functions of private dwellings involves thinking of the living environment as a whole system. For future studies, investigation of the usability of the living environment rather than the dwelling as an isolated phenomenon is important. The physical qualities related to the surroundings of the dwellings are often more important to residents than the qualities of the dwelling itself (Steffansen 2012). Some studies have shown that smaller dwellings in compact urban areas compensate by extending living space into shared spaces, such as commercial and public services where carbon emissions thus created can exceed the gain from reducing their private dwelling space (Heinonen et al. 2013). This indicates the importance of investigating the implications that constraining dwelling sizes have for residents' quality of life and for neighbourhood urban planning.

Location

Diversity and distance between the dwelling and various neighbourhood facilities may influence the desired size and functions of the private dwelling. Residents living in central parts of a city usually have shorter distances than those living in suburbs to various facilities – grocery stores, services, restaurants, cafes, cultural services and sporting facilities – that could compensate for a small and simple dwelling. In most cities, the residents of the most central areas have far more job opportunities near home than those living in outer districts (Næss et al. 2017).

Urban density

Urban density or population density is a measure of the number of people inhabiting a given urbanised area – a key policy strategy for accommodating population growth, enhancing community liveability and addressing sustainability by minimising automobile reliance (Howley 2009; Næss 2012). However, many residents view high-density living as an undesirable long-term housing option. Since limiting the average size of new dwellings can contribute to urban densification, perceptions of density are very important for the study of perceived dwelling quality of small dwellings, especially because the same degree of density may be acheived by different housing types. Skyscrapers, for example, do not necessarily lead to higher density than lower and denser housing structures if the spacing between the buildings is large, say, for car parking.

Earlier studies have shown that measures of density and perception of density do not always coincide. It was not high density per se that produced dissatisfaction according to a Dublin study but, rather, related factors such as environmental quality, noise, lack of community involvement, traffic and lack of services and facilities (Howley 2009). Design plays a significant role, the position of the dwelling in the complex, the dwelling's layout and sizes of rooms, in addition to facilities such as sanitation and communal facilities (such as pool and laundry) (Buys and Miller 2012).

Dwelling quality

Factors of importance for the perceived quality of the private dwelling unit and its surroundings include mainly three types – based on functional qualities, atmospheric qualities and qualities associated with social interaction – and might depend on the private dwelling unit or the neighbourhood or relate to interactions between both.

Functional quality

Functional quality refers to the extent to which a building might support internal uses, provide sufficient space arranged efficiently and comprehensibly, be sufficiently flexible and provide spatial and physical conditions to ensure a safe, healthy and pleasant physical environment (Voordt and Wegen 2005).

Definitions of 'quality' have mainly focused on functionality, i.e. dwelling quality mainly related to dwelling sizes, their number of rooms, potential uses and layouts (for Norway, see Manum 2005; Guttu 2003, 2011; Hansen 2007; Schmidt 2009). Requirements for minimum floor area and specific functions to secure functional quality of the life within the dwelling as defined by, for instance, the Norwegian State Housing Bank and building code may have led to increasing sizes of dwellings. A degrowth perspective would argue that basic needs should be satisfied modestly, avoiding luxury.

The prevailing discourses on quality of small dwellings have emphasised spatial efficiency to acquire quality. Worldwide, architects and designers are taking the challenge to design small dwellings for one and two person households that are functional and spatially efficient in terms of flexible uses and, say, employ convertible furniture (Post 2014).

Increased housing costs have led to a greater focus on 'saving by sharing' through cohousing, a housing concept with common spaces and shared facilities (Lietart 2010). Space is saved by needing fewer private rooms than in noncollective living, including a large kitchen, dining area, laundry and outdoor spaces, such as gardens. From this perspective, cohousing fits perfectly well with degrowth theories (see Chapters 4 and 21). From a social interaction perspective, households have potential to cooperate with other inhabitants of the collective. Cohousing as a phenomenon started in Scandinavia about 50 years ago, particularly in Denmark but also numerous projects have been built over the past decades in Sweden and the Netherlands, though fewer in Norway (Vestbro 2012). The idea has spread internationally, with similar ambitions and strong information flows through publications and websites of cohousing networks (Tummers 2015). However, it is probably too farfetched to say that cohousing is a generic solution. Moreover, Tummers (2015) argues that cohousing will only be fully understood by taking into account the planning context.

Functional quality, to fulfil physiological and safety needs, is taken account of by laws and regulations, mainly by instructions involving spatial and physical measurements. However, such measurements do not directly apply to psychological needs even if physical characteristics of the built environment influence how psychological needs can be fulfilled (Gehl 1971). Functional quality is no guarantee that psychological needs are fulfilled in the design of a dwelling and the immediate surroundings. Additionally, building smaller dwellings can diminish functionality, say in terms of flexibility.

Atmospheric quality

Although functional quality can be studied and defined separately, as has been the dominant approach in earlier studies on dwelling quality, aesthetics is an inseparable part of design quality. Aesthetics relate to fulfilling an aspect of psychological needs (see below), including the extent to which a dwelling and its immediate surroundings are perceived as beautiful, stimulating or original, pleasant, cosy, spacious or homely experiences (Voordt and Wegen 2005). Emotional experiences can be associated with, for example, enjoyment and are independent of function (Stefánsdóttir 2014). However, functional quality and aesthetic quality are interrelated, for example, when functional quality permits or enhances aesthetic experiences (Heath 1988). In terms of individual satisfaction, aesthetics is of vital importance to senses of wellbeing (Porteous 1996).

The concept of atmosphere proposed by Böhme (1993), as related to aesthetic quality of the built environment, offers a unique opportunity to examine the complex and often fluid affective relationships between people, things and physical surroundings, without prioritising human intentionality (Daniels 2015). Daniels argues that, by exploring the complex entanglements of ideal and actual atmospheres, we might gain a more comprehensive understanding of intimacy within different cultural contexts. For instance, atmospheric tensions may occur among household members who have contradictory understandings of what it means to 'feel at home' and to be free to do what one wants, with discrepancies between social needs of the family group and desires of its individual members (ibid.).

Quality of social interaction

People have psychological needs for different kinds of contact with other people: seeing other people, listening to or speaking with others and doing things together. People need privacy, to withdraw from others and from external stimulation. The need for contact appears with varying degrees of involvement and social changes occur in, for example, family relations. Dimensions and arrangements of the surrounds and dwelling location physically influence possibilities for contact. Desired privacy is important, such as protection against noise and overlooking (Gehl 1971). Good social interaction between neighbours may create a good atmosphere while the need for privacy limits the minimum size of the dwelling unit.

In England, people who tend to be overrepresented in inner-urban living include youths, particularly males, one-person households and couples with similar socioeconomic status who live there temporarily (Allen and Blandy 2004; Bromley et al. 2007). Although not a universal requirement, ensuring social mix in residential areas can avoid long-term problems of gentrification due to an imbalance in the age and household type of new residents (Seo 2002). City centres should not feature gentrification as the central city might become socially exclusive and demographically limited by being appropriate for young people, but not for families or older residents (ibid.).

Household

The household theme includes issues related to users' perception of dwelling quality and factors influencing interpretation of liveable dwellings.

Needs

It is important to be aware of households' needs as relative and dynamic phenomena influenced by cultural factors. It is important to distinguish between 'needs' and 'wants' (Næss and Xue 2016). Therefore, definitions of household needs should be regularly reconsidered.

The interplay between living environments, physical and social aspects, and experiences, and the behaviour and feelings of residents (Gehl 1971) is of importance to liveability. Needs may be divided into physiological needs (such as sleep or rest, food, hygiene, air, light and sun), safety and psychological needs. The latter include: contact, experience, structuring, identification and aesthetics (ibid.).

Household size and the ages of household members change over time. For some households, the number of household members might change from day to day because of combined families, shared custody of children and mobile workforce participants. For such households, flexibility in dwelling space is beneficial. Cities need to move beyond fixed, old-fashioned ideas of what they think people need (Post 2014).

Perception and interpretation

The way a household member perceives and interprets the quality (or lack thereof) of a dwelling arises from the confrontation between the individual household member, and the physical components of the dwelling and its surrounding environment. This leads to three different perspectives: the individual's perception, the elements of the physical surroundings, and the ways the perceived physical surroundings are interpreted into meanings for the individual perceiver.

How an individual evaluates the quality of the physical components of the dwelling and its immediate surroundings starts with sensual perceptions. The most valuable senses for interpreting and sensing the quality of surroundings are vision, hearing, smelling and touch (Porteous 1996). For this reason, characteristics perceived and interpreted as part of a dwelling's quality include types of light, shapes of rooms, smell from food and sounds from neighbours or garden birds.

Motivational factors, both cultural and individual, influence how perceived information is interpreted into meanings. Individual factors include objectives, attitude and expectations (Stefánsdóttir 2014). Not everyone experiences surroundings the same way because perception is not the passive receipt of sensory signals but shaped by learning, memory and expectations (Goldstein 2007). Perception is influenced by every lived experience, which has a dynamic and fluid background (Dahlberg et al. 2001). Lived experience relates to how perception is influenced by the living conditions of an individual and includes material and immaterial circumstances. Motivational factors, including lived experience, may influence perception of, say, density. A study on the perception of urban atmosphere in Oslo and Stavanger found that some people experience street life in city centres as stimulating while others experience it in a negative way, depending on the persons' past experiences of such environments (Stefánsdóttir 2017).

Stage of life influences how people tend to situate themselves in specific dwelling types (McAuley and Nutty 1982; Smith and Olaru 2013). Households of different types, for example number of members and age, can be expected to have different values and attitudes towards lifestyle in a small dwelling, for example in terms of flexibility. The stage in a household's life cycle, and satisfaction with both the dwelling and the neighbourhood, emerge as significant predictors of intended future mobility patterns (Howley 2009). Howley's study also indicated that individuals who lived in multi-person households were almost twice as likely as respondents living in single-person households to feel like moving in the next five years.

Cultural factors include societal influences and the contextual built environment in which a person lives. City size and different urban contexts can influence motivational factors. Attitude and expectations towards particular quality factors of the dwelling and its surrounding can change with time, as both are in continuous transformation. Stimulation can be shaped by experiences of the urban environment and the attitude towards the importance of certain functional qualities or dwelling size. Mere quantity may lose its meaning once a level of satisfaction is attained. Value, then, turns on the degree of choice offered among accessible resources (Stefánsdóttir 2014).

The conceptual framework

The discussed themes involved in perceived dwelling quality and influencing subjective wellbeing of households are shown in a conceptual framework in Figure 14.1. The conceptual framework includes three main groups of themes that interact internally and dynamically: household needs, perception and interpretation of physical components of the dwelling influence dwelling quality in terms of functional quality, atmospheric quality and quality of social interaction. The physical components of the dwelling include the private dwelling unit, its location and neighbourhood as well as housing density. All groups of themes are important when studying how dwelling quality might influence perceived wellbeing. All the themes, sub-themes and related keywords have been incorporated in Figure 14.1 by combining different factors that constitute perceived wellbeing associated with a dwelling.

Conclusion

The conceptual framework shows that many different physical components may influence perceived dwelling quality in terms of liveability, depending on the motivational factors of the household, individual and culture. Motivational factors are dynamic, changing as both the built environment and society are in constant transformation. It is important to be critical towards household needs and influences on perception of dwelling quality when studying how dwellings may be built smaller to live in for long periods. Dwelling size and other physical functional factors influence this quality, as does the atmosphere created by the design of those factors and the possibilities for social interaction. The last two should be emphasised to greater extent in future research, not least because good atmosphere and desirable social interaction may play important roles in making small dwellings more acceptable.

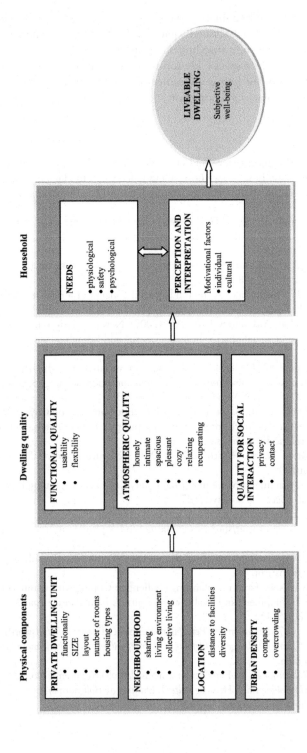

Figure 14.1 A theory of dwelling quality influencing subjective wellbeing

When aiming at building smaller dwellings, more awareness should be put on fulfilling psychological needs. Friendly parks and outdoor space where people can go to when they leave their dwelling, for example, may be important to compensate for lack of indoor spaces. For future studies it is, therefore, important to investigate the uses of the living environment rather than simply the usability of the dwelling as an isolated phenomenon.

References

Aall, C. (2013) 'Why has the level of household energy consumption stopped increasing in Norway – and how can we bring about a decrease', in Hansson, L., Holmberg, U. and Brembeck, H. (eds.) *Making Sense of Consumption*. Göteborg: University of Gothenburg.

Allen, C. and Blandy, S. (2004) *The Future of City Centre Living: Implications for Urban Policy. Final Report*. Centre for Regional Economic and Social Research. Sheffield: Sheffield Hallam University.

Andreoni, V. and Galmarini, S. (2014) 'How to increase well-being in a context of degrowth', *Futures* 55: 78–89.

Böhme, G. (1993) 'Atmosphere as the fundamental concept of a new aesthetics', *Thesis Eleven* 36(1): 113–26.

Bromley, R.D., Tallon, A.R. and Roberts, A.J. (2007) 'New populations in the British city centre: Evidence of social change from the census and household surveys', *Geoforum* 38(1): 138–54.

Buys, L. and Miller, E. (2012) 'Residential satisfaction in inner urban higher-density Brisbane, Australia: Role of dwelling design, neighbourhood and neighbours', *Journal of Environmental Planning and Management* 55(3): 319–38.

Costanza, R., Fisher, B., Ali, S., Beer, C., Bond, L., Boumans, R. and Gayer, D.E. (2007) 'Quality of life: An approach integrating opportunities, human needs, and subjective well-being', *Ecological Economics* 61(2): 267–76.

Dahlberg, K., Drew, N. and Nyström, M. (2001) *Reflective Lifeworld Research*. Lund: Studentlitteratur.

Daniels, I. (2015) 'Feeling at home in contemporary Japan: Space, atmosphere and intimacy', *Emotion, Space and Society* 15: 47–55.

Eurostat. (2017) 'Household composition statistics', *Eurostat Statistics Explained*, August – http://ec.europa.eu/eurostat/statistics-explained/index.php/Household_composition_statistics

Gehl, I. (1971) *Living Environment.* (English summary.) Report 71. Copenhagen: Stat ens Byggesorsknings Institut.

Godschalk, D.R. (2004) 'Land use planning challenges: Coping with conflicts in visions of sustainable development and livable communities', *Journal of the American Planning Association* 70(1): 5–13.

Goldstein, E.B. (2007) *Sensation and Perception*. Belmont: Thomson/Wadsworth.

Guttu, J. (2003) *"Den gode boligen": fagfolks oppfatning av boligkvalitet gjennom 50 år*. Oslo: Arkitekthøgskolen.

——— (2011) *Boligvisjoner: Tti Forbilder for den Sosiale Boligbyggingen*. Oslo: Forlaget Press.

Hansen, T. (2007) *Bolignormer, Helse og Velferd. Drøfting av Bolignormer, Deres Grunnlag og Rolle i Boligpolitikk og Planlegging*. Oslo: SINTEF byggforsk.

Heath, T.F. (1988) 'Behavioral and perceptual aspects of the aesthetics of urban environments', in Nasar, J.L. (ed.) *Environmental Aesthetics: Theory, Research, and Applications*. Cambridge: Cambridge University Press: 6–10.

Heinonen, J., Jalas, M., Juntunen, J.K., Ala-Mantila, S. and Junnila, S. (2013) 'Situated lifestyles: I. How lifestyles change along with the level of urbanization and what the greenhouse gas implications are – a study of Finland', *Environmental Research Letters* 8(2): 025003, 1–13.

Hershberger, R. (2015) *Architectural Programming and Predesign Manager*. London/New York: Routledge.

Howley, P. (2009) 'Attitudes towards compact city living: Towards a greater understanding of residential behaviour', *Land Use Policy* 26(3): 792–8.

Høyer, K.G. and Holden, E. (2001) 'Housing as basis for sustainable consumption', *International Journal of Sustainable Development* 4(3): 48–59.

Jenks, M., Burton, E. and Williams, K. (1996): *The Compact City: A Sustainable Urban Form?* Oxford: Oxford Brookes University and FN Spon (Taylor & Francis Group).

Jenks, M. and Jones, C. (eds.) (2010) *Dimensions of the Sustainable City*. Vol 2. London: SpringerLink, Springer Science + Business Media B.V.

Lietart, M. (2010) 'Cohousing's relevance to degrowth theories', *Journal of Cleaner Production* 18: 576–80.

Manum, B. (2005) 'Generality versus specificity: A study on the interior space of apartments', in *Proceedings of the Fifth International Space Syntax Symposium*. West Lafayette: Purdue University Press.

McAuley, W.J. and Nutty, C.L. (1982) 'Residential preferences and moving behavior: A family life-cycle analysis', *Journal of Marriage and the Family* 44: 301–9.

Mouratidis, K. (2017) 'Rethinking how built environments influence subjective well-being: A new conceptual framework', *Journal of Urbanism: International Research on Placemaking and Urban Sustainability* 11(1): 1–17.

Næss, P. (2001) 'Urban planning and sustainable development', *European Planning Studies* 9(4): 503–24.

—— (2012) 'Urban form and travel behavior: Experience from a Nordic context', *Journal of Transport and Land Use* 5(2): 21–45.

Næss, P. and Xue, J. (2016) 'Housing standards, environmental sustainability and social welfare', in Næss, P. and Price, L. (eds.) *Crisis System: A Critical Realist and Critical Environmental Critique of Contemporary Economics*. London: Routledge.

Næss, P., Strand, A., Wolday, F. and Stefansdottir, H. (2017) 'Residential location, commuting and non-work travel in two urban areas of different size and with different center structures', *Progress in Planning* – https://doi.org/10.1016/j.progress.2017.10.002.

Newman, P.W.G. and Kenworthy, J.R. (1999) *Sustainability and Cities: Overcoming Automobile Dependence*. Washington, DC/Covelo: Island Press.

OECD. (2012) *Compact City Policies: A Comparative Assessment*. OECD Green Growth Studies. Paris: OECD Publishing.

Porteous, J.D. (1996) *Environmental Aesthetics: Ideas, Politics and Planning*. London: Routledge.

Post, R. (2014) 'Are tiny houses and micro-dwellings the future of urban homes?' *The Guardian*, 25 August – www.theguardian.com/sustainable-business/2014/aug/25/tiny-houses-micro-living-urban-cities-population-newyork-hongkong-tokyo

Priemus, H. (2005) 'How to make housing sustainable? The Dutch experience', *Environment and Planning B* 32(1): 5–19.

Schmidt, L. (2009) 'Små boliger – en kunnskapsoversikt', *NIBR-Rapport*: 1.

Seo, J.K. (2002) 'Re-urbanisation in regenerated areas of Manchester and Glasgow: New residents and the problems of sustainability', *Cities* 19(2): 113–21.

Smith, B. and Olaru, D. (2013) 'Lifecycle stages and residential location choice in the presence of latent preference heterogeneity', *Environment and Planning A* 45(10): 2495–514.

Stefánsdóttir, H. (2014) 'A theoretical perspective on how bicycle commuters might experience aesthetic features of urban space', *Journal of Urban Design* 19(4): 496–510.

–––––– (2017) 'The role of urban atmospheres for none work activity locations', *Journal of Urban Design*, pub. online 16 October – https://doi.org/10.1080/13574809.2017.1383150

Steffansen, R.N. (2012) *Dwelling Ideals and Reality*. Masters thesis submitted to Urban Planning and Development, University of Aalborg – http://projekter.aau.dk/projekter/files/63615383/Master_thesis_Dwelling_ideals_and_reality.pdf

Swan, L.G. and Ugursal, V.I. (2009) 'Modeling of end-use energy consumption in the residential sector: A review of modeling techniques', *Renewable and Sustainable Energy Reviews* 13(8): 1819–35.

Tummers, L. (2015) 'Understanding co-housing from a planning perspective: Why and how?' *Urban Research and Practice* 8(1): 64–78.

Veenhoven, R. (2012) 'Happiness: Also known as "Life Satisfaction" and "Subjective Well-being"', in Land, K.C., Michalos, A.C. and Sirgy, J. (eds.) *Handbook of Social Indicators and Quality of Life Research*. Dordrecht: Springer: 63–77.

Vestbro, D.U. (2012) 'Saving by sharing – Collective housing for sustainable lifestyles in the Swedish context', in *Proceedings of the 3rd International Conference on Degrowth for Ecological Sustainability and Social Equity*, Venice, 19–23 September – www.degrowth.info/en/catalogue-entry/saving-by-sharing-collective-housing-for-sustainable-lifestyles-in-the-swedish-context/

Voordt, D.J.M. van der and Wegen, H.B. (2005) *Architecture in Use: An Introduction to the Programming, Design and Evaluation of Buildings*. Amsterdam: Elsevier/Architectural Press.

Xue, J. (2014) 'Sustainable housing development: Decoupling or degrowth? A comparative study of Copenhagen and Hangzhou', *Environment and Planning C* 33: 620–39.

Part VI
Whither urbanisation?

Prefatory note

This part of the collection demonstrates that degrowth is still in an emergent phase with respect to strategic theory. Most advocates and supporters are united on the direction of degrowth as a current critique of growth but diverge on ultimate visions of such post-growth and strategies for achieving it. Therefore, the movement and its discourses embody diversity, even confusion, and strive for clarity. To display this state of the movement and to advance open engagement, we sought two provocative contributions by Jin Xue and Aaron Vansintjan, two respondents, and include our critiques of Xue and Vansintjan. This exercise reveals the inside of the degrowth movement as an open network of activists and scholars engaged in collectively visioning a new world and determining the most appropriate strategies for action. Most significantly, it functions as a discussion starter for those inside and outside of the movement.

Part VI
Whither urbanisation?

15 Housing for degrowth

Space, planning and distribution

Jin Xue

As an overarching societal paradigm, the building of a degrowth future poses various challenges and engages all dimensions of a society. This complexity also applies to housing for degrowth. At an abstract level, housing has social, environmental, financial and cultural aspects. As such, solutions to housing for degrowth entail an interdisciplinary approach and require coordinating the various options in a consistent and systematic way. Insofar as this book covers a broad range of responses, this chapter aims to discuss how urban and regional planning can contribute to housing for degrowth.

Housing has been a long-standing topic in urban planning since its origins. Accounting for a large proportion of built-up areas, housing is an essential element in spatial planning. Variations in dwelling type and size, residential area density, location and housing-related infrastructure affect the environment in different ways and to different extents. Meanwhile, with privatisation and marketisation of the housing sector, the development of housing projects has increasingly raised issues of inequality and injustice. Therefore, how planners deal with residential development impacts significantly on environmental sustainability and social justice.

To fulfil a degrowth future, the goals of housing development need to be reconsidered and current planning strategies revised. This chapter offers a preliminary discussion of such issues by, first, interrogating the goals of urban planning for housing for degrowth based on a normative understanding of sustainable welfare and, second, critically reflecting on three topics relevant to housing development: residential decentralisation, localisation of politics and principles of distributive justice. The discussion is based on the geographical scale of 'urban regions'. This theoretical inquiry is mainly based on the Scandinavian context, where living standards are among the highest in the world. Nevertheless, the discussions are relevant to other affluent, and soon-to-be affluent, countries.

Sustainable welfare, normativity of urban planning and housing for degrowth

Degrowth depicts a desirable future society that is ecologically sustainable, enhances quality of life and achieves social justice (Martinez-Alier et al. 2010;

Schneider et al. 2010). This means achieving social welfare and social justice while shrinking our levels of production and consumption due to the existence of ecological limits. Both research and social practices need to bridge the domains of welfare and environmental sustainability. For urban planners, the integration of both domains raises a question: What is required to make a sustainable city socially just, or, to make welfare societies ecologically sustainable in the urban context?

In attempting to approach this question, Koch and Mont (2016) applied the term 'sustainable welfare' to argue that, from intergenerational and global perspectives, an objective, human needs-based understanding of welfare is essential to meet the external sustainability proviso (Brandstedt and Emmelin 2016). That is to say, certain subjective preferences and wants have to be held in check and we must sacrifice individual welfare (where welfare is explained in subjective accounts as 'preferences'). To what extent needs and wants over and above basic needs can be satisfied within Earth's carrying capacity limits is determined by advances in scientific knowledge and, thus, remains relative (ibid.).

Although theories of human needs differ, having adequate housing is a human basic need (Gough 2014), meaning it is non-negotiable and failure to gratify it will cause serious harm. However, satisfiers of this need vary across cultures and over time. For instance, the need for shelter can be satisfied by compact apartments in high-rise residential buildings prevalent in Asia, or by spacious single-family houses dominant in Scandinavian countries. However, living in spacious houses is more of a want than a basic need. In countries like Denmark and Norway, per capita residential floor area has grown to more than 50 square metres, among the highest in the world. Although the critical threshold for universally meeting the need for housing space is still subject to scientific scrutiny, universalising Nordic housing standards seems implausible environmentally. Degrowth or, at least no further growth, in average floor area per capita in affluent countries is necessary to accomplish the sustainability proviso.

Given the moral imperative to facilitate the satisfaction of basic human needs for everyone (Frankfurt 1984; Koch and Buch-Hansen 2016), facilitating adequate housing for all is a moral necessity recognised as a human right in the United Nations (UN) Human Rights Declaration (UN 1948) with a distributive justice dimension implying that everyone has a right to a minimum standard of housing. By implication, urban regional planning for housing development should contribute to the overarching goal of building a sustainable welfare society. More specific goals include reducing the environmental impacts of housing development, stabilising or degrowing residential floor area per capita, and facilitating the satisfaction of meeting a minimum standard of housing for everyone. Propositions and beliefs relating to housing for degrowth need to be evaluated against these goals in order to determine whether their potential impacts contribute to or hinder degrowth transformation.

The following discussions revolve around three topics: residential decentralisation, localisation of politics and principles of distributive justice. The first two topics relate to the widely accepted belief in localism as a degrowth strategy (Fotopoulos 2007; Latouche 2009; Trainer 2012). In addition, degrowth advocates display a general interest in exploring degrowth prospects in housing projects at the neighbourhood level. However, the neglect of housing development on higher geographical scales may constitute an obstacle to a successful degrowth transformation. Distributive justice and distributive institutions are crucially relevant to degrowth to avoid aggravating existing poverty and severe social conflicts. Justice has been insufficiently discussed in degrowth debates (Muraca 2012).

The rest of this chapter scrutinises the contentious idea of localism, evaluating different principles of distributive justice against aforementioned planning goals for housing development, in terms of whether, and to what extent, various propositions and beliefs contribute to achieving sustainable welfare goals. From the urban planning perspective, these three topics link to three key elements in the planning profession: space, planning process and planning ethics.

Residential decentralisation versus high-density, compact urban and housing development

The argument for localisation as a degrowth strategy is primarily motivated by negative social and environmental impacts of globalisation and neoliberal capitalism. Instead, self-sufficiency in production and consumption using local resources is seen as improving energy efficiency, reducing energy need for transportation, encouraging the use of local renewables and enhancing environmental sensitivity and accountability (Cato 2011; Latouche 2009). Moreover, degrowth advocates believe that embedding human activities in local contexts creates a harmonious relationship between people and nature. The self-sufficiency vision entails a decentralised self-reliant society which is small-scale and ecologically harmonious.

Relying largely on immense quantities of fossil fuels and over-consuming resources to overshoot their ecological footprint, cities are usually regarded as inappropriate to be self-sufficient (Cato 2011). By contrast, decentralised small-scale human settlements tailored to the characteristics and resources of a region, and low-density, spacious residential areas are better able to utilise local resources and realise self-sufficiency (Owen 2012). Mixed land use is often suggested as a planning principle in the development of such habitats. To be optimally self-sufficient, food production and materials for other basic needs, like shelter and cloth, are mainly produced locally or within the community bioregion. Production is decentralised in each local settlement. Some go as far as to argue for the backyard as the main production site (see, for example, Chapter 10). This means creating a relatively sparse and open structure to accommodate farms, market gardens and backyards. The aspiration to self-sufficiency in energy requires spacious and low-density single-family dwellings to capture optimum local renewables, like solar energy.

The environmental performance of decentralised, small-scale, self-contained human settlements partly depends on how such local units are spatially structured internally and linked externally to other units. Since self-sufficiency and re-localisation do not equate to autarky, as some degrowth proponents have argued, exchange of goods and services with neighbouring villages is necessary. For villages to specialise in different trades and exchange products they must be located in different bioregions, which implies that either a village trades with villages further away than neighbouring ones, or villages are scattered to enable them to specialise in different kinds of production. Neither case dramatically reduces transport demand. The smaller the village, the lower the self-sufficiency and the greater requirement for transportation of goods. Furthermore, many services and infrastructure, particularly public facilities, are unlikely due to the small population base. Since most facilities are currently located in traditional urban cores, low-density and scattered distribution of settlements will result in longer travelling distances and higher possibilities of using motorised transport modes.

If we do not dramatically modify the existing urban residential fabric to fit the 'ideal' residential decentralisation, new decentralised small-scale settlements will mean low-density spatial extension of urbanised land. Such developments in and of themselves might decrease the ecological footprint for food production and waste absorption, but the footprint for built-up land will increase, imposing a great threat to biodiversity conservation due to habitat fragmentation for other species (Liu et al. 2003). If the 'ideal' spatial model is universalised globally, it will require large-scale demolition and rebuilding, consuming vast amounts of natural resources.

Countering the assumption that mixed land use and provision of a range of local facilities will lead to less environmentally harmful patterns of localised activity, UK case studies show that residents transgress the limits of local areas (Tait 2003). Factors such as location of employment and other functional destinations, and mobility capability impact on people's activities.

In summary, residential decentralisation promoted by some degrowth proponents does not necessarily reduce the need for energy and material consumption and, undoubtedly, will increase the conversion of natural land into built-up areas. So, what is the ideal spatial residential form for a degrowth vision according to planning studies? The most commonly suggested and adopted instrument for the purpose of reducing energy consumption from housing and housing-related transport is a concentrated urban developmental pattern, a 'compact city' (Newman and Kenworthy 1999; Stead and Marshall 2001; Næss 2012). Compared to decentralised, low-density habitats, a dense urban structure is particularly advantageous in protecting agricultural land, natural landscapes and biodiversity, because less land is required for building and encroachments on natural landscapes and farmland are reduced. Concentrated buildings, such as apartments and row houses, are required in a compact city, indicating high energy-efficiency and low absolute energy consumption by the housing sector. While decentralised, small-scale human settlement provides very limited freedom to make individual choices, compact cities allow and facilitate certain levels of freedom of choice while reducing consumption levels and environmental impacts. Since high-density urban development means compact residential buildings, it will contribute to stabilising and even reducing residential floor area per capita.

Localisation of politics versus centralisation and planning

In terms of planning, the call for political re-localisation implies that planning power and process should be decentralised to the level of many small communities. Decisions on issues such as land use, dwelling types and infrastructure provision will be made by local citizens using public participation and communication. The assumption is that political decentralisation and localisation will lead to the achievement of a degrowth society that is democratic, just and sustainable. In this section I argue that such an assumption is untenable; there is no logical necessity between localism and these degrowth goals.

According to Maston (2000), scale is socially constructed; scale is not fixed but continuously remade through social actions, so outcomes of any scalar strategy are contingent on who are empowered and their agendas (Brenner 2001; Delaney and Leitner 1997). Localising control over space through direct decision-making by citizens has no a priori consequence, whether greater democracy or other degrowth goals (Purcell 2006). The tendency to equate devolution of authority to local-scale with greater democracy and other goals is framed by Purcell (2006, 1924) as a 'local trap', which 'assumes something inherent about the local scale'.

In degrowth debates, emphasis on political decentralisation is partly grounded on the belief that it can make decision-making process more democratic and a general tendency to advocate for a more direct form of democracy than representative democracy (Asara et al. 2013; Fotopoulos 2007; Ott 2012). Direct democracy implies greater citizenry participation, communication and deliberation so empowered residents have more influence and control in their neighbourhoods. Apparently, there is more potential and convenience in local-scale than in larger-scale communities exercising direct democracy.

In the planning profession, these arguments resonate with the turn to 'collaborative planning', which gained in theoretical popularity from the 1990s (Allmendinger 2002/2009). Collaborative planning emphasises the process of planning characterised by collective communication involving diverse communities and public participation (Forester 1989; Healey 1992, 1997/2006). Instead of specifying the goal of a plan, supporters of collaborative planning claim that purposes, options and actions should be decided in collective processes of communicative practices and inter-subjective understanding (Healey 1992; Innes 1996). Despite the claimed merits of decentralising planning power by deliberation, serious scepticism arises when applied to housing for degrowth goals.

Decision-making based on communicative rationality has an exclusive focus on planning processes and leaves open the outcome of the communication process (Healey 1992). Various outcomes might be generated depending, say, on who are empowered and the conditions of negotiation. There is no guarantee that these outcomes will lead to the normative project of a transition to degrowth. For example, a group of citizens might collectively decide to build spacious single-family houses violating the goal of reducing residential floor area per capita.

To ensure a minimum standard of housing for everyone requires a fair distribution beyond the local level. In particular, a simple lifestyle and reducing residential floor area do not reflect prevailing lifestyles in affluent countries. Unless there is strong environmental awareness and altruism, locals are unlikely to propose a plan against currently displayed preferences. Locals would also need some expertise on spatial solutions to sustainable urban and housing development. Urban planners' expert knowledge based on scientific knowledge of relationships between goals and means is very necessary and important (Næss 2001). In addition, the 'democratic dilemma' means that the capacity for making universal decisions decreases as the political unit is downscaled (Latouche 2009), hindering local citizens from decision-making beyond their territorial limit. For housing development, this applies to issues like residential location, and transport infrastructure at urban and regional scales. Planning for these issues needs coordination between sectors at municipal and regional levels.

Discussion of the limitations of localisation and deliberation does not necessarily deny the importance of this strategy but, rather, the fallacy of resorting to an exclusive scale and democratic form to achieve degrowth. Purcell (2006) has argued that specific goals should be distinguished from scalar strategies used to pursue them. I consider that different scalar strategies and planning styles should be combined and selected according to the issues in question. In the context of planning housing development for degrowth, some centralisation of planning power in a hierarchical form is necessary and even crucial because degrowth is a normative project with clearly articulated goals, such as reducing housing consumption per capita and safeguarding a minimum housing standard for everyone.

An overarching and centralised planning power can bring elements of a substantive agenda, such as goals and strategies, that are indispensable for realising housing for degrowth. To reduce our levels of housing consumption, setting a maximum size limit for new dwellings and forbidding the construction of single-family houses is necessary (Næss and Xue 2016). These higher-order constraints function as counteracting forces to the likely overconsumption of housing by local regimes. Apart from setting a maximum limit, setting a minimum size of new dwellings by a higher planning authority is necessary to safeguard universal satisfaction of the basic need for housing. Moreover, a higher level of territorial planning organisation can function as a distributive body, ensuring a fair distribution of housing among citizens.

Another argument in support of some centralisation of planning power is that decentralised communities can be easily co-opted by neoliberal politics and be utilised by vested interests for the pursuit of local economic growth (Harvey 2012). Due to power inequality and unequal esteem between capital and citizens, the communicative planning process and outcome might be dominated by market interests with a hegemonic social position and, even unintentionally, serve the interests of capital. Moreover, localisation and deliberation can be used to justify neoliberal urban polices due to their seemingly inclusionary processes of democracy.

In summary, localism and deliberation alone do not offer good ways to fulfil sustainable welfare goals in the field of housing development. Degrowth should be pursued at multiple scales; local participation and deliberation should be incorporated and combined with centralisation and hierarchical forms of planning. Only at national and urban levels can maximum and minimum housing standards be determined to, say, stabilise or reduce per capita residential floor areas, or to effectively safeguard a fair distribution of housing. Therefore, democratic decision-making at the local level can be made compatible with environmental limits. I advocate participant diversity, democratic discussion and transparency, which not only increase the legitimacy of planning and applicability of goal-directed planning strategies, but also facilitate satisfying the basic need for housing. In deliberative planning, planners can advocate for the disadvantaged and interject their demands into participatory planning processes (Rankin 2012).

Principles of distributive justice in the context of housing for degrowth

Distributive justice concerns moral guidance on how benefits and burdens are distributed in societies. Theories of distributive justice vary with respect to what is distributed and patterns of distribution. In this section, I briefly scrutinise the limits and potential of different principles of distributive justice – derived from the *Stanford Encyclopedia of Philosophy* by Lamont and Favor (2017) – with respect to the goals of realising sustainable welfare in housing for degrowth.

A relatively simple and straightforward principle of distributive justice is strict egalitarianism, which calls for allocating equal material goods to all members of society, justified on the grounds that people are morally equal. Although strict egalitarianism neglects environmental limits, it is not conditioned on perpetual economic growth. It is 'neutral' in applicability to both growth and degrowth paradigms. In the context of housing for degrowth, lessening inequality in per capita floor area in situations of non-growth or degrowth would mean reallocating floor areas from residents with high housing standards to those living in substandard conditions. This reallocation would realise the welfare right to a minimum housing size. However, even though I think reducing inequality would be beneficial for social solidarity and the mental and physiological wellbeing of citizens, completely eliminating inequality (as suggested by strict egalitarianism) seems to leave no room for people to make free choices. No doubt a degrowth society would constrain freedom of choice and individualistic behaviours in varying degrees. For instance, conspicuous consumption of positional goods would be limited; living in luxury, spacious houses and owning more than one home should be forbidden. However, some may like to live in a bigger dwelling while forgoing other material goods. Allowing some level of 'inequality' would make a degree of individual choice possible. However, the level of inequality should not endanger the welfare right of the most poorly situated to a decent living standard while the average floor area per capita should not breach environmental limits.

The most widely debated theory of distributive justice is proposed by John Rawls (1971). His Difference Principle permits diverging from strict equality on the condition that such inequalities bring greater benefits to the least advantaged in society than under strict equality. The economic view inspiring this principle is that wealth is most readily increased in systems where the more productive earn greater incomes (Lamont and Favor 2017) and overall growth will benefit the worst-off more than any equal distribution. This principle has been adopted by the World Bank: the economy of rich countries should continue to grow as rapidly as possible to provide markets for the poor and to accumulate capital to invest in poor countries (Daly 2008). While Rawls's primary focus is enhancing the absolute position of the poor, his approach resorts to growth and violates the goal of environmental sustainability. Moreover, the Rawlsian principle of distribution depicts the dominant distributive pattern in contemporary welfare societies based on a growing economy as one where everyone benefits. In fact, while 'trickle down' from growth has enhanced the absolute conditions of the poor, it has benefited the rich considerably more, therefore, increasing inequality.

The welfare-based principle guides distributive justice via utilitarianism, where justice is based on 'the greatest good of the greatest number', suggesting that the majority of entitlements should benefit the majority of people. This distributive pattern ignores how welfare is distributed among individuals and, thus, the welfare of certain groups can be sacrificed to the benefit of others, as long as total satisfaction increases. Providing housing as luxury and spacious dwellings unaffordable to poor households would be just provided that the utility and benefits arising from satisfying the rich exceed the losses and suffering of the poor. The utilitarian principle of distributive justice cannot safeguard the satisfaction of the basic need for housing for everyone. Although enhancing welfare by satisfying preferences cannot be equated with supplying increased material goods (Brandstedt and Emmelin 2016), in reality increased purchasing power and growth in consumption resulting from economic growth are often seen to fulfil the majority of private preferences (Sen 1993). Thus, the application of utilitarian distributive justice implies perpetual economic growth, in conflict with the goal of downscaling consumption levels.

The libertarian distributive principle does not propose a pattern of distribution but advocates believe that just outcomes will arise if exchanges permitted in the market satisfy the conditions of just acquisition and exchange. According to the best known version of libertarianism, Robert Nozick's Entitlement Theory, if a person justly acquires some part of the material world – say, neither through fraud nor stealing – then they gain the permanent exclusive property right over it. Nozick (1974) argues that exclusive acquisition is justified because the initial acquisition does not worsen the position of others to use the resources (an argument also known as a weaker version of Lockean Proviso). According to the libertarian principle, if a person inherits several luxury spacious dwellings, they are entitled to own and use them as they wish. Likewise, if a poor person cannot afford to buy or even rent a dwelling through the market, they have to endure homelessness or substandard conditions.

Therefore, implementing libertarian distributive principles potentially leads to huge housing inequality and some people's basic needs may not be fulfilled. An initially just acquisition does not mean that its use later will not make other people worse off. In a finite world where population increases, fewer resources are available for each person and exclusive use of several dwellings by an individual who acquired them in a just way means less resources available for others. Libertarian distributive principle theory fails to take account of environmental constraints.

In summary, none of the major theories of distributive justice meet the challenges of environmental sustainability and welfare rights simultaneously. If no growth in housing consumption per capita is allowed due to the existence of environmental constraints, to safeguard the welfare right for housing for all would only mean redistribution from those who have high levels of housing consumption per capita to those whose consumption levels are lower. Policies should focus on disadvantaged people in poor living conditions. Rawls's focus on improving the worst-off is relevant but, instead of resorting to economic growth to realise such improvements, more direct redistributive policies targeting the most poorly situated should be pursued. Within this framework, certain degrees of inequality should be considered acceptable in order for people to choose the levels of housing consumption according to their preferences.

Conclusion

Housing for degrowth embraces both dimensions of environmental sustainability and welfare rights. To make housing development compatible with the sustainability proviso, a concept of welfare based on needs was put forward to stabilise or even degrow per capita housing consumption. As a basic need, the satisfaction of housing to a minimum standard is a human welfare right. Using these criteria, this chapter discussed to what extent the localism advocated by some degrowth proponents might not achieve housing for degrowth.

Residential decentralisation can lead to various social and environmental consequences contradicting the goals of housing for degrowth. Localising and decentralising decision-making in the planning process might not lead to just and sustainable housing developments. Instead, multi-scalar strategies and combinations of centralised planning powers with local democratic public participation in planning would effectively allow pursuit of degrowth goals. Furthermore, I scrutinised the limitations and potentials of different theories of distributive justice in fulfilling both sustainability and welfare goals, suggesting that policies focusing on redistribution from rich to poor and directly targeting the disadvantaged was necessary if both sustainability and welfare are to be safeguarded.

References

Allmendinger, P. (2002/2009) *Planning Theory*. Hampshire: Palgrave Macmillan.
Asara, V., Profumi, E. and Kallis, G. (2013) 'Degrowth, democracy and autonomy', *Environmental Values* 22: 217–39.
Brandstedt, E. and Emmelin, M. (2016) 'The concept of sustainable welfare', in Koch, M. and Mont, O. (eds.) *Sustainability and the Political Economy of Welfare*. Oxon/New York: Routledge: 15–28.
Brenner, N. (2001) 'The limits to scale? Methodological reflections on scalar structuration', *Progress in Human Geography* 25: 591–614.
Cato, M.S. (2011) 'Home economics: Planting the seeds of a research agenda for the bioregional economy', *Environmental Values* 20: 481–501.
Daly, H.E. (2008) *A Steady-State Economy: A Failed Growth Economy and a Steady-State Economy Are Not the Same Thing; They Are the Very Different Alternatives We Face*, Report to Sustainable Development Commission – http://www.sd-commission.org.uk/publications.php@id=775.html
Delaney, D. and Leitner, H. (1997) 'The political construction of scale', *Political Geography* 16: 93–7.
Forester, J. (1989) *Planning in the Face of Power*. Berkeley: University of California Press.
Fotopoulos, T. (2007) 'Is degrowth compatible with a market economy?' *The International Journal of Inclusive Democracy* 3(1) – www.inclusivedemocracy.org/journal/vol3/vol3_no1_Takis_degrowth.htm
Frankfurt, H.G. (1984) 'Necessity and desire', *Philosophy and Phenomenological Research* 45: 1–13.
Gough, I. (2014) *Lists and Thresholds: Comparing Our Theory of Human Need with Nussbaum's Capabilities Approach*. Cambridge: Cambridge University Press.
Harvey, D. (2012) *Rebel Cities: From the Right to the City to the Urban Revolution*. London: Verso.
Healey, P. (1992) 'Planning through debate: The communicative turn in planning theory', *Town Planning Review* 63: 143–62.
―――― (1997/2006) *Collaborative planning, Shaping Places in Fragmented Societies*. Second edition. London: Palgrave Macmillan.
Innes, J.E. (1996) 'Planning through consensus building: A new view of the comprehensive planning ideal', *Journal of American Planning Association* 62: 460–72.
Koch, M. and Buch-Hansen, H. (2016) 'Human needs, steady-state economics and sustainable welfare', in Koch, M. and Mont, O. (eds.) *Sustainability and the Political Economy of Welfare*. Oxon/New York: Routledge: 29–43.
Koch, M. and Mont, O. (eds.) (2016) *Sustainability and the Political Economy of Welfare*. Oxon/New York: Routledge.
Lamont, J. and Favor, C. (2017 Winter) 'Distributive Justice', *The Stanford Encyclopedia of Philosophy* (online) – https://plato.stanford.edu/archives/win2017/entries/justice-distributive/
Latouche, S. (2009) *Farewell to Growth*. Cambridge: Polity Press.
Liu, J., Daily, G.C., Ehrlich, P.R. and Luck, G.W. (2003) 'Effects of household dynamics on resource consumption and biodiversity', *Nature* 421: 530–3.
Martinez-Alier, J., Pascual, U., Vivien, F. and Zaccai, E. (2010) 'Sustainable de-growth: Mapping the context, criticisms and future prospects of an emergent paradigm', *Ecological Economics* 69: 1741–7.
Maston, S.A. (2000) 'The social construction of scale', *Progress in Human Geography* 24: 219–42.

Muraca, B. (2012) 'Towards a fair degrowth-society: Justice and the right to a "good life" beyond growth', *Futures* 44: 535–45.

Næss, P. (2001) 'Urban planning and sustainable development', *European Planning Studies* 9: 503–24.

––––––– (2012) 'Urban form and travel behavior: Experience from a Nordic context', *Journal of Transport and Land Use* 5: 21–45.

Næss, P. and Xue, J. (2016) 'Housing standards, environmental sustainability and social welfare', in Næss, P. and Price, L. (eds.) *Crisis System: A Critical Realist and Critical Environmental Critique of Contemporary Economics*. London: Routledge: 130–48.

Newman, P.W.G. and Kenworthy, J.R. (1999) *Sustainability and Cities: Overcoming Automobile Dependence*. Washington, DC: Island Press.

Nozick, R. (1974) *Anarchy, State, and Utopia*. New York: Basic Books.

Ott, K. (2012) 'Variants of de-growth and deliberative democracy: A Habermasian proposal', *Futures* 44: 571–81.

Owen, D. (2012) *The Conundrum: How Trying to Save the Planet Is Making Our Climate Problems Worse*. London: Short Books.

Purcell, M. (2006) 'Urban democracy and the local trap', *Urban Studies* 43: 1921–41.

Rankin, K.N. (2012) 'The praxis of planning and the contributions of critical development studies', in Brenner, N., Marcuse, P. and Mayer, M. (eds.) *Cities for People, not for Profit: Critical Urban Theory and the Right to the City*. Oxon: Routledge: 102–16.

Rawls, J. (1971) *A Theory of Justice*. Cambridge: Belknap Press of Harvard University Press.

Schneider, F., Kallis, G. and Martinez-Alier, J. (2010) 'Crisis or opportunity? Economic degrowth for social equity and ecological sustainability. Introduction to this special issue', *Journal of Cleaner Production* 18: 511–18.

Sen, A. (1993) 'Markets and freedoms: Achievements and limitations of the market mechanism in promoting individual freedoms', *Oxford Economic Papers* New Series 45: 519–41.

Stead, D. and Marshall, S. (2001) 'The relationships between urban form and travel patterns: An international review and evaluation', *European Journal of Transport and Infrastructure Research* 1: 113–41.

Tait, M. (2003) 'Urban villages as self-sufficient, integrated communities: A case study in London's Docklands', *Urban Design International* 8: 37–52.

Trainer, T. (2012) 'De-growth: Do you realize what it means?' *Futures* 44: 590–9.

UN. (1948) *The Universal Declaration of Human Rights*. Paris: United Nations.

16 Urbanisation as the death of politics
Sketches of degrowth municipalism

Aaron Vansintjan

Degrowth is both an ideological strike against unquestioned faith in economic growth, and a concrete demand to scale down society's metabolism, to transition to an economic system that is both more just and less materially and energetically intensive. In this respect, it has been conceived of as a response to the limits of a highly extractive system that breaches planetary boundaries (Rockstrom et al. 2009; Schneider et al. 2011). Much of the literature resuscitates the language of the neo-Malthusians of the 1970s, who argued that a growth-based economy could not be sustainable and would eventually face collapse (Meadows et al. 1972). To avoid this, many advocate relocalising the economy and decentralising political power (Latouche 2009; Trainer 2012).

For others, though, degrowth represents an insufficiently radical and apolitical environmentalism. Marxists have challenged the degrowth movement to engage with the problems of labour and capital (Brownhill et al. 2012; Barca forthcoming), while critical theorists have pointed to the role of 'limits to growth' discourse in furthering the neoliberal narrative (Nelson 2014). Talk about 'limits' can fall into the trap of population biologists, who focus on demographic drivers rather than political economic dynamics to explain today's environmental crises, leading many to pursue development programmes that amount to eugenics of the poor and lifeboat ethics (Commoner 1972; Angus and Butler 2011). Further, localist and back-to-the-land proposals have a history of parochial views on immigration and ethnicity, and there have been documented instances of a 'fascist creep' in communities promoting bioregionalism and localism (Park 2013; Ross 2017).

Some also see degrowth as a primitivist flight from modernity. For example, 'accelerationists' reject the 'small is beautiful' ethos and localism associated with environmentalism, arguing that it is precisely at this point that we have to embrace technological innovation and the possibility of material abundance and luxury (Merchant 2015; Srnicek and Williams 2015). Calling for a renewal of utopian ideas, these thinkers argue that the environmentalist's call for limits shuts down political possibilities. To demand limits at this moment is to miss our chance for a new politics of abundance.

To overcome simplistic Malthusianism, degrowth scholars such as D'Alisa et al. (2014) and Kallis (2016) have argued that degrowth is not about imposing apolitical limits on society, but creating a political space to set limits collectively. It is about firing a missile into the ideology of growth (Ariès 2005) and making room for different visions of progress (Escobar 2011; Acosta 2013; Kothari 2016). Furthermore, some advocate 'open localism' to distinguish degrowth localism from eco-fascist proposals (Schneider and Sekulova 2014). However, there has been little discussion of what 'setting limits collectively' would look like at a municipal level. Does the call for the reduction of energetic and material throughput necessarily mean that human settlements must be forced to live in scarcity? Is degrowth only possible through a mass demographic shift away from cities toward the countryside? Yet, as a democratic and liberatory movement, wouldn't degrowth require lifting limits on urban life, making municipalities vibrant and liberatory?

This essay is an attempt to stir up and encourage debates on limits, scarcity and abundance in the city. Relying largely on the work of Murray Bookchin (1992), I argue that the process of urbanisation imposes 'scarcity' (i.e. people's inability to use their milieu to generate resources) by hampering vibrant, organic, political engagement. The answer, however, is not to move everyone to the country. While rural life is historically marked by parochialism, cities are characterised by openness to difference and the possibility of vibrant politics. Degrowth municipalism, understood here as the politicisation and downscaling of municipalities' social metabolism necessary to achieve a more just society, will require the creation of an organic citizenship or the citification of urban space.

To make my case, I start by relating personal experiences of London (England) and Hanoi (Vietnam), illustrating how scarcity and abundance play out in urban lives. Then, following Bookchin, I suggest a distinction between 'the city' and 'the urban'. While urbanisation relies on imposed and regulated scarcity, it also floods the world with synthetic abundance. A degrowth municipality, properly understood, would be oriented toward openness, collective sufficiency and organic abundance, i.e. the multiplication of relationships required to develop a robust democratic system. This, I argue, is different from proposals such as the 'ecovillage' or 'urban village', which do not adequately take into account scale and a politics of difference. As we are being faced with the deployment of urban space globally and drawn into an interconnected 'mesh' of power and material flows (Merrifield 2013), the creation of a political sphere becomes ever more critical. Therefore, the main challenge for degrowth-oriented municipalism is neither to impose more rules and limits on urban residents in the name of sustainability and efficiency (the technocratic, authoritarian solution), nor to bring about a demographic shift to the countryside (the localist solution). Rather, the primary challenge is to institutionalise and cultivate an active, organic, political life.

Scarcity in London

In August 2015, I moved to a council estate in Bethnal Green, London. My flatmate and I decided that we would like to compost our food waste. But the more we looked into it, the more impossible it seemed. Our borough didn't have a municipal composting system. When we learnt that the next borough did,

I started stealthily dropping off our compost there only to notice that their compost container was mostly used as a trash bin and, even after several months, had never been collected.

Our redbrick council building was home to 40 households, surrounded by a lawn cordoned off by an impassable fence. 'Can't I just put a big bucket on the lawn, hidden under a bush?' I asked my flatmate. 'The groundskeeper will see it', he responded. We could get into trouble with the council, it might start smelling, or our neighbours might use it as a trash bin.

I continued to eye the big lawn (circa 250 square metres). Even if everyone in the building composted, we'd take up maybe 5 square metres of the lawn, less space than a car or those poorly pruned rose bushes. I imagined building a big compost unit at night, then hosting workshops for residents on how to use it to nourish the rose bushes. One day we'd tear down the fences around the lawn, kids would play ball games without scraping their knees on the pavement, we'd plant runner beans up the south-facing wall, we'd graft edible apples onto the crab-apple tree and turn the parking space into a terrace, where we'd trade baked goods and recipes.

But, in reality, I knew my flatmate was right: there were too many rules and regulations. It was absurd not to be able to find a tiny spot for compost in a vast expanse of open space. This, to me, symbolised our inability to participate in our immediate surroundings. Urban life is marked by scarcity. That scarcity isn't natural, it is actively imposed on us; layers of rules and regulations prevent us from taking advantage of the abundance of the earth around us.

Abundance in Hanoi

Gardening in public is ubiquitous in Hanoi, where I lived for six months in 2016. Every inch of land is productive. Even in wealthier areas, residents put large planters on the sidewalk and take over public parks. People freely modify, rearrange and transform the urban environment. A short walk away from my apartment, a public lake had been drained. Within days, nearby residents started ploughing the bed of the lake, planting seeds and setting up their garden plots. Gardeners grew vegetables for their family, but most also shared produce with neighbours.

While this activity resulted in monetary benefits to disadvantaged people – rural migrants relied on street vending to send money back to their families – it also vitalised dynamic networks and connections, bringing residents together and establishing strong community ties. As urbanisation envelops the countryside, people recreate village life by practising gift economies and participating in public life. It is barely possible in authoritarian Vietnam to organise political groups; these community ties and broader networks provide a much-needed social safety net when times are tough which, in turn, empowers residents to resist development projects that would push them off their land (Wells-Dang 2010; Labbé 2014).

Vietnamese urbanites take up public space to garden, sell street food, exercise, play, dine, drink tea and hang out. Even as these activities are eroding – the state is trying to criminalise street vending by imposing regulations on the use of public space – a certain spirit of abundance remains. The ubiquity of street vending and urban agriculture multiplies day-to-day interactions and helps develop support networks. As local officials look away, people use their milieu to create resources seemingly out of thin air, and the public becomes political.

The city as an ecocommunity

'The city at its best is an ecocommunity'. This is the first line of Bookchin's *Urbanization without Cities: The Rise and Decline of Citizenship*. The book can be read as a history of cities, complementing Bookchin's other work, such as *The Ecology of Freedom* and *Post-Scarcity Anarchism*. It advances a wider framework of radical municipalism or what Bookchin calls 'communalism': a politics that, in the wake of a collapse of labour organising and the neoliberal counter-revolution, places importance on citizens' movements that go beyond class and race boundaries and advocates the strategic importance of democratic and place-based control over municipalities. The book's major theme is a theoretical distinction between the 'urban' and 'the city', typologies of human settlement whose evolution and transformation Bookchin traces throughout history. Here, I first define 'the city' and 'the urban'. Second, I distinguish between what Bookchin calls an 'ecocommunity' and more localist proposals like ecovillages, urban villages and bioregionalism.

For Bookchin, the city is a unique place, coinciding with the birthplace of a politics of difference. Following Aristotle, Hannah Arendt and Jurgen Habermas, Bookchin is a firm believer in the 'political', the sphere wherein people manage collective concerns *across* differences. Bookchin explains how the rise of the city corresponded to the creation of spaces where 'insiders' and 'outsiders' met and decided their affairs together, spaces where citizenship was a constantly reworked, dynamic and organic process. In this way, at best, political decision-making in cities was independent of ties of kinship or ethnicity. Accordingly, 'the city' is a type of settlement where 'people advance beyond the kinship bond to share, create, and develop the means for life, culturally as well as economically, as human beings' (Bookchin 1992, 173).

The concept of 'organic' citizenship helps Bookchin explain how he views the 'political': an 'inorganic' being is an outsider unable to participate in decision-making; an 'organic' being is able to engage in the active political life of the community. The biological connotation is not accidental; for Bookchin, political life looks a lot like an ecosystem – diverse, 'biotic' and shifting.

Bookchin focuses on the nature of politics in ancient Athens, which saw the development of a unique political system based on democratic decision-making. Of course, the Athenian *polis* depended on hierarchies and exclusions, where neither women nor slaves were able to participate in democracy. Nevertheless, the ideal of the city became crystallised as an intentional, bottom-up *and* top-down institutionalisation of democracy.

As an example, Bookchin (ibid., 61) details life around the agora, where vendors and citizens would constantly interact:

> In its emphasis on direct, almost protoplasmic contact, full participatory involvement and its dealing in variety and diversity, there is a sense in which the agora formed the space for a genuine ecological community within the polis itself. Thus politics, which found its most ordered and institutionalized expression in the ekklesia [the citizens' assembly], originated in the daily ferment of ordinary life in the agora.

Reading this reminded me of the informal markets in Hanoi's back alleys and public squares. There, local residents and migrant workers sold wares, each with their own relationships to the food they sold and their regular customers. The phrase 'daily ferment of ordinary life' is especially appropriate here: vendors would often ferment day-old vegetables in jars, popular and important in Vietnamese cuisine. The diversity of goods and relationships was breathtaking – essential for those looking for a room to rent and vital when development projects threatened people's livelihoods. We can only speculate what 'daily ferments' appeared at the agora in Athens; nevertheless, Bookchin's insight that politics is intrinsically tied to the dynamic use of public space is astute and fecund.

Thus, for Bookchin, the realm of politics is not just in meeting rooms, assemblies or parliament but also in the market square, face-to-face interactions, meetings of strangers in public space, through food making, in feasts and cultural celebrations. Keeping in mind the exclusions of the ancient *polis*, this view makes space for feminist, decolonial and Indigenous politics beyond the workplace, the street or city hall (Federici 2012; Zibechi 2012; Simpson 2014).

Moreover, Bookchin (1992, 247) carefully distinguishes between what he calls 'administration', such as planning infrastructure and building roads, and 'policy':

> To debate and decide the need for a road, including the choice of its site and the suitability of its design, is a political process. If the distinction between policy making and administration is kept clearly in mind, the role of popular assemblies and the people who administer their decisions easily unscrambles logistical problems from political ones.

This distinction leaves room for the need for administrative questions to be addressed, while acknowledging that these decisions often become subservient to techno-managerial and bureaucratic institutions and, eventually, can be used as excuses to deaden the use of public space, as in Hanoi's regulation and criminalisation of open markets.

The Athenian polis was also characterised by its non-local, scaled, political institutions. Allied in a confederation with neighbouring city-states, Athenian democracy defended itself from outside aggressors, learnt from its allies, developed a robust system of economic exchange and spread democratic practices beyond its own city walls. Municipalism is not decentralised localism; it is only possible at scale, extending beyond the individual municipality to form a network of autonomous, but collaborative, settlements.

Another feature of the polis is that it is characterised by a political appreciation of limits – here we start to see what is meant by 'ecocommunity'. Bookchin (1992, 36–7) refers to Aristotle (1932), noting that he 'derides the view that a community's greatness is to be judged by its demographic and territorial size'. For Aristotle (1932, 1326a30–40), 'beauty' accorded with a 'due magnitude . . . as there is for all things' and 'the best limiting principle for a polis is the largest expansion of the population with a view to self-sufficiency that can be taken in at one view'. For Bookchin, Aristotle's argumentation for human scale was not on the 'logistical, demographic, and aesthetic' grounds commonly used by urban planners today, but rather 'on ethical, indeed metaphysical, grounds'. Bookchin (1992, 251) points out that citizenship requires some limits, namely 'a humanly scaled, comprehensible, and institutionally accessible municipality'. Here one may note the similarities with Castoriadis (1999, 2005) who has similar views on 'autonomy' and 'self-limitation' as a political pursuit, also inspired by Aristotle (see Asara et al. 2013).

As such, an 'ecocommunity' or ecological city doesn't necessarily confine itself to localism of the sort in contemporary fads like the '100-mile diet' but, rather, may conceivably engage in trade with far-off allies. An ecological city, a city of 'human scale', is primarily characterised by democratic political control over its own economic activities. Perhaps counter-intuitively, this self-rule cannot be based on an economy of scarcity. The self-limitation Bookchin (1992, 276) advocates depends on *multiplying* relationships of exchange; a robust political sphere requires free exchange of materials:

> the direct sale of locally grown food from farmer to consumer . . . more barter, comprehensive mutual aid networks, and the use of public land to foster domestic gardening – these are only some of the many possible projects that could give tangibility to a moral economy.

Significantly, this vibrant fusion between politics and economy does not mean a refusal of technology and tools but ensures the political means to control technology, deliberate its relative benefits and capture its liberatory potential. Thus, Bookchin (1971, 13) describes the condition of 'post-scarcity' as 'the fulfilment of the social and cultural potentialities latent in a technology of abundance'. For Bookchin, capitalism 'destroys the capacity for abundance' by imposing a cash nexus, where all interactions are subordinated to monetary exchange and survival outside the monetary sphere is impossible. Modern-day technologies produce unprecedented stuff and 'furnish the state with historically unprecedented means for manipulating and mobilising the entire environment of life – and for perpetuating hierarchy, exploitation and unfreedom' (ibid., 57). Thus, one can distinguish between a system of organic, democratic abundance and contemporary synthetic abundance and imposed scarcity (for a discussion on degrowth and post-scarcity, see Finley 2017).

In summary, there are at least five key characteristics of Bookchin's liberatory municipality. First, a settlement governed according to municipalist principles is characterised by diversity, non-rigid institutions and dynamic relationships based on material interactions. Second, such a politics would distinguish between management and governance, separating technocratic 'tasks' from political decision-making processes. Third, and crucially, municipalism requires a politics of scale, a strong system of solidarity and collaboration between other cities in a confederacy. (Without this, citizenship would stagnate in its isolation.) Fourth, through political control over its economic activity, an ecocommunity necessitates self-limitation and self-sufficiency, in short, the politicisation of social metabolism. Finally, such a city is defined by an economy of abundance (not scarcity), where public spaces are sites of production, consumption and interaction as essential preconditions for creating and maintaining a dynamic biotic community.

Urban scarcity

Understanding Bookchin's definition of an ecocommunity prepares us for his concept of 'the urban', here confined to four descriptors: scarcity, synthetic relationships, techno-managerialism and a depoliticised metabolism. For Bookchin, the urban is a deadened space – a regulated, concrete environment that resists and undermines the possibility of organic interactions. Urbanisation is 'the dissolution of the city's wealth of variety' and 'a force that makes for municipal homogeneity and formlessness' (Bookchin 1992, 173). The expansion of urban space generates capital and scarcity: 'growth . . . has affected what we still persist in calling the "city" by leading to the expansion of pavements, streets . . . and retail structures over the entire landscape just as a cancer spreads over the body and invades its deepest recesses' (ibid., 202).

These spaces are characterised by the 'cash nexus', which generates material and synthetic abundance but limits the full use of the environment and technology. Fabricated abundance and socialised scarcity undermines politics:

> urbanization not only removes [the arena for interconnection outside the workplace] from the individual's control; it undermines, simplifies, and literally fossilizes them such that people and their habitats become entirely inorganic, indeed synthetic objects that can be easily manipulated and ultimately divested of all their living attributes.
>
> (ibid., 267)

Instead of organic relationships and dynamic encounters, interactions become pre-programmed. What should be as simple as putting a compost bin on a lawn becomes unusual, even illicit.

This deployment of urban space globally is maintained by a vast network of bureaucratic institutions, which substitutes 'an active community life' with 'the police officer . . . the last custodian of order in disintegrating neighbourhoods and the social worker . . . the last custodian of order in domestic life' (ibid., 223). Without a political sphere, administrative questions decided upon by elites and elected representatives become what we today derisively call 'politics'. In Hanoi, the use of public space is increasingly deadened by regulations disguised as concern for 'safety', 'cleanliness' and 'civilization'. What passes for political decision-making becomes a means to further sterilise public space to make it more manageable. Divested of the power to guide society, people become embroiled in endless bureaucratic and administrative institutions, binding us in what Giorgio Agamben (1998) calls 'bare life', the inability to intervene in the body politic or take control over social surplus.

If urbanisation were just the opposite of the city in these respects, it would be benign, boring space: endless lawns and poorly maintained rose bushes. But, for Bookchin (1992, 194), such characteristics threaten the very survival of humanity: the urban is not just a governmental regime, it is material, relying on infrastructure and technology that depends on high energetic and material metabolism. Urbanisation meant creating a system of transport infrastructures and 'market towns that fostered the monetization, commercialization, and industrialization of nations' and 'the effective centralization of the state along national lines'. This 'new, continent wide commercial nexus' would 'cut across the moral relationships fostered by traditional society' by creating 'material dependencies' between people and undermining their ability to create self-sufficient systems (ibid., 132). Active repression of democratic movements in cities enabled this accelerating social metabolism, further deprecating political life. By highlighting the material dependency of urban space, Bookchin prefigures urban political ecology, connecting the rise of urbanisation with the development of global metabolic flows (Kaika and Swyngedouw 2014).

This depoliticised metabolism threatens our very existence today: undermining our ability to take control over our consumption and production and leading to an 'ever-expansive, accumulative, [and] cancerous economic system whose "law of life" is to "grow or die"' (Bookchin 1992, 202). Urbanisation doesn't just destroy the city, but also 'the psyche, and ultimately the natural world' – 'from organic to synthetic human and biotic relationships' (ibid., 222). The repetitive extension of streetscapes becomes a 'structural gigantism that replaces all the organic sinews that held precapitalist society together' (ibid., 201). This techno-managerial-material assemblage drives ecological and social crises, our over-reach of planetary boundaries, violently imposes limits and accelerates the energetic and material metabolism of the global economy today.

More than ecovillages

Bookchin's conception of municipalism is distinct from 'ecovillage' or 'urban village' proposals made in the broader 'vocabulary' and practice of degrowth (Homs 2007; Delambre 2010; Trainer 2012; D'Alisa et al. 2014; Xue 2014). These proposals often assume that economic relocalisation and regionalisation is necessary (Latouche 2009) because cities are perceived as inadequate for a sustainable transition. Cities are resource-intensive and rely heavily on centralised energy sources (primarily fossil fuels) and massive infrastructures, leading to ecological overshoot. In contrast, low-density, rural and small-scale villages and towns have greater control over their metabolism. Relocalising the economy and dispersing populations provides an opportunity for, and even requires relocalised politics and decentralised political power (Latouche 2009; Trainer 2012; Asara et al. 2013). Ecovillage and urban village proposals are mainly concerned with demographic decentralisation with emphasis on land use diversity (mixing production and consumption), ideally leading to reduced travel and transportation. Everything in walking or biking distance means increasing interactions and encouraging community autonomy (Delambre 2010; Trainer 2012; D'Alisa et al. 2014; Xue 2014).

At first glance, these proposals sound similar to Bookchin's ecocommunity. However, there are some differences. First, he distinguishes the ecocommunity from the village by the composition of an 'outside'. Self-sufficient villages are more likely to be bound by kinship relationships and reject strangers while the ecocommunity, a dynamic node for commerce, must accept difference and outsiders. Importantly, Bookchin's strong stance as a humanist means strong opposition to any form of fascism while certain green imaginaries of decentralisation have long had a strong appeal to fascists and neo-fascists (Park 2013; Schneider and Sekulova 2014).

Another crucial difference between municipalism and the proposals for decentralisation mentioned above is acknowledging (or not) the need for scale in politics. Many forms of localism reduce sustainability to an imperative of local over global (Born and Purcell 2006). In contrast, Bookchin's municipalism is open to distant municipalities engaging in trade. Going beyond economic considerations, an isolated ecocommunity is impossible: it depends on a community of ecocommunities to survive and flourish. In the context of global urbanisation, the ecovillage is an isolated social experiment that cannot, in itself, scale up.

Furthermore, often the feasibility of ecovillage and decentralisation proposals are discussed in terms of technical and demographic limitations and possibilities (Xue 2014). For Bookchin (1992), population does not appear as a problem *de jure* but rather as a political question. He does not pinpoint when a community becomes 'too large' – as is often done in discussions about the 'ideal' ecovillage. Rather, political institutions ought to be organic enough to respond to demographic shifts and impose self-limitations when face-to-face interactions no longer become possible and material needs are over-extended. By distinguishing 'governance' and 'policy' from 'administration' and technical questions, Bookchin is careful to let political questions drive the cart of demography or economy, rather than the other way around.

Moreover Bookchin's municipalist framework is neither primitivist nor blindly modernist. Distinguishing the urban from the city conceptually separates the qualities of modern urban living that inhibit or encourage citizenship. Without calling for a large-scale return to the countryside, as some degrowth advocates do, he still problematises the total acceptance of urbanisation by ecomodernists, accelerationists and other contemporary progressive modernist strains. The distinction between urban and city keeps intact the political nature of social metabolism and today's environmental crisis. Given that urbanisation is only possible by eroding organic political life, a metabolic transition must be, first and foremost, a political transition. Some proposals for relocalisation are guided by assumptions that 'smaller' is necessarily better (socially, environmentally and economically) and political questions come later. Without foregrounding the political, such assumptions are little more than one-size-fits-all panaceas.

Obviously, cities are not inherently liberatory or ecological but, as Bookchin makes clear, historically, cities have fostered unique spaces of human interaction, simply because they existed at the intersection of differences, of insiders and outsiders. If ecovillages can create this kind of political space, and are able to scale up politically, then there is no reason why they should not be significant actors in a degrowth future. But the historical record suggests that this is unlikely.

Planetary urbanisation

Increasingly, geographers are using the term 'planetary urbanisation' to describe a global regime where the city, as Bookchin would have defined it, has become absorbed into a 'shapeless, formless, and apparently boundless' mesh intricately woven across the globe (Merrifield 2013, 210). For these theorists, distinguishing urban from rural no longer makes much sense. Traditional 'hinterlands' have become sites of urban space. Peasants have become rural-urban migrants subordinated to the ebbs and flows of global economic patterns.

This literature also emphasises the techno-managerial regimes that make this kind of urbanisation possible (Brenner 2014). In this vision, nature is both 'out there' and to be managed by experts. Even pro-sustainability policies are characterised by technical 'fixes' and apolitical 'solutions' that ride on the backs of concerns to devise new strategies of capital accumulation, economic growth and regulation of urban space (Kaika and Swyngedouw 2014).

Consequentially, our era is being called 'post-political': no real alternative to neoliberal governance seems to exist; politics has become a spectacle. We are bombarded by constant cycles of elections, referenda, polls and consultations, but fundamentally little has changed in our (in)ability to intervene or participate in political decision-making. This 'limited world' is one of political, not natural limits and 'true' citizenship appears as a distant dream. As intuited by Lefebvre (1968; Merrifield 2013) in 1968, as urbanisation threatens to swallow the political sphere, we have to rethink concepts such as the 'right to the city'. When we no longer have cities, is it even possible to do politics?

Leaving the question of political strategy aside, it's worth noting that the literature on planetary urbanisation does little to contradict Bookchin's analysis. Indeed, it extends it, allowing us to see how this urban 'mesh' has become a globally expanding latticework and highlighting the increased urgency, and sheer magnitude, of our problems. Thus urbanisation appears as the main challenge for degrowth: inhibiting our ability to take collective control over political and economic systems and dependent on the ever-expanding metabolism of materials and energy. As both the literature on planetary urbanisation and Bookchin's work illustrate, this is a *political* crisis: the urban represents the materially and socially fixed erosion of our capacity to 'do' politics.

The citification of urbanisation: a sketch of degrowth municipalism

Recently, I interviewed 'Cristina' (a pseudonym), who was involved in Montreal's transition movement. Cristina emigrated to Montreal from Romania as a 16-year-old. For her, the role of the transition movement is to encourage a cultural shift, where use of public space is not stigmatised:

> We want to see people living with abundance and not scarcity. We want to break down those barriers of access to food.

When I asked Cristina about those barriers, she described a project trying to plant fruit trees throughout the city: 'zoning is really strict so we couldn't . . . every single square inch belongs to someone, and you have to get their OK'.

For Cristina, scarcity was directly tied to zoning, regulations and bureaucratic hurdles: 'There is no common space in Montreal'. Cristina contrasted this to Romania, remembering how, in Bucharest, she could stop and eat from mulberry trees, and no one found it strange. This experience helped her envision an alternative of abundance and led her to participate in local politics, and she was even planning to run for borough councillor.

As in Hanoi and ancient Athens, Cristina knew that the everyday thrift of the market and active use of public space allows a political subject to emerge. She used 'scarcity' to describe urban life and 'abundance' to describe the world she envisioned. In contrast, the 'framing' of the degrowth movement often focuses on the need to limit, not maximise, consumption. Recognising the need for positive narratives, degrowth literature refers instead to words like 'conviviality' and 'flourishing'. But conversations with residents in London, Hanoi and Montreal revealed a childish wonder at the sheer possibilities of urban space once they had acted to modify it. They'd point at empty lots and parking spaces, saying things like 'can you imagine all the stuff you can do with all that space?' This was often paired with frustration: once they did intervene in the environment, they started learning all the strategies authorities use to regulate or take over these spaces.

Words like 'conviviality' and 'flourishing' don't quite capture Earth's propensity to provide, to create wealth out of thin soil and air. The abundance Cristina talked about has potential to vitalise citizenship and encourage people to get involved in politics. Perhaps our task is not to limit ourselves in the face of scarcity, but to multiply our capacity to access abundance. This abundance is not quantitative but organic, vibrant and fluid. Will such 'organic abundance' lead us to over-extending our use of resources? On the contrary, multiplying organic relationships to create a vibrant citizenship makes self-limitation possible. Following

Aristotle, Bookchin and Castoriadis, a robust political sphere enables societies to choose to limit themselves.

In closing his book, Bookchin highlights some conditions for such a political milieu. The first is the creation of organic citizens, involving education, vibrant city life and the multiplication of day-to-day interactions. Second, economic innovations in wealth generation, communal control over production and productive use of public space, potentially increase the self-sufficiency of disadvantaged groups and inspire political participation. The third condition is a political sphere, an autonomous institution, where citizens come together to make decisions, enacting the politics of their neighbourhoods and cities. Fourth, confederation enables assemblies to meet across scale, proliferating political experimentation, mutual aid and solidarity.

This recipe indicates the need to push degrowth beyond its current paradigm in several ways. First, the project to degrow urbanised space should be a project to reject 'natural' limits and undo the scarcity that defines our urban lives. Second, going beyond the 'local trap' means acknowledging that local and small are not inherently more sustainable. Third, this would be neither a primitivist anti-modern stance nor macho economodernism. Technology is neither the problem nor the solution. Rather, the deadening of organic relationships is the root of current crises, as represented by the scarcity imposed on us through the urbanisation of the world.

Many environmentalists advocate the ruralisation of the city, losing sight of what makes cities unique and risking an increase in isolationist parochialism. Degrowth should be about the citification of urbanisation. Now that our planet has become a vast mesh of deadening urban space, the politicisation of limits is only possible by creating political beings – the institutionalisation of vibrant city life.

References

Acosta, A. (2013) *El Buen Vivir: Sumak Kawsay, Una Oportunidad para Imaginar Otros Mundos*. Barcelona: Icaria.
Agamben, G. (1998) *Homo Sacer: Sovereign Power and Bare Life*. Palo Alto: Stanford University Press.
Angus, I. and Butler, S. (2011) *Too Many People? Population, Immigration, and the Environmental Crisis*. Chicago: Haymarket Books.
Ariès, P. (2005) *Décroissance ou Barbarie*. Lyon: Golias.
Aristotle. (1932) *Politics*. London: Loeb Classical Library.
Asara, V., Profumi, E. and Kallis, G. (2013) 'Degrowth, democracy and autonomy', *Environmental Values* 22(2): 217–39.
Barca, S. (forthcoming) 'The labor(s) of degrowth', *Capitalism Nature Socialism* – https://doi.org/10.1080/10455752.2017.1373300
Bookchin, M. (1971) *Post-Scarcity Anarchism*. Berkeley: Ramparts Press.
——— (1992) *Urbanization without Cities: The Rise and Decline of Citizenship*. Montreal: Black Rose Books.
Born, B. and Purcell, M. (2006) 'Avoiding the local trap: Scale and food systems in planning research', *Journal of Planning Education and Research* 26(2): 195–207.

Brenner, N. (2014) *Implosions/Explosions*. Berlin: Jovis.
Brownhill, L., Turner, T.E. and Kaara, W. (2012) 'Degrowth? How about some "De-alienation"?' *Capitalism Nature Socialism* 23(1): 93–104.
Castoriadis, C. (1999) *Figures du Pensable*. Paris: Ed. Seuil.
—— (2005) *Une Société à la Dérive*. Paris: Ed. Seuil.
Commoner, B. (1972) 'A bulletin dialogue: On "The Closing Circle" – response', *Bulletin of the Atomic Scientists*: 17–56.
D'Alisa, G., Demaria, F. and Kallis, G. (2014) *Degrowth: A Vocabulary for a New Era*. London/New York: Routledge.
Delambre, M.G. (2010) 'Sustainable communities of practice and eco-villages as mediation tool for degrowth process', in *Conference Proceedings of the 2nd Conference on Economic Degrowth for Ecological Sustainability and Social Equity*, 26–29 March 2010, Barcelona.
Escobar, A. (2011) *Encountering Development: The Making and Unmaking of the Third World*. Princeton: Princeton University Press.
Federici, S. (2012) *Revolution at Point Zero: Housework, Reproduction, and Feminist Struggle*. Oakland: PM Press.
Finley, E. (2017) 'Beyond the limits of nature: A social-ecological view of growth and degrowth', *Entitle Blog* – https://entitleblog.org/2017/02/07/beyond-the-limits-of-nature-a-social-ecological-view-of-growth-and-degrowth/
Homs, C. (2007) 'Localism and the city: The example of "urban village"', *International Journal of Inclusive Democracy* 3.
Kaika, M. and Swyngedouw, E. (2014) 'Radical urban political-ecological imaginaries: Planetary urbanization and politicizing nature', *Derive Journal* 15.
Kallis, G. (2016) 'Limits without scarcity: Why Malthus was wrong', *Leverhulme Lecture*, SOAS – www.youtube.com/watch?v=ENZX0xj0eSg
Kothari, A. (2016) 'Radical ecological democracy: Some more reflections from the South on Degrowth', *Degrowth.de* – www.degrowth.de/de/2016/12/radical-ecological-democracy-some-more-reflections-from-the-south-on-degrowth/
Labbé, D. (2014) *Land Politics and Livelihoods on the Margins of Hanoi, 1920–2010*. Vancouver: UBC Press.
Latouche, S. (2009) *Farewell to Growth*. Cambridge: Polity Press.
Lefebvre, H. (1968) *Le Droit à la Ville*. Paris: Anthropos.
Meadows, D.H., Meadows, D.L., Randers, J. and Behrens, W.W. (1972) *The Limits to Growth*. New York: Universe.
Merchant, B. (2015) 'Fully automated luxury communism', *The Guardian* – www.theguardian.com/sustainable-business/2015/mar/18/fully-automated-luxury-communism-robots-employment
Merrifield, A. (2013) 'The urban question under planetary urbanization', *International Journal of Urban and Regional Research* 37(3): 909–22.
Nelson, S.H. (2014) 'Resilience and the neoliberal counter-revolution: From ecologies of control to production of the common', *Resilience* 2(1): 1–17.
Park, M. (2013) 'The trouble with eco-politics of localism: Too close to the far right? Debates on ecology and globalization', *Interface: A Journal for and about Social Movements* 5(2): 319–44.
Rockström, J., Steffen, W., Noone, K., Persson, Å., Chapin III, F. S., Lambin, E. . . . and Nykvist, B. (2009). 'Planetary boundaries: Exploring the safe operating space for humanity', *Ecology and Society*, 14(2) – http://www.ecologyandsociety.org/vol14/iss2/art32/
Ross, A.R. (2017) *Against the Fascist Creep*. Oakland: AK Press.

Schneider, F., Martinez-Alier, J. and Kallis, G. (2011) 'Sustainable degrowth', *Journal of Industrial Ecology* 15(5): 654–6.

Schneider, F. and Sekulova, F. (2014) 'Open localism', *Degrowth Conference Leipzig 2014* – www.degrowth.info/en/catalogue-entry/open-localism/

Simpson, A. (2014) *Mohawk Interruptus: Political Life across the Borders of Settler States*. Durham: Duke University Press.

Srnicek, N. and Williams, A. (2015) *Inventing the Future: Postcapitalism and a World Without Work*. London/New York: Verso Books.

Trainer, T. (2012) 'De-growth: Do you realise what it means?' *Futures* 44(6): 590–9.

Wells-Dang, A. (2010) 'Political space in Vietnam: A view from the "rice-roots"', *The Pacific Review* 23(1): 93–112.

Xue, J. (2014) 'Is eco-village/urban village the future of a degrowth society? An urban planner's perspective', *Ecological Economics* 105: 130–8.

Zibechi, R. (2012) *Territories in Resistance: A Cartography of Latin American Social Movements*. Oakland: AK Press.

17 Scale, place and degrowth
Getting from here to 'there' – on Xue and Vansintjan I

Andreas Exner

I start with an observation from my field research, in 2015, into urban development in Vienna, which might seem a great leap from the general reflections on degrowth principles in housing issues in Jin Xue (Chapter 15) and Aaron Vansintjan (Chapter 16), both questioning what they denounce as the 'local trap'. Yet, starting with some observations in the field allows me to acknowledge the specific character of such a local trap and, thus, to pose the question of a degrowth perspective on a particular issue in a particular place more precisely. In this vein, I attempt to outline dimensions of possible answers to the problem of urban growth from a place-specific perspective, using Vienna to briefly illustrate some of the practical challenges of housing policies for degrowth, while emphasising that degrowth should recognise multiple scales of politics.

Snippets from field research

Sitting in the hot summer sun of an early afternoon, I observe a group of rather disgruntled citizens staring at a bunch of wooden blocks that lie scattered on a table covered by a large map. Someone, a planner, speaks. I am attending a workshop of a so-called citizen participation process in Vienna (Austria) in an area called the Donaufeld. It reminds me (and others) of rural landscapes. The city of Vienna seems distant, surrounded by vast arable fields, sometimes growing salads in chequered colours of bright green and dark red, sometimes covered by pumpkins that extend their twines and large leaves all over. When I arrived, seeing a greenhouse bordering the little group protected from the excess of heat by an awning, I recognised the impressive change of landscape, coming here from the inner city.

The planner is radiating self-confidence. His arguments are well rehearsed. I have come across them many times in urban policy documents, media texts and political speeches. 'Cities are growing', he declares in front of the crowd of neighbours, 'Well, at least those that are successful'. The arguments sound authentic. 'Without building more houses, rents will rise; one might well look at Munich'. As external developments enforce urban growth, he repeats, social policy goals compel local governments to invest in extending housing areas and public infrastructures. The planner believes what he says. But the listening crowd do not.

Repeatedly, he is interrupted by refutations that the city has to grow. A planning office colleague seems to become anxious: the one who in an interview prior to this workshop declared some citizens tedious, poor at expressing themselves and impeding participation processes. The colleague is not right wing; I have seen a German radical gardening book on participatory knowledge production lying on his desk. His job kills his intentions, I think. The issue here is getting participation done, not theory but practice. This requires 'decent' citizens.

Some of the citizens here make some trouble. Members of a local citizens group for several years opposed to the kind of urban development envisaged by the municipal government put effort into carving out constructive arguments. After all, the workshop is on building densities, and wooden blocks symbolising future houses carefully prepared for this occasion are spread out on a map representing the Donaufeld, its fields – soon to be covered by houses and by streets. The participants are expected to move the blocks around at this event.

Well before the planner ends his speech, three women produce a few baskets filled with different sorts of vegetables, carry them towards the planner and put them on the map amidst the little wooden blocks. A leaflet is going around, and people are invited to take the vegetables, the 'harvest of local peasants', as it is said. One of the women raises her voice, criticising green space that is not farmed, lauding farmers who 'plant until 2am', not like the 'bums and strollers' occupying 'unused green space'. In fact, the Donaufeld development plan gives prominence to such 'lazy' green space instead of 'sweaty' fields – never mind that these brave late-night farmers are mostly poorly paid and from foreign countries.

The speaker's colleague wrings his hands. 'Is anyone interested in discussing building density?' he asks in a frustrated and mildly desperate undertone. While the group and its attention dissolves and shifts, I wonder if anyone is recording the results of this awkward exercise. Some days after, I find a reasonably accurate report of the event on the website of the participation management, even showing the vegetable baskets proudly standing on the map.

Urban growth and the smart city

After the event, I interview a few bystanders, including a former factory worker in his sixties, who complains about 'the many people cramping up the tramway recently'. Only after a while do I understand that 'people', here, actually means 'foreigners'. Attracted by new housing areas, he believes, they will compete for space. He decries having suffered discrimination due to foreigners when applying for one of the public housing flats that characterise Vienna's social policy. Red Vienna has been commemorated ever since because of its public housing projects. The municipality reports that two-thirds of all residents live in public housing or in publicly subsidised housing areas, with every fourth Viennese citizen inhabiting a public housing area (City of Vienna 2016). Today, we are far from the 'good old times' of Red Vienna; the Social Democratic government practically destroyed the housing market in feverish construction efforts led by top-notch architects infused by high modernist, progressive ideas of the times, probably boosted by a radical settlers' movement co-opted into so-called superblocks of Austro-Marxism (Novy 1981; Eigner et al. 1999; Becker and Novy 1999; and Kadi 2015 for recent developments). Far from Red Vienna – obviously not as socialist as it is often depicted because it was quickly overruled by National Socialists who turned Vienna into a capital of the *Novemberpogrome* of 1938 – but not far enough away.

My snippet illustrates the sort of real-world contradictions that degrowth has to tackle, such as: massive urban growth in a social environment shaped by racist attitudes against immigrants, intermingling with ecological arguments for protecting arable land. In such contexts, reflections about ideal spatial and social forms may inspire concrete action and provide orientation but do not necessarily connect sufficiently with the materiality of spatial and societal relations that, in fact, mostly impede shortcuts to utopias. Since the built environment is a condensation of past struggles, shaping us as spatial beings, future spaces can rarely arise as a radical break. Moreover, degrowth is about resource conservation, which implies conserving the built environment, not realising an ideal through a completely new construction. Real innovations notwithstanding, degrowth will mostly involve reusing and recycling, sorting out, re-contextualising, reinterpreting and modifying – a transformation rather than the tabula rasa approach of many modernist projects attempting to forge ideal societal and spatial forms (Scott 1998).

The modernist discourse of ideal spatial forms is prominent in contemporary Vienna. In addition to piecemeal extensions of urban space in areas with lower building densities, the municipality follows a greenfield approach to peripheral urban development. The Donaufeld will have to wait for its new housing space, due to fragmented property relations. But on a former airfield nearby, in 22nd district, the heavy black topsoil transpiring fertility in certain appreciating eyes has already been turned into a neat, nice and cool urban Seestadt Aspern development project. The city government has emphasised that it is one of the biggest urban development projects in Middle Europe, framing the Seestadt as a key project of its smart city strategy. Everything, it seems, is perfect here in the red-green terms of the coalition government, from gendered street names to smart metres, combining the image of a business park with queer co-housing.

But a large fraction of the new inhabitants of the Seestadt Aspern voted for the right-wing extremist FPÖ (Freedom Party of Austria) at the last municipal election (Wittstock 2016). This is ironic, given the Seestadt Aspern is explained as an indispensible part of Vienna's smart strategy to manage city growth due to immigration from foreign countries. Most migration is from Serbia, followed by Turkey, Germany and Poland. Asian immigrants are increasing, apparently partly due to people escaping war-torn Afghanistan and Syria. Immigrants from Iran, Iraq, China, India and other countries seem to be considerable as well. Overall, immigration from Eastern Europe is sizeable and increasing. About half of the Viennese population has a migrant background.

The city government hails the achievements of Red Vienna of the 1920s as proof that Vienna has always been smart (City of Vienna 2014, 11). The Municipal Councillor for housing does not hesitate to proclaim rent rises, and increasing singles and small families have led him to promote smaller smart houses, and flexible architecture allowing adaptations of flat size (Fernsebner-Kokert and Heigl 2012, 9). Here, smart is small. Certainly, the trend in rising sizes of flats (MA 18 2005, 104) needs reversing. The attempt by smart planning to reduce flat sizes without reducing comfort is a positive example of an approach similar to Jin Xue's degrowth planning principles. Vienna's smart housing policy is reserved for those who cannot, or can only just, afford private housing; a large public housing stock at least allows such measures with societal impact. For degrowth housing to succeed, property relations are important. Of course, theoretically, flat sizes may be capped across public and private housing but with the current power relations, it would be difficult to formulate as policy and to enforce.

Smart city discourses, projects and their corresponding imaginaries have two immediate roots: smart growth and the idea of the compact city (Gibbs et al. 2013). An important principle of Xue's degrowth planning for housing is, thus, already visible in contemporary urban development discourse, which includes the goal of the compact city. Vienna illustrates that this is not mere rhetoric. Although falling short of more radical ecological approaches to housing, Seestadt Aspern is a mainstreamed version of the car-free city, where pedestrians, public transport and bike use are facilitated and cars deterred. Well-integrated working, living and leisure, short distances and a radical shift from fossil-fuel driven traffic are authentic aspects of Vienna's smart city strategy. High technology 'gimmicks' are secondary and data security is no more (or even less) of an issue than elsewhere in a city where all urban infrastructures are owned by the municipality. Smart cities are diverse, and Vienna's version is a particular one (Exner et al. 2018).

However, while certain sustainability goals are similar, a smart city does not mean degrowth. First, this imaginary is closely connected to conventional business geared towards economic growth, even if Vienna is not a typical neoliberal space. Second, Vienna has been shaped by urban growth for many years. So, I return to the group of disgruntled citizens, engaged planners and vegetable baskets amid wooden blocks on the map of an area to be radically transformed for affordable housing for new inhabitants, mainly from other countries. This project will destroy some of the largest areas of highly fertile soil closest to the largest mass of Austrian consumers. In general, peri-urban agricultural land is of great importance for us in the near future, as the shift from the 'subterranean forest' of fossil fuels to aboveground biomass will increase demands on land even further. The idea of local self-determination certainly enters a harsh contradiction, here, with issues beyond citizens' reach.

The multiple scales of degrowth

The deeper conditions of immigration to Vienna are not substantially determined at the local scale. Vienna's attractiveness is not an essential property of this place but, rather, expresses a relational position of this city with regard to other cities in a broader social field. Vienna's attractiveness rises as livelihood potential in peripheries from Eastern Europe to Afghanistan is destroyed. Even movements of people from Germany to Vienna can reflect such conditions; many students circumvent the more restrictive access to German universities by moving to Austria and, even if official data is scarce, it appears that many German workers in Austria are from the Eastern region.

Vienna is subject to a mode of development that prioritises competition and economic growth. Although the city executive has not pursued urban growth as a policy goal explicitly, it reacts to conditions set by the European Union and broader dynamics of globalisation. Attempts to reposition Vienna as an international city have been visible since the late 1970s. Vienna aims for political and economic leadership in relation to Eastern Europe and, especially, proximate regions. Although the importance of Vienna as an investment hub between West and East may have diminished, Austrian capital (together with German capital) is very much engaged in Eastern Europe and, thus, co-responsible for living conditions (Exner et al. 2016).

The current situation cannot be directly compared to the late nineteenth and early twentieth century, when Vienna experienced its last explosive phase of growth and population reached a peak before World Wars I and II reduced not only its population but also its international relevance tremendously; there are similar processes at work. Capital is still driving processes involving manifold forms of dispossessions and, within Europe this initially meant the dismantling of socialist industries, agriculture and social infrastructures. Romania, for instance, is one of several countries most affected internationally by questionable large-scale land deals, with a notable participation of Austrian investors (Nolte et al. 2016). And Austrian capital has greatly profited from expansion into Eastern European markets, especially in banking (Becker 2010). Agents in the European peripheries are in weak positions in relation to those at the centre, to which Vienna belongs. Furthermore, European capital and state policies are affecting many other regions ranging from Africa to Asia. Thus, we see the general similarity between the immigration of dispossessed smallholders and artisans during the Habsburg monarchy, and contemporary capitalism.

So, what does degrowth mean here, where international structures and dynamics play out in a specific way due to local relations of social forces? Simply closing off borders is neither feasible nor acceptable in a degrowth perspective. First, closing borders is ethically intolerable because no one has the exclusive right to a piece of earth as private property, but may only exert a temporary stewardship in the name of humanity as a whole. Second, refuge must be provided unconditionally to those fleeing economic, political or cultural hardships. Third, economies are tightly interlinked in many ways today which can, and should, be upheld to a certain degree in a degrowth perspective. Closing borders for human movements while maintaining the exchange of goods and services is contradictory and expresses the prioritisation of things over people. Moreover, movements of people certainly improve, or are even at the core of, the vibrancy of cities. The politics of difference that Aaron Vansintjan quite rightly praises require difference, after all, and migration is one of its most powerful creators. Vienna is a case in point. After the bloody destruction of the high level of social and cultural diversity of the city, Vienna had become socially almost unbearably suffocating in the 1950s and 1960s for those of a lively mind, body and heart.

Certainly there is some potential to create affordable housing for the tens of thousands projected to make Vienna their new home in upcoming years and decades without putting arable fields in jeopardy. First, making unused housing space available for those who need it may alleviate some of the challenges and conserve resources. Even the mayor has declared an interest in gathering reliable information on the extent of such space in the city.

Second, building heights are a topic of considerable potential, since there are hardly any tall buildings in Vienna to date. While forbidden in the inner city districts, which are under protection as UNESCO world heritage, there is no reason for low building heights other than the prevailing planning culture and possible resistance from affected neighbours in urban development.

Third, an unknown but perhaps significant amount of space is lost on uses such as parking lots and could be put to better use for housing or soil conservation measures. Probably, some sealing of soil will be unavoidable in the short run – highly problematic in a country with high rates of soil sealing (GLOBAL 2000 2015). A change in property relations retrenching private housing would certainly be beneficial: reducing speculative building projects that create unused space, especially in office buildings (which, however, could partly be transformed into flats); and reducing private housing prices and, later, the costs of new communal buildings, too, since these suffer rising expenses due to rising land prices. Ultimately, though, one of the root causes of net immigration from peripheries to centres is social inequality on regional, international and world scales. To tackle these, local democracy is not sufficient or may even be an obstacle, since higher scale problems are not necessarily treated best on lower scales.

Conclusion

Clearly the sorts of real-world problems that confront the degrowth movement – as indicated above – require practical as well as radical solutions that open up and safeguard possibilities of deeper future transformations. Although local solutions to local problems are reasonable and often feasible, many problems have an international, even global, dimension. Although they are crucial for degrowth, local initiatives are not sufficient to put the full potential of degrowth as a multi-level approach to socio-ecological transformation into practice. Indeed, the rise of cities as political actors propelled by a broader pro-urban discourse – that has even taken hold of United Nations agendas (Caprotti et al. 2017) – might point towards the promise of a progressive municipalism explained by Aaron Vansintjan. At the same time, this approach might inappropriately bias degrowth measures at other particular scales, especially if the limitations of local politics go unnoticed and remain institutionally unchecked.

References

Becker, J. (2010) 'EU in der krise: Bruchlinien zwischen zentrum und peripherie', *Kurswechsel* 1: 6–23.
Becker, J. and Novy, A. (1999) 'Divergence and convergence of national and local regulation: The case of Austria and Vienna', *European Urban and Regional Studies* 6(2): 127–43.
Caprotti, F., Cowley, R., Datta, A., Broto, V.C., Gao, E., Georgeson, L., Herrick, C., Odendaal, N. and Joss, S. (2017) 'The new urban agenda: Key opportunities and challenges for policy and practice', *Urban Research & Practice* 10(3): 367–78.
City of Vienna. (2014) *Smart City Framework Strategy*, Smart City Vienna – https://smartcity.wien.gv.at/site/files/2014/09/SmartCityWien_FrameworkStrategy_english_doublepage.pdf
——— (2016) *Municipal Housing in Vienna*, History, facts and figures – www.wienerwohnen.at/wiener-gemeindebau/wiener-gemeindebau-heute.html
Eigner, P., Matis, H. and Resch, A. (1999) 'Sozialer wohnbau in Wien. Eine historische Bestandsaufnahme', *Jahrbuch des Vereins für die Geschichte der Stadt Wien 1999*: 49–100 – www.demokratiezentrum.org/fileadmin/media/pdf/matis_wohnbau.pdf
Exner, A., Cepoiu, L., Weinzierl, C. and Asara, V. (2018) *Performing Smartness Differently. Strategic Enactments of a Global Imaginary in Three European Cities*. Report of the project Smart City as a Living Vision funded by the City of Vienna WU Jubilee Fund, 2016-2017. SRE-Discussion 2018/05. Vienna: Institute for Multi-Level Governance and Development, Vienna Business University.
Exner, A., Kumnig, S., Krobath, P.A., Schützenberger, I. and Brand, U. (2016) 'Stadtentwicklung, urbane Landwirtschaft und zivilgesellschaftlich gestalteter Grünraum in Wien', in Tomaschek, N. and Fritz, J. (eds.) *Beiträge zum lebensbegleitenden Lernen und Wissenstransfer 5: Gesellschaft im Wandel*. Münster: Waxmann: 247–58.
Fernsebner-Kokert, B. and Heigl, A. (2012) 'Schlauer wohnen mit den Wiener Roten', *Der Standard*, 16 March.
Gibbs, D., Krueger, R. and MacLeod, G. (2013) 'Grappling with smart city politics in an era of market triumphalism', *Urban Studies* 50(11), 2151–7.
GLOBAL 2000. (ed.) (2015) *Bodenatlas 2015*. Heinrich-Böll-Stiftung/Institute for Advanced Sustainability Studies/Bund für Umwelt- und Naturschutz Deutschland/Le Monde diplomatique – www.global2000.at/en/node/5531
Kadi, J. (2015) 'Recommodifying housing in formerly "Red" Vienna?' *Housing, Theory and Society* 32(3): 247–65.
MA 18. (2005) STEP 05. *Stadtentwicklung Wien 2005*. MA 18 – Stadtentwicklung und Stadtplanung. Wien: Magistrat der Stadt Wien.
Nolte, K., Chamberlain, W. and Giger, M. (2016) *International Land Deals for Agriculture: Fresh Insights from the Land Matrix: Analytical Report II*. Bern, Montpellier, Hamburg, Pretoria: CDE/CIRAD/GIGA/University of Pretoria.
Novy, K. (1981) 'Selbsthilfe als reformbewegung. Der kampf der wiener siedler nach dem 1. Weltkrieg', *Arch+* 55: 26–40.
Scott, J. (1998) *Seeing Like a State: How Certain Schemes to Improve the Human Condition Have Failed*. New Haven/London: Yale University Press.
Wittstock, B. (2016) 'Der Aspern-Blues', *Falter* 39: 38–41.

18 Geography matters

Ideas for a degrowth spatial planning paradigm – on Xue and Vansintjan II

Karl Krähmer

Both Vansintjan and Xue (this volume) present important arguments, effectively criticising the frequent tendency to localist approaches to the spatial organisation of human settlements in ecological and degrowth thinking. Instead, I would argue for a more differentiated vision. Even though Vansintjan and, similarly, Xue reject 'one-size-fits-all solutions' – a central criticism that I share to localist approaches – they risk falling into the same trap, when ferociously defending the city.

In as much as Xue's and Vansintjan's arguments centre on the political organisation of settlements, I largely agree with them. However, I propose to abandon the *tabula rasa* approach of any universal model for the ideal spatial organisation of society, considering them unrealisable for, at least, the following reasons. First, due to the material cost of rebuilding from scratch everything – be it for an ideal city or an ideal village – if we decided to follow such a model. Second, such a transformation has never happened before. One of the most successful ideal city models, the modernist approach of the Charter of Athens, unintentionally led to very problematic, car-dependent and socially exclusive cities while radical proposals, such as Corbusier's to demolish and rebuild Paris were never realised, fortunately. Third, such a wholesale transition is incompatible with the short period available for a transition, if degrowth is to address problems such as climate change. Fourth, and most importantly, such approaches are based on an ignorance of geography.

Not surprisingly, my answer to the question 'What is the right solution, the city or the (eco)village?' is: It depends! Neither a localist nor a compact city paradigm can claim to be the right universal approach for housing for degrowth. Rather, place-dependent solutions need to be developed that consider context, start from the existing situation and take into account each place's natural and human geography and the function(s) that each human settlement has and/or shall assume: the same principles of spatial and social organisation appropriate to a university city can hardly be applied to a rural settlement oriented to food production. (I hope that university cities will continue to exist in a future degrowth society.) Consequently, I elaborate this position by discussing geography, planning guidelines, some examples, perspectives and an agenda.

Geography matters

I invite you to conduct a simple thought experiment: think about two landscapes you know and then imagine them without human trace. You might imagine Central European plains and hills covered by beech forests, the vast Saharan desert, tropical islands with coconut palms and lush rainforest, or Alpine heights with glaciers, rocks, some grassland and forests below. Different forms of human use, different societies and different settlements have developed in such diverse geographical landscapes. I don't want suggest, in any determinist way, that the human settlements in these different natural geographical settings were certain and led to a sort of stable equilibrium, but these outcomes depend on natural geographic opportunities and limits. In certain places big cities surged and in others small villages, according to the availability of resources, climate, protection of a location and its connectedness to other places.

At the same time, from the moment that human beings appeared on earth, they began to interact with nature, transforming their surroundings and creating history (Diamond 1998). Today, after several thousand years, the two landscapes we thought about look quite different. Large parts of the Central European beech forests have been cleared. In their place intensively used agricultural land is cultivated, many villages and mostly medium-sized cities do exist and (in Germany) a third of the land is forest although most are monocultures of spruce and pine. Certain tropical islands remain relatively 'pristine' from an ecological point of view with a mainly 'indigenous' human presence, while others in strategic locations, such as Java or Singapore, have been heavily urbanised, filled with infrastructure, deforested and used for agriculture. The Sahara is still a desert, but with human presences: nomads, refugees or culturally significant cities like Timbuktu. Finally, the Alps have been used for hundreds of years by humans living off pasture, enriching the landscape's biodiversity (Bätzing 2015). However, with industrialisation, some people began to migrate to cities in the plains, abandoning land – with consequent expansion of the forest leading to a loss rather than increase of biodiversity – and certain tourism produced ecological damage in relatively few places.

To forget the importance of place is to fall into the classical error of the modernists who degrowth theorists criticise. It is as if globalisation annihilated the importance of place; from the perspective of 'real business', '"time" is equated with movement and progress' whereas '"space"/"place" is equated with stasis and reaction' (Massey 1994, 5). These ideas do not correspond to reality. Instead, the acceleration of globalisation increased spatial inequalities. Air flights connect places and increase the isolation of others where airports do not exist or are small: Massey (1994, 6) points out that places as well as people now have multiple identities, so some citizens in their multicultural neighbourhood of London feel strongly related to Ireland and the IRA, and others to India and its *saris*, all of which socially and culturally constructs their neighbourhood. Importantly, Massey emphasises that place is not defined by drawing its 'enclosing boundaries' but, rather, by such intrinsic qualitites.

The point I finally want to make is that geography matters if we want to think about such a thing as a 'degrowth spatial planning paradigm'. Even if we take into account the possibility of major catastrophes and epochal transformations of human societies, it doesn't make a lot of sense to imagine a European ecovillage in an ideal central place, at a crossroads of human exchange, with access to water, fertile soil and existing housing and infrastructures for many inhabitants or to suggest building *new towns* for residents of remote rural areas, oriented around agriculture, where diffuse control of the land is important for ecological reasons (for example in the Alps) and functioning community structures still exist.

Therefore, both visions of a world of ecovillages and bioregions with cities of fixed maximum sizes or of a world full of efficiently organised, vibrant and democratic cities are misleading even if such ideals offer useful points for analysis.

Guidelines for a degrowth spatial planning paradigm

This criticism of universal models does not imply that things should stay the same. On the contrary, a degrowth spatial planning paradigm should be developed – one that is truly bottom-up and leaves the populations of each place to decide how to realise the goals of degrowth, with more or less urbanisation, according to the following criteria:

- consumption of space and fragmentation of ecosystems
- energy consumption, especially for housing and transport of people and goods
- qualities of public spaces for social, cultural and political interaction
- spatial justice in accessing services and questions of the private absorption of rent.

Considering these criteria in an analysis of existing settlement forms and structures I can only agree with Vansintjan when he identifies the central problem as the planetary diffusion of 'the urban', in other words 'the periurban', 'rurban', 'sprawl', 'edge city', 'diffuse city' – middle- to low-density settlement structures organised around single-family houses, highways and malls, with huge space and energy consumption and highly car-dependent. This urbanisation coincided with the period in which we began to exceed planetary limits and has rated badly in respect to all the above established criteria. What is required, then, are strategies to both densify these territories and bring back their rural or natural status (Wächter 2013), a difficult challenge in as much as most inhabitants of periurban single- and two-family homes have no intention to give up this lifestyle.

Preuß and Ferber (2008) present a circular land use management approach, basically avoiding urbanisation of new land and focusing on reusing abandoned land in already urbanised contexts. As human settlements for all kinds of social and economic reasons grow or shrink, they introduce a compensation (or offset) scheme to only urbanise new land in growth areas if renaturalising land in other locations. Their model is not framed by, but certainly their instruments could be adapted to, degrowth goals. Transit-oriented development (Dittmar and Ohland 2012) – to create dense, mixed-use walkable neighbourhoods around stations of efficient transit lines – should also be integrated in existing low-density suburbs, thereby reducing car-dependency. In a degrowth perspective the long-term aim should be to renaturalise land freed by urban functions becoming concentrated in a smaller area. Therefore, diffusion of electric cars might have negative effects, moving attention from the priority of transport systems to motor techniques with the risk of repopularising the car, and its devastating consumption of land and public space.

A perhaps less obvious point to be considered is private property in land. Landlords live on rent they extract 'from land', a socially constructed value dependent on the surrounding urban context that the whole society built (Smith 1979; Harvey 2012). Private appropriation of socially created value, continuously becoming more centralised and financialised, is the source of our cities becoming evermore consumption-oriented, dominated by big companies and tourists, instead of being vibrant places of everyday life and local economies. Expelling economically weak inhabitants and functions from central neighbourhoods through high land prices (gentrification) leads to problems of spatial justice and pressures urbanisation on cheaper rural land at the urban fringes. As outlined by Olsen et al. (this volume), Rome is a good (negative) example of a large high-quality historical centre expelling poorer residents who move to flat-flung newly built peripheries, with few facilities and completely car-dependent. As the total population remains roughly stable, this capitalist dynamic leads to the city's massive expansion onto erstwhile rural land.

Consequently if we aim for a compact and just city and make the use of instruments discussed above feasible – as much more bottom-up experiments show below – we should reflect on how to strongly limit extensive private landed property and rent extraction, beginning with intelligent land value taxation.

Case studies

There are good empirical case studies illustrating the argument that certain types of large and small cities and certain types of villages point in the direction of a degrowth society. They include both traditional settlements and innovative "nowtopia" experiments. The medieval *Comuni* of central Italy should be studied for having been a relatively democratically governed town with great public spaces and a very close relationship with the landscape, the famous Lorenzetti fresco of *Buongoverno* in Siena being their manifesto – the well-governed city inserted harmoniously within an agricultural landscape – while his equally allegorical fresco of 'bad government' shows both the land and the city in war.

Well-structured neighbourhoods offer good examples of foundation stones for an efficiently functioning large city with reduced per capita living spaces and car use (Owen 2010). Certain alpine villages have shown how, for centuries, rural communities successfully and sustainably managed their land on the basis of commons (pastures), without being autarchic (Bätzing 2015).

Two examples of nowtopias that I know personally are the Cavallerizza Reale in the city centre of Turin, and Mondeggi in the countryside close to Florence. Both squatted spaces self-organise on principles of the commons (Bailey and Mattei 2013). The former operates as a centre of independent arts, culture and politics, providing the political space for experimentation with different ways of sharing space. It sustains precarious workers (such as artists) through an urban gardening project and enhances the relationship with agriculture by providing market spaces to farmers of Genuino Clandestino.

Genuino Clandestino is an Italian network organised on an assembly level as the instrument to guarantee product quality, connected to small farms so as to promote an agriculture respectful of land, environment and people. The network is anti-racist, anti-fascist and anti-sexist, operating somewhat illegally (hence 'Clandestino') because of their opposition to the ways that big enterprises add value to agricultural products making traditional farm-based food processing more-or-less impossible and as they try to restitute closer relationships between city inhabitants and farmers. Within Genuino Clandestino, Mondeggi combines sustainable usage of land for food production and collective living with the defence of an historically significant place, struggling against the commodification of an old rural estate which has been public property but planned to be privatised.

Perspectives and agenda

What can we do? Let's abandon the sterile debate of a 'compact city versus ecovillage' and develop a research agenda based on the real global problem of sprawling urbanisation.

Let's find ways to appreciate the obvious differences between central, large-scale settlements (cities) and peripheral, small-scale settlements (villages) and aim to reduce any consequential injustices without attempting to annihilate these differences. Let's engage in local practices and political struggles that make where we live better places. In cities, we should transform streets back to public spaces, and think about transforming parking lots into orchards. In rural areas we should fight against new roads and new single-family house settlements and develop positive associations between the rural land and the cities embedded in them, learning from cases such as medieval Siena and contemporary Genuino Clandestino.

These pursuits can be achieved by both researchers and activists alike. We should support and increase the number and quality of 'nowtopias', real anticipations of potential degrowth practices in both rural and in urban contexts.

References

Bailey, S. and Mattei, U. (2013) 'Social movements as constituent power: The Italian struggle for the commons', *Indiana Journal of Global Legal Studies* 20(20): 965–1013.

Bätzing, W. (2015) *Die Alpen: Geschichte und Zukunft einer Europäischen Kulturlandschaft*. München: CH Beck.

Diamond, J. (1998) *Guns, Germs, and Steel.* New York: Vintage Books.
Dittmar, H. and Ohland, G. (eds.) (2012) *The New Transit Town: Best Practices in Transit-Oriented Development.* Washington, DC: Island Press.
Harvey, D. (2012) *Rebel Cities: From the Right to the City to the Urban Revolution.* New York: Goodreads.
Massey, D. (1994) 'A global sense of place', in Massey, D. (ed.) *Place, Space and Gender.* Minneapolis: University of Minnesota.
Owen, D. (2010) *Green Metropolis: Why Living Smaller, Living Closer, and Driving Less Are the Keys to Sustainability.* New York: Riverhead Books.
Preuß, T. and Ferber, U. (2008) *Circular Land Use Management in Cities and Urban Regions – A Policy Mix Utilizing Existing and Newly Conceived Instruments to Implement an Innovative Strategic and Policy Approach.* Difu-Paper. Berlin: Deutsches Institut für Urbanistik (Difu).
Smith, N. (1979) 'Toward a theory of gentrification a back to the city movement by capital, not people', *Journal of the American Planning Association* 45(4): 538–48.
Wächter, P. (2013) 'The impacts of spatial planning on degrowth', *Sustainability* 5(3): 1067–79.

19 'Open localism' – on Xue and Vansintjan III

François Schneider and Anitra Nelson

First, we make some general comments on Xue's chapter and, second, Vansintjan's chapter and, third, given confusion around 'localism', we make a substantive statement on 'open localism' as a preferred degrowth position.

Jin Xue: 'Housing for degrowth: space, planning and distribution'

Xue's critique of the localisation strategy and vision of many degrowth advocates is erudite – attracting debate in the degrowth movement when her original article appeared in 2014, in international journal *Ecological Economics*. Xue's contribution is significant, even if simultaneously marred, because her position reflects many professional and mainstream perspectives on degrowth. Our rebuttal aims to elaborate how and why many of us support localisation, or decentralisation, and direct democracy, and what those terms mean to us.

First, Xue somewhat misconstrues the localisation position when she writes that adherents not only seek 'decentralised small-scale human settlements tailored to the characteristics and resources of a region' but also believe that '*low-density, spacious residential areas* are better able to utilise local resources and realise self-sufficiency' (our italics). A localisation or decentralisation position is often compatible with compact living, and degrowth's small footprint criterion rules out spaciousness. Many in the degrowth movement are European, where traditional villages display homes a couple of storeys high, clustered together and surrounded by productive space. Other models of decentralisation incorporate eco-collaborative living where eco-cohousing and ecovillages achieve one planet lifestyles through mixes of shared living and collective sufficiency (Nelson 2018).

Second, while a localisation strategy involves minimising external exchange, Xue grossly exaggerates when she suggests that, because of bioregional limitations and sparsely spread specialisations, localisation cannot significantly reduce environmental costs associated with transport. There is a massive difference in the environmental implications of a household pantry, say 80 percent full of locally produced goods and the rest gained from the nearest source possible, compared with a pantry typical of the global city householder where all goods might have been produced in any other part of the globe. Neighbouring settlements can contain a variety of sub-bioregional, ecotone and microclimate environments and discrete resources. By way of an example, the 28 villages composing the Blue Mountains City Council (New South Wales, Australia) – a sub-sub-bioregion within the Sydney Basin bioregion – grow a complex variety of plants from cold temperate to sub-tropical climates, providing food and other products.

Third, as Olsen et al. (Chapter 3) and Cattaneo (Chapter 4) indicate, degrowth advocates neither envisage nor support decentralisation by way of new waves of colonisation even though economic circumstances force them to take up opportunities that abound in repopulating, depopulating or deserted rural, and even urban, areas. Xue romanticises the urban solution in as much as she writes, for instance, that 'compact cities allow and facilitate certain levels of freedom of choice while reducing consumption levels and environmental impacts'. Irrespective of economies of scale, there is little empirical evidence of this seemly logical planner's assumption. In fact, cities are foci of growth and consumption even as they become more compact (Nelson 2018, 61–2). Choice exists because the city depends, in an environmentally unsustainable way, on a vast global productive hinterland to support its residents. Moreover, many compact urban areas are characterised by gentrification, high land prices and maximum profits.

Fourth, throughout the 'localisation of politics, centralisation and planning' discussion, claims are made that degrowth advocates assume that localised settlement enhances direct democracy. This is not the case for the many degrowth advocates who strive to develop and share skills of collective decision-making, aware that they are learned social skills. An allied slip conflates foiled attempts at collaborative planning in currently existing capitalism with models of direct democracy in a post-growth future. It is not surprising that neighbourhood participatory processes fail when conducted in an environment where state and market forces dominate participants' everyday lives and thoughts. In contrast, many degrowth advocates of direct democracy draw inspiration from anti-capitalist anarchist, new left and Occupy movements, and active degrowth centres such as Can Decreix (Cerbère, France).

Fifth, many activists have reached positions supporting grassroots activity and power because the hierarchical power structures of the state and market do not seem capable of achieving socially and environmentally beneficial outcomes. If, theoretically, state and city powers can regulate maximum sizes for dwellings and minimum sizes for households, where has this happened, is happening or is likely to be successfully implemented in progressive, degrowth, ways? Given the unsustainable state of the planet, we need to urgently achieve change. The direct democracy and localisation strategy achieves in practice not only theory; it is widely acknowledged that the greatest strides in implementing policies to reduce carbon emissions and adapt to climate change have occurred at the municipal rather than regional, state and international scales. Many sustainability programmes within municipalities scale down to neighbourhoods and evolved from grassroots pressure.

Sixth, a direct democracy and decentralisation strategy does not preclude collective decision-making at broader scales than the locale. Even if relatively autonomous cell-like communities populated the planet, they would want and need to collaborate on common environmental and social concerns using direct and collective decision-making. Our degrowth vision integrates horizontalism, which is neither hierarchical nor centralised (Adamovsky 2008/2011). At a universal (global) level we would require that key environmental and social values and principles substitute for prices and property in the current system. The framing of most direct democracy and decentralisation strategy discourse is anticapitalist and postcapitalist. This strategy cannot work in market dynamics that currently prevail but that does not mean that direct democracy is not appropriate to the world we are in the process of making possible.

Seventh, the philosophical concepts of justice considered in the final section of Xue's chapter are less relevant to degrowth discourses than significant work in environmental justice literature (to which the author of our foreword, Joan Martinez-Alier, has greatly contributed). For instance, Xue discusses justice and strict egalitarianism whereas, since the nineteenth century and exemplified in the writings of Marx and Engels, the broad left of socialists and trade unionists have developed sophisticated concepts of fairness, need and social contributions. In other words, we call for a reorientation towards mutually agreed upon referents for terms such as 'justice' in order to continue useful strategic discourse within and without the degrowth movement. Meanwhile, we welcome further interventions by critics such as Xue.

Aaron Vansintjan: degrowth, scarcity and the citification of an urbanised world

Just as we found Xue's contribution overly determined by a planner's perspective, Vansintjan's critique of degrowth centres on the political – 'the primary challenge is to institutionalise and cultivate an active, organic, political life' – to the detriment of the materiality of degrowth politics (a sustainable planet and sustainable humanity). Moreover, Vansintjan writes almost exclusively from the vantage of Bookchin's work analysing current urbanisation through the lens of a highly sympathetic and theoretical reading of 'the city'.

Therefore, we iterate frustrations with disciplinary and positional straitjackets and romantic views confusing what the city might be with how we experience it as agents of change. This is especially the case with Vansintjan whose negative views of the rural have him resort twice to an inflammatory conflation of village culture with fascism. He links a publication of Schneider and Sekulova (2014) to one such claim when they, in fact, explain that supporters of closing borders and even a few ethnic separatists exist among both critics and supporters of growth. Demonising the rural village and ecovillages seems rather unreasonable at a time when global cities and family homes are acknowledged sites of violence and urban areas are rife with terrorism, intolerance and rising income inequality. Instead, many degrowth advocates recognise the need to heal country–city rifts through listening together, mutual respect and coordination.

Fortunately, Vansintjan's analysis contains nuanced discussion, say recognising that globalisation has flattened the contours of what might be seen as city and country. But, we wonder where case studies of thriving, tolerant and connected rural centres such as Castlemaine in Victoria, Australia (Nelson 2017) or the compact Los Angeles Eco-Village (Nelson 2018, 138–43), whose outreach is exponential, fit in this framework of stark conceptual separations between the parochial locale and the progressive city?

Unfortunately, Bookchin's conceptual distinction between urbanisation (bad) and the city (good) often appears as a convenient mask for the argument that democratic decision-making naturally forms in the womb of the city, its markets and politics. Other chapters in this volume show how people's lived urban experiences are deficient. While some resort to, or yearn for, the rural, in reality many degrowth activists situate themselves in cities and urban politics. Moreover, those of us who practise degrowth in regional areas have had much more complex experiences than Bookchin's simplistic arguments suggest (Nelson, this volume).

While Vansintjan criticises an apparent obsession with population size on the part of localisation advocates, could not Xue's and Vansintjan's obsession with scale, specifically scaling up, be similarly criticised? Neither mention the capitalist state and global city nexus, political dominance of the international bourgeoisie, and structural-cum-political reorganisation required to successfully implement either central authority (Xue) or participatory democracy (Vansintjan).

The accusation that the term 'degrowth' is as off-putting as a diet is well-taken, but Vansintjan walks on thin ice when he points the finger at 'conviviality' as a weak motivation compared with the apparent attraction of Bookchin's sense of 'abundance'. The shorthand 'abundance' shares with 'degrowth' vagary and a tendency to produce confusion. In reality, solidarity, sharing and empowerment are integrated social skills. In fact, degrowth advocate Latouche (2014) promoted the concept of 'frugal abundance' referring to the abundance created by consuming modestly, yet fulfilling our needs, so there is security (not fear related to scarcity). Frugal innovation could open a new utopia of frugal abundance with much to invent in this new direction.

We share with Bookchin and Vansintjan sympathies with dynamising politics and underscoring the engine of collective will but question the glorification of cities at the expense of the village. The city must be challenged as an environmentally viable unit at a point in history when unsustainability threatens the very future of our species. In short, the political is central for the degrowth movement but so is the material world. These are connected as form (politics) is to content (natural and artificial environments), which can only be separated in the abstract but cannot be untangled in reality.

We completely agree with reducing regulations that limit fulfilling simple needs, such as Vansintjan's compost example. But rules and regulation can create more liberty. Take Bangalore, where the powerful wildly urbanise, the sprawl resulting from lack of regulation (see Chapter 11). We need balance. Aren't limits necessary? Citizen deliberations are needed for residents to decide between uses of public space – a green space, carpark or buildings – based on neighbourhood, city and societal (versus private) interests. Regulations against cars, sport-utility vehicles and inappropriate urban development opens urban space to green alternatives.

Finally, we thank Vansintjan for his stimulating contribution.

'Open localism'

Xue and Vansintjan, and the other rejoinders, circumnavigate 'open localism' so our commentary as follows specifically elaborates this concept. The position needs contextualising, which is where this section starts.

Closure

Writing early 2018, it seems that more people have been voting for extreme right parties. Concepts of closure and nationalism seem widespread, borders and doors are closing, flags are waved, and policies are stiffening to defend the nation state and the gated community. At the same time, the dream of living without conflict and misery forces thousands of refugees to emigrate. The closure policies of rich countries make it tragic: thousands of refugees are dying at the gates of Europe, the United States and Australia. Anti-immigration policies not only create more deaths and misery, but also fail to either manage or prevent immigration, which can only continue but in more difficult conditions. Meanwhile, certain neoliberal supporters of 'open borders' tend to create new borders by closing themselves in secure residences, and the 'no-border' movement attempts to practise solidarity in a courageous way.

Why closure? Simply to defend, and limit access to material privileges? We are in a 'schizophrenic' situation where advertising and television series celebrate our consumer lifestyles to the world but, at the same time, deny access. Moreover, the Global North's overuse of planetary resources destroys the very ecosystems that might allow the Global South to live modestly or, at least, simply survive. The result is profound inequality and huge frustration, generating violence and armed conflict to hand over natural resources, causing even more economic and political refugees. This situation generates more fear, closure and crises of identity that, in turn, generate direct violence in the form of extreme right or religious fundamentalist attacks and indirect violence, such as border patrols and bombings.

Localism

In contrast, degrowth promotes voluntary simplicity and economic shrinkage, favouring all of us to reduce our needs to modest but diverse lifestyles, which would reduce resource demands for energy, food and finances, and harmonise relations between us. According to Latouche (2006), 'localism' constitutes one of the masterpieces of degrowth. But which definition of localism is specifically appropriate for degrowth? Is it a territorial partitioning with well-defined boundaries, a sovereign territory or autarkic? Is localism directly associated with intolerant and divisive concepts of closure?

We prefer 'open localism': attention to listening, feeling what is around us, reducing separation and distance, self-production and self-management at different levels from farms and neighbourhoods to villages and regions, in short, a localism without closure. Open localism (sometimes referred to as 'neo-localism') is cosmopolitan and diversified, and consists of reorienting the organisation of human communities towards personal relationships of proximity, and reduces that distance that has grown with production for trade and related economic, social and political management.

In contrast, closure is a process of drawing boundaries, building identities and communities to monopolise resources for the singular group with which one identifies, thus excluding access to such resources to others. Localism does not require such closure. Open localism has evolved within the grassroots movement of degrowth yet has been less attractive to theoreticians of degrowth. A further cause of confusion is that, while the concept of open localism has been defended by degrowth proponents since 2001, some other critics of growth now support the concept of closure.

Critics of growth who defend borders

Some Keynesians have defended reducing imports at national borders, customs officers controlling imports and payments of import taxes. Instead, open localism develops policies such as reducing expenditures on highways and supports citizen actions against large 'useless and imposed' infrastructures, with measures such as eco-taxes on air transport, trucks and fuel. Open localism advocates reducing the distance between producers and consumers without erecting walls; the 'local' might be on the other side of any socially construed border.

Other critics of growth, such as Daly (2015) and Sourrouille (2014), defend closing borders to immigrants, arguing that populations in rich countries must decrease or stabilise and that birth rates are not declining sufficiently nor quickly enough; therefore immigration to rich countries must be reduced. 'If southerners come north, they will adopt their consumer lifestyles', they say, arguing that growth advocates want immigration to foster growth. Starting from an ecologist's position, they end up close to an extreme nationalist right anti-immigration position.

Logically, immigrants are attracted to privileged, high-consuming countries. Both closure of borders and inequalities create frustration because the excluded emulate the rich and seek to join them in their citadel, especially as privileges are touted as symbols of success. It is not immigrants who need to be challenged, but the existence of overconsumption creating frustration through artificial scarcity and endless desires. Those with rich lifestyles need to become frugal, rather than defending unsustainable behaviours by closure of borders.

An author of the extreme right and expert in perverting leftist ideas, De Benoist, prominent theoretician of ethnic separatism between communities, wrote a 'degrowth' book (De Benoist 2007). His vision contorts the concept of diversity dear to the left, where diversity exists at all scales, including the local, which implies important work to facilitate social and cultural interrelations, and make advances on commons and agreements. On the contrary, De Benoist's 'diversity' at the global level corresponds to an ethnic homogenisation at the local level, containing, in germ, 'global apartheid' and ethnic wars (Deland et al. 2014).

Therefore, the concept of diversity must be defended between countries, localities and at all scales. Open localism rejects the closing of identity (patriotism). In contrast to De Benoist, the degrowth concept of open localism requires bonding with the environment surrounding us with all its diversity. It is about spending the evening in the local bar with Moroccans, rather than going on holiday in Morocco. For 'open localism' identity is negotiable and, based on dialogue, it is a relational identity. Open localism involves belonging to different open communities with different foci at different scales. It is about developing communities of projects by creating institutions that transcend social closures. I can have a French national identity, but find myself in a neighbourhood association with people of other nationalities, and organise, say a community supported agriculture group, with socio-economic variety.

Scale and context

In open localism the appropriate scale varies: vegetable production can be done within a few kilometres, while producing steel or dentists' chairs will happen at nodes at larger scales. Indeed, human rights issues or CO_2 emissions affecting the climate will be dealt with at a global level. We advocate a type of 'glocalism' that is not capitalist. Open and cosmopolitan localism does not exclude an ecological reserve, a sanctuary of resources, but prioritises conserving mineral and fossil resources, and frugal knowledge for the good of all.

This localism would mainly safeguard frugal lifestyles from being destroyed by infrastructures related to growth, such as high-speed transport infrastructures, roads and dams in pristine forests. The degrowth concept of open localism supports limiting material consumption to allow greater diversity. We need limits to liberate us, not standardisation that blocks us. For example, living without a car opens up a variety of alternative means of transport (such as cycling, walking and riding on a scooter) that, otherwise, are unlikely or impossible.

However, closure has a place: in some extreme cases, for instance defending frugal lifestyles – as with an endangered frugal Amazonian tribe under risk of unwanted assimilation by global capitalism – some defensive closure might be justified, if the tribe preferred it. Rich communities wishing to safeguard their opulent lifestyles find this type of closure hard to understand. Our approach challenges closure related to the defence of privilege.

Open localism defies the identification of success with markers of consumption, which tend to generate economic wars. In open localism, degrowth in consumption and production reduces pressure on resources and makes cooperation possible. Management of commons, ecosystems, water and mineral resources requires great cooperation across a great scale. Similarly, ensuring justice in access for all, including future generations. Commons become easier to operate and save when competition for resources is reduced. Reduced pressure on resources must be accompanied by sharp reduction in inequalities, to reduce frustration and consumer lifestyles that lead to desperate emigration.

Localism has a place in degrowth because many things can be more sustainably managed locally, but degrowth cannot be wholly realised on a small territory and must be societal. Degrowth is not about reducing consumption in one place only to increase it elsewhere! The degrowth movement proposes open localism and challenges borders along with supporting measures such as sharing work, leaving resources underground and withdrawing the right of banks to issue money. Degrowth brings to the fore the right to free and slow travel without discrimination. Open localism promotes spaces of hospitality and supports mobility by long-distance journeys on foot, by bike and train, and advocates long-stays. Open localism is a cultural struggle against taking a plane to the other side of the ocean for a weekend holiday.

To conclude, open localism does not defend a universalism imposed from above. In particular, degrowth does not support generalising the reign of individual profit. Degrowth does not defend the vision of a culturally segregated world. Open localism implies a type of universal diversity (the Diversal), a non-conquering universalism evolving from below.

References

Adamovsky, E. (2008 [2011]) *Anti-Capitalism: The New Generation of Emancipatory Movements*. New York: Seven Stories Press.
Daly, H. (2015) 'Mass migration and border policy', *Real-World Economics Review* 73: 130–33.
De Benoist, A. (2007) *Demain, la Décroissance! Penser l'Écologie Jusqu'au Bout*. Paris: Éditions Edite.
Deland, M., Minkenberg, M. and Mays, C. (2014) *In the Tracks of Breivik: Far Right Networks in Northern and Eastern Europe*. Berlin: Lit Verlag.
Latouche, S. (2006) *Le Pari de la Décroissance*. Paris: Fayard.
——— (2014) *Essays on Frugal Abundance*. Simplicity Institute Report 14c. Simplicity Institute – http://simplicityinstitute.org/
Nelson, A. (2017) 'Castlemaine: Climate change, consciousness and art', *Arcadia: Online Explorations in Environmental History* 30, Autumn – www.environmentandsociety.org/arcadia/castlemaine-climate-change-consciousness-and-art
——— (2018) *Small Is Necessary: Shared Living on a Shared Planet*. London: Pluto Press.
Schneider, F. and Sekulova, F. (2014) 'Open localism', *Stirring Paper zur Degrowth Konferenz Leipzig 2014* (Research & Degrowth).
Sourrouille, M. (2014) *Moins Nombreux, Plus Heureux – L'urgence Écologique de Repenser la Démographie*. Paris: Sang de la Terre.

Part VII
Anti-capitalist values and relations

20 Mietshäuser Syndikat

Collective ownership, the 'housing question' and degrowth

Lina Hurlin

The global urban population has never been so high: since 2008, more than half of the world's population lives in cities (World Bank 2017). The worldwide trend towards city living sets up new, and expanding, questions concerning housing. Addressing social injustice and degrowth requires attention to housing as developed in the neoliberal real estate market. This chapter considers the situation in Germany, where a common slogan is the 'return of the housing question'. This is a reference to a series of questions with a history as long as capitalism. In *Zur Wohnungsfrage* (*The Housing Question*), written in the early 1870s, Friedrich Engels (1948) contributed to a major debate in the worker and progressive press on the housing shortage for the expanding numbers of workers living in Germany's major industrial centres.

In this chapter, I highlight one solution to the current housing question: collectively owned houses on the model of the Mietshäuser Syndikat (literally translated as a 'syndicate of tenements'). Although 'degrowth' as a concept and movement is neither central to the Mietshäuser Syndikat nor the German Right to the City movement, I identify commonalities and discuss related questions. Both the Mietshäuser Syndikat and degrowth advocates are aware that capitalism cannot deliver a good life for all, and try to show how we can live secure, modest and fulfilling lives without aspiring to be individual property owners with expanding wealth. The chapter starts by outlining key characteristics of life as a tenant in Germany today, then discusses the concept and practices of the Mietshäuser Syndikat, and its application of housing for degrowth. Unless indicated otherwise, information about the syndicate is sourced from the Mietshäuser Syndikat (2017) and personal experience.

A brief selective history of tenancy in Germany

This analysis focuses on the situation in Germany, where the development of the Mietshäuser Syndikat is tailored to the German legal system. This is not to say that similar concepts do not exist in other nations. Indeed, around the same time that the Mietshäuser Syndikat formed, so did Radical Routes (2017), a cooperative of cooperatives in the United Kingdom. The latter network has differences as well as similarities in the way that it promotes a cooperative approach to the housing question. Other projects, such as Vrijcoop (2017) in the Netherlands and HabiTAT (2017) in Austria, have tried to adapt the Mietshäuser Syndikat organisation within their legal systems.

In order to analyse potential housing solutions and their limitations we need to understand the tenants' views of the currently absurd real estate and rental market. The abrogation of the law benefiting housing for the common, public, interest through tax benefits, the *Wohnungsgemeinnützigkeit* (detailed below) and the global financial crisis (GFC) 2007–2008 resulted in some brutal outcomes for tenants. Horlitz (2013, 3) highlights 'a major conflict and even a fundamental contradiction between the commodity and speculative aspects of housing and its most crucial purpose: providing decent homes for everyone'. In the capitalist market real estate is seen as a profit-making investment rather than as fulfilling a human need.

Susanne Heeg (2013, 76–7) identifies three reasons for the financialisation of the housing market, whereby the house became a financial product or asset rather than a simple commodity. First, in the context of liberalised financial markets, the regime which had been dominated by a logic of the industrialisation of work and technological innovation moved towards a regime that is based on financial accumulation by investment. Second, real estate gained in status as a financial investment, partly due to the growing privatisation of housing. The housing shortage following World War II (WWII) made German municipalities invest public money in building activity for the first time. As public housing was introduced, a new tenant's law was passed and, slowly, a complicated web of aid programmes, public housing and tax benefits evolved favouring financialisation (Holm 2014, 98ff).

The third point made by Heeg needs further explanation. The state can use tax regulations to steer activities in a specific policy direction, which resulted in the *Wohnungsgemeinnützigkeit*. In short, investors who provided social housing got tax benefits. Unfortunately, since this law was abolished in 1988, the investment market has become the driver of housing. From a capitalist's perspective it seems to make most sense to invest in apartments for those on higher incomes so social (public rental) housing has almost disappeared. Andrej Holm (2014, 32) points out that homelessness is not recognised as a supply gap within a market logic because the homeless have no money and could not rent anyway. Markets do not see needs, only monetary-backed demand.

In retrospect, the post-WWII period was the most favourable for German tenants, even if the housing sector was still part of the free market. Then the support programmes ended, the key law was changed and, adopting a neoliberal rationale, municipalities basically sold their social housing assets. One famous example is Dresden where, in 2006, the municipality sold all their dwelling stock to an American finance-investor (Holm 2014, 124). These more (or less) drastic steps meant that municipalities – and the state in general – relinquished their influence on who lived where, and under what circumstances, consequently marginalising the 'housing question' from the political debate. Government influence can be broken down into one of three spheres of influence: law, money or public property. If laws are changed, money is scarce or property is sold off, public influence in the area of housing becomes very limited.

Social tenancy law: a clue to solving the housing question?

Internationally, German tenancy law is regarded one of the best: its stipulations protect tenants relatively well. Rent increases conform to strict regulations and tenants' agreements protect them from eviction. Therefore, tenants seem secure once they sign a contract. However, in reality, things are rather different. Even though, in an international comparison, tenants in Germany are relatively secure, exceptions are increasingly raised in public protests and scholarly critiques. Apart from the possibility of terminating a contract when rent has not been paid for more than two months, the landlord can claim the flat or house for personal use, which is a legal loophole used to get rid of a tenant and then rent out the dwelling for a higher rent (Holm 2014, 105, 112).

Another way of effectively evicting a tenant for a more lucrative rent is by pressuring them to move out 'voluntarily'. Documented cases show mostly large real estate companies tyrannising tenants until they move out. They exert psychological pressure, say cutting off their heating system or even hiring people to hassle them at home (Supe 2016). Several protest movements have developed to support tenants threatened by either forced or 'voluntary' eviction. Stop Evictions Berlin (*Bündnis Zwangsräumungen Verhindern*) is an activist organisation that uses various forms of protest to stop evictions. They highlight the strategic question of how to achieve reasonable housing for all.

Although the housing bubble was seen as the flashpoint of the GFC and ensuing great recession, investment in property is increasing. Especially in bigger cities, where capital investment in real estate is particularly lucrative, the outcome of the neoliberal housing market is a visible concern. However, alternatives have been invented. Although the ultimate solution to stop this process would be decommodification of real estate (Holm 2014, 7), the Mietshäuser Syndikat is an initiative of people wanting to solve the housing question by removing houses from the market and collectivising them. This means protection from market forces, at least at a small scale.

Concept and functions of the Mietshäuser Syndikat

The Mietshäuser Syndikat covers a conglomeration of housing projects in Germany: in April 2017, there were 124 projects housing more than 3000 residents – and still expanding. '*Häuser denen, die drin wohnen!*' ('houses for those who dwell in them') is the central vision, to be realised by isolating private capital interests from owning housing property. The autonomy of each project is respected as much as the power of the syndicate of which it is a member. (Mietshäuser Syndikat 2016, esp. 80.)

An important guarantee is that a Mietshäuser Syndikat house will never be thrown back on the real estate market. This hazard of other types of premises is particularly evident when debts need to be written off, the market value of the dwelling rises, or a project's purpose is lost over time (Rost 2014, 286). The strategy to prevent re-privatisation in practice can be achieved through a combination of simple and complicated legal forms, understandable by closely examining the structure of the organisation formed to achieve such objectives.

Initially, all the people who live in – or plan to live together in – the Mietshäuser Syndikat house form themselves into an association. An association is relatively easy to form and establish but, if a corporate body bought the house it could easily be resold, say, if the residents developed an intransigent conflict, needed money or simply had new ambitions or ideals. Therefore, another corporate body is brought into play, the *Gesellschaft mit beschränkter Haftung* (*GmbH*), which is similar to a limited liability company.

At first glance, a thoroughly capitalist corporate body needs to be established by every housing project, a body then divided into two types of company shares. The association of the house's tenants owns one share (51%) and the Mietshäuser Syndikat *GmbH* solely owns the other (49%) share. The Mietshäuser Syndikat only has a few voting rights, the most important regarding resale of the house: the organisation will always say 'No' to selling the property. Reprivatisation of real estate covered by the syndicate is almost impossible. The Mietshäuser Syndikat association consists of memberships of all the housing projects in the syndicate, plus interested groups or persons, and is the formal link that holds this alliance together. This – as shown graphically in Figure 20.1 – seems complicated but

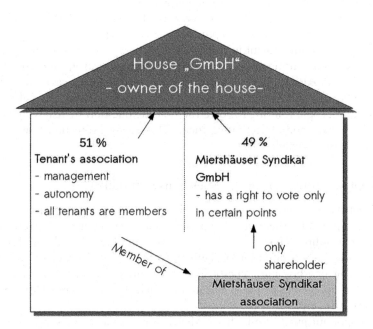

Figure 20.1 Roles and relations in the Mietshäuser Syndikat association

provides a safe model for each project's participation and autonomy and prevents re-privatisation.

The syndicate in action

Given the complicated juggling of legal forms to create a more or less anti-capitalist model within a capitalist system, the everyday workings of the syndicate need explanation. Basically all the projects retain full autonomy in their decision-making processes and in organising how they live together (such as deciding what colour to paint the kitchen wall). All projects, irrespective of size, have to contribute to the budget for their house association and the *GmbH*. There is a wide variety of dwellings associated with the syndicate. Some look like normal apartment buildings with small apartments, others practise alternative ways of living together, such as engaging in a collective economy, raising children together and sharing the work of reproduction and care. The syndicate determines none of this; members of each project negotiate their internal organisation.

Alternative models of living together are easier to experiment with if the household decides its structure as a group. For example, many house projects have big common rooms that they all share. This kind of collaboration and coordination is hard to find on the free market and is an illustration of how the model expresses potential for degrowth ideals and aims – enabling community-oriented living and shared spaces.

Central to the platform and process by which decisions are made within the *GmbH*, every few months, the Mietshäuser Syndikat holds a general meeting of members. Usually, most houses send a few representatives, and between 150 and 250 people attend such meetings. The venue changes but most meetings are in cities where numbers of projects exist and they share the responsibilities and work for organising the meeting. In those meetings all the main decisions concerning structural changes or new projects are made. Moreover, it is a platform for information and exchange between members, for example about new laws or how to deal with conflicts in groups. All decisions are made through processes of achieving consensus and everybody has the opportunity to speak and discuss. This certainly is a challenge. There are often trials of new methods to get more people participating in the processes and to create room for everybody to be heard. These meetings take up one full day, side-by-side with two-day work-group meetings, for example, about internationalisation of, or structural changes in, the syndicate. Furthermore, they involve an exchange of knowledge, consultation and counselling of members in new projects.

Starting a new project has many hurdles and challenges, although new groups do not need to reinvent the wheel. Every new project has one or two advisers, mostly from other projects. The advisers accompany the group as they become a part of the syndicate and inform new projects or suggest experts who might be able to inform them. Contracts and statutes do not have to be created anew; standard templates exist that can be used or adapted by the projects. Beyond funding legal forms, planning the construction phase, or financial plan, advisors from established projects inform the projects' social processes.

Most structural forms of residential groups are created in the 'construction phase' both in ideal and practical ways. It is not unusual that conflicts are seen, initially, 'as threats rather than something normal that has to be dealt with'. Therefore, support from experienced members of other projects help to co-create 'solidarity, open-minded, non-hierarchical, and respectful behaviour'.

Most significantly, all work for the Mietshäuser Syndikat is honorary, except for one part-time administration job in the Freiburg office. All the counselling, organisation of meetings and workshops, and reading of contracts is unpaid, relying on the shared values and ideology that nobody should make a profit from other people's dwellings.

Investing collectively

The funding of projects shows where and how the Mietshäuser Syndikat must accommodate capitalism even as it tries to extricate itself from the system. The GmbH of the house requires capital to buy and renovate a building or, in some rare cases, to build a new one. Financing is the responsibility of those who form and found the house project together but an established community-based financing model for syndicate projects often assists them.

Interest on bank loans increases the rent and the bank usually lends only a part of the investment costs, generally requiring a basic equity between 20 percent and 30 percent. This basic equity is often raised through the savings of resident members or friends and supporters, sometimes allowing for larger bank loans. In the beginning of every new project, members seek funds from acquaintances, ethical investments in so far as these projects are recognised as realising social, environmental and sustainability-oriented values and goals. Moreover, the project usually pays interest on such loans, which is attractive for friendly investors. Although rarely eliminating the need for bank loans, this funding gives the banker greater confidence and, often, interest rates on private loans are lower than on bank loans.

Rent

The GmbH needs to cover all expenses and annuities to pay back both bank and private loans. Consequently, all house dwellers pay rent to the GmbH. The amount is calculated, with the support of local advisers, in a financial plan in the initial phase of each project and depends on aspects such as the length of the loan, prevailing interest rates, purchase price, maintenance costs and taxes. The internal distribution of liabilities differs from project to project. Some adjust rental levels according to personal incomes, others per capita or by the size of space in each dwelling. Yet others introduce principles of solidarity and communal support, an area of project autonomy with each project ruling on such internal affairs.

Transfers based on solidarity

Under normal conditions one can imagine that, once loans are repaid (usually taking approximately 30 years) the houses are paid off and residents pay less rent. From the syndicate's point of view this seemed unfair: the 'first generation' in the house was burdened by planning, establishing and organising the project while paying higher rent than members who joined the project later and without need for such efforts. For this reason, a solidarity transfer was invented: existing projects would contribute a slowly increasing amount of money into a Solidarity Fund to support new house projects through the initial stages of establishment. Thus, each project begins by contributing 10 cents per square metre of floor space per month. This amount grows by 0.5 percent, although there is a ceiling of 80 percent on such increases.

With this money, say €12,400 worth of shares for the new house association is paid, some infrastructure expenses are covered and, sometimes, short-term loans are given to projects needing financial support. Hence, the transfer is based on solidarity between younger and older projects, a kind of intergenerational contract. Over the years, larger proportions of rent are paid to the Solidarity Fund, while other liabilities reduce in size. If the rent increases such that rental in the free market becomes cheaper than living in the syndicate house, then the group can apply for a reduction in the level of payment to the fund. The objective is to keep dwelling costs at a low level and make housing possible for people on low incomes.

Housing syndicate: challenges and limits

Challenges and limits of the Mietshäuser Syndikat focus on four questions, as follows. How can the model be scaled up? Is such a model simply a niche reform or capable of being mainstreamed? What commitments do syndicate associations have regarding housing activism more generally? Is proprietorship a genuine solution to the housing question?

Limited scale?

Given that the ideals of the syndicate are to create housing for everybody in non-profit-making ways, the final goal is to collectivise all existing houses and grounds. As mentioned, in April 2017, there were 124 projects in the syndicate, providing dwellings for about 3000 people. As an achievement of self-organised voluntary work, this number is quite high, but its influence on the general rental market is still marginal. In fact, around half of Germans live in rental housing but only a fraction lives in collectively owned housing. To have a recognisable influence on the rental market, the syndicate either has to grow immensely – indicating the need for a new structure – or more, similar, syndicates need to be launched.

A strength of the syndicate is its handling of democratic decision-making processes. The quantity of people involved in decisions is impressive, given that discussions are open for all members and the underlying principle of consensus. No decision can be made if someone uses their veto power. Currently, between 200 and 300 people come to meetings held every few months. As the number of projects increase, it is likely to be more and more difficult to find larger rooms to hold bigger meetings and to create a space where everyone attending can participate in discussions. Either the syndicate needs to split up into several syndicates, or the structure will need to change so that, for example, a constellation of smaller soviets work on different topics.

Niche or mainstream?

A common critique that the syndicate faces is that it is 'subcultural'. While there have been no reliable studies on the sociological composition of the syndicate or, indeed, on cohousing in general, the accusation is made that such models only cater for an academic middle class. In response to such critiques, and after showing the more general relevance of such models to householders of all incomes, Christiane Droste (2015, 80) asks if 'the growing number of projects as well as the emergence of entire co-housing neighborhoods suggests that the time has come for municipalities to ask whether they should support the concept to move from "niche to mainstreaming"'.

Droste (2015, 89) sees many ways for municipalities to support the mainstreaming of cohousing, from financial support in the form of loans or grants to special conditions for providing property (Simbirger 2008, 355), and refers to such models as win-win solutions for projects and municipalities to the extent that 'residents and neighborhoods appreciate co-housing because of its hybridity, diversity and the openness of the approaches, even though individual projects function as closed internal communities'. Following Droste, municipalities could be given the responsibility for bringing projects in from niche to mainstream.

Mainstreaming can also be progressed by house project associations that open up both their spaces for co-living and their facilities and organisation to their neighbourhoods. For instance, many projects have some open rooms for neighbourhoods, emergency and guest rooms for people in need or shared workspaces and tools. Such developments support degrowth approaches to living economically and efficiently with existing resources being shared as commons.

Housing activism

On the one hand, Horlitz (2013, 10) claims that activists in the syndicate 'focus on projects and not on protest and carrying through policy measures' in order to mount the argument that 'the successful enforcement of policy measures, for example rent control, will eventually benefit a much larger amount of people than those singular projects can'. On the other hand, projects are often a main hub for (protest) groups, projects and communities to hold meetings, activities publicising the housing question and other political issues. Certainly, the housing activism of each project varies and the impacts of the syndicate as a whole depend entirely on the activities of its current member householders.

Proprietorship as a solution?

The idea of the syndicate came about in the 1990s, in Freiburg, and was born out of the squatter's movement. Squatting of houses has been a strategy for criticising unused vacant property, and property more generally. The ideal of separating profit-making from people's dwellings still exists in the syndicate, although the solution of creating collective property is sometimes criticised, first, for failing to eliminate the ideal of owning houses and, second, for creating housing for some but not everybody. Syndicate houses are owned by the people living in them, who are part of an association that excludes others from the privilege of a dwelling. Moreover, living in syndicate projects still requires paying rent. Even if cheaper than on the free market this does not make it possible to dwell without money at all. While total de-commodification of real estate is commonly seen as the final solution, strategies to achieve this, and appropriate compromises, remain hotly debated.

Affordability

Given that profit-making is eliminated in this form of housing, it is cheaper than living in surrounding housing, and residents are often willing to work at supporting it. For example, the prevailing 'standard' is to provide housing at a price that people dependent on social welfare could afford, so that as few people as possible are excluded for financial reasons. While affordable housing for everyone remains an ideal of the syndicate and all its associated house projects, Horlitz (2013, 10) highlights critics who charge that such a model is 'privately doing the job the state actually is supposed to do – to redistribute resources in order to provide housing for low-income people – and thus in a way cushions, legitimises, or even indirectly strengthens current neoliberal politics'.

This returns us to the question of scaling up. Can such syndicates provide housing for more than a marginal number of householders who are, consequently, singled out as constituting a subculture? Could the model have a positive impact on housing politics or might it only take over the government's task of providing decent and affordable housing? Is there a limit to scaling up the model and, if so, what kinds of structural changes are needed to keep the democratic structure of the syndicate?

Mietshäuser Syndikat and the concept of degrowth

The word 'degrowth' is hard to find in discussions within, or about, the Mietshäuser Syndikat partly because the degrowth debate in Germany is quite young – only several years old in many political circles – whereas the syndicate was founded in the 1990s. Moreover, much degrowth debate takes place in academia as a theoretical draft for an economy beyond growth whereas the syndicate arose from urgent and practical housing struggles. Although developing in different contexts, both share certain ideas and could improve their political position and visibility, if they worked together.

Xue (2012, 20) nominates two forms of growth, and ipso facto degrowth, relevant to housing: 'the growth in the physical housing stock and the growth in the economic value of the housing sector'. Neither the syndicate nor the degrowth movement is interested in rising house prices and rents. Fair housing is only possible when houses are decommodified or at least collectivised (as with the syndicate). So, in a good-life-for-all degrowth utopia, the profitable housing sector must shrink or, better, disappear.

Furthermore, highlighting the fact that the practical use value of housing has been displaced by its market value, Gómez-Baggethun (2015, 68) defines degrowth as 'a critique of the colonizing expansion of market values, logic, and language into novel social and ecological domains'. Here Mietshäuser Syndikat creates and reproduces values, arguments and language appropriate to housing needs, real social demands, and has successfully developed social and economic organisations that challenge everyday speculative practices of housing developers and investors. Furthermore, their governance practices enhance equity and consensus.

Many degrowth advocates argue for reducing the average size of dwellings. This argument might by environmentally sound but raises issues of class and power. Collective housing, as in certain Mietshäuser Syndikat projects, often uses less space per capita by sharing rooms, such as kitchens, bathrooms and workspaces. While people who can afford it might reduce the space in which they live by choice, it would be entirely different and reproduce hegemonic power if, say social housing policy makers, targeted those on low incomes who struggle to afford an apartment. So, as an organisation steeped in issues of social justice and grassroots democracy, the Mietshäuser Syndikat would scrutinise all the strategies for environmental efficiencies that might be pursued by the degrowth movement (Martinez-Alier 2015).

Conclusion

This chapter has discussed a German model for financing and organising housing as an alternative to the mainstream market and state provision of housing. The ideals behind the Mietshäuser Syndikat centre on housing justice in an otherwise inequitable commercial sector. Compatible with degrowth ideals, the Mietshäuser Syndikat eschews profit, which implicitly drives growth, encourages conviviality and the sharing of resources, skills and responsibilities for collectively managed housing. As such, the Mietshäuser Syndikat has a place in a suite of degrowth measures that include other forms of cohousing, self-managed social housing and squatting. The connections to anti-capitalist degrowth ideals and practices are obvious, but activists within the Mietshäuser Syndikat would also challenge degrowth activists to address questions about housing for social justice and adequate space for all, including in growing cities.

References

Droste, C. (2015) 'German co-housing: An opportunity for municipalities to foster socially inclusive urban development?' *Journal of Urban Research & Practice* 8(1): 79–92.
Engels, F. (1948) *Zur Wohnungsfrage*. Berlin: Dietz.
Gómez-Baggethun, E. (2015) 'Commodification', in D'Alisa, G., Demaria, F. and Kallis, G (eds.) *Degrowth: A Vocabulary for a New Era*. Oxon: Routledge.
HabiTAT. (2017) Über uns', *HabiTAT* – https://habitat.servus.at
Heeg, S. (2013) 'Wohnungen als Finanzanlage. Auswirkungen von Responsibilisierung und Finanzialisierung im Bereich des Wohnens', *suburban: zeitschrift für kritische stadtforschung* 1: 75–99.
Holm, A. (2014) *Mietenwahnsinn*. München: Knaur.
Horlitz, S. (2013) *Movements and Initiatives to Decommodify Housing*. Paper presented at the Resourceful Cities International RC 21 Conference 29–31 August, Berlin – www.rc21.org/conferences/berlin2013/RC21-Berlin-Papers-3/26-2-Horlitz.pdf
Martinez-Alier, J. (2015) 'Environmentalism, currents of', in D'Alisa, G., Demaria, F. and Kallis, G. (eds.) *Degrowth: A Vocabulary for a New Era*. Oxon: Routledge.
Mietshäuser Syndikat. (2016) *Die Häuser denen, die drin wohnen*. Freiburg: Mietshäuser Syndikat GmbH.
——— (2017) *Mietshäuser Syndikat* – www.syndikat.org/
Radical Routes. (2017) 'Aims and Principles' – www.radicalroutes.org.uk/aims-and-principles.html
Rost, S. (2014) 'Das Mietshäuser Syndikat', in Helfrich, S. and Heinrich-Böll-Stiftung (eds.) *Commons: Für Eine Neue Politik Jenseits Von Markt Und Staat*. Second edition. Bielefeld: Transcript: 285–7.
Simbirger, A. (2008) 'Von der Nische zur Serie. Zur Bedeutung von gemeinschaftlichen Wohnprojekten in der Bestandsentwicklung', in Schmitt, G. and Klaus, H. (eds.) *Bestand? Perspektiven für das Wohnen in der Stadt*. Dortmund: Rohn.
Supe, J. (2016) *Plötzlich Fremde in der Küche*. Berlin: Junge Welt – www.jungewelt.de/artikel/286783.plötzlich-fremde-in-der-küche.html
Vrijcoop. (2017) 'Collectief kopen, en samen huren' – https://vrijcoop.org/
World Bank. (2017) 'Urban population, % total, 1960–2016', 28 September – http://data.worldbank.org/indicator/sp.urb.totl.in.zs
Xue, J. (2012) 'Potentials for decoupling housing-related environmental impacts from economic growth', *Environmental Development* 4: 18–35.

21 Nonmonetary eco-collaborative living for degrowth

Anitra Nelson

The attraction of living in eco-collaborative housing has increased as housing has become less affordable, average household sizes have diminished and environmental concerns have grown. Collaborative housing refers to a range of 'alternative' housing and households whose members live in intentional, collectively governed, residential communities sharing resources, skills and spaces. Examples include shared houses (joint households), cohousing, squats and ecovillages (LaFond and Honeck 2012; Litfin 2014; Nelson 2018). For instance, cohousing is comprised of clusters of dwellings, often attached, whose households share indoor and outdoor spaces for collective activities such as dining, gardening, playing and hosting guests. Eco-collaborative living offers potential environmental, economic and social efficiencies. Arguably, along the spectrum of reformist to radical cases, intentionally transformative models that aim for collective sustainability have the most degrowth potential.

This discussion of benefits and limits of collaborative living to drive environmental, cultural and political developments to achieve degrowth makes an anti-capitalist point. Elsewhere, I have argued that capitalist growth and money are so integrated that degrowth requires us to develop relations of production and modes of exchange that eschew money, monetary relationships, production for trade and associated markets (Nelson 2016). This is a distinctly different strategy for degrowth than creating alternative currencies, community banks or community-oriented financial cooperatives. Anti-money arguments point out that monetary values (prices) are based on social dynamics, particularly supply and demand, that market-based processes neither concern nor account for environmental sustainability, and that growth imperatives and endemic competition inevitably lead production for trade towards ecological unsustainability. In other words, capitalist economies automatically reproduce a material dualism between humans and nature.

In short, if we are to live modestly, collectively meeting our basic needs, then production and distribution must rely on ecological and humane principles neither interrupted nor contorted by monetary values, negotiations and calculations. Consequently, effective governance techniques and processes for meeting our basic needs through localised and collective planning, production and distribution are paramount to living sustainably within the regenerative capacities of

Earth and enable us to move beyond money. Drawing on auto-ethnography, informal interviews and relevant literature, this chapter compares and contrasts two well-established eco-collaborative housing models to demonstrate such points.

Round the Bend Conservation Co-operative (RBCC) is in Christmas Hills on the peri-urban fringe of Melbourne (Victoria, Australia). In 1971, RBCC's founders bought 132ha of Australian box-ironbark eucalypt woodlands intending to preserve it while living there.[1] Members were keen to disprove the argument that native forests were best kept as a pristine reserve as the Wilderness Society (a prominent Australian environmental organisation) claimed. RBCC aimed to show that a residential community using appropriate practices and governance could live in such woodlands with low impact. Functionally, RBCC is an atypical eco-cohousing model: members live in detached dwellings and do not share built, only outdoor, space. In mid-2017, RBCC had around 50 adult members living, with their children, in 22 dwellings with ten more house sites available for development.

The second case is an ecovillage, a relatively self-contained settlement of dwellings pursuing collective sufficiency and ecological balance within Earth's local and global regenerative potential and limits. The income-sharing Twin Oaks community near Louisa in Virginia (United States [US]) has around 90 adult residents, most of whom work onsite, and 15 children.[2] In the second half of 2017, Twin Oaks community celebrated its 50th year of existence, owned 182ha and was seeking crowdfunding to purchase an adjacent 42.5ha to prevent it being clear-cut and enhance their collective sufficiency.

This analysis examines three key areas: land and dwelling ownership and use, governance and work, and political and economic integration. I aim to show how both cases of eco-collaborative housing have more potential for residents to practice degrowth than if they lived in mainstream individualised housing. I argue that members of Twin Oaks have more potential to achieve degrowth because they have a high level of collective sufficiency, minimise trade and production for trade, treat their property as commons, and share their collective product and monetary income rather than maintain private property and separate incomes as in RBCC and typical cohousing projects.

Land and dwellings: ownership and use rights

RBCC and Twin Oaks own private property as institutions so that members' use rights are distinct from householders' individualised private property in mainstream real estate trading in property titles. However, they have distinctly different legal and financial models for members' rights and responsibilities, and members' relationships with their land.

Land and dwellings: Round the Bend Conservation Co-operative

Becoming a full member of RBCC means purchasing a share, entitling the shareholder household to one of 32, 1500 square metre, sites on which members can establish their house, an evapotranspiration bed processing 'waste' water from the dwelling (often covered by a netted kitchen garden), firewood storage, garden sheds and tanks for water collection and household use. Sites were decided on by the cooperative's earliest members, who located them off three tracks.

RBCC membership commits one to home ownership; investors with tenants are not allowed. Dwellings can only temporarily accommodate visitors or tenants while owners are away. Shares have remained well below market value for a comparable lot of land adjacent to the cooperative and members benefit from joint use rights over their land. However, the cost of either both a share and building or of purchasing a share with a home included still require considerable savings or a private credit arrangement. Mainstream bank loans have not been available unless the whole cooperative guaranteed them, which members have felt too uncomfortable to do. This circumstance encouraged shareowners to self-build, often in stages.

In the 1990s, I bought a share associated with a vacant site and built a small (60m^2) mud-brick house with savings and an A\$20,000 loan from a fellow traveller. After gaining a fixed-term part-time academic research position a year or later, I paid off the debt by borrowing a smaller personal bank loan at a high interest rate – forcing me to save and pay it off within a few years – an entirely different experience from typical mortgage sagas (see Chapter 1).

Most RBCC homes are made of mud-brick, timber and recycled materials. House designs and other plans for a site must pass cooperative rules more stringent than any state and local council building and planning regulations. Policies focus on conservation, protecting the woodlands from undue disturbance and social factors (Nelson 2001). Many details, say regarding house materials, construction practices, finishes and the siting of sheds, woodpiles and water tanks, must be approved by RBCC directors and their delegates. Members are very helpful so these processes are not as daunting as dealing with, say, an impersonal shire council resistant to innovation. Moreover, group action can be powerful: RBCC members pioneered their environmentally friendly – ultimately council-approved – hybrid septic and evapotranspiration bed grey and black water treatment systems.

The main purpose of RBCC is to 'co-operatively live on and manage the land in order to protect, conserve and enjoy its indigenous nature'. RBCC defines 'conservation' ('what we do'), cooperation ('how we do it') and 'governance' as fundamental to its objectives. RBCC has adopted a cooperative model: constitutions of cooperatives spell out responsibilities and rights of members, which can involve sharing incomes and treating property as commons rather than including privately owned and negotiable lots. Membership of RBCC is very different from engaging in mainstream real estate. Even RBCC's lengthy membership approval process slows down entry and exit.

Land and dwellings: Twin Oaks community

An intentional income-sharing community, Twin Oaks has self-proclaimed 'values of cooperation, sharing, nonviolence, equality, and ecology'. For US taxation purposes, Twin Oaks is categorised alongside monasteries although Twin Oaks is not a religious organisation, rather harbouring diverse beliefs and philosophies in a secular culture. Still, Twin Oaks does mimic the simple living and collective sufficiency of many traditional monasteries, say, during the middle ages of feudalism in Europe. Unlike most cooperative arrangements no one, even in a partial way as a member of a collective, owns Twin Oaks but membership permits egalitarian use rights to and governance of all its resources and amenities.

In effect, Twin Oaks community operates as commons, benefitting from past accumulation of farming land and forest, equipment for various businesses, housing and people skills and knowledge. On entry, approved members can only bring as much personal property as will fit into a small bedroom space. Other things they bring will be shared – effectively donated to the community. A member can still own assets outside Twin Oaks but, for the duration of their membership, income earned from such assets is shared with the rest of the community. On exiting, they can resume full ownership rights to use and/or income from reserved assets. Most significantly, members neither need to bring on entry nor extract on exit any monetary or other resources from the community. This is probably the most straightforward, efficient, effective and fair standard communal living arrangement of which I know. Certainly it is a framework for a future degrowth society where no one owns any part of Earth yet gains benefits from, and has responsibilities for, bounded land and associated resources as stewards.

Most of the community's modest functional buildings were constructed by members, who participated in their design, from timber found on site and recycled materials. There are seven large group houses. All householders can communally share main meals in a big dining area, various equipment (including a fleet of vehicles), other spaces and resources, such as a big room of 'commie' clothes laundered as communal work. Group houses have kitchen and other common areas and a private room for each household member, where they keep personal property such as clothes that they clean themselves. There is relative autonomy around organising each household such as protocol on personal behaviour, including making noise.

Buildings are well insulated, with passive solar design, solar hot water and heating using wood sustainably grown onsite and their sawmill scrap. Design benefits from permaculture approaches and multiple uses of all spaces by numerous users. One of the households, Kaweah, is environmentally oriented with a totally off-grid solar photovoltaic electric system. Other buildings benefit from a grid-connected array of solar panels. Energy-efficient practices produce major savings. Similarly, there is minimal use of their 18 fuel-driven vehicles of various sizes and capacities. Bikes lie, or sit in stands, around the whole farm. You pick one up to get somewhere and leave it for someone else to use. Bikes are procured second-hand, repaired and maintained in a workshop on site.

Governance and work

Governance of RBCC is similar to many cohousing projects where consensual decision-making processes are modified by voting when, ultimately, necessary.

All households are independent with respect to incomes and cooperative duties centre on a relatively small amount of conservation-oriented activities. In contrast, the Twin Oaks labour policy is central to members' lives: the community is relatively collectively sufficient, most work is full-time and its governance processes include collectively determining details of everyday work tasks.

Governance of Round the Bend Conservation Co-operative

Although households work and live independently, gaining and spending their own incomes, shareholders co-manage their land for conservation ends, partner with like organisations on conservation projects, socialise together and organise their association through quarterly general meetings. Quarterly assemblies, a board of seven elected directors meeting monthy and numerous working parties act in transparent and horizontal ways to manage internal matters. Householders participate in several half-day working bees held annually (rarely paying a levy in lieu). Some working parties, say regarding pest animals and plants (weeds), are permanent. Others are task-oriented and, therefore, temporary. For instance, initially, trenches were dug along each of three tracks to lay communication and electrical cables underground to service each site (Victorian Collections 2017). Later, monthly half-day work parties laboriously laid second-hand household bricks in herringbone pattern over dirt tracks and used bricks to form drainage swales across these brick roads over numbers of years.

RBCC collectively focuses on maintaining its natural environment in ecologically sensitive ways. Self-sufficiency, let alone collective sufficiency, is off the radar. RBCC land has little potential for growing food or husbanding animals. Rainfall averages less than 650mm per annum and the shallow soil is nutritionally poor with sparse native undergrowth. Residents are permitted to establish and maintain relatively small, private kitchen gardens over used-water treatment sites, which permaculture practices can make highly productive. Produce can be used, gifted or sold. Elsewhere the bush is left to function as naturally as possible. Any plants non-indigenous to the local area outside the kitchen garden (or in pots adjacent to or inside the house) are considered weeds. Similarly, non-indigenous animals are forbidden, even if brought with visitors. Seasonal site inspections ensure that tenants and resident members abide by these rules.

Mainstream private property owners and government agencies regulating their use rights divide and clash over environmental management of a host of aspects such as nature strips, trees, water ways and bores, and citizen groups develop to influence national, state and council policies. However, RBCC shows how direct land management makes community members grapple collectively with processes for sorting out the most appropriate practices for conserving their particular land. Members have developed in-depth knowledge and skills to manage it. At the same time RBCC is open and transparent enough to acknowledge discrepancies and discomfort with certain decisions made.

While constitutional rules set out members' rights and responsibilities, the Land Management Plan is a flexible work in progress yet permanent enough in its guidelines to offer RBCC stability. Probably the most controversial policy relates to an intent to cool burn 10 percent of the property every year, to prevent inhabitants and the bush from intense and relatively frequent natural and artificial fires to which the state of Victoria, and the local Bend of Islands area, is particularly prone. A 'cool burn', 'prescribed burn' or 'controlled burn' is a carefully managed slow burn of undergrowth, a hazard reduction burn. Cool burns aim to eliminate easily burnable bark, ground litter and certain low vegetation. Policies over such burns are highly controversial in Victoria, and Australia, more generally (Vigilante and Thornton 2016; Thornton 2015).

The cool burn policy is somewhat at odds with, or limits, the cooperative's conservation policy, which stipulates that fallen branches and trees are left on the ground as habitat for birds, marsupials and reptiles. Still, many Australian species rely on fire for germination so cool burns have a conservation purpose. Cool burns were practiced for millennia by traditional owners before white settlement and recently integrated into government policies. Cool burns must be lit on appropriately calm and cool days when adversarial winds, rain or warmth are not forecast. RBCC's policy can be undermined by residents who disagree with it not volunteering to work on cool burns when required: to clear leaf litter and twigs on the bush floor before the burn, to manage the cool burn (lighting and controlling the fire) – including having Country Fire Authority tankers and teams ready to fight any uncontrollable outbreaks – and to be constantly vigilant day and night for a week or so afterwards because fires fuelled by roots underground can break out anytime.

Like other Australian residents with similar sentiments – but with the added benefit of pooling energies and influence – members constantly struggle against locally 'inappropriate' (read 'environmentally insensitive') developments, certain council policies and practices and the frequently poor practices of electricity and water service providers, say cutting down unnecessary vegetation or failing to manage weeds on public property bordering the cooperative. Still, as a non-income-sharing cooperative without any joint income-earning enterprises, RBCC is much less onerous governance-wise than Twin Oaks, and less communal to the same extent. Members are free to select and vary their level of social and communal activities while they live there.

There is a higher level of sharing than in the average suburban neighbourhood context. However, lack of extensive sharing diminishes householders' potential environmental sustainability; for instance, car use is essential in such a remote area not serviced by public transport but, beyond a household, neither car sharing nor car lifts are commonplace. Rather than as formal protocol, a relatively low level of sharing of all kinds happens as a voluntary ad hoc habit between certain members acting on personal choice and connections.

Twin Oaks: work and governance

The Twin Oaks community as a whole deems what activities constitute communal work. By the mid-2010s, they collectively and organically produced a lot of their food, via extensive vegetable gardens, plants in two complementary greenhouses and an orchard. They used tractors, other mechanical tools and a lot of direct human labour. Vegetables were harvested and walked to the kitchen so transport costs and refrigeration were negligible. A herd of cows provided unpasteurised milk, cheese, yoghourt and beef (slaughtered on site). Chickens were kept for eggs and poultry and, intermittently, pigs or other animals if individuals cared to drive such programmes. The orchard included apple and pear trees, blueberries and raspberries, and grapevines. Beside washing and cleaning, milking cows and making cheese, cutting down timber from their forests and making wood products, gardening, childcare and food preparation, there were tasks in a range of businesses producing cash for the community, mainly: making tofu, hammocks, indexing books and growing seeds for heirloom plants.

Despite the complex range of working and living activities undertaken by Twin Oaks members, the community has developed effective forms of participatory direct democracy. Policies and processes span a range of issues such as nudity (where and when), who gets which rooms for their personal space, and deciding who to trade with, and on what terms, as well as mediating unresolved personal disputes. Twin Oaks' level of collective sufficiency demonstrates that, if people apply appropriate technologies sufficient to satisfy their basic needs and keep numbers of members at a manageable level, direct democracy is a successful governance model for a communal economy and produces superior results to production for trade using money as the ruling principle (Kincade with Twin Oaks community 2011).

Techniques for direct democracy developed over decades of practice are inclusive, simple and straightforward. There are notice boards for proposals, to start open discussion on changes and new ventures. People can volunteer for all kinds of regularly rotating executive positions. Governance is non-hierarchical with committees, managers and planners executing policies made by the community. Managers and planners need to be transparent, responsible and effective and are open to challenge and retirement. Thus, the authority of the collective is paramount. No one is so much of a specialist that they usurp another's decision-making power as they do regularly in capitalism. Members practice collective governance by focusing on deep listening and fully participatory discussion in decision-making. Consensual decision-making, inclusive of resorting to voting occasionally for reasons of expediency, is successful. An array of solutions is sought, the successful one leaving the most people relatively content.

Members work around 42 hours per week on communal domestic tasks, collective sufficiency and trading businesses but their workload reduces annually after they turn 50 years of age. In return, all their basic needs are met and, in the mid-2010s, they received around $1200 per annum 'pocket money'. Their workload equates with the average world rate of paid work (WorldAtlas 2016), making the Twin Oaks workload significantly lower than many national averages that include remunerated and domestic work.

The Twin Oaks work schedule is determined each week, incorporating all the regular and special work necessary, as indicated by work area managers. Renwick (2017) explains:

> The Labor Assigner essentially has a list of all the jobs that need to be done that week, and they work their magic to match up the open jobs with the people who sign up to do that type of work. At once flexible enough to allow members to do only the work they want to do, and structured enough to fill several hundred workshifts a week, the Labor System is a thing of administrative beauty . . . the backbone of the community and some people believe what kept us from folding like so many other 60s communes.

Along with regular half-day tours for those interested in seeing how the community functions, there are three-week visitor intensives, mandatory for those considering membership. Visitors are scheduled to work so that they get to know regular routines, protocol and activities.

Degrowth futures: political and economic integration

RBCC and Twin Oaks have developed within and against prevailing political and economic structures. They can be seen to further degrowth futures by collectively managing local environments. Furthermore, Twin Oaks community prefigures communal low impact living economies.

Round the Bend Conservation Co-operative: environmental living zone

RBCC evolved from a broader local environmental campaign that founded the Bend of Islands Conservation Association (BICA) in the late 1960s. Subsequently, RBCC worked with BICA to establish a unique environmental living zone (ELZ), extending many of the cooperative's conservation principles across 635ha of local private properties 'to maintain and enhance the positive environmental qualities of landscape, vegetation, habitat for flora and fauna, and to protect specific sensitive areas from damage to the natural systems, consistent with the maintenance of existing occupation'.[3] Although the 'environmental living' proposal became part of the prevailing Shire of Healesville Planning Scheme with an Interim Development Order in 1976, it took more than 20 years for its successor, Nillumbik Shire Council, to approve Special Use Zone 2 Bend of Islands/Environmental Living Zone in its planning scheme (1999) and for the State of Victoria to gazette associated legislation (2000).

Anyone buying into the ELZ is alerted by real estate agents, and advised and monitored by BICA, to abide by ELZ conservation regulations. Provisions cover private and public space. For instance, while horses can be ridden on most Victorian roads, they are banned from the ELZ. BICA informs, trains and skills residents, and runs working bees that assist in applying their policies on public and private lands. A 'phone tree' and neighbourly support with bushfire alerts and emergency procedures are available to ELZ residents. RBCC insists on inspecting member household's bushfire preparedness in annual fire response rehearsals. A unique practice, in bushfire prone areas such security is really a basic need relevant to human safety and carbon emissions. In widespread fires surrounding and impinging on this area in 2009: 173 people died, many more were injured and left deeply traumatised, 2,133 houses were destroyed, along with other kinds of private and public buildings, basic infrastructure and agricultural resources (Teague et al. 2010, 1 and 13). These types of circumstances emphasise the significance of conservation and bushfire measures pursued by RBCC and the wider ELZ for broader human settlements now and in the future. In a degrowth future, such mobilisations would complement the application of simple and convivial living principles.

Moreover, the invisible as it were 'ecological housekeeping' of RBCC benefits non-members. Collective intents and practices cover communal ownership of erstwhile private property fragmented in lots with landowners acting in ad hoc ways subject only to weakly monitored council regulations with illegal practices, such as clearing vegetation, readily taking place. By collectively conserving woodland, RBCC residents contribute to preventing and abating global carbon emissions associated with most other land uses. This is a gift to present and future generations. Moreover, the ELZ proves the cooperative's influence as a role model.

Twin Oaks: relationships and exchanges beyond the community

Justifiably, Twin Oaks claims an ecovillage status, listing achievements in energy conservation and use of renewable energy, local organic food production and a 'sustainable culture', including the pooling of all their resources, skills and knowledge. A member of global ecovillage and intentional community networks, Twin Oaks acts as a role model and demonstration space advocating the conservation of Earth and offering governance techniques for low impact living. Characteristically, what is scheduled and deemed 'work' at Twin Oaks includes certain political activities, such as involvement in the Occupy movement.

Twin Oaks community makes labour, product and service exchanges in non-monetary and monetary forms with like-communities but relies on trade within capitalist markets to the tune of around US$5000 per capita. In trade and non-monetary exchange, members make ethical choices about trading partners, terms and conditions. Production for trade includes making hammocks; organic soy products, such as plain, herbed or exotically marinated extra firm tofu, tempeh and spiced soy sausages; book indexes; seeds, herb plants and cut flowers. Soy products are made from local non-genetically modified organism soybeans, fresh additive-free artisanal well water (heated with renewable energy), and organically grown herbs and seasonings. Moreover, the community reuses the nitrogen-rich liquid bi-product of tofu manufacture as a fertiliser.

Twin Oaks shows the potential of reducing impacts collectively through nonmonetary collective sufficiency and carefully managed necessary trade based on democratically decided social and environmental ethics.

Conclusion

Many types of eco-collaborative housing offer practices appropriate for advancing degrowth, interpreted as just socio-economic and political structures that aim to establish and maintain a balance in the interdependent relations between humans and Earth. This reading conceptualises degrowth in terms of 'use values' (the qualities, purposes and uses to which things might be put) and using a minimum of natural and artificial resources. Degrowth focuses on diminishing over-consumption of use values so the focus moves from 'exchange values' to reducing consumption of Earth's use values to levels capable of regeneration.

If degrowth strategies are to conform to our vision, means need to parallel ends. We need to work with urgency because the state of Earth is dire and natural readjustments in train – namely climate change – threaten the species existence of humans. Therefore, a bottom-up response is particularly appropriate and necessary; if people everywhere can work on similar principles locally we can achieve necessary change quickly. This implies direct democracy with as-local-as-is-feasible production focusing on people's basic needs, so future distribution is decided simultaneously with collectively agreeing on productive goals and ways of achieving them. No money or financial sectors or capitalists are necessary, simply a vision that implies that the means of production are owned and controlled by popular power.

The two cases contrasted in this chapter exemplify different aspects of living for degrowth, focusing on the extent to which they challenge capitalist ways and establish alternative degrowth practices. Both show concerted and successful community-based activism demonstrating that more socially and environmentally sensitive alternatives to conventional household and housing arrangements are feasible. Successfully maintained for decades, they have actively demonstrated alternatives for people to observe and read about, visit, stay in and experience – belying the charge that such communities are closed, selfish, insular and unworldly institutions (Tummers 2016).

Twin Oaks community, in particular, demonstrates that collective action is a breeding ground for non-hierarchical techniques for communicating, relating and acting together, pointing to post-capitalism. RBCC has fewer anti-systemic goals but remains community-driven and self-managing. RBCC has challenged, and occasionally subverted, state and local government institutions. Moreover, if those settling new areas and residents of existing neighbourhoods pulled down fences between their properties and respected the land as a joint responsibility and amenity under conservation principles, then we could develop ELZs in multiple locations with regulations appropriate to each biome or bioregion. Earth badly needs such nurturing. The ELZ suggests feasible, if concerted, neighbourhood action might be readily achievable within the current system and, if applied, would be empowering to behold.

Furthermore, this comparison suggests that higher levels of collective sufficiency in eco-collaborative living enable greater empowerment, marginalising the capitalist market and production for trade. In short the comparison shows the close connection between the intensity and extensiveness of communal governance and relative autonomy and the level and variety of basic needs which the community controls. Both cases suggest that non-hierarchical decision-making can be successful in governing the production and exchange of a range of residents' basic needs; people power can be a much deeper and more extensive force than protesting in street marches or even temporary occupations. Twin Oaks, in particular, offers a hybrid model, stained by this world but prefiguring a degrowth Earth.

Notes

1 Unless indicated otherwise, data on RBCC derives from their site – www.roundthebend.org.au/
2 Unless indicated otherwise, data on Twin Oaks derives from their site – www.twinoaks.org and http://twinoakstofu.com/
3 Unless indicated otherwise, data on BICA derives from their site – https://bendofislands.wordpress.com/

References

Kincade, K. with Twin Oaks community. (2011) 'Labour credit – Twin Oaks community', in Nelson, A. and Timmerman, F. (eds.) *Life without Money: Building Fair and Sustainable Economies*. London: Pluto Press: 173–91.
LaFond, M. and Honeck, T. (eds.) (2012) *CoHousing Cultures: Handbuch für Selbstorganisiertes, Gemeinschaftliches Und Nachhaltiges Wohnen/Handbook for Self- Organized, Community Oriented and Sustainable Housing*. Berlin: Jovis.
Litfin, K. (2014) *Ecovillages: Lessons for Sustainable Community*. Cambridge/Malden: Polity Press.
Nelson, A. (2001) 'Two models of residential conservation: Communal life in an Australian box ironbark forest', *International Journal of Heritage Studies* 7(3): 249–72.
——— (2016) '"Your money or your life": Money and socialist transformation', *Capitalism Nature Socialism* 27(4): 40–60.
——— (2018) *Small Is Necessary: Shared Living on a Shared Planet*. London: Pluto Press.
Renwick, V. (2017) 'Twin Oaks over time', *The Leaves of Twin Oaks* 125, Fall.
Teague, B., McLeod, R. and Pascoe, S. (2010) *2009 Victorian Bushfires Royal Commission Final Report: Summary*. Melbourne: Parliament of Victoria.
Thornton, R. (2015) 'To burn or not to burn', *Wildfire*, March – April. Posted at Bushfire and Natural Hazards CRC site – www.bnhcrc.com.au/news/2015/burn-or-not-burn

Tummers, L. (2016) 'The re-emergence of self-managed co-housing in Europe: A critical review of co-housing research', *Urban Studies* 53(10): 2023–40.
Victorian Collections. (2017) *Round the Bend Conservation Co-operative Bend of Islands, Victoria* – https://victoriancollections.net.au/organisations/round-bend-conservation-cooperative#collection-records
Vigilante, T. and Thornton, R. (2016) 'Bushfires 2: Managing landscapes', *Nova (Australian Academy of Science)* – www.nova.org.au/earth-environment/bushfires-managing landscapes
WorldAtlas. (2016) 'Average working time by country', *WorldAtlas* – www.worldatlas.com/articles/average-working-time-by-country.html

22 Summary and research futures for housing for degrowth

Anitra Nelson and François Schneider

This collection on housing for degrowth has offered various windows into realities of degrowth resistance and experimentation, as well as imagined and real transformations breaking through the dominant narrative and practice of mainstream housing for growth. On many occasions contributors have shown the potent connections between degrowth and other similar movements, underlining existing collaborations and pointing to future alliances. In this summary chapter we integrate ideas for future research rising from each chapter and the entire collection.

Although many themes intertwine across housing, we sought to categorise chapters in seven clusters, highlighting the book's sub-title 'principles, models, challenges and opportunities': simple living for all; housing justice; housing sufficiency; reducing demand (i.e. market demand versus need); ecological housing and planning; a debate, 'whither urbanisation?'; and, anti-capitalist values and relations. Further research will challenge and refine our approach in a field that is as central to human needs as food and deserves greater attention.

Simple living for all

Within the field of housing studies more generally, we hope that this book will be seen as a fresh and coherent contribution that constructively highlights the inefficiencies and ineffectiveness of capitalist growth economies. The latter seems to be clearly shown if measured by the social and environmental values and criteria on which degrowth is based. We have aimed to show the integration between singular struggles and a future vision, including legal and regulatory changes that might ease and support the pathway to degrowth. Furthermore, we have argued that degrowth is not a simple reversal or downsizing but has a qualitatively different dynamic and set of societal principles. In this sense, contributors have variously discussed the transformation of everyday practices and changes to policies and social perspectives required.

In the field of degrowth studies this book is an unusual intervention to the extent that it highlights the collective practice of degrowth practitioners and traces links between activities that are often perceived by the mainstream as marginal, fragmented and small-scale actions driven by isolated agents. This logic of change is drawn out in the narrative framework of rippling interconnected and holistic change offered by Schneider (Chapter 2), a theoretical framework developed by collective effort grounded in known everyday practices.

The housing for degrowth narrative is based on an activist reality of organic networking, developing models and principles based on clear values and evolving relationships that promise transformation. Schneider suggests a collective scholarly-activist method for understanding and motivating holistic change in the everyday acts of housing struggles based on solidarity. This research approach could be applied across a suite of other practical fronts within degrowth activism, such as transport or food provisioning, to strengthen practices and emphasise both their actual and potential impacts. Further research would extend and develop this approach as well as identify other constructive approaches for application by the degrowth movement.

Housing justice

Olsen, Orefice and Pietrangeli (Chapter 3) offer an exemplary intertwining of general radical urban change theory and the specifics of everyday practice in their analysis of the housing movement in Rome (Italy). Developing on the well-known concept of the 'right to the city' and the lesser known 'right to metabolism', they demonstrate that the micro- and macro-politics of distribution and justice are prevalent in efforts to downscale flows of matter and energy in urban metabolisms. They reveal that struggles of 'marginalised and precarious urban dwellers' are, or can be made to be, coherent within the grander sustainable degrowth theory, in ways similar to E.P. Thompson's feat for the lower classes in his classic *The Making of the English Working Class* (1963). This chapter by Olsen et al. invokes the concept of 'degrowth injustice' to highlight that degrowth analyses need explanatory as well as visionary potential. Furthermore, they demonstrate that the metabolic framework anchored in use values offers great potency for further applications in degrowth literature and discourse.

Cattaneo (Chapter 4) draws out the separate and combined logics of aligned movements in his insightful analysis of the squatters' and degrowth movements in Barcelona. He applies an ecological economics lens, draws on auto-ethnography, focuses on the 'community squat' model and identifies both the politics and materiality of squatting as jointly significant for degrowth outcomes. Thus, he concludes, first, by identifying three characteristics of successful and politicised squatting that offer strategies for a degrowth future and, second, with a proposal 'to start movements devoted to high-level radicalism that cannot be confused with the heterogeneous squatting movement because they explicitly identify with the possibility of a wide-spread urban movement'. His contribution highlights the consciousness-raising and strategic significance of theory for practice, action research and learning.

Housing sufficiency

In contrast to mainstream marginalisation and maligning of the 'domestic', Pernilla Hagbert (Chapter 5) situates the 'home' as an organ of societal pressures, values and relations. She draws on Swedish examples. The home is a space of mediation, a 'node'. A feminist and socio-political analysis, the chapter supports the experiential finding that home, especially when the household is a collective, can be a potent site for degrowth radicalism (as explicitly shown in Chapters 4 and 21). Hagbert's feminist slant raises, even though it does not engage with, similarities between the women's and degrowth movements as yet insufficiently explored in the wider degrowth and feminist literatures. Specifically, 'the personal is the political' resonates with any movement that involves changing everyday practices, relations and values – as does the realisation of 'the good life'. Such cross-field research and analyses would not be of simple historical interest but would benefit discourse across both fields.

April Anson's Chapter 6, on the movement advocating 'tiny houses', critically addresses how tiny houses might, do and do not contribute to degrowth ideals. A tiny house builder and resident, Anson charges the North American movement with mimicking the 'frontier rhetoric of pioneering, homesteading and individual freedom tied to histories of class and racial violence' and argues that 'the tiny house miniaturises instead of challenges class distinctions'. She criticises degrowth advocates and practitioners with certain similar failings. Thus the sustainability discourse is stretched and challenged by an environmental politics framing. Yet Anson sees that both movements have the potential to shake mainstream imaginaries, specifically of our challenged and uncertain future, and argues that they encourage transformative integration of humans and nature. For researchers, Anson's analysis highlights the weaknesses of focusing on built environment initiatives alone to either read or transform residents, a learning pertinent to general degrowth analyses that might focus on the material.

While degrowth activities and discourses have centred on Europe, Christie and Salong (Chapter 7) critically report on the South Pacific Ocean nation of Vanuatu where 'there is no consciously labelled degrowth movement' but the typical self-sufficient, convivial and non-market based ni-Vanuatu way of life might be considered a living example of degrowth. They show how collectively building simple, appropriate and affordable dwellings with natural local and recycled building materials expresses low impact living. Moreover, they highlight outcomes from the dramatic Tropical Cyclone Pam (2015) and grassroots ni-Vanuatu achievements post-cyclone to show the advantages of the frugal and collective do-it-ourselves resilience (in contrast to the top-down and market-based official response). Further research selectively embracing the know-how of Indigenous peoples worldwide will extend degrowth fields of literature and discourse.

Reducing demand

In Chapter 8, Verco presents the housing system for around 900 residents within Christiania (aka Freetown), an enclave in Copenhagen (Denmark), as a practical example of degrowth principles. From 1971, in the face of growing state pressures, the effective squat Christiania worked hard to establish and maintain fair processes of use rights to land and housing based on need, capacity and self-governance. In this analysis, Verco offers Christiania's housing system as 'a messy colourful "poster child"' of degrowth ideals of self-sufficiency, frugality, autonomy and environmental respect. Moreover, she defends eco-collaborative housing as a degrowth model – pre-empting debates in Part VI on the controversial topic of urbanisation within degrowth discourses. Finally, Verco defends a radical, even confrontational and oppositional, position against growth-oriented capitalism, arguing that politico-economic compromises risk weakening the basic principles of degrowth in practice. Verco's chapter demonstrates the critical need for historic and detailed degrowth analyses of such case studies.

Ferreri (Chapter 9) addresses a degrowth principle of continued use of existing buildings (i.e. 'refurbishment versus demolition') with respect to low-income social housing, now an endangered sector due to neo-liberal practices. Centring her analysis on a highly visible campaign against the demolition of the Heygate Estate, Southwark (London, United Kingdom), Ferreri's arguments focus on the 'politics of valuation'. She highlights the environmental and social inefficiencies of mainstream approaches to housing provision. As such, Ferreri carefully reframes and draws out degrowth concerns within a wider movement struggling for social housing per se. This kind of exercise, performed by several contributors in this book who read a conflict in degrowth terms – even if the protagonists and antagonists are unconscious of this perspective – offers a useful way for degrowth research to expand, simultaneously emphasising its relevance to twenty-first century challenges and solutions.

In Chapter 10, Trainer authentically shares his personal living experience of developing a degrowth centre, based at his home, around self-sufficiency, do-it-yourself and frugal living principles. Testimonial-style analyses from activist-scholars elaborate degrowth motivations, visions and experiences. Pigface Point, near Sydney, is a place of frugal innovation with experiments linking arts with simple green engineering disconnected from the urban grid. Trainer shows that housing can be cheap, sustainable and even, maybe, beautiful. He introduces what he calls the 'Simpler Way' – integrating aspects of households from the bottom-up, the house(hold) scaled up independent from strong market pressures. Trainer presents a degrowth vision explaining frugal practices in terms of future society-wide change.

Ecological housing and planning

Vishwanath (Chapter 11) presents another Global South perspective, this time from the point of view and current practice of an innovative architecture studio in the increasingly urbanised high-tech city Bengalura (formerly Bangalore), South India. She shows not only how natural, renewable and erstwhile waste resources of the city can be used to build new sustainable dwellings but also how deskilled, competitive and precarious building industry work can be transformed to encourage self-building and sharing between households in the building stage. As such, Vishwanath offers a model contribution to degrowth discourse from and for professionals that, in this case, integrates well with social and solidarity economy and sharing city approaches. Further housing for degrowth research must uncover such innovative practices and submit them to diverse critiques and comparative reviews.

The personal journeys of Dale, Marwege and Humburg (Chapter 12) reveal the centrality of home within low impact living. At the same time, they show how a dwelling reflects and engages with its social, economic, material and environmental surrounds. Their self-builds were established in West Wales and in rural Germany and show the significance of both formal regulatory and informal social processes associated with degrowth networks and conviviality in construction and lifestyles. There are great opportunities for more contributions that take this form, of self-critical personal experience set in the context of wider literatures and mainstream pressures. Here 'the personal is the political' framing reveals barriers beyond housing design and building materials and techniques that mainstream structures raise against alternatives to show how tenacity and ingenuity can break through such barriers.

P.M. with François Schneider (Chapter 13) presents a detailed degrowth utopia from 'neighbourhood' (basic democratic clusters with inclusive, egalitarian participation) through to planetary scales. This 'symbolic' vision is based on the principles of commons and resilience and aimed to stir and motive people to debate, organise and act. P.M.'s utopia incorporates quite a few ideas raised elsewhere in this volume, developing an open-localist vision at multiple scales, promoting the collective and city life without undermining other compatible approaches. The 'modules' he describes demonstrate links between degrowth housing at all scales, including the planetary one. This is not a cold mathematical demonstration but, rather, serves to open our imaginary to new possibilities. Such thought experiments – also conducted by Trainer in Chapter 10 – serve critical functions as explanatory devices for future researchers to understand and challenge degrowth perspectives.

Stefánsdóttir and Xue (Chapter 14) systematically analyse how significant current building and planning standards and regulations fail to incorporate degrowth criteria for smaller dwellings, better designed and more liveable dwellings, and eco-collaborative housing for conviviality and neighbourhood sustainability. Drawing on international literature, they focus on Norwegian examples and psychological as well as material needs, moving beyond function and aesthetics to levels of emotional satisfaction. This chapter raises the important point that we need to intervene more – to open up public discussion on the size and unsustainability of our built environment, the distinction between needs and wants, and the significance of population control and overconsumption. Stefánsdóttir and Xue take a fully professional approach to the degrowth discourse, elucidating how and why professionals and their daily practice need to be overhauled to achieve degrowth futures. They suggest further research topics and open discussion on appropriate degrowth research methods and theories.

Whither urbanisation?

A novelty of the collection is the debate on urbanisation, which airs one of the deepest controversies within the degrowth movement and a very significant controversy for housing. Research discourse via engagement and provocation challenges theories with empirical evidence and seeks to understand and logically overturn opponents' arguments. We approached two authors, Xue and Vansintjan, who had already presented views supporting and problematising urbanisation in distinctive ways, to write chapters. Then we sought commentaries from Exner and Krähmer. Furthermore, given that the initial contributions were so provocative, co-editors Schneider and Nelson could not resist addressing certain points.

Xue's Chapter 15 draws on, updates and revises an article published in 2014 in the esteemed *Ecological Economics* journal. With reference to Scandinavian countries, Xue's contribution applies specific political and social science concepts with respect to scale in urban and regional planning. To simplify her position, we would say that Xue argues 'for urbanisation' in ways which, of course, greatly modify and qualify that statement.

In contrast, Vansintjan (Chapter 16) uses personal experiences in London and Hanoi to reorient the debate around concepts derived from Murray Bookchin's libertarian municipalism. Thus, Vansintjan argues that (bad) 'urbanisation' processes impose artificial 'scarcity' by depriving residents of political agency and culture whereas a (good) 'degrowth municipalism' would be based on citification based on 'the politicisation and downscaling of municipalities' social metabolism necessary to achieve a more just society' and 'the creation of an organic citizenship or the citification of urban space'.

Despite Vansintjan's labelling of urbanisation as 'the death of politics', his and Xue's elaborations can be rendered as 'pro-urbanisation'. Certainly both criticise the decentralisation and localisation currents in the degrowth movement. Thus, in lieu of a straight forward commentary on Xue and Vansintjan, and to great effect, Exner (Chapter 17) tests some of their perspectives, concepts and arguments in 'place-specific' cases of planning and social urban developments in contemporary Vienna. In his commentary, Krähmer (Chapter 18) moves to 'abandon the *tabula rasa* approach of any universal model for the ideal spatial organisation of society' (as appears in Xue and Vantsinjan) and, instead, argues for 'a more differentiated vision' with reference to wider theories and European examples. The final commentary by Schneider and Nelson (Chapter 19) centres on 'open localism' but makes several other points.

This exercise prompts us to argue that degrowth, as a field of studies, is now sufficiently mature and sophisticated to greatly benefit from respectful discussion of the complexities and subtleties of a range of such topics both within and beyond housing for degrowth.

Anti-capitalist values and relations

The last two substantive chapters in this collection question financial and monetary values within capitalism and examine real-life models that exist to varying degrees in active opposition to conventional financial and monetary structures along certain degrowth principles and practices. In a certain sense, this part of our collection points to, without directly engaging in, a central area of degrowth debate: Is post-growth also post-capitalism?

In Chapter 20, Hurlin analyses the German umbrella Mietshäuser Syndikat of housing cooperatives, residential cooperatives that develop in semi-autonomous ways to promote affordable and self-managed housing within processes and practices that express collective solidarity. Nelson (Chapter 21) compares and contrasts two eco-collaborative housing models in terms of their processes for, and levels of, collective governance; their models of land ownership and use rights; and degree of collective sufficiency.

These chapters venture into an, arguably, weak area of broader degrowth research involving finance and monetary relations, including alternative currencies and banking schemes, and the specific significance of non-monetary values (use values) and relations. They offer insights into cooperatives and shared eco-collaborative housing as structures which can, in various ways, encompass degrowth strategies and achieve degrowth goals. They raise questions around degrowth and characteristics of ownership and tenancy about which various contributors make contradictory remarks. Again these kinds of analyses offer activists and scholars rich material for further developing degrowth concepts and theories, as the results of a variety of practical endeavours deliver strategic lessons.

Research questions and housing for degrowth narratives

A whole range of questions raised by contributors beg further research, such as: How might squatters responding to housing dilemmas avoid the insecurities of risks of eviction? How might the use of empty houses by people in need be better supported? How might the state favour social housing fulfilling inhabitants' preferences? For social justice, questions around basic and maximum incomes are crucial. How can we best design basic and optimal housing? Many such questions demand clearer degrowth perspectives on 'the state', 'the market' and 'the grassroots'.

Cattaneo and Olsen et al. show how squatting creates political agents for degrowth and ways to encourage and favour such agents. But generic questions, as follow, require much more interrogation. How can we create large movements against speculation and for housing justice? How can actors struggling for social and environmental justice integrate associated degrowth strategies? Verco indicates the significance of making crucial agreements with governing powers yet still working radically even if at a different scale. How are other crucial degrowth experiments, both individual and collective, being maintained and challenged in currently difficult societal and political contexts?

There are the dilemmas of following 'simplicity', for example living in smaller houses theoretically makes us less susceptible to co-option. But, in practice, degrowth strategies can be simply integrated into capitalism. Anson shows these risks in those forms of neo-colonisation generated by tiny houses. An associated challenge is finding the balance between reshaping and keeping what is already built. Similarly, Vishwanath's chapter raises questions – yet to be addressed – about adequately addressing the massive recycling required by overconsumption without generating more pollutants and challenges for future disposals.

How can we alter our housing habits successfully? How do we integrate, say, the imaginative innovations of Trainer and careful house design as described by Stefánsdóttir? People are conditioned by habits, sociotechnical systems and oppressive consumerist cultures. How do we inspire more voluntary housing for degrowth, whether through tiny houses, house sharing, cap and share, compact settlements or frugal innovations? Moreover, Christie and Salong show that defending certain existing cultures is required. Can we introduce new degrowth ideas and perspectives – such as sharing housing – without being overly missionary in our approach?

Other questions surround governance. What is the ideal form of planning in degrowth futures – participative (Exner), consultative or expert-led? Vishwanath and Xue, for instance, point to misinformed participative processes. Hagbert, Trainer and Dale et al. situate action emanating from the home. P.M. proposes organising in neighbourhoods and within larger democratic processes simultaneously. Is there a preferred scale of departure? Or, is a coalition of participative actors working at different scales necessary?

What line might triumph in the city versus decentralisation debate? Krähmer argues that both can support degrowth. But how do we adapt and apply these approaches to specific contexts as Exner does for Vienna? If demand for housing reduces, urbanisation and its impacts reduce, along with speculation and injustice. But, how do we initiate such a virtuous housing for degrowth revolution? All contributors point to risks of failure. Is this because a particular focus often leads to reductionism, indicating the limit of a typical scientific approach where a singular change is studied in isolation rather than integrating broader aspects?

Key questions remain around support and collective agency. Might all the different proposals combined in a coalition of themes adequately deal with existing contradictions, create a real convergence of housing struggles, and result in a revolutionary transformation of housing that could even apply to other sectors? Where are more case studies to show whether this kind of logic is either being realised or is found wanting?

Behind the 'story' of the housing for degrowth narrative there are societal institutions, namely the state in all its functions and forms and multi-dimensional market forces, i.e. decision-making structures, effectively re-creating the powerful and the rest of us. Rich analyses of more case studies are needed to address a growing list of questions about changing structures.

Conclusion

We do not want to suggest a research agenda rigidly identifying 'the way' but, rather, a deepening and expanding narrative, where all actors present distinctive ideas and engage with and transform one another to generate a collective creation. We want diversity but need to work towards dialogue and shared perspectives. We intended this book to show that housing for degrowth can represent a long-term mutually integrative zone with transformative capacities. This means a strong future for housing action and housing for degrowth analyses. We encourage you to seek, contribute and experiment more to build the necessary praxis for a degrowth future.

Index

Page numbers in *italics* indicate a table and **bold** numbers indicate a figure.

ABC *see* Anti-Boredom Centres
Agamben, G. 203
Alexander, S. 76
alternative housing 3, 11, 36, 57, 61, 62, 64, 110, 120, 121, 244; radical 77; *see also* Simpler Way
Alternative Science and Technology for Rural Areas 137
'amateur economy' 50
Anson, A. 22, 258, 262
Anti-Boredom Centres (ABC) 165, 166, 167
Architectural Digest 72
Arendt, H. 199
Aristotle 199, 201, 207
Arts and Crafts movement 75
aspirational narrative 3–5
ATER 35
atmospheric quality 175–6, 178
Auroville Earth Institute 137
autogestione 37–8
autonomia operaia 37
autonomy 23, 37, 47, 61–2, 74, 88, 94, 100, 168, 201, 204, 235, 237, 238, 247, 254, 259
autorecupero 36, 38–9, 40
average ratio of household debt to disposable income in select countries 9

back-to-the land 63, 73, 196
Bangalore 133, 134, 137, 226, 259
Bangalore Development Authority (BDA) 135–6
Bauwagenplatz 77
BDA *see* Bangalore Development Authority
beauty 201
'B economy' 50

Bend of Islands 249; Conservation Association 251; Environmental Living Zone 251
bene comune urbano 38, 39, 40
Bengaluru, South India 133–44; basement being constructed *139*; basement in use *141*; comparing roof areas for their potential 143; computer keyboards embedded in concrete roof *142*; house with basement *138*; model 137–43; political background to environmentally unsustainable development 133–5; smart roof functionality 143; soil quantity available from basements of various projects **140**; twenty-first-century changes in economic and building practices 135–7
Better Elephant 114
Biome Environmental Solutions 137, 140
Bookchin, M. 197; *The Ecology of Freedom* 199; *Post-Scarcity Anarchism* 199; *Urbanization without Cities* 199
bottom-up 7, 14, 15, 18, 19, 21, 24, 39, 46, 199, 219, 220 253, 259
Bradley, K. 61
Buen Vivir 77
buying houses 3, 21, 104

carbon emissions 7, 10, 11, 47, 75, 115, 137, 158, 171, 173, 224, 252
Castlemaine (Victoria, Australia) 226
Castoriadis, C. 201, 207
Cattaneo, C. 21, 22, 26, 33, 40, 46, 102, 103, 105, 224, 257
Christiania (Freetown) 24, 99–106, 258–9; degrowth 99–101; degrowth and housing style 101–4; housing outside the market 104–5

Christie, W. 23, 81, 258, 263
Cigales 26
circular narrative 15, 20
citification of urbanisation 197, 206–7, 225–7, 261
city as an ecocommunity 199–202
Clarke, C. 75
climate change 10–1, 23, 80–94, 156, 217, 224, 253; Global South and Global North 91–3; island dwelling 81–3; Nguna Island dwellings 83; Port Vila main street 84; Taloa Farea 82; Taloa village 81; Tropical Cyclone Pam 23, 80, 85–91, 92, 93, 258; urban dwelling 83–5
cohousing 23, 24, 44, 45, 48, 49, 50, 51, 61, 62, 64, 104, 175, 240, 242, 244, 247; eco- 223, 245
Coiffier, C. 83, 85
collaborative planning 189, 224
Collserola Natural Park 46
commodification 45, 46, 59–60, 68, 76, 105, 106, 221, 235, 241
Community First! 78
communal living: contribute to material degrowth 47–8; contribute to monetary degrowth 48–50; contribute to political dimensions of degrowth 50–1
community squat 46, 257
Compressed Stabilised Earth Blocks (CSEBs) 137, 139, 140
Compulsory Purchase Order (CPO) 114; beyond the Heygate 115–16; Heygate public inquiry 114–15
conviviality 16, 19, 24, 26, 27, 41, 47, 143, 153–4, 206, 226, 242, 260; self-sufficiency 62–4
Corbyn, J. 22
corporate green movement 74
CPO *see* Compulsory Purchase Order
Cronon, W. 73
CSEBs *see* Compressed Stabilised Earth Blocks
cybernetics 15

Dale, J. 26, 260, 263
Dale, S. 148, 149
D'Alisa, G. 47
Daly, H. 228
d'Amour, B. 7
Dancing Rabbit Ecovillage 124
Daneshpour, A. 101
De Benoist, A. 228–9

debound effect 19
Decide Roma 35, 39
deforestion 7, 160, 218
degrowth: circular narrative 20; definition 3, 14–15; housing 16–19; housing and monetary relationships 26; housing justice 21–2, 77, 242, 257, 262; narratives 14–27; reducing ecological impacts of housing 19, 25–6; reducing housing demand 22, 23–4; reducing urbanisation 24–5; sufficiency 22–3
demolition waste 7, 140
Difference Principle 192
direct democracy 47, 189, 223, 224, 225, 250, 253
disposable income 6, 8–9; average ratio of household debt to disposable income in select countries 9; high 50
distributive justice in the context of housing for degrowth 49, 185, 186–7, 191–3
Donaufeld 210–2
Droit au Logement 21, 22, 33
Droste, C. 240
Dunbar, R. I. M. 159

ecological housing 14, 47, 146, 256; planning 259–60; reduction 19, 25–6; squatting communities 102
ecovillages 24, 101, 104, 122, 127, 128, 197, 199, 221, 223, 225, 244, 245, 252; European 219; more than 203–5; Pescomaggiore 92–3; *see also* Dancing Rabbit Ecovillage; Lammas
Edward Woods Estate 113
Elephant Amenity Network 112
Elephant & Castle 112, 114, 115
El Niño 87
ELZ *see* environmental living zone
energy consumption 21, 136, 188, 219; EU-27 7; Italy 7; London 113; Poland 7; Twin Oaks 252
Engel-Di Mauro, S. 33
Engels, F.: *Zur Wohnungsfrage* 225
Entitlement Theory 192
environmental cost of dwellings 6–8
environmental living zone (ELZ) 251–2, 254
Essen, C. 111
European Commission 3, 16
European Grands Projets Inutiles et Imposés 24–5
Exner, A. 26, 261, 263

Fairlie, S. 145
Favor, C.: *Stanford Encyclopedia of Philosophy* 191
feminism, material 160
feminist ecologies 60
feminist engagement 57, 258
feminist politics 200
feminist re-imaginations of everyday life 64–5
Ferber, U. 219
Ferreri, M. 24, 259
5 Stars Movement (M5S) 35, 36, 37
food sovereignty 150
Foster, J. B.: *What Every Environmentalist Needs to Know about Capitalism* 74, 77
Freedom Party of Austria 212
Freetown *see* Christiania
frugal abundance 226
frugal innovation 15, 18–19, 226, 259, 263
functional quality 174–5, 176, 178

Gavaldá, M. 33, 46, 102, 103, 105
Geddes, P. 19
Gensler 113–14
Genuino Clandestino 221
geography matters 217–21; case studies 220–1; guidelines for degrowth spatial planning paradigm 219–220
Germany 5, 26, 45, 214, 260; *see also* Bauwagenplatz; Heckenbeck alternative, self-run school ; Holzen roundhouse; Mietshäuser Syndikat
German Right to the City movement 233
Gescal fund 34, 36
Gesellschaft mit beschränkter Haftung (GmbH) 236, 237, 238
Gestione Case per I Lavoratori 34
GFC *see* global financial crisis
Gibson-Graham, J. K. 65
global financial crisis (GFC) 9, 10, 35, 91, 109, 234
GmbH *see Gesellschaft mit beschränkter Haftung*
Gómez-Baggethun, E. 242
Grand Designs 4
Grazioli, M. 37
green amenities 113
green areas 112, 113, 134
Green Empire 72
greenfields 26, 212
green imaginaries of decentralisation 204
green living 60
green movements 72, 74
green space 211, 227, 227
Grenfell Tower 117

Habermas, J. 199
HabiTAT 234
Hagbert, P. 22, 61, 258, 263
Hanoi 197, 198–9, 200, 203, 206, 261
Haraway, D. 65
Hardin, G.: 'The Tragedy of the Commons' 76
Harvey, D. 38, 77
He, Y. 23
Heckenbeck alternative, self-run school 154
Heeg, S. 234
Herczeg, M. 7
Heygate Estate 110–14, 259; CPO public inquiry 114–16
Heynen, N. C. 38
hinterland 134, 143, 166, 205, 224
Holm, A. 234
Holzen roundhouse 149–54, *152*; debarking day *153*; planning 151–4; practical process 150–1
HOME 113, 114
home: origination of term 58
home as a node for transition 57–66; autonomy through collaboration 61–2; commodification 59–60; conviviality and self-sufficiency 62–4; feminist re-imaginations of everyday life 64–5; finding home 57–8; home as political agenda 58–9; reconceptualising home as part of degrowth transitions 60–5
homelessness 4, 5, 6, 21, 24, 78, 129, 193, 234
home ownership 3–5, 6, 8, 59, 246
Homes and Communities Agency's Grants Programme 113
HOPP 63
Horlitz, S. 234, 240, 241
household 176–8; needs 176–7; perception and interpretation 177–8
house sharing 23, 24, 263
housing demand 134; increases 133; reducing 22, 23–4
housing-for-growth narratives 3–11; aspirational narrative 3–5; average ratio of household debt to disposable income in select countries 9; environmental cost of dwellings 6–8; home ownership 3–5; insufficiency

5–6; recession and degrowth 9–10; system change not climate change 10–1; tenancy, squatting and homelessness 4–5; ties that bind 8–9; unaffordability 5–6; underbelly 5–10
housing justice 21–2, 77, 242, 257, 262
housing question 35, 45, 233–5, 241; solving 235, 239
housing sovereignty 149–54; debarking day 153; Holzen 149–54, 152; planning 151–4; practical process 150–1
housing struggle 45, 242, 257, 263
Humburg, A. 26, 260
Hurlin, L. 26, 262

Idle No More 77
INA Casa 34
Indian Ecological Swaraj 77
Intergovernmental Panel on Climate Change 10
International Monetary Fund 6, 168
Italian Civil Protection Department 92

Jacobin: 'The Tiny House Fantasy' 69
justice, housing 21–2, 77, 242, 257, 262
Just Space 115

Kahn, L.: Shelter 72
Kinder Morgan Transmountain pipeline 77
knock down and rebuild 122
Knock It Down or Do It Up 115–16
Koch, M. 186
Kothari, A. 77
Krahmer, K. 26, 261, 263

LAB!Puzzle 34, 39
Lammas ecovillage 26, 147–9, 148, 151
Lamont, J.: Stanford Encyclopedia of Philosophy 191
Lancaster West Estate 117
The Land Is Ours (TLIO) 145–6
land use planning 25, 89
Latouche, S. 15, 226, 227
Le Corbusier 19
Lefebvre, H. 33, 35, 37–8, 205
libertarian distributive principle 192–3
libertarian municipalism 261
Lietaert, M. 23
The Limits of Growth 75
localisation of politics versus centralisation and planning 185, 186, 189–91, 224

Lockean: justification for resource 76; private property 75; Proviso 192
London 5, 24, 109, 110, 114, 115–16, 117, 206, 218, 259, 261; municipal 111; scarcity 197–8; see also Edward Woods Estate; Heygate Estate
London Tenants Federation 115
low-budget housing 34
'low hanging fruit' 7, 10
low impact living 145–54; development 145–6; Heckenbeck alternative, self-run school 154; Holzen roundhouse 149–54, 152; housing sovereignty 149–54; Lammas ecovillage 147–9, 148, 151; permaculture 146–7; Undercroft 147–9, 148
Lupi, M. 36

Magdoff, F.: What Every Environmentalist Needs to Know about Capitalism 74, 77
Mahadevia, D. 136
mainstream housing 3, 7, 126, 256
Malthusianism 196
Malvatumauri 85–6
Martínez, M. 33, 40
Martinez-Alier, J. 225
Marwege, R. 26, 260
Marx, K. 225
Marxism 196, 212
Maston, S. A. 189
material feminism 160
Max-Neef, M. A. 16
Mayer, P. W. 23
McCloud, K. 4
M5S see 5 Stars Movement
Mietshäuser Syndikat 26, 233–43, 262; affordability 241; brief selective history of tenancy in Germany 233–5; concept and functions 235–41; concept of degrowth 241–2; housing activism 240–1; housing syndicate 239; investing collectively 238; limited scale 239–40; niche or mainstream 240; proprietorship as solution 241; rent 238; roles and relations 236; social tenancy law 235; syndicate in action 236–7; transfers based on solidarity 238
Milkman, A. 74; 'The Tiny House Fantasy' 69
monetary relationships 26, 244
Mont, O. 186
Montreal 206

Moore, J. 58, 84
Movimento 5 Stelle 36
Mumford, L. 19
municipal housing 115; low-income 110; London 110, 111, 115

Nash, R.: *Wilderness and the American Mind* 73
National Building Code for Vanuatu 87
National Forest System 7–8
National Geographic 72
neighbourhoods as basic module of global commons 156–69; borough *165*; borough or town 164–6; living more efficiently 163–4; micro-agro linked *159*; microcenter, ground floor *163*; neighbourhoods 157–60; neighbourhoods in a borough *161*; parachutes from capitalism pillars of degrowth *157*; planet 168–9; region 166–8; rural areas 160–3; territories 168; world map of possible territories *169*
Nelson, A. 24, 26, 102, 261, 262
Neuman, M. 101
New Labour 111
The New Yorker 69, 72
no-border movement 227
nonmonetary eco-collaborative living 244–54; governance and work 247–51; land and dwellings: ownership and use of rights 245; political and economic integration 251; Round the Bend Conservation Co-operative: environmental living zone 251–2; Round the Bend Co-operative: governance 248–9; Round the Bend Conservation Co-operative: land and dwellings 245–6;Twin Oaks: governance and work 249–51; Twin Oaks: land and dwellings 246–7: Twin Oaks: relationships and exchanges beyond the community 252–3
Norgard, J. 50
Nozick, R. 192

Occupy Madison 77–8
Occupy Wall Street 76, 164
OECD *see* Organisation for Economic Co-operation and Development
Olsen, E. S. 21, 22, 220, 224, 257, 262
One Planet Development 146, 147
one planet lifestyles 162, 223
One Planet Policy 149

open localism 227–30; closure 227; critics of growth who defend borders 228–9; localism 227–8
Opportunity Villages 78; scale and context 229–30
Orefice, M. 21, 257
organic citizenship 197, 199, 207, 261
Organisation for Economic Co-operation and Development (OECD) 4, 6, 10
Ostrom, E. 156, 157
Othello and Quixote Villages 78
Outside 69
owner-occupiers 8, 9

PAH *see* Plataforma de Afectados por la Hipoteca
Pauling, C. 5
Paulson, S. 40
Payne, H.: 'Home, Sweet Home' 57
Peck, J. 111
'People's Home' 59
permaculture 63, 123, 146–7, 148, 149, 150, 247, 248
Piano Casa 36
Pietrangeli, G. 257
planetary urbanisation 205–6
Plataforma de Afectados por la Hipoteca (PAH) 21, 45, 50
Polanyi, K. 47
polis 199–200, 201
post-growth 18, 24, 63, 183, 224, 262
Preuß, T. 219
Purcell, M. 189, 190

quality of small dwelling 171–80; atmospheric quality 175–6, *178*; conceptual framework *178*; dwelling quality 174–6; functional quality 174–5, 176, *178*; household 176–8; liveable dwellings 172; physical components of dwelling and surroundings 173–4; quality of social interaction *178*; theory of dwelling quality influencing subjective wellbeing 179; urban density 84, 136, 173, 174
quality of social interaction 178

Radical Routes 233
Raggi, V. 36
Rasmusen, S. 102
Rawls, J. 192, 193
RBCC *see* Round the Bend Conservation Co-operative

rebound effect 19
recession 25, 33, 76, 235; degrowth 9–10
reducing ecological impacts of housing 19, 25–6, 27
reducing urbanisation 24–5
red Vienna 211–2
refurbishment 24, 26, 109, 110, 112, 113; versus demolition 114–17, 259
rental regulation 5
renting houses 3, 4, 5, 21
residential decentralisation versus high-density, compact urban and housing development 185, 186, 187–9, 193
RESPONDER 16, *17*, *18*
Resurrection Village 78
right to inhabit 33, 35, 36, 37–40, 41
'right to metabolism' 33, 34, 37, 38, 40, 257
'right to the city' 33, 35, 37, 38, 45, 205, 257
Rodman, M. 85
Round the Bend Conservation Co-operative (RBCC) 245–6, 247, 248–9, 251, 252, 253; environmental living zone 251–2; governance 248–9; land and dwellings 245–6

Salong, J. 258, 263
Sandstedt, E. 62
scale, place and degrowth 210–15; field research 210–1; scales of degrowth 213–15; urban growth and smart city 211–13
scales of degrowth 213–15
Schneider, F. 16, 26, 47, 99, 156, 225, 257, 260, 261
Second International Degrowth Conference 44
Seestadt Aspern development project 212–13
Sekulova, F. 225
self-recuperation 36, 38
self-sufficiency 61, 62–4, 100, 104, 120, 149, 187–8, 201, 202, 207, 223, 248, 259
Sendai Framework for Disaster Risk Reduction 87, 93
Sethman, A. 35, 36, 37
Shafer, J. 72
Shakibamanesh, A. 101
Simpler Way 23, 120–9, 259; centre 120–11; economic and social restructuring 126–7; general model 122–4; housing at Pigface Point 121–2; housing design 124–6; key approach 128–9; psychological, social and 'spiritual' benefits 127–8
small dwelling quality 171–80; atmospheric quality 175–6, 178; conceptual framework 178; dwelling quality 174–6; functional quality 174–5, 176, 178; household 176–8; liveable dwellings 172; physical components of dwelling and surroundings 173–4; quality of social interaction 178; theory of dwelling quality influencing subjective wellbeing 179; urban density 84, 136, 173, 174
smart cities 14, 212, 213
social centre 35, 44, 45, 46
Social Democratic government 211
social housing 4, 6, 21, 24, 35, 109–17, 234, 242; assets 234; demolition of Heygate Estate in London 109, 110; future 116; holistic approach 115; imaginary 117; lack of in Spain 45; low-income 109, 259; retrofitting Edward Woods Estate 113; self-managed 242
soft revolutions 15
Sourrouille, M. 228
Southwark Housing Stock Condition Survey 112
space, planning and distribution 185–93; localisation of politics versus centralisation and planning 185, 186, 189–91, 224; principles of distributive justice in the context of housing for degrowth 49, 185, 186–7, 191–3; residential decentralisation versus high-density, compact urban and housing development 185, 186, 187–9, 193; sustainable welfare, normativity of urban planning and housing for degrowth 185–7, 191
spatial planning 91, 185; paradigm 219–220
spiralling narratives 15
SquareOne 78
squatting 5, 33, 34; communal living contribute to material degrowth 47–8; communal living contribute to monetary degrowth 48–50; communal living contribute to political dimensions of degrowth 50–1; contribute to degrowth 44–51; political act 46–7
Squatting Europe Kollective 77

Stefánsdóttir, H. 22, 101, 260, 263
Stein, S. 7–8
Stop Evictions Berlin 235
sufficiency in housing 22–3
Sundaresan, J. 134
Susanka, S.: *The Not So Big House* 72
sustainable housing 16, 25, 66, 77, 101, 124, 193
sustainable welfare, normativity of urban planning and housing for degrowth 185–7, 191
Swedish Social Democratic 'People's Home' 59
system change not climate change 10–1

Taller Contra la violencia Inmobiliaria e Urbanistica 45
Taloa Farea 82, 82, 83, 85
tenancy 262; Germany 233–5; social law 235; squatting and homelessness 4–5
Thompson, E. P.: *The Making of the English Working Class* 257
Thoreau, H. D. 72–73, 75
Thörn, C. 113
THOWs *see* tiny homes on wheels
Tickell, A. 111
tiny homes on wheels (THOWs) 68, 69, 73–4, 76, 77
tiny house mobility 68–78, 70–1; ecological revolution 77–8; framing (with) degrowth 75–6; romance and reality 69–72; settler capital 72–5
Tiny Houses Greensborgo 78
TLIO *see* The Land Is Ours
top-down 5, 7, 14, 19, 22, 25, 62, 65, 100, 100, 258
Trainer, T. 50, 259, 260, 263; Simpler Way 23
transition, home as a node for 57–66; autonomy through collaboration 61–2; commodification 59–60; conviviality and self-sufficiency 62–4; feminist re-imaginations of everyday life 64–5; finding home 57–8; home as political agenda 58–9; reconceptualising home as part of degrowth transitions 60–5
transit-oriented development 220
Tropical Cyclone Pam 23, 80, 85–91, 92, 93, 258; 'Building Back Safer' 86; 'Disaster Risk Reduction' 86; formal rebuilding response 86–7; grassroots rebuilding response 87–91; National Building Code for Vanuatu 87; Post

Disaster Needs Report 85; Pre- 88; Vanuatu Shelter Cluster 85, 86, 87
Tumbleweed Tiny House Company 72
Twin Oaks: governance and work 249–51; land and dwellings 246–7: relationships and exchanges beyond the community 252–3
2008 Master Plan for Rome 38

UCL Urban Lab and Engineering Exchange 115
Undercroft 147–9, *148*
United Nations 16, 168, 215; Human Rights Declaration 186
unsustainable housing 65, 150
urban commons 38, 39
urban density 84, 136, 173, 174
urbanisation, reducing 24–5
urbanisation as the death of politics 196–207; abundance in Hanoi 197, 198–9, 200, 203, 206, 261; citification of urbanisation 197, 206–7, 225–7, 261; city as an ecocommunity 199–202; more than ecovillages 203–5; planetary urbanisation 205–6; scarcity in London 197–8; urban scarcity 202–3
urban sprawl 18, 19, 25, 47, 149

Van der Steen, B. 77
Vansintjan, A. 25, 26, 183, 210, 214, 215, 217, 219, 223; degrowth, scarcity and citification of urbanised world 225–7; urbanisation 261
Vanuatu *see* Tropical Cyclone Pam
Vanuatu Cultural Centre 80
Vanuatu Shelter Cluster 85, 86, 87
Vanuatu 2030 90
Verco, N. 24, 258, 259, 262
Videira, N. 15
Vienna 210–15, 261, 263; *see also* Donaufeld
Vietnam *see* Hanoi
Vishwanath, C. 25, 259, 263

Wales *see* Lammas ecovillage; One Planet Development
Walker, L.: *Tiny, Tiny Houses* 72
Welzer, H. 15
Westin, S. 62
Widmer, H. 25, 156
World War I 214
World War II 34, 111, 234

Xue, J. 22, 25, 26, 183; building and planning standards and regulations 260; central authority 226; degrowth and housing 101, 210, 223–5, 260; degrowth spatial planning paradigm 217; governance 263; growth 242; 'open localism' 227; urbanisation 261

zero cemento 38, 39, 41